# VULCAN 607

## Rowland White

## BANTAM PRESS

LONDON · TORONTO · SYDNEY · AUCKLAND · JOHANNESBURG

TRANSWORLD PUBLISHERS
61–63 Uxbridge Road, London W5 5SA
a division of The Random House Group Ltd

RANDOM HOUSE AUSTRALIA (PTY) LTD
20 Alfred Street, Milsons Point, Sydney,
New South Wales 2061, Australia

RANDOM HOUSE NEW ZEALAND LTD
18 Poland Road, Glenfield, Auckland 10, New Zealand

RANDOM HOUSE SOUTH AFRICA (PTY) LTD
Isle of Houghton, Corner of Boundary and Carse O'Gowrie Roads,
Houghton 2198, South Africa

Published 2006 by Bantam Press
a division of Transworld Publishers

A catalogue record for this book is available
from the British Library.
ISBN 978 0593 053911 (cased) (from Jan 07)
ISBN 0593 053915 (cased)
ISBN 978 0593 053928 (tpb) (from Jan 07)
ISBN 0593 053923 (tpb)

Typeset in 11.5/14pt Sabon by
Falcon Oast Graphic Art Ltd

Printed and bound in Great Britain by
Mackays of Chatham, Chatham, Kent

3 5 7 9 10 8 6 4

Papers used by Transworld Publishers are natural, recyclable products
made from wood grown in sustainable forests. The manufacturing processes
conform to the environmental regulations of the country of origin.

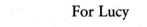
For Lucy

# Contents

# Author's Note

Everything that follows is, to the best of my knowledge, a true and accurate account of what happened. I've not had to join the dots to make the story work. Inevitably memories fade, and in interviewing so many people for the book I've been presented with sometimes contradictory accounts. On the rare occasions when this has happened, I've done my best to establish a consensus. I've drawn on a variety of different sources and this is reflected in the dialogue in the book. Where it appears in quotation marks it's either what I've been told was said, or what's been reported in previous accounts or records, published and unpublished. Where speech is in italics – often the call-and-response checks that accompany any military flying – it represents genuine dialogue that has been taken from another source to add richness to a scene. I hope it can be argued, with a degree of certainty, that it's what would have been said. Finally, where internal thoughts are included in italics, they are accurate recordings of what participants told me they were thinking at the time.

I hope I've written a book that does justice to those who took part. Needless to say, any mistakes are my own.

R.W.
Nant-y-Feinen
March 2006

# Acknowledgements

I owe a huge debt of gratitude to large numbers of people without whom I could not have even entertained the idea of writing this book. Martin Withers, 607's Captain, was the first to commit himself to the project. Had he not done so – and so enthusiastically – it would never have happened. Marshal of the Royal Air Force Sir Michael Beetham was also quick to offer his encouragement and Sir Michael's support proved crucial. His involvement underpinned the book's credibility at a very early stage, then facilitated my visit to the Falkland Islands and Ascension Island and a place on a recent RAF air-refuelling sortie.

Apart from Martin, I spoke to a large number of the aircrew who took part. All were open, welcoming and generous with their time and hospitality – sometimes enduring repeated visits and long follow-up phone calls. The list is a long one: Peter Taylor; Hugh Prior; Bob Wright; Dick Russell; John Reeve; James Vinales; Mick Cooper; Barry Masefield (who also kindly arranged for me to join him and the rest of the crew of Wellesbourne Mountford's Vulcan while it was taxied); Don Dibbens; Alastair Montgomery; Neil McDougall; Bob Tuxford; Ernie Wallis; Alan Bowman; Barry Neal (particular thanks are due here for the guided tour around Victor 'Lusty Lindy'); Paul Foot; Simon Hamilton.

Help wasn't limited to those who actually flew the Vulcan

and Victors, however. Simon Baldwin was an enthusiastic supporter and great host whose work on the manuscript was kind and invaluable. John Laycock's guided tour of a Vulcan cockpit and invitation to both the 44 (R) and V-force reunion were hugely appreciated. Jeremy Price and Air Chief Marshal Sir Michael Knight could not have been more friendly or supportive. Air Marshal Sir John Curtiss, Air Vice-Marshal George Chesworth and Keith Filbey were also kind enough to cast their minds back to answer my questions. I'm also extremely grateful to Sir John Nott for making time to see me.

A number of people dedicated to preserving both working examples and memories of the Vulcan and Victor also helped my cause: Felicity Irwin and Dr Robert Pleming of Vulcan to the Sky; Derek and Mark at Wellesbourne Mountford for allowing me aboard their beautifully preserved Vulcan, XM655 on two separate occasions; Richard Clarkson and Dave Griffiths of the Vulcan Restoration Trust; and Bill O'Sullivan of the Newark Air Museum who kindly opened up the cockpit of the museum's resident Vulcan to me.

Particular thanks should go to David Thomas, Mike Pollit, Barry Masefield (again . . .), Andy Marson and Al McDicken, who crewed XM655 during the two ground runs I sat in on.

Still with the RAF, but slightly further removed from the action, Air Vice-Marshal Nigel Baldwin and Wing Commander Jeff Jefford of the RAF Historical Branch were helpful in getting the ball rolling and subsequently. Squadron Leader Andy Sinclair, Kate Sesaver and Ken Johnston made smooth arrangements for me to fly with 101 Squadron and to the Falkland Islands. I'm grateful to the crew of VC10 Tartan 41, Squadron Leader Andy Kellett, Flight Lieutenant Marc Rodriguez, Squadron Leader Hugh Davies and Master Air Engineer Rick Gomez. And on my flight south to the Falklands I was very privileged to fly as a guest of Air Marshal Sir Glen Torpy and Captain David Swain, RN. At RAF Waddington, I'd like to thank both Station Commander Group Captain Jeremy Fradgley and Wing Commander Tom Whittingham – who was kind enough to show me round.

Still with the UK armed forces, I'm grateful to Rear-Admiral Roger Lane-Nott for shining a light on HMS *Splendid*'s contribution to the war. Lieutenant General Sir Hew Pike and Major General Julian Thompson were also kind enough to help me.

I was to benefit from an unusual perspective on events when Lieutenant Colonel William Bryden, USAF, took the time and trouble to talk to me.

After arriving on the Falkland Islands themselves, I could not have been made to feel more welcome. Sukey Cameron, the Falkland Islands government representative in the UK, helped point me in the right direction before I left. When I landed at Mount Pleasant, Captain Ben Taylor made sure I was well looked after (despite having left my wallet in the back of a taxi at RAF Brize Norton . . .). After that, Maria Strange, Jane Cameron and Jenny Cockwell, editor of *Penguin News*, were generous with their time and consideration. So too were all those I interviewed: Gerald Cheek; John Smith; Hilda Parry; Peter Biggs; Leona Vidal; Liz Elliot; Joe King and Don Bonner. In addition, I should thank Carl Stroud, manager of the excellent Malvina House Hotel, who also helped me manage without cards and cash.

I'd like to thank as well Martin Rappalini, who strove to put me in touch with Argentine Air Force personnel, and Comodoro Héctor Rusticcini, who was kind enough to take the time to answer my questions.

Closer to home there are many people to thank. James Holland was one of the first people I spoke to about writing this book, and he was a source of encouragement from that point on. Harrie Evans, too, was an early confidant and supporter, and a chance to compare notes was always welcome. Lalla Hitchings, who transcribed hours and hours of interviews, relieved me of an overwhelming burden and was instrumental in making the whole thing possible. Ana-Maria Rivera was kind enough to translate Spanish to English and vice versa. Tom Weldon also has to be mentioned for a leap of faith he made ten years ago that changed everything.

When my agent, Mark Lucas, agreed to take the book on, I felt I must be doing something right. His enthusiasm has been reassuring and his input considered and welcome. The same is true of my editor Bill Scott-Kerr. Bill's been a joy to work with and his faith in the book has been a source of great encouragement. My copy editor, Mark Handsley, has been careful and flexible. I'm grateful to him. And at Transworld I'd like to thank Laura Gammell, Vivien Garrett, Simon Thorogood and everyone in the design department, marketing team and sales force who has worked so hard on the book's behalf.

A special mention needs to go to my parents, who gave me every opportunity. On occasions I've given them cause to question the wisdom of that.

Lastly, I want to thank my amazing wife, Lucy. Over the last couple of years I've been absent, preoccupied and short of time – either no fun to be around or not around at all. I don't know how you've put up with me, but the truth is I couldn't have done it without you, hon.

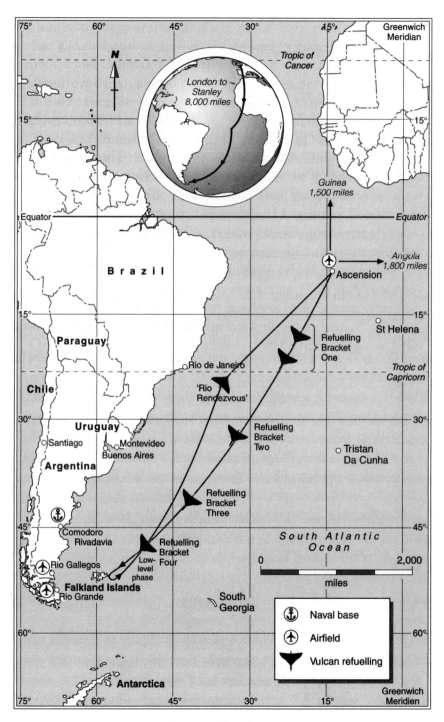

**Black Buck 1**

Ascension Island

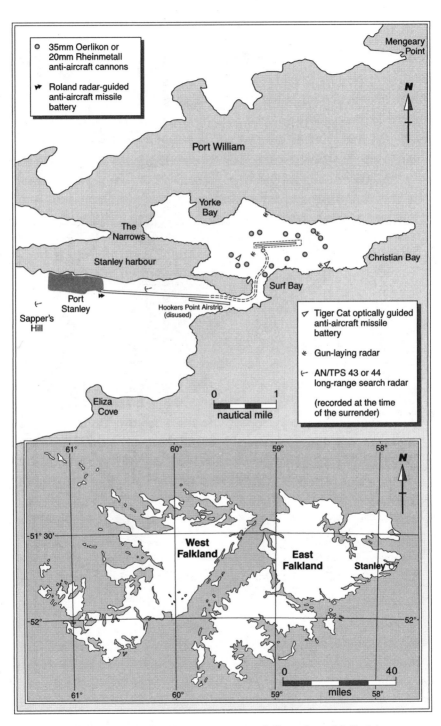

**Anti-Aircraft Defences around Stanley Airfield**

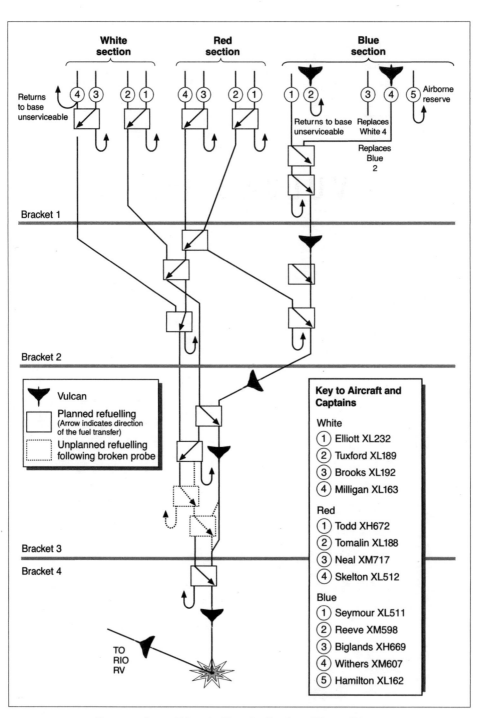

# Operation Black Buck Refuelling Plan

# VULCAN 607

# Prologue

## Down in Flames

*At Farnborough in September 1952, a prototype, then called the Avro 698, in the hands of Roly Falk, put on a flying display that remains in my memory more vividly than any other. The aircraft was new, having first flown only two days before the show opened. It was, like so many other British aircraft at the time, highly secret. It was a dramatic new shape that even people totally disinterested in aviation knew was called a delta. It was impressively large; Avro announced its skin plating would cover a football pitch. It was painted glossy white overall, making it look like the sail of a fantastic yacht. Above all, Falk did not take his amazing vehicle gently past the crowds, but thundered round in tight turns, with a white vortex writhing from the wingtip only just clear of the ground.*

Bill Gunston, *Aeroplane Monthly*, October 1980

# 8 January 1971

Looming cloud ahead meant that any further low-level flying would have to be abandoned. Flight Lieutenant Bob Alcock told the rest of his five-man Vulcan crew they were scrubbing it and smoothly increased the power to 85 per cent. He raised the nose and the big delta began its climb above the weather.

A moment later, a massive explosion rocked the bomber. Metal fatigue had caused the failure of a turbine blade in the number 1 engine. The blade jammed in the spinning engine until the catastrophic vibration ruptured the engine casing. Unharnessed, the whole turbine broke up. Debris ripped through the wing like gunfire. As the bomber absorbed the impact it lurched violently to the left. A catalogue of devastation unfolded in an instant.

Flight Lieutenant Jim Vinales flinched at the force of the blast, his whole body jerking with the shock of it. His first, instinctive, thought was that they must have hit the ground. But that couldn't be right – they were all still alive.

From the Captain's seat, Alcock and his co-pilot, Flying Officer Peter Harkyns, watched the rpm on the number 1 engine unwind as the jet pipe temperature rose rapidly. Then the fire-warning light in the centre of the control panel blinked on. Red. He shut it down and pressed the 'Fire' button. In the back of the crew cabin, Air Electronics Officer Jim Power switched off and isolated the engine's alternator and scanned the back of the jet for damage using his rear-view periscope. The big bomber continued to climb on the three remaining engines. When the fire-warning light went out it appeared the problem had been contained. Relaxing a little, Jim Vinales and Flying Officer Rodger Barker, the Navigator Radar to his left, exchanged a glance that acknowledged the unfamiliarity of it all. *What's going on?*, their faces asked, while at the same time confirming that they were in it together. There was no panic. They'd lost an engine, but the Vulcan was blessed with surplus power. They could maintain the climb to altitude on three engines. What they didn't know was that the destruction caused by the shattered number 1 engine hadn't yet properly revealed itself.

It didn't take long. Alcock noticed the jet pipe temperature on the number 2 engine rising alarmingly, followed quickly by its own fire-warning light. 'Fire in the number 2 engine,' he shouted to the crew. It was time to 'drop the rat' – the Ram Air Turbine that would help provide electrical power once the second engine and its alternator shut down. He reached forward and pulled the yellow and black handle.

With that, angry swarms of warning lights lit up around the cockpit and Vinales' navigation gear froze solid as all non-essential electrics shut down. They could do without it. When it boiled down to it, what mattered most was keeping the flow to the powered flight controls. Without *them*, the bomber was out of control. And for the time being at least, while he needed bootfuls of right rudder to keep her straight, Alcock did still have control.

Then the number 2 engine fire-warning light went out too. It was a brief respite, but barely more than an opportunity to declare an emergency. As they flew south over Northumberland towards Newcastle, Vinales passed a plot of their position to the Captain. Alcock thumbed the transmit button on the control column. 'Mayday, Mayday, Mayday,' he began.

With the fire-warning lights out, they weren't out of the woods, but they did have some breathing space. Vinales and

Barker looked at each other again, relieved that the situation, while serious, was no longer quite so acute. Then, to his right, Vinales noticed something catch Power's eye. While the AEO had been working through the detailed checks laid out on his flight reference cards, he'd caught a flicker in his rear-view periscope.

'Fire's not out!' he shouted through the intercom. 'Fire's not out!' As he watched the flames lick and burn underneath the jet's big delta wing, the number 2 fire-warning light came on again.

They were going to have to bail out.

Air Traffic Control responded to the 'Mayday', suggesting they try to put the burning bomber down at Ouston, a small airfield west of Newcastle. No good, Alcock told them. He was going to try to make it south to the Master Diversion Airfield, RAF Leeming, near Thirsk. Only a frontline station had the kind of emergency facilities that might be able to cope with their arrival.

It was becoming clear, though, that even that was too far. As the jet climbed to 9,000 feet, it was beginning to handle raggedly. Alcock knew he had to save the lives of those on board. But only he and his co-pilot had ejection seats. Instead, the backseaters had swivelling seats with inflatable 'assister cushions'. Pulling the yellow and black handle didn't fire the men clear of the aircraft, but merely helped them up and forward out of their seats. They were going to have to jump.

'Prepare to abandon aircraft,' Alcock ordered. Vinales, sitting in the middle, was pinioned until the men on either side of him vacated their chairs. Rodger Barker moved first. His chair swivelled to the right to release him and he clambered down to crouch at the front of the crew hatch on the floor of the bomber's cabin. Vinales pulled the cabin depressurization handle.

'Ready,' each of the three backseaters called out in turn.

'Static line,' instructed the Captain. 'Jump! Jump!'

From next to the crew hatch, Barker turned and pulled at the lever that opened the door. At the same time, Vinales hit the switch at the Nav Plotter's station that operated the door electrically. Failsafe. The parachutes, attached with a static line to the roof of the Vulcan's cabin, would open automatically.

As the two pneumatic rams pushed the door out into the slipstream, a cloud of dust ballooned up into the cockpit. Barker raised his knees up to his chest, clutched his arms around his ankles and vanished from view out of the 3-foot by 6-foot hole in the cockpit floor.

Jim Power was the next to go. Vinales looked at the AEO to his right – he seemed to be struggling with his oxygen mask, unable to free it. Vinales saw the concern in his eyes and quickly moved to help. As he reached out to tear it off, the mask came clear and Power too clambered down over the jump seat to the sill of the open crew hatch. He curled into a tight ball before sliding down the crew door and out towards the Cheviot Hills 9,000 feet below.

With Power gone, Vinales pushed his seat back on its runners. Unlike Power and Barker he didn't trigger the assister cushion. Received wisdom among the Nav Plotters held that it would only wedge you under the chart table and trap your legs. Vinales wasn't going to test the theory. He unstrapped, got up and climbed down towards the front of the door. A well-rehearsed escape drill. Second nature. He tucked up tight and let go, plunging quickly along the smooth metal door into the sky below.

As Vinales dropped out into the slipstream, from the corner of his eye he caught sight of the two pneumatic rams flashing past on either side of him. Then the elemental roar of the two remaining engines, straining on full power to keep the doomed bomber in the air, overwhelmed him. It was horrendous – an over-amped, thunderous howl that kept any immediate thought of safety at bay.

The parachute jerked open two seconds later and forced his chin down on to his chest. The lines were snarled. It might have spooked him, but Vinales was fortunate. An experienced sports parachutist, he knew there was no real cause for concern. He just had to ride it out and let the twisted risers unwind. But there *was* a downside to his confidence. He knew he'd never have chosen to jump for fun with a 25-knot wind coursing over rock-strewn hills below. He'd be lucky, he thought, to escape with only a broken leg.

As the receding sound of the burning Vulcan shrank to a low rumble, he struggled to catch sight of it. He strained to look over his shoulder as the parachute lines uncoiled, but a last glimpse of the dying jet carrying away the two pilots eluded him.

*They've got ejection seats*, he thought, *they'll live*. He was more concerned now with his own predicament, because if the fates were against him when he hit the ground, *he might not*. And, with the way the day had gone so far, it was hard to say whether luck was on his side or not . . .

# PART ONE

An Ungentlemanly Act

*This was a colony which could never be independent, for it never could be able to maintain itself. The necessary supplies were annually sent from England, at an expense which the admiralty began to think would not quickly be repaid. But shame of deserting a project, and unwillingness to contend with a projector that meant well, continued the garrison, and supplied it with a regular remittance of stores and provision. That of which we were most weary ourselves, we did not expect any one to envy; and, therefore, supposed that we should be permitted to reside in Falkland's island, the undisputed lords of tempest-beaten barrenness.*

*Thoughts on the Late Transactions Respecting Falkland's Islands*, Samuel Johnson, 1771

# Chapter 1

## January 1982

The road trip was going well. A few days' break from flying had presented too good an opportunity to miss. Flight Lieutenant Martin Withers, Pilot Leader of 101 Squadron, RAF, had hired a vast American station wagon and with his five-man crew headed south into California. Hertz had been very clear. Whatever you do, don't take the car into Mexico, they'd said. But that, of course, had only encouraged them. The RAF men all thoroughly enjoyed their day trip over the border to Tijuana.

Now, after a night staying with friends of Withers' parents outside San Diego, they were drinking in a bar near Disneyland. And honour was at stake.

'Weenies!' the bullet-headed American Marine had called them. They'd only left the motel to have a couple of cocktails before heading out for something to eat, but that was the kind of challenge that Withers' Navigator, Flight Lieutenant Gordon Graham, couldn't let go. With dark good looks and a raffish moustache worn with conviction, Graham seemed every inch the dashing RAF officer. His precious Lotus Europa in its black and gold John Player Special livery only underlined that impression. As a patriotic Scot, Graham might have pre-ferred a good malt, but on this occasion he'd make an exception. Tequila it was.

Round followed brutal round, but the odds were always

stacked against the big American. He was competing alone, while Graham was part of a team, and the more he drank, the less he noticed. And he'd stopped noticing that Graham was passing drinks to his captain, Withers, and the rest of the crew. The Marine refused to be beaten. *Semper fi.* And then he passed out.

Even sharing the drinking, though, Withers' crew were all over the place. If it hadn't been for the pretty barmaid taking a shine to them they might have gone the same way as their loud-mouthed opponent, but she'd kept them going, plying them with coffee. Just as well too, because as the drinking had intensified, all thoughts of food fell by the wayside.

There were wide grins on their faces as the crew spilled out of the bar into the Californian night. If Withers' grin was wider than the others', it was with good reason: he had the barmaid's address and phone number in his pocket.

Martin Withers was enjoying himself, really enjoying himself, for the first time in months. And that was supposed to have been why he'd joined the Air Force in the first place. He'd abandoned a career in law. As his then boss had gently pointed out, all he ever did was talk about flying and stare out of the window whenever an aeroplane flew past. Withers still had vivid memories of a summer spent at RAF Binbrook as a member of his University Air Squadron. To his student eyes, the lifestyle of the young Lightning pilots was seductive. In 1968 he joined as a graduate entrant and was soon enjoying all that life as a young RAF officer had to offer. He was posted to Vulcans and, although he still harboured an ambition to fly fighters, life was good. By the end of 1981, though, it had all gone sour. Withers' wife, Amanda, had recently left him to return home to Australia. He'd been washed out of a fast-jet training course after the death of another student had cast a shadow over the whole class. Before his final check flight he was told that it didn't matter how well he flew, they weren't going to pass him. So, instead of a tour as a Qualified Flying Instructor on a Gnat he spent three years as an instructor on the less glamorous Jet Provost. Then, despite appearing to be an ideal candidate, he'd been overlooked for an exchange posting flying Alpha Jets with the Armée de l'Air in Toulouse. The weather in the south of France, he had thought, might be his only hope of persuading Amanda to come back. Instead he was sent back to the Lincolnshire fens where he had previously been stationed and back to the Vulcan Operational Conversion Unit. The OCU was the training squadron for all Vulcan bomber aircrew, but it was being shut down in anticipation of the jet's imminent retirement. By the time Withers was qualified to instruct, there was time to take just one student through before the outfit closed and he was sent back to a frontline bomber squadron. To cap it all, now separated, he no longer qualified for free RAF mess accommodation and was living alone in a little two-bedroom maisonette on the edge of a Lincoln council estate. All of a sudden he had very little fondness for the RAF.

Then, at the end of the year, he was chosen to participate in RED FLAG. Withers seized the opportunity to put aside his unhappiness and began to prepare himself and his crew to fly the Vulcan in America in the most realistic series of war games ever devised.

In December, as the Withers crew trained, Admiral Jorge Anaya, the ascetic, sharp-faced political head of the Argentine Navy, lent his support to General Leopoldo Galtieri's bid to take power in Argentina. Galtieri would replace President Viola, the weakened head of the country's ruling military junta. The price for Anaya's blessing was approval for the navy's plan to seize Las Malvinas, the Falkland Islands, the disputed British colony barely 300 miles off their southern shores. Galtieri was easily persuaded. The two men were also confident that they could carry international opinion with them. They had seen how, when Portugal was removed from Goa by India in 1961, the world had done nothing. Throwing out the colonial power from Las Malvinas would surely be seen as a similar piece of legitimate anti-colonialism. Especially with the

United States on their side. Only recently, the US government had been courting Galtieri as an ally for their operations in El Salvador. On a visit to America in 1981, Galtieri had been feted with genuine red-carpet treatment, enjoying time with those at the highest levels of government. After four years in isolation following Argentina's military coup, the country was being welcomed back into the fold.

The date Galtieri and Anaya had in mind was 9 July 1982 – the anniversary of Argentina's independence. By then, Britain's Antarctic patrol ship, HMS *Endurance*, would have been decommissioned, conscripts could be trained, delivery of French Super Étendard attack planes and their sea-skimming Exocet missiles would be complete and, in any case, the British would be powerless to intervene in the face of the extremes of the southern winter.

That was if the British responded at all. History suggested that they were, at best, ambivalent about their distant possession.

Withers and his crew arrived in Nevada in style – determined to start as they meant to continue. Inbound to Nellis Air Force Base, the air base near Las Vegas that hosted RED FLAG, Martin Withers had spied the vast scar of the Grand Canyon thousands of feet below. He radioed Air Traffic Control, asking to abandon his flight plan and finish the transit under Visual Flight Rules. He pulled back the throttle levers of his Avro Vulcan B2, swooped down with a smile on his face, and told his crew to find themselves a vantage point. While Withers flew, his young red-haired co-pilot, Flying Officer Pete Taylor, took snaps for everyone on board with the collection of cameras that hung round his neck – it was always said, after all, that Vulcan co-pilots carried *everything* but the responsibility. Tourists enjoying the breathtaking panorama of the canyon must have been unnerved to find themselves looking *down* on the huge delta wings of a British Vulcan bomber sweeping by below them, followed quickly by a second jet, flying past more cautiously, above the lip of the gorge.

Once on the ground at Nellis, with the skyscrapers of Las Vegas's mega-casinos visible from the vast flightline, Withers was joined by Squadron Leader Alastair 'Monty' Montgomery, the diminutive, hyperactive Scottish captain of the second Vulcan, and his crew. The two crews walked towards the collection of functional white low-rise buildings and hangars that lined the concrete pan. Withers, his face boyish despite his thinning hair, was popular, self-deprecating and friendly. As he entered Building 201, RED FLAG's HQ, and began to get his bearings, he looked up at the board that displayed the day's flying programme and winced. Over a map of the Grand Canyon was an unmissable red mark bearing the words 'NOT BELOW 20,000 FEET'. *Wonderful scenery though*, he thought.

As a teenager, Monty had, like Withers, been inspired to join the Air Force by the glamour of being a fighter pilot. The moment an English Electric Lightning taxied past at an air-show with the canopy raised, its scarf-wearing pilot waving insouciantly at the crowd, Monty had been hooked. RED FLAG was the kind of thing they'd signed up for and both men knew that it was a privilege to be involved. The RAF were first invited to take part in 1977. And since then they'd earned a reputation for low, aggressive flying. 'Those RAF boys truly part the sand and shave the rocks,' said one admiring American fighter pilot. Only the best crews were sent and com-petition for places on the RAF detachment was fierce. Over the month that followed, Withers and Monty would be tested as pilots and captains like never before. And they would become, despite their very different personalities, firm friends.

RED FLAG was born out of necessity. During the Vietnam War, the North Vietnamese ace Nguyen Van Bay shot down thirteen American fighters. These weren't the kind of numbers that sat happily with the USAF. While the war was still being fought they commissioned the 'Red Baron' Report into what was going wrong. American training taught the crews every-thing but how to fight. Good, but raw, young pilots were being overwhelmed by the experience of combat. If they lived through the first ten hours or so of combat, though, the odds on surviving the rest of the tour improved dramatically. The solution was RED FLAG, which first took place in 1975.

Flown over the deserts and ridges of Nevada, on weapons ranges the size of Switzerland, RED FLAG was a series of ultra-realistic war games. Participants were divided into blue and red forces, good guys and bad guys. Radars tuned to Warsaw Pact frequencies searched the skies while anti-aircraft units fired harmless but convincing Smoky SAMs – simulated surface-to-air missiles. RED FLAG also boasted its own 'enemy' fighters in the shape of the 64th Aggressor Squadron, a unit trained to fly and fight like the Soviets. Through all of this, the good guys had to try to get through to their targets. It was the closest training got to going to war for real. If combat was Red, and peacetime Green, then RED FLAG was Amber.

Inside Building 201, the walls were covered with signed pictures and plaques left behind by visiting units. In the offices of RED FLAG's Commanding Officer, though, one poster stood out. It celebrated the time a low-flying RAF jet scraped a scar into the scrub with its wingtip. The same year, another crew took out a powerline when they flew *up* into it. When the engineers went out to repair the line they recorded its height from the ground: just 42 feet. And aircrew and engineers still talked about the photo taken of a Vulcan with a chunk of Joshua tree jammed behind its control surfaces. But what might appear reckless was in fact the lifeblood of the RAF strike force in 1982. Low-level flying was their main defence. It stopped search radars seeing them until the last minute, denied fire-control radars the time to get a lock and confused the air-to-air radars of defending fighters as they struggled to pick up their attackers against clutter thrown up by the ground features.

During the first week of the exercises, a minimum altitude of 200 feet was imposed – organizers didn't want participants killing themselves – but as crews familiarized themselves with the terrain that restriction was lifted. When anyone asked

Martin Withers how low he'd take his Vulcan through the Nellis ranges he'd smile mischievously and tell them 'never below eighty feet' – less than the wingspan of the Vulcan he was flying. At this height, the vortices spiralling off his wings could roll tumbleweed in the big bomber's wake. A sneeze could send the crew into the ground in a twitch. But it was the big jet's combination of size and low-down agility that so impressed the Americans. Their lumbering B-52s simply couldn't twist and turn below the ridgelines like their British counterparts. As the Vulcans swept past it was an epic sight. The American crews who manned the Smoky SAM sites would whoop and holler at the sight of such a large aircraft being flown so low and so hard through the hot, viscous desert air. Even in the relative cool of January in Nevada the Vulcan crews would finish a sortie wet with sweat from physical exertion.

Alone on Withers' crew, AEO, Flight Lieutenant Hugh Prior had been to RED FLAG before. Chosen as the most qualified Vulcan AEO for that first RAF deployment in 1977, he knew well the dangers the Nellis ranges presented. That year a Blackburn Buccaneer S2, trying to negotiate its way through the jagged Nevada peaks at 100 feet and 500 knots, was lost. On one occasion, Prior had thought the same fate awaited his Vulcan. As his two pilots scanned the ridgelines looking for gaps through to the next valley, one told the other, 'We're not going to make it.' To Prior and the two navigators seated facing to the rear, without a view out, it was a statement open to misinterpretation at the very least. The pilot was lucky any of the three backseaters climbed into a plane with him ever again.

The Vulcans were at the Nellis ranges to practise for one thing only: to deliver a nuclear bomb. And on Martin Withers' crew ultimate responsibility for the success of that fell to the amiable young Navigator Radar, Flying Officer Bob Wright. And even getting to a frontline squadron had been far from plain sailing for him. Wright had wanted to be a pilot, but had been told after three attempts that he didn't have the aptitude for it. Hand–eye co-ordination, they'd said. Poor A-level results didn't help either. But he still wanted to fly and so he accepted the knock-back and joined the RAF as a Navigator, eyeing the possibility of a posting to a fast-jet squadron. Then he flunked Navigator training. He got through the second time, but then had to endure watching other students get postings to the Buccaneers and Phantoms he wanted while he got Vulcans. But as soon as he arrived at Waddington things started looking up. Being on the squadron was exactly what he'd needed. He was learning and improving with every sortie. On a five-man crew, the others were able to support and nurture the new boy. Wright, the Navigator Radar, operated the Navigation and Bombing System (NBS). This included a powerful radar which he used to fix the aircraft's position against distinctive ground features. Low over the ridges and valleys of the Nevada scrub, he also served another vital function – providing back-up to the pilots who used their own Terrain-Following Radar (TFR) to fly clear of obstacles. Sitting at his right shoulder, Navigator Plotter Gordon Graham planned the route, and navigated the aircraft around it. He controlled the jet's primary navigation system: the Ground Position Indicator Mk 6. The GPI6 provided a continuous read-out of the aircraft's position over the ground in latitude and longitude. Graham's system was linked to Wright's NBS, and information could be passed between the two. The two navigators worked together, and as RED FLAG progressed each began to develop an instinct for how the other operated. They were becoming a strong team. In the end though, while Graham could navigate the aircraft, the pilots Withers and Taylor could follow his directions, and AEO Hugh Prior could try to make sure they stayed safe from the attentions of enemy air defences, it was still Wright who had to drop the bomb on target. And that alone was the Vulcan's *raison d'être*.

# Chapter 2

Galtieri's accession to Argentina's presidency meant that Anaya's plot to invade Las Islas Malvinas became a priority. In so doing, it displaced an earlier initiative to test Britain's resolve in the region. In July 1981, encouraged by signals from London suggesting a waning interest in the South Atlantic, Anaya and Vice-Admiral Juan Lombardo, the Commander-in-Chief of the Argentine fleet, had begun planning a different operation. In 1976 the two men had put fifty naval technicians and scientists ashore on the frozen British island of Southern Thule, one of the chain of South Sandwich Islands that lie 400 miles to the south-east of South Georgia. The Argentinians quietly constructed a permanent weather station there and, beyond protesting, the British did nothing to remove them.

Anaya and Lombardo proposed to repeat the operation on South Georgia itself. The plan was christened Operation ALPHA and was designed to establish an Argentine claim on the remote outpost. But with Galtieri in power, ALPHA was relegated, quickly overtaken in Anaya's imagination by the greater prize: taking possession of Las Malvinas. Plans for ALPHA, however, remained in place. Lombardo quickly realized that Operation BLUE, as the Falklands plan became known, would be jeopardized if Operation ALPHA was allowed to go ahead. The British were certain, he thought, to send a nuclear hunter-killer submarine in response to any move on South Georgia and the Argentine Navy simply had no answer to a weapon of such stealth and sophistication.

Lombardo signalled Anaya in Buenos Aires from his base at Puerto Belgrano on 15 January in order to make his point and was told by Anaya that ALPHA had been cancelled. Reassured, Lombardo and his staff carried on with detailed planning for Operation BLUE. The Falkland Islands' long and messy history was about to become manifest.

Early disputes over sovereignty were characterized by their half-heartedness – that is, until any rival displayed an interest. Sightings of the islands by ships rounding Cape Horn date back to the sixteenth century, but it was the British who were the first to record setting foot on the islands, when a privateer, Captain John Strong, *en route* to Chile, was forced to take refuge there from a storm. Few, however, seemed particularly enamoured of the bleak, treeless islands that sat like a pair of lungs, either side of Falkland Sound – the channel of water named by Strong after the then Lord of the Admiralty. It was over sixty years before a more permanent presence on the islands was established. And it was French. Antoine de Bougainville created the small settlement of Port Louis on East Falkland in 1764, claiming the islands for the French king. Three years later, in an attempt to strengthen an alliance with Spain, the colony was sold to her for the modern-day equivalent of £250,000 and Port Louis became Puerto Soledad. And Les Malouines – named after the French port of Saint-Malo – became Las Malvinas. And that would have been that: the islands would have passed from Spain to Argentina as that country came into existence in the early 1800s, assuming in- dependence and control of Spain's South American territories.

Or it would have been were it not for the fact that, while all this was going on, the British had arrived on Saunders Island off West Falkland in 1765, fenced off and planted a vegetable garden, and named the whole enterprise Port Egmont. But although the British mission might have been motivated by French interest in the region, the men on the ground appear to have been entirely ignorant of the rival French settlement at Port Louis.

When the British conducted a more thorough reconnaissance the following year, however, they stumbled on de Bougainville's colony, now numbering around 250 people. Offered a choice by the British expedition's leader, Captain John McBride, of leaving or swearing allegiance to George III, the colonists called his bluff and a humiliated McBride was forced to return to England, leaving behind only a small contingent of marines at Port Egmont.

Two years later, those thirteen marines gave themselves up to the Spanish commodore commanding the fleet of five frigates sent from Buenos Aires to expel them. The shame provoked a public outcry in Britain and a demand that national honour be avenged. Neither Britain nor Spain – without French support, at least – wanted war, however, so while Dr Johnson, commissioned by the British government, wrote a pamphlet trying to devalue the islands in the mind of the nation, a compromise with Spain was negotiated.

For three years, the British colony returned to Port Egmont before quitting for good in 1774, leaving behind only a plaque restating Britain's sovereignty, which read: 'Be it known to all nations that Falkland's Ysland, with this fort, the storehouses, wharf, harbour, bays, and creeks thereunto belonging, are the sole right and property of His Most Sacred Majesty George III.'

And with that, the islands remained under the control of Spain and her inheritors, the United Provinces of Rio de la Plata and that new state's successor, Argentina, for the next sixty years, until the brutal intervention of an American warship, the USS *Lexington*, in 1831.

Spain removed her colonial authorities from Puerto Soledad in 1810, and from that point on the islands became little more than a base for American sealers, who were used to operating without rules or administration. So when the United Provinces appointed a governor in 1823, his relationship with the lawless residents was always going to be a difficult one. The simmering distrust between Buenos Aires and the unruly residents of Puerto Soledad came to a head after the appointment of a new governor, Louis Vernet. Vernet imposed restrictions on the number of seals killed, and in trying to enforce them arrested an American ship and escorted her to Buenos Aires to make the captain stand trial.

Vernet's great misfortune was that the USS *Lexington*, under her captain Silas Duncan, was at port in Buenos Aires. Demanding that Vernet be arrested as a pirate, Duncan immediately set sail for Puerto Soledad, where, on arrival, he destroyed the settlement, declared the islands 'Free of all government' and left.

The British government quickly saw an opportunity both to reassert its own sovereignty and head off any possibility of the Americans establishing a permanent naval presence in the South Atlantic. In 1833 HMS *Clio* and HMS *Tyne* took and held the Falkland Islands and they have remained British ever since. But what seemed an almost casual reassertion of the status quo for the British hurt Argentina badly. For this newly independent young country it was and remained an illegal occupation, a humiliating stain on the nation's self-image and a source of simmering resentment. They mattered to her in a way that they could never matter to Britain.

By 1982, little appeared to have changed on that front. Now, though, these windswept southerly islands had a 1,800-strong population who were passionately and defiantly British. And the Argentinians had decided to do something about it.

# Chapter 3

The Avro Vulcan was conceived in the reign of King George VI as a nuclear bomber. She was designed by a team led by the legendary Lancaster, Sir Roy Chadwick at A. V. Roe, to meet an ambitious 1947 Air Staff Requirement for an aircraft that could cruise at 500 knots at an altitude of 50,000 feet for nearly 4,000 miles to deliver a 'special bomb'. With a piston-engined RAF bomber force barely capable of flying 2,000 miles at 200 knots and 20,000 feet, it was to be quite a feat of engineering.

Chadwick's solution was radical: a giant delta, her nose and cockpit extending forward of the triangular planform like the head and neck of a pterodactyl. It's hard to appreciate the impact this imposing combination of power and purpose must have made when she first roared overhead, powered by four of the same Rolls-Royce Olympus engines that would be developed to propel Concorde through the sound barrier. In 1952 – two years before the last Lancaster was retired by the RAF – she must have looked like she'd soared straight out of the pages of 'Dan Dare' in the *Eagle* comic. And the public weren't the only ones who seemed left behind by Britain's most advanced jet bomber. When the test pilot Roly Falk wowed the crowds at the Farnborough air show, 'the pinstriped pilot' did so wearing a tweed suit and tie.

After entering service in 1956, the Vulcan bore most of the weight of Britain's independent nuclear deterent and did so convincingly.

In 1961, RAF Bomber Command was invited to participate

in SKYSHIELD, a major exercise designed to test North America's sophisticated air defences. Eight Vulcans took part. Four, flying from Scotland, attacked from the north. The rest approached from the south out of Kindley Air Force Base in Bermuda. Preceded by American B-47s and B-52s, the northern component streamed in at 56,000 feet, a greater height than any of the defending USAF fighters could reach. One of the British bombers picked up the fire-control radar from an American F-101 Voodoo, but it was jammed by her AEO and she made it through unscathed. The other three were untouched. From the south, the four Vulcans spread themselves across a front 200 miles across. As the line approached the American east coast, the most southerly aircraft turned sharply north and, screened by electronic jamming from the three other bombers, staged a completely undetected mock attack on New York.

Since responsibility for Britain's independent nuclear deterrent passed to the Royal Navy's Polaris fleet in June 1969, however, the Vulcans had been relegated to the second wave, but they remained declared to NATO as a nuclear force. Crews joked about the tiny 28lb practice bomb that dropped foolishly from the Vulcan's cavernous bomb bay on to the RED FLAG targets, but the pint-sized bomb perfectly simulated the ballistics of the WE177C 400-kiloton nuclear bombs the Vulcans would in theory carry into war. Hitting the target with the little 'terror weapon' was, ultimately, the thing that mattered at RED FLAG, the planes' only real measure of success.

But it *was* getting ever tougher for them to get through. The demands on the crews coaxing the best out of what was now very outdated equipment were becoming more intense, and the risks in doing so becoming greater. The Vulcans were the only part of the RAF cleared to fly at low level at night in any weather. In fact they depended on it. But flying through ugly thunderheads that had grounded all the American participants at RED FLAG, Monty had thought he was going to lose the jet – that she'd break up in the violent skies. Once safely back on the ground, Monty felt that, on this occasion, discretion might have been the better part of valour. *Shouldn't have ever left the ground,* he thought. And when he was told by a severely shaken member of another Vulcan crew that they too had just all but hit the desert floor, he knew he wasn't the only one riding his luck.

Breaching the defences at night, in bad weather, below the radar, the Vulcans could still live with the hi-tech, swing-wing, supersonic USAF F-111s (which, in the early 1970s, the RAF had expected to *replace* the Vulcans) and completely out-classed the big B-52s. But by day, their big deltas casting long shadows on the desert floor, they were easy pickings for the new generation of American F-15 Eagles with their powerful look down–shoot down radars and guided missiles. When one Vulcan captain, breaking hard into a turn, found himself sand-wiched between two F-15s he knew his number was up. The Eagle jockeys were hardly breaking sweat – one even had the impudence to wave. In the right conditions, determined crews believed, the Vulcans could reach the target to deliver their 'bucket of sunshine', but working with navigation and bomb-ing equipment that hadn't been substantially upgraded for twenty years, they now had to rely to a frightening extent on their own skills and experience. The truth was that in 1982 the Vulcans were really starting to show their age.

That year would be the Vulcan's last appearance at RED FLAG, but there was little in the commitment or performance of the Vulcan detachment to suggest it. On or off the ground the pace was intense. In Vegas, the crews made the most of what was on offer. For many of them it was nights out with the boys, for some the slot machines featured. For John Hathaway, Monty's AEO, it was the satisfaction of staying awake late enough to catch the hotel's 99-cent breakfast before going to bed. By wading his way through another in the morning he was feeding himself for $1.98 a day. And RED FLAG had been known to lay on less innocent entertainment too: strippers provided by the wife of an American Lieutenant Colonel who ran her own booking agency. If the girls could cope with the big egos and testosterone of Happy Hour in the Nellis Officers' Club during RED FLAG, the lady reckoned, they were probably ready for anything.

But if the crews displayed big appetites for life on the ground, it was only because the enormous pressure of operating in the crowded, hostile skies out of Nellis demanded that kind of pressure valve. During the weeks at RED FLAG the Vulcan crews put themselves through the most challenging flying of their careers. By the time they took off from the long Nellis runway for the last time – their bomb bays stuffed with teddy bears and cuddly toys won in the Vegas arcades – all were holding their heads a little higher. Fuelled by that self-confidence, Withers and his crew were unable to resist a final flourish as they headed for home. But as they descended again towards the Grand Canyon, none of them imagined for a moment that they would soon be asked to draw on all they had learnt, or that self-confidence was about to become an extremely valuable commodity.

Martin Withers began his journey home from RED FLAG on 15 February 1982. As his Vulcan flew east across America, the final draft of Vice-Admiral Lombardo's plan to recover Las Islas Malvinas was passed to the Argentine junta. Reassured that ALPHA, the South Georgia operation, had been scrubbed and his work on BLUE approved, Lombardo went on holiday to an exclusive Uruguayan resort with his family.

The whole of Stanley – the world's most southerly capital – faced north, lining the south side of a large natural harbour. Whatever sun its remote latitude afforded it, it captured. There were a few trees – almost entirely absent outside town – but most of them were hunched like old women, because of the strong prevailing winds. Many of the houses were wooden and painted white. There were a few more permanent-looking constructions, but all seemed to share the same corrugated-iron roofs. Despite its small size and highlands and islands feel, though, Stanley had the infrastructure of a much larger settlement. So far from Britain and even the South American mainland, the little town needed its own power station, hospital, primary and secondary schools, and government buildings to support its population of barely 1,000 people.

Joe King's house, surrounded by immaculately manicured hedges, looked down the hill towards the waterfront. King had enjoyed drawing cartoons for the local paper until realizing that every time he lampooned the events of the day – usually another crashed Land-Rover – someone would take it personally. In an island community which, in and out of Stanley, totalled just 1,800 people, he knew he'd end up offending everyone. A laugh and a joke over a drink seemed safer, he'd decided. In the first months of 1982, though, his easy good humour was coming under threat from another source: Argentina. Something was up – he could smell it. Successive British government ministers had visited, suggesting compromise and accommodation with Argentina, but for King and many others, it was simple: they were British and wanted to remain so. And they wanted to get on with their lives without concerns over Britain's commitment and Argentina's ambition hanging over them.

On 6 March 1982 an Argentine C-130 Hercules approached Stanley airfield. On board was the local agent – an Argentine Air Force officer – for Lineas Aéreas del Estado (LADE). Since the new airport had opened five years earlier, this quasi-civilian Argentine transport airline had operated the air link between Comodoro Rivadavia on the mainland and the islands. In the tower, Gerald Cheek, the bearded, red-haired Director of Civil Aviation on the islands, manned the radio. All appeared normal until the crew of the big turboprop radioed to say they couldn't lower the landing gear and were aborting the landing. They flew straight down the length of the runway then simply continued west in the direction of Argentina. As the Hercules flew overhead, HMS *Endurance*, the Royal Navy's ice patrol ship, steamed off Cape Pembroke, to the east of the islands. For many years she had been the only British warship permanently stationed in the South Atlantic and, militarily at least, she was of limited value. But she was a visible presence and signalled Britain's continuing interest in the region. This was to be her final season, however, before being decommissioned without replacement.

The announcement, made in June 1981, that *Endurance* was to be withdrawn had been opposed by the British Foreign Office for fear that it would send the wrong message to Argentina. It did. Along with the decision to withhold full British citizenship to nearly half the Falklands population and the imminent closure of the British Antarctic Survey base on South Georgia, it sent a very clear message to Argentina: Britain does not really care about the South Atlantic.

The Hercules returned to Stanley later the same day. This time there were no problems with the landing gear. Gerald Cheek watched from the side of the apron as the camouflaged transport plane taxied to the terminal and drew to a quick stop without shutting down the engines. The stairs at the front of the plane swung down and the LADE agent stepped down to the concrete. Then before any of the airport ground crew could get near, the door was closed and the Hercules was taxiing back to the end of the runway for an immediate departure. *There's something not right about this*, thought Cheek.

Then the Chief Engineer of FIGAS – the Falkland Islands Government Air Service – turned to him and told him that the Hercules had a camera pod attached to the wing.

There were other causes for concern. In a separate incident, another Argentine Hercules had declared an emergency and landed unexpectedly at Stanley airport, where she'd been surrounded by armed Royal Marines from Naval Party 8901. This tiny detachment of lightly armed marines who, on Guy Fawkes night, would fire flares into the sky in lieu of fireworks, were in effect the only defence provided by Britain for the Falklands. The British government simply didn't take the Argentine threat seriously.

Bilateral talks held at the UN in early March between the two countries ended inconclusively. The British delegation offered nothing beyond further talks and a restatement of the principle that the wishes of the islanders were paramount and that sovereignty was not up for negotiation. The idea that there was no timeline nor any prospect of something more tangible than an agreement to talk again was rejected out of hand in Buenos Aires.

The two-man delegation from the Falklands that attended the talks returned from New York to Stanley sworn to secrecy, but making it quite clear that the situation was grave.

Joe King felt as if a noose was slowly tightening.

An Argentine entrepreneur, Constantino Davidoff, thought South Georgia would be his ticket to big money. At 105 miles long, but just eighteen and a half miles across at its widest point, the island's dramatic, mountainous landscape rises from sea level to nearly 10,000 feet. Reputed to endure the worst weather in the world, South Georgia was most well known for providing the daunting setting for the final act of Shackleton's epic journey to save his stranded men. It was the island's defunct whaling industry that attracted Davidoff. Between 1904 and 1965, when whaling operations finally ceased, over 175,000 of the million and a half whales taken from Antarctica were processed on the island. Such was the efficiency of the operation there that a ninety-foot blue whale weighing 150 tons could be flensed and processed in barely an hour. Davidoff's interest was in the derelict plant machinery, littering Leith, Stromness and Grytviken, that the whaling industry had left behind. He estimated that it was worth £7.5 million and could cost him £3 million to remove.

In 1978 Davidoff agreed a contract with the Scottish firm Christian Salvesen, who still owned the South Georgian leases. And then he tried to raise the money to pursue his grand scheme. While Davidoff kept the British embassy informed of his plans, little more was heard from him until December 1981, when he set sail for his El Dorado for the first time aboard the Argentine Navy icebreaker *Almirante Irizar*.

Davidoff needed only a few hours ashore at Leith to decide that there were indeed rich pickings for him on the island. Before setting sail the small landing party took notes and pictures and left behind cigarette butts, film packaging and a message scrawled in chalk, '*Las Malvinas son Argentinas –*

*20 December*', but it was what they didn't do that caused ripples. While Davidoff had alerted the British embassy and Salvesen's of his departure, he failed to obtain permission to land on South Georgia at King Edward Point, the official port of entry – thus making his landing illegal.

Despite delivering a formal protest over the incident – which was rejected by Argentina – the British embassy in Buenos Aires gave Davidoff permission to mount his recovery operation. Davidoff told the British that he would not be returning himself. This effectively meant that control of the expedition lay with the Argentine Navy, who were happily providing Davidoff with a 3,100-ton naval transport, *Bahia Buen Suceso*, for four months at the bargain price of just $40,000. It would soon become apparent to everyone that their motives were far from altruistic. *Bahia Buen Suceso* set sail for South Georgia on 11 March carrying Argentine marines.

Anchored off Grytviken, HMS *Endurance* was visiting South Georgia for the last time before returning to the UK for good. Her captain, Captain Nick Barker, knew of the *Bahia*'s departure, but had heard nothing more from her. It was usual for ships to broadcast regular weather updates, but *Endurance*'s operators heard none. The *Bahia*'s radio silence seemed suspicious to Barker, an officer with long experience in the region, but wasn't, in itself, a reason for staying put. Fuel and stores on the 'Red Plum', as *Endurance* was known because of her red-painted hull, were running low. So, concerned as he was, Barker couldn't wait for something that might never happen, and late in the afternoon on 16 March he sailed west for Stanley, leaving behind the small contingent of British Antarctic Survey scientists who were spending winter on the island.

In March 1982, *Endurance* wasn't the only British asset facing the prospect of imminent retirement. While she and the *Bahia Buen Suceso* criss-crossed the South Atlantic, Martin Withers delivered a Vulcan bomber to the Imperial War Museum at Duxford in Cambridgeshire. The big jet came in low over the

M11 motorway, performing two touch-and-goes for an air-show crowd on the museum's short runway before shutting down the engines for the last time. It wasn't even such an unusual day's work for the aircraft's crew. Other Vulcans were being flown into museums around the country. RED FLAG had been an Indian summer; the writing was on the wall for the old bombers.

By the time the Argentine negotiating team returned from New York, the mood in Argentina had hardened. The outcome of the talks no longer mattered. The Argentine Navy – in particular, Admiral Anaya – now seemed to be setting the agenda. And had the plan delivered by Vice-Admiral Lombardo on 15 February been acted on, it might even have worked. Instead, Anaya's unfortunate deputy was completely wrong-footed.

His plan to take Las Malvinas had contained one clear warning: if the British deployed a hunter-killer, the Argentine Navy would effectively be restricted to Argentina's home waters. So when news reached him at his Punta del Este resort that Davidoff's scrap metal dealers had raised the Argentine flag on South Georgia, he knew that Anaya had lied to him. The scrap dealers were no more than a cover story. ALPHA, he realized, was under way and the British, he felt certain, would dispatch a nuclear submarine south. Once it arrived on station, BLUE was off. He had, he calculated, about ten days to act.

# Chapter 4

'How do you feel about the Argentines hoisting their flag on South Georgia?'

The news took John Smith by surprise – he was frustrated that he was learning of events so close to home from a friend over 8,000 miles away in the UK. He felt it acutely too. Now running Sparrowhawk House guesthouse in the west of Stanley, he'd once worked for the British Antarctic Survey and had visited South Georgia before spending the next twenty years working for the FIC, the Falkland Islands Company. Although he had been born in Southampton, his roots were now in the Falklands. He'd been a resident for twenty-five years and been married to an islander, Ileen, for twenty-one of them. They had four children, two boys and two girls. Smith loved the islands, cherishing and recording their unique history – a job which included regular inspections of the rusting hulks of ships that had made it to Stanley harbour but no further.

Staying at the guesthouse when Smith heard the news of the scrap dealers' action on South Georgia was Captain Goffoglio of the Argentine Navy. That evening Goffoglio walked down the hill, past the children's playing field in front of Sparrowhawk House, to join the islanders at a town hall dance. He spent the evening dancing with a blonde Argentine teacher who was in Stanley to teach Spanish. As they reeled around, both wore knowing, contented smiles. Upset by events on South Georgia, John Smith found it uncomfortable to watch.

*

Goffoglio's cheerful reaction to the news from South Georgia contrasted greatly with that of his superior. A horrified Vice-Admiral Juan Lombardo was racing back to Puerto Belgrano against a British submarine that he was sure was on its way. But instead of sending an attack submarine, Britain ordered HMS *Endurance* to return to South Georgia, stand off Grytviken and await further orders. While 'Red Plum' embarked nine extra Marines from the Falklands garrison, fitted the two 20mm cannon that were normally stowed below decks and left her hydrographers behind, she set sail armed with little more than a firm set of the jaw.

In Stanley, ten-year-old Leona Vidal had been looking forward to an excursion aboard *Endurance* before the ship returned to the UK for winter. She and her classmates had been excited about it for weeks. With their trip scheduled for 1 April, the children planned a practical joke: to pretend one of them had fallen overboard. With *Endurance* gone, they were upset that their April Fools' Day prank was off – probably no bad thing. And in any case, their disappointment would soon seem very insignificant. As *Endurance* steamed east her radio operators intercepted traffic from Argentina to the *Bahía Buen Suceso* congratulating her on her mission's success. The situation was very finely poised and the dispatch of *Endurance* was about to tip the balance.

Air Chief Marshal Sir Michael Beetham sat in his office on the sixth floor of the Ministry of Defence building on Whitehall. As 1950s blocks go, he thought, it wasn't too bad. A bit of wood panelling here and there helped to dress it up, along with a few oil paintings from the MoD archives. Beetham was a compact, precise man whose kindly demeanour gave little hint of the fierce reputation he'd earned as a young squadron commander.

In the summer of 1940, Beetham had spent the school holidays with his father. A veteran of the First World War, but too old to fight in the Second, he had been posted by the army to Hillsea Barracks on the hills overlooking Portsmouth. Although tales of the trenches didn't fill the boy with much enthusiasm, his father was keen for him to join the army and the young Beetham expected to follow in his father's footsteps. Until, that is, from his vantage point at Hillsea, he watched scenes from the Battle of Britain unfold. As the Hurricanes and Spitfires took on the attacking German bombers they cast a spell on him. *That's what I want to do!*, he thought.

'Sorry about the army,' he told his father, 'I want to be a fighter pilot and fly one of those!' He joined the Air Force a year later, but by then the RAF needed bomber pilots. And in the winter of 1943 he was posted to 50 Squadron to fly Lancasters.

His squadron's next target had been Berlin. Beetham's crew weren't on the list to go. His Squadron Commander took him aside and told him he felt that such a heavily defended target might be too much on his first-ever raid. The next night, though, their names were on the list. And the target was again Berlin. 'We're going to be going to Berlin a lot,' the CO told him. 'I can't hold you back any more.' Beetham went on to fly thirty missions over Germany. Ten of them were over Berlin, but it was Augsburg that was mentioned in the citation for his DFC. Deep into southern Germany near the Austrian border, Augsburg and back was a long haul. His crew had completed their bomb-run and had turned for home, when the flight engineer spoke over the RT. The coolant temperature on one of the port engines had begun to rise alarmingly.

'Temperature's too high,' said the engineer. 'We've got to feather it. If we don't do something about it . . .' His voice trailed off.

If they didn't shut the Merlin down they'd have a fire on their hands. Beetham cut the power. Flying on three engines, they lost height and dropped behind the stream of bombers. Then, for the next 600 miles over enemy territory, they were on their own.

Now, thirty-seven years after the end of that war, he was in his fifth year as Chief of the Air Staff, the professional head of the Royal Air Force, and he was finding reports of scrap metal merchants raising the Argentine flag on South Georgia difficult to get too worked up about. After all, he'd seen it all before. He remembered earlier Argentine feints: the incident on Southern Thule in 1976, threats to British ships in the South Atlantic, even the deranged Operation CONDOR, when a group of Argentine radicals landed an airliner on Stanley racecourse and claimed the islands for Argentina.

In 1982, the entire MoD planning was focused on NATO and the Cold War. Intelligence-gathering, weapons systems, orders of battle and training were all concerned with keeping at bay the Soviet threat from the east. NATO forces faced nearly overwhelming numerical superiority and the UK could ill afford to be distracted by the regular routine contingency planning for every potential troublespot around the globe. At six-month intervals the chiefs would review possible theatres of operation throughout the world. Belize, the ex-colony of British Honduras that Guatemala had designs on, would always figure. So too would the Falklands. But unlike Central America, which was relatively easy to reinforce, whenever the Falklands came up, the conclusions would be the same – as things stood, the islands were practically indefensible. Although defence contingency plans ranged from sending a submarine to mounting a task force to ward off any threat, without proper resources being committed to the Falklands the plan for its defence amounted to little more than a hope that it wouldn't be necessary to defend it. And faced with the prospect of an occupation, it was thought unlikely that the islands could even *be* won back through force of arms.

But no one in Whitehall, it seemed, believed it would come to that. Beetham was not alone in failing to appreciate the significance of what was unfolding in the South Atlantic. After reviewing defence contingency plans for the Falklands and drawing little encouragement from them, the Defence Secretary, Sir John Nott, left for a NATO planning meeting in Colorado Springs on 22 March. The Chief of the Defence

Staff, Admiral Sir Terence Lewin, flew to New Zealand on an official visit, while Lord Carrington, the Foreign Secretary, left for Israel after agreeing to the dispatch of *Endurance* on 20 March.

There appeared to be a complete dislocation between Argentina's view of what was happening and London's. In the end, it was the mistaken assumption by Argentina that Britain had taken her seriously that triggered the immediate invasion of the Falklands. In sending *Endurance*, the British visibly demonstrated the gravity with which they regarded Operation ALPHA, but the patrol vessel was a paper tiger. Lombardo assumed, reasonably enough, that his opponent's response would make military sense. He never considered that *Endurance* might represent the sum total of Britain's reaction. He had, he believed, only until the submarine arrived to act.

While Lombardo scrambled to get back to Buenos Aires, the British press began to take an interest in the story. 'NAVY GUN BOAT SAILS TO REPEL INVADERS' read the most excitable of the headlines on offer. At RAF Waddington, Martin Withers registered the story, but like so many other people in Britain viewed it as a little local difficulty in a far-away place that would soon blow over. Before returning to the Vulcan force, he'd completed a tour as a Qualified Flying Instructor flying Jet Provosts. Used to the enormous Vulcan, he'd enjoyed flying the nimble two-seat trainers and jumped at the chance to keep his hand in. On 23 March, the day he threw the little JP around the sky for an exhilarating three-quarters of an hour of aerobatics, Lombardo was confronting Anaya. He demanded to know what was going on, but Anaya never gave him an answer. Instead, he simply asked his subordinate, 'Are we in a position to implement the Malvinas plan?'

As drafted, the answer could only be no. While 9 July had been suggested as the patriotic date to launch the operation, the earliest date given was in the middle of May. Now, with a week to go before the expected arrival of the submarine, the plan was in disarray. Lombardo had carefully designed Operation BLUE to use – and be *seen* quite clearly to be using – the minimum possible force. When the small main body of troops flew in by helicopter, one component of the invasion force would already be staying as paying guests in Stanley's Upland Goose Hotel. But his plan relied on the two transport ships and their helicopters that were now tied up in the South Georgia operation. Lombardo told Anaya he would need to consult his planning team and report back.

At Puerto Belgrano, Lombardo and his team frantically reworked the plan. He would now have to use warships and landing craft to deliver the troops to Las Malvinas. Despite his care to avoid it, Operation BLUE would now appear to be exactly what it was: a forceful, military annexation. But it could be done. Anaya was going to get his invasion.

On 28 March, a task force that included destroyers, frigates, a submarine and an aircraft carrier, *Veinticinco de Mayo*, set sail for the Falkland Islands.

# Chapter 5

## 30 March 1982

Commander Roger Lane-Nott, RN, was at war. Below the chill waters of the north-western approaches to Scotland his nuclear-powered hunter-killer submarine was on the frontline of the Cold War. HMS *Splendid* was the newest attack boat in the fleet and she had a contact. The control room, charged with adrenalin, focused on collecting and checking every snippet of information, every piece of intelligence and every sound. And then interpreting it.

Driving a submarine was as much an art as a science – nearly everything was subjective. The control room was tightly packed with machinery, valves, gauges and pipes. At action stations, fifteen or sixteen people were squeezed in, each with his own area of responsibility: ship control, navigation, information organization, fire control. In the middle, side by side, were the periscopes. It was an intense, claustrophobic environment in which everybody knew what was expected of him and his colleagues. There were no secrets in the control room of a nuclear submarine.

For Lane-Nott, *Splendid*'s war was personal and that's the way he wanted it. Stuck on the bulkhead in the mast well of the boat's control room were pictures of Soviet submarine commanders. He wasn't fighting an enemy boat, he was fighting its Captain. He had to outwit him; be *better* than him.

*Splendid* had been at sea continuously now for nearly three months. But the success or failure of the patrol had been distilled into the last forty minutes. For sixteen hours she'd been vectored into position by RAF Nimrods. Intelligence from the RAF patrol planes would be sent back to Northwood HQ then on to *Splendid* via 'the broadcast', a very-low-frequency transmission sent from an aerial in Northamptonshire. The reports could be received at any depth just thirteen minutes after first being made by the RAF. The beauty of 'the broadcast' was that at no point did the submarine have to advertise its position – the submariner's worst fear. Not for nothing were *Splendid* and her sister ships known as 'Sneaky Boats'.

The Nimrods worked closely with the attack boats. Submariners would fly with Nimrod crews to understand how they thought and operated and vice versa. Now that close co-operation had paid off, and *Splendid* had to maintain her contact without alerting the enemy boat.

To minimize noise from her screws and maximize the value of the intelligence he was gathering, Lane-Nott followed silently between a mile and a half and two miles to port and aft of the Soviet boat. He was aware that at any time the enemy could do something unexpected. It wouldn't have been the first time. In 1972, a Soviet submarine entered the Clyde Channel for the first time. Lane-Nott was a young navigator aboard HMS *Conqueror*, the boat given the simple order to 'Chase him out.' On being discovered, a very aggressive Soviet captain turned his submarine and drove it straight at *Conqueror*. It had been an *extremely* close call. There had been other occasions when harassed Russians had fired torpedoes to scare off trails. British attack boats never went to sea without live weapons in the tubes.

This is what it was all about. Lane-Nott felt energized that he'd found his quarry so quickly. Now there was no need to rush things. A nuclear submarine had endurance to burn. As long as his sonar operators maintained contact he could stay with her as long as he liked. The indications were that she was something new, a 'Victor 3' or 'Akula' class. Something they didn't have much intelligence on. By the time *Splendid* turned for home, they'd be groaning with it. Every minute of the patrol was recorded. There would be miles of tape to analyse.

They were in difficult water though, and before continuing the trail Lane-Nott wanted to know precisely where he was rather than rely on what the Inertial Navigation System was telling him. Without breaking contact with the Soviet boat he rose to periscope depth to fix his position. The shallower water also made communication easier and as *Splendid* returned to depth the Captain was interrupted by one of his radio signals men.

'There's a Blue Key message for you, sir.' For the Captain's eyes only. *Fucking hell*, he thought, *I don't want this now. I'm in the middle of a bloody trail.* Lane-Nott had been waiting his entire career for a Blue Key message and he was excited by the prospect of new, significant intelligence on the Russian, but a Blue Key meant that he had to decrypt it personally. Crypto codes changed every four hours and his personal safe was stuffed with the crypto cards and deciphers. Reluctantly, he left *Splendid* in the hands of his First Lieutenant.

As he decrypted the message he couldn't believe what he was reading. So he did it a second time. It seemed inexplicable. He had orders to abandon the trail, return to base under radio silence, and to store for war in preparation for another mission. He was to 'Proceed with all dispatch' – an expression that dated back to Nelson's time and all in the Navy understood. In naval terms, Lane-Nott's orders could not have been put more forcefully.

By three o'clock the following afternoon, *Splendid* was tied up in number 1 berth at Faslane naval base.

Air Vice-Marshal George Chesworth was furious. Since the early 1960s Chesworth's career had been devoted to finding and tracking Soviet submarines. Perhaps more than anyone else in the RAF, he'd been behind the introduction of the Nimrod into the service. He'd written the Air Staff Requirement, commanded the first squadron and now was Chief of Staff at 18 Group at Northwood HQ with operational responsibility for the entire Nimrod force. Nestled among the golf courses of London's leafy north-west suburbs, Northwood had since 1938 been the headquarters of the old Coastal Command, 18 Group's predecessor. By 1982, it was also home to the Navy. The two services worked closely and well together in an era when joint operations were not the norm. But what on earth, Chesworth wanted to know, were they up to now?

His Nimrods had painstakingly steered HMS *Splendid* to within striking distance of a Soviet boat. At Northwood, his team had been poring over the analysis of the tapes made by his aircraft, examining the signature of the boat, looking for new developments. And now, just as he thought the operation was about to pay off, the Navy were pulling their boat out. A bitterly disappointed Chesworth berated his naval counterpart.

'It's not our fault' was the only explanation he was given.

The decision was out of the Navy's hands. Political. And no one could tell him why. But by the time Chesworth travelled north with his family to their cottage in Scotland the following weekend, he, like everyone else in the country, knew exactly where the problem lay.

The MoD was finally acting on the contingency plans that had so depressed the Defence Secretary, John Nott, when he'd first read them a week earlier. He'd returned from the NATO summit in America to realize that the South Georgia situation had escalated. Over the weekend he read intelligence reports telling him that two Argentine destroyers armed with Exocet missiles had been ordered to sea following the diversion of *Endurance* to Grytviken. Nott decided it was time to send the submarines. *Splendid* was the second submarine being prepared to head south. Her sister ship, HMS *Spartan*, had been ordered into Gibraltar docks to take on stores on Monday. But with the Argentine fleet already at sea, there was nothing either boat would be able to do to stop the invasion. Without expecting to unearth anything that hadn't already been considered and dismissed, Nott discussed other possibilities with Sir Michael Beetham – with the Chief of the Defence Staff, Admiral of the Fleet Sir Terry Lewin, in New Zealand, the

Chief of the Air Staff was holding the reins. *Could the Falklands garrison destroy the runway to prevent the Argentinians flying in men and equipment?* They didn't have the explosives to do it. *Could the Parachute Regiment be flown into the islands by C-130?* The dependable old work-horses of RAF's transport fleet simply didn't have the range to cover the vast distances involved. The only comfort was a false one. Both men believed they were still discussing contingencies. At this point neither Nott nor Beetham knew that the Argentine invasion force was just a day away from the islands.

By six o'clock the following evening, they were in no doubt.

The Chief of the Naval Staff, Admiral Sir Henry Leach, returned to his office in Whitehall from a visit to the Admiralty Surface Weapons Establishment at Portsdown Hill. He'd been forced to cancel the trip three times already because of complications arising from a Defence Review that he believed would decimate the Royal Navy. Waiting on his desk was an intelligence report that stated unequivocally that an Argentine invasion of the Falklands was likely to take place before dawn on Friday, 2 April. Accompanying it were a number of briefs counselling that no more should be done. Leach had joined the Navy as a thirteen-year-old cadet in 1937. A sailor of the engage-the-enemy-more-closely Nelsonian tradition, Leach found the contradictory signals baffling and nonsensical. *What the hell is the point of having a Navy*, he thought, *if it was not used for this sort of thing?*, and he strode off to find John Nott, his nemesis over the offending defence review. But the Defence Secretary wasn't in his office. Alarmed by the same intelligence seen by Leach, he was already in the Prime Minister's room in the House of Commons, briefing her on the situation. Leach was invited in. The Defence Chiefs normally conducted their business in Whitehall in civilian business suits. Uniform was reserved for when a point needed to be made, but, just back from an official visit, Leach was wearing his naval uniform. Coincidentally, he also had a point to make.

'Admiral, what do you think?' he was asked.

Leach was unstinting: everything suggested the islands would be invaded in the next few days. Nothing could now be done to deter the Argentinians and nothing could be done to stop them. To recover the islands or not was a political decision, but to do so would require a large naval task force. He went on to outline the ships that could make up the task force. Questions came quickly. *How quickly could a task force be assembled? How long would the task force take to get to the Falkland Islands? What about air cover?* Then came the one that really mattered.

'Could we really recapture the islands if they were invaded?'

'Yes,' Leach answered deliberately, 'we *could* and in my judgement – though it is not my business to say so – we *should*.'

'Why do you say that?' the Prime Minister came back quickly.

Leach finished with a flourish. 'Because if we do not, or if we pussyfoot in our actions and do not achieve complete success, in another few months we shall be living in a different country whose word counts for little.'

Margaret Thatcher nodded and Leach thought she looked relieved. He left with orders to sail a third attack submarine south and with full authority to prepare a task force he'd said could be ready in forty-eight hours.

The Prime Minister turned to her Defence Secretary. 'I suppose you realize, John,' she said, 'that this is going to be the worst week of our lives.'

'Well, that may be so,' Nott responded, 'but I imagine that each successive week will be worse than the last,' and felt immediately that his reply was less than helpful.

Back in his office at the MoD, Leach telephoned Sir Michael Beetham. The news of the Admiral's decisive intervention caught Beetham on the back foot. Ideally, he and Leach would have spoken beforehand, but it was clear Leach's action had been unplanned – a consequence of events developing a momentum of their own.

*

With the invasion now inevitable, *Endurance* was ordered to return from South Georgia to Stanley, leaving behind her force of twenty-two Royal Marines to defend the island should the Argentine mission – still operating under the cover of Davidoff's scrap dealers – make its intention clear. Captain Barker was mindful of the odds stacked against the meagre contingent of Marines.

'In three weeks' time this place is going to be surrounded by tall grey ships, but we're not going to be able to help you if you're dead,' Barker told Lieutenant Mills, the young officer in command of the soldiers. He went on to suggest that about half an hour's spirited resistance before surrendering to overwhelming Argentine forces might be about right.

'Fuck half an hour,' Mills was overheard saying as he disembarked. 'I'm going to make their eyes water.'

That night, 'Red Plum' slipped away from South Georgia to the east, hugging the jagged shoreline to avoid being picked up on Argentine radar.

# Chapter 6

## 1 April 1982

A 25lb gold-painted bomb enjoyed pride of place in Flight Lieutenant Mick Cooper's house. Since he joined the Air Force, bombing had been his obsession. And he was good at it too. Throughout the 1970s Cooper's reputation as a bomb-aimer had grown steadily. The bomb he now displayed at home had been blagged by his crew, a gift to mark Cooper's outstanding performance in the RAF's annual bombing competition against the Americans. Contemporary newspaper reports described Cooper, brought up in Essex, as a 'cockney bombing ace'. By 1982, the chain-smoking Navigator Radar with the straggly red hair was, perhaps, the best in the business and that was all he ever wanted to be. His Captain on 50 Squadron reckoned the 'Green Porridge', the glowing cathode ray tube that displayed Cooper's radar picture, spoke to him. The RAF may have regarded him as 'overspecialized', but so what. His job was to get the bomb on target. End of story. The Vulcan was simply transport, its sole purpose to get him to the right place to drop a nuclear bomb.

Cooper would tell people he regretted never having had the chance to do just that. It wasn't Armageddon he was after, just the satisfaction of knowing he could do the job he'd been trained to do.

In spring 1982, though, with the Cold War reaching its endgame, the possibility that he'd get his chance felt very real.

Brezhnev was still General Secretary of the Communist Party and the Soviet Union's three-year-old invasion of Afghanistan provided a reminder of how high the stakes were – as if the vast armies, air forces and navies that faced each other, waiting for their opponent to blink, weren't reminder enough. In Britain, the publication of Raymond Briggs' graphic novel *When the Wind Blows* vividly reflected many people's genuine fear. Just around the corner lay Ronald Reagan's description of the USSR as the 'Evil Empire'. And yet despite the ratcheting up of East–West tension, Cooper wasn't going to get to do his job in a V-bomber. By summer, the last four Vulcan squadrons would be gone and RAF Waddington reduced to care and maintenance. On the far side of the station – an old Second World War bomber base built on fens south of Lincoln – decommissioned Vulcans were already being torn apart for scrap. Sitting unloved with panels missing and wires hanging off them, they were a sorry sight for long-serving crews who regarded the old jets with fondness.

Despite the destruction, morale on the station was still high. For the time being, Cold War notwithstanding, a flying club atmosphere persisted. Waddington had its own golf course and, of course, its own Officer i/c Golf. Work hard, play hard. Many of the men had been on the Vulcan force for years. Squadrons shuffled around and nearly everyone had been on the same squadron as nearly everyone else at some point in his career. With responsibility for Britain's nuclear deterrent in the hands of the Navy, the crews usually had weekends off, so Friday night's Happy Hour became a focal point. It usually carried on all night. Formal dining in the evening also provided opportunities to let off steam. And the sight of well-lubricated bomber crews performing 'carrier landings', launching themselves off tables through the windows of the Officers' Mess, would have struck a chord with anyone who'd watched similar scenes of chaos in movies like *The Dambusters*. Boys will be boys.

Mick Cooper wasn't sure about it all. He liked a glass of wine over dinner with his wife Sharon, but didn't care for being a piss artist. It didn't mean he didn't enjoy a joke though.

As he sat reading the alarming-sounding headlines on 1 April, he couldn't resist the temptation to make mischief. It was April Fools' Day after all, and Argentine designs on British islands in the South Atlantic all seemed so far away and unlikely. Cooper phoned the station Medical Officer and told him he was going to ring around the squadron and ask who had 1,000lb conventional bombing experience and was fully jabbed up for the South Atlantic. Would the MO go along with it, he asked. The Doc agreed to and Cooper began asking for volunteers.

Two weeks later it would no longer seem so funny. And the joke would, in any case, be very firmly on Cooper himself.

'This is the worst day of my life,' wrote Captain Nick Barker as *Endurance* steamed impotently between South Georgia and the Falklands into a force ten gale. The bottom line was that he and his ship couldn't be in two places at once. Barker had left South Georgia reluctantly, feeling that, lightly armed as she was, at least here *Endurance* and her Wasp helicopters could influence events – even stop any Argentine aggression in its tracks. Barker spoke to his tactical team aboard *Endurance*, his words reflecting the desperate frustration he felt: 'There must be something we can do to zap these bastards.'

The options were limited. They could try to enter Stanley harbour in the face of the Argentine task force and stall an invasion that would already be well under way. *Probably suicidal.* Or they could try ramming the Argentine support tanker using *Endurance*'s reinforced, ice-breaking bow. Without fuel, the Argentine fleet might be vulnerable to his little Wasps with their AS12 wire-guided missiles. It wasn't much of a plan, but it was better than nothing. *Endurance* ploughed on west through the storm.

In London, despite Leach's bravura performance, there was still unease about sending a task force. Because of the strength of feeling there had been over the Defence Review, John Nott couldn't quite bring himself to accept Leach's judgement at face value. Sir Michael Beetham, too, urged caution. If the fleet sailed it would be a minimum of three weeks before it arrived off the islands. Three weeks of inactivity with the world watching seemed to make them a hostage to fortune. Beetham also worried that, without being able to guarantee air superiority through what would be a comparatively tiny force of Sea Harriers, an amphibious landing might not even be practical. But in an atmosphere where a feeling that *we must do something* held sway, the reservations of both Beetham and the country's senior soldier, Chief of the General Staff, Field Marshal Sir Edwin Bramall, were swept aside.

'Look,' said Margaret Thatcher, cutting across the debate to settle the matter, 'we're not committing anything, just sailing.'

Any decision to actually *use* the Task Force could be made later. *Who could object to that?*, Beetham thought, his mind already turning to the formidable problems the distances posed to the use of airpower.

Eighteen hours after she'd put in to Faslane, HMS *Splendid* sailed out of the Clyde and dived off the Isle of Arran. Not a single item of stores was outstanding and she carried a full load of torpedoes. As she headed south through the Irish Sea, the submarine's crew tested everything, checking every bit of kit. By lunchtime they were at periscope depth between Fastnet and the Welsh coast. Roger Lane-Nott tuned in to Radio 4's *The World at One*. As he listened, the new reality hit him. This was no longer some show of strength. An enemy would be trying to sink him and he would have to try to sink them.

*Splendid* dived deeper. As soon as she was clear of the continental shelf, Lane-Nott ordered maximum revolutions. Full-power state. They were on their way.

On the Falklands, the day before the invasion, there was an air of unreality. Everyone felt something terrible was just around the corner and yet nothing really tangible had happened. The previous day Gerald Cheek had been up at the airfield with one of the islands' Cable and Wireless engineers when the regular LADE flight came. The engineer could tell from the boxes that it was Collins' radio gear and went to take a closer look. The Argentinians wouldn't let him near it.

'I don't know what's going on,' he said to Cheek, 'but they've brought in some very sophisticated equipment on that flight.' *What did that mean though?* A member of the FIDF, the Falkland Islands Defence Force, Cheek found out at 4.30 p.m. the next day when he was summoned to Government House by Sir Rex Hunt, the Governor of the islands. A similar outfit to the Second World War's Home Guard, the FIDF prepared themselves for the invasion. Along with six others, Cheek moved up to the racecourse. At 7 p.m., the FIGAS Islander landed there, approaching low over Stanley. They planned to fly a reconnaissance sortie at first light the next morning. Armed with standard British Army SLR assault rifles and general-purpose machine-guns (GPMGs), they had orders from Hunt to shoot down any Argentine helicopters that might try to land.

Peter Biggs, just six days into a new job as the Falkland Islands government taxation officer, was still in the dark. He left his pregnant wife Fran at home to go for a run. On his way back as he jogged down Sapper's Hill, he passed a marine, carrying an SLR, who seemed to jump several feet in the air as Biggs ran up behind him and passed him. *Why so jumpy?*, he wondered.

Half an hour later, it all became clear.

With the decision to send the Task Force made, Beetham focused on the possible contribution the RAF could make to the islands' recapture. But with the distances involved, the use of air power was going to be, he thought, *bloody difficult*. The Falklands were as far from London as Hawaii.

He consulted his closest adviser, Assistant Chief of the Air Staff (Operations), Air Vice-Marshal Ken Hayr. An intellectually acute New Zealander with a carefully groomed moustache and dapper appearance, Hayr could have passed for David Niven's brother. The two of them chewed over the difficulties and spoke with other senior staff to discuss the options, continually asking themselves the questions: *How can we help? What can we do?* At such extreme range there were simply no easy answers. In fact, on the day of the invasion there was only *one* aircraft in the entire Air Force fleet that even had the ability to fly to the Falklands and back from a friendly base: the Handley Page Victor K2. Along with the Vulcan and a third bomber, the Vickers Valiant, the Victor had made up the RAF's V-bomber force. For the last ten years, though, the remaining Victors had served exclusively as air-to-air refuelling tankers. It was this ability to transfer fuel while airborne that now made them so crucial. The Navy were on their way though, and Beetham asked Leach what the Air Force could do to support their efforts. Leach had seized the opportunity for the Navy to show its value and, consequently, demonstrate the wrongheadedness of Nott's proposed cuts. He asked Beetham for just three C-130 Hercules transports to provide logistical support for the fleet. Trying to anticipate events, Beetham thought that such a small number would be inadequate – if not absurd – and told Hayr: 'Get the whole of the transport fleet on standby, recall them from wherever they are, we're going to need a big effort!'

One other thing was also immediately clear. If the RAF was going to contribute anything at all beyond ferrying kit around for the Navy, that effort was going to involve the sleepy little mid-Atlantic outpost of Ascension Island. Many people were now discovering its existence for the first time. Almost exactly equidistant between Britain and the Falklands, this tiny little volcanic island with its very long runway was, at the very least, Beetham thought, *bloody convenient.*

John Smith's wife Ileen and their daughter Anya were trying to make a trifle without success when, at 8.15 local time, the evening's programming on FIBS, the Falkland Islands Broadcasting Service, was interrupted. The Governor had an important announcement to make. Unaware of what was coming, the Canadian announcer Mike Smallwood didn't quite strike the right tone: 'Get your ears tuned in for the Governor, folks.'

'Good evening,' Hunt began, before explaining the situation in detail. 'There is mounting evidence that the Argentine armed forces are preparing to invade the Falkland Islands.' He asked people to stay calm, stay off the streets and keep listening to FIBS. The British government, he told them, was seeking an immediate meeting of the UN Security Council, but if that failed to halt the Argentinians, 'I expect to have to declare a state of emergency, perhaps before dawn tomorrow.' But there was never any possibility of reprieve at this stage. The Argentine junta, faced with riots on the streets of Buenos Aires, had already played their joker, announcing that 'by tomorrow, Las Malvinas will be ours'. There was no pulling back from such a statement.

Despite the mood of the last few weeks, Smith greeted the news with disbelief. People never really thought they'd be crazy enough to do it. John and Ileen's sons, Jeremy and Martyn – both members of FIDF – changed into combat gear and left for the drill hall. The trifle was forgotten.

Across town, Stanley residents made what preparations they could. Joe King hid the ammunition for his rifle under the public jetty. He'd always kept the old gun as a souvenir of his target-shooting days, but it too had to go. On Davis Street in the east of town, Elizabeth Goss, a 23-year-old mother of two, went round the house gathering up photos of her children, Karina and Roger, and put them in a little bag. She didn't know what lay ahead, but if she had to leave, the one material possession she wanted to hold on to was her collection of family photos.

Jeremy and Martyn Smith returned home to Sparrowhawk House to pick up sandwiches and tea to keep them going through the night. The second farewell to the boys, while quick, hit harder. They were going off to fight alongside the Royal Marines. Once they'd gone, their parents prayed for them.

'Oi! What do you think you're doing?' At 2.30 a.m., Joe King sneaked out of his house to check one last time on his aunt who lived down the road. He'd offered to look after her in his own home, but she wasn't having any of it. 'I'm not leaving my house,' she'd told him, not open to debate. Now he'd been rumbled. As he crept along the grass verge he was spotted by the police. They'd been told to enforce Sir Rex Hunt's request that people stay inside.

'If you're not careful, we'll arrest you and you'll spend the night in gaol!' they threatened.

King knew them both, explained what he was up to and their tone softened.

'There don't seem to be any lights on, so I expect she's all right. You'd better get yourself under cover.'

With that King scuttled back.

As he was welcomed home by his wife, ninety-two Argentine Marines of the Amphibious Commando Company had already been ashore for three hours. They'd split into two groups and were making slow progress towards the Royal Marines' Moody Brook barracks at the far west of Stanley harbour. And towards Government House.

# Chapter 7

## 2 April 1982

Claudette Mozley was on her porch on Friday morning when a Royal Marine crawled out of the undergrowth in her garden. These were the same Marines who would play Santa for the children at Christmas time. They were friendly, familiar faces.

'Is that you Figgy?' she asked. 'Would you like some coffee?'

'Get on the bloody floor, you silly bitch!' came the urgent reply. 'There's an invasion on.'

At a quarter to six, the firing had started. As dawn broke, John Smith picked out the threatening shape of the Argentine Type 42 destroyer *Santisima Trinidad* steaming off the Cape Pembroke lighthouse. As the gunfire intensified, he and Ileen worried terribly about their two sons.

In Port William, outside the harbour, the Argentine landing ship *Cabo San Antonio* disgorged her cargo of twenty Amtrac amphibious APCs – armoured personnel carriers. By 6.30 the first of them was driving up the beach. They quickly secured the undefended airfield and a vanguard unit of three continued into the capital.

On the outskirts of Stanley, a hundred yards or so back from the waterfront, Government House watched over the harbour. Surrounded by more than its fair share of Stanley's few trees, it was a tangle of extensions and conservatories covered with an olive green corrugated roof. On the eastern side of the Falkland Islands' grandest property was a flagpole, supported by cables against the strong winds. Inside, alongside the Governor's family and staff, were thirty-one Royal Marines and eleven sailors from *Endurance*. At 6.15, the Argentine attack began. At first, the assault from the ridge behind the building appeared to be a shot across the bows, designed to coerce, not to kill and destroy. But that changed when six Argentine Commandos came over the back wall and tried to reach the house. Three of them were cut down by semi-automatic fire from defending Royal Marines. The other three took cover in the maids' quarters. For the next fifteen minutes there were fierce but inconclusive exchanges of fire. Sunrise was still an hour away and the British Commandos had difficulty in picking out the Argentine muzzle flashes. Then, just before seven o'clock, the shooting stopped. Instead, the Argentinians called for Governor Hunt to surrender. Hunt let the Marines speak on his behalf: *Fuck off, you spic bastards.*

But the unsuccessful end to the initial Argentine efforts to capture the British residence could only delay the inevitable.

On Davis Street, the only road connecting Stanley to the airport, Elizabeth Goss heard a horrendous rumbling sound. The brutal-looking Argentine Amtracs were going to have to come right past her house. Each APC had three forward hatches manned by the commander, its driver and a gunner. Along their sides there were long horizontal hatches through which the vehicle's occupants could fire their weapons. She looked out of the window to see a column of them grinding along, their guns pointing straight at her.

Goss grabbed Karina and Roger. If she could take them into town to her in-laws on Ross Road, they'd be safer there. Not so exposed. At the moment she put her hand on the door handle, gunshots rang out close by. She and the kids were going nowhere. Bullets were sniping around the house from all directions. She took Karina and Roger back into the bedroom, where she pulled the mattresses off the bed and piled them up against the wall. Then they huddled there in the corner. At five years old, Karina didn't really understand what was going on, but at least she could be reasoned with. The toddler, Roger, just sixteen months old, was more of a handful. He was into everything. Liz gave him her little alarm clock, which he pulled to bits, keeping him distracted until the firing stopped.

That took just over an hour. At 8.30, with Argentine reinforcements rolling into town, Major Norman, the British officer commanding the defence of Government House, advised the Governor that their position was untenable. By 10.30 Governor Hunt had ordered his outgunned, outnumbered Marines to surrender and the Union Jack over Government House had been replaced by the sky blue and white of Argentina. The Royal Marines had always had an impossible task on their hands. But the spirit of their resistance to the invasion provided an indication of the British reaction to it. They'd sunk a landing craft, destroyed an Amtrac APC and killed as many as five Argentine soldiers in the defence of Government House.

'We came second,' admitted Major Norman, 'but we won the body count.'

Shrapnel littered Liz Goss's backyard. The brick wall that stood between her house and her neighbour's was pitted with bullet scars. As she and her kids had huddled inside their wooden house they'd been just beyond the protection afforded by the wall. She shuddered at the thought of how close it had been.

Her house was searched three times. Each time the soldiers ordered the family outside and held them at gunpoint – their weapons trained on the children. Liz found it almost unbearable. Later in the day, as she and the children moved into town to stay with her husband's parents, she felt overcome by a feeling of utter hopelessness.

At 8.30 in the morning local time, Lieutenant Colonel William Bryden, USAF, commander of Ascension Auxiliary Air Force Base, had a call put through.

'What support', asked the reporter from the London *Evening Standard*, 'is Ascension Island going to provide for the British fleet being prepared to sail for the Falkland Islands?'

Bryden didn't have a clue what the man was talking about. He'd heard of the Falklands, but knew little about them – he'd certainly heard nothing about any threat of an invasion. As the two men spoke, the Argentine Amphibious Commando Company were using tear gas to clear the buildings of the Royal Marines' Moody Brook barracks.

The reporter persisted. 'How far is it from Ascension to the Falklands?'

Again, Bryden didn't know, but he wanted to help. 'If you hold on a minute, I'll take a look,' he offered and got up to check the map pinned to his office wall. He quickly gauged the distance and got back to the phone. 'About 4,000 miles?' he told the reporter but, from the reaction, knew that he was helping rather less than had been hoped for. The reporter carried on as if Bryden were trying to keep something from him.

Bryden had been on Ascension for nearly a year, and he and his wife loved it. A navigator who'd seen combat flying AC-119-K gunships in Vietnam – a vital mission in a bad aeroplane that the crews labelled 'The Flying Coffin' – Bryden had twisted people's arms to get a posting that had proved to be every bit as unique and satisfying as he'd hoped.

Just 34 square miles in area, the British colony of Ascension is an extinct volcano stranded in the mid-Atlantic 1,200 miles from Brazil to the west and northern Angola to the east. Rising sharply out of the sea towards the 2,817-foot summit of Green Mountain, she's part of a sub-oceanic ridge that also broaches the surface further south in the shape of St Helena and Tristan da Cunha. The British first established a settlement there in 1815, when a garrison was stationed to guard against any attempt by the French to rescue Napoleon, imprisoned on St Helena, 700 miles away to the south-east.

Now, though, she was home to little more than an airfield, radars, listening posts and relay stations for NASA, Cable and Wireless and the BBC, who for a brief period had even been responsible for the island's administration. The routine work of sending and receiving data from orbiting spacecraft was punctuated by intercontinental ballistic missile tests from submarines sitting off the coast of Florida. By day the missiles were too fast to see. At night, though, you could trace them coming in as you heard the sonic boom following re-entry. The missile's impact, as close as six miles away, was all the excitement Ascension needed.

Although the island was British, Wideawake airfield – named after a seabird, also known as the sooty tern, that returns to Ascension every eight months to lay and hatch its eggs – was leased to the Americans. Under the terms of the lease, the British could use the airhead and expect 'logistical support'. The arrangement worked well. The British simply never used Wideawake. Perhaps it was hardly surprising, after the reception given to the first British visitors from the air.

On 29 March 1942, over 1,000 officers and men from the US Corps of Engineers came ashore, unimpressed by Ascension's barren volcanic appearance. They carried with them the road-building machinery and supplies necessary to build an airfield that would be an important stepping stone to Europe. Both the Stars and Stripes and Union Flag flew above the capital, Georgetown, and a draft agreement formalizing the status of the new American base was drawn up. By 12 June their commander, Colonel Robert E. Coughlin, was able to telegraph Washington to tell them their runway was ready.

Three days later, a Royal Navy Swordfish torpedo bomber from the escort carrier HMS *Archer* approached the island. Her crew, the pilot Lieutenant E. Dixon Child, RN, Sub-Lieutenant Shaw, RN, and Petty Officer Townson bore grim news. A merchantman, the SS *Lyle Park*, had been sunk near St Helena by a German raider and her survivors machine-gunned in their rafts. *Archer*'s Captain realized it would be suicidal to break radio silence and instead sent his Senior Pilot to drop a message bag with a raider warning for the Cable and Wireless office in Georgetown. Dixon Child was unaware of the US presence but saw no reason not to use the unexpected and by now nearly complete runway. He fired a recognition signal and began his approach. As he descended to 400 feet US engineers blocked the runway and opened fire on his unfamiliar biplane. Dixon Child felt a hard thump on his shoulder as he dived out to sea, his swearing ringing in his Observer's ears. Out of range, the crew tried to decide whether they were thought to be German or Japanese. They decided to give it another go. Making sure to fire a second recognition signal out to sea to avoid making things worse, he was relieved to see them clear the runway of vehicles. Dixon Child managed to get his 'Stringbag' down without casualties. As he jumped down off the wing, a bullet, stopped by the buckle of his Sutton harness, fell to the ground.

But if, since that first visit, British aircraft had not visited Ascension as often as they might have done, forty years later they were about to make up for lost time.

By midday on 2 April, Bryden had received a message from the Eastern Range Headquarters at Patrick Air Force Base in Florida. He was brought up to speed about the international situation. Soon afterwards, at lunch with the heads of all the island's various organizations – including the British administrator – what information they had was shared. It was clear that Ascension was going to be involved. Bryden had already been asked if he could support three RAF C-130s over the next five days. There was an embassy support flight due in from the US imminently. *It's going to be cramped,* Bryden thought, *but we can handle it.* None of them really had the slightest inkling of what was about to hit them.

Bryden usually asked for three days' notice of any incoming flights. That luxury was the first thing sacrificed to necessity. The first British Hercules was already on her way. Loaded with stores, she'd left RAF Lyneham in Wiltshire hours earlier. Sir Michael Beetham's 'big effort' was under way. And, unlikely as it seemed at lunchtime on 2 April, Ascension Auxiliary Air Force Base was about to displace Chicago O'Hare as the busiest airfield in the world.

Flight Lieutenant Jim Vinales and his wife Jean were in the kitchen of their new house in the picturesque Lincolnshire village of Colby when they heard news of the invasion on the radio. Vinales joined the Royal Air Force as a Navigator in 1965 after hitch-hiking through Europe from his Gibraltar home to demonstrate initiative to the recruiting officers. His Spanish mother hadn't approved. Growing up, on the Rock, English hadn't been Vinales' first language, but he spoke it now with the fruity vowels and precise diction of a Shakespearean actor. Now bilingual, he couldn't help but take an interest in Latin-American affairs, and the mess Argentina was getting herself into concerned him greatly. The couple watched what news they could on television and, on Saturday the 3rd, tuned in to the emergency parliamentary debate called to discuss the invasion. They heard the Prime Minister tell a febrile House that something would be done, but it wasn't clear to him what, exactly, *could* be done. It certainly never occurred to him that he might be involved. A full-blown war seemed unlikely and a possible role for his Vulcan squadron even more remote.

The entire Vulcan force came under the command of the RAF's 1 Group, which in turn reported to Strike Command. The Air Officer Commanding, or AOC 1 Group, was Air Vice-Marshal Michael Knight. A no-nonsense, popular figure, the ruddy-faced Knight had split loyalties. He loved the Air Force, but he also loved rugby. Today, though, he was able to combine the two. As one of two RAF members of the RFU committee he was going to watch the RAF play the Army at Twickenham. He was looking forward to it. After the game he planned to drive straight on to north Devon on leave. Driving south from HQ 1 Group at RAF Bawtry in Lincolnshire, he tuned into the parliamentary debate on the car radio. As the debate raged, he realized that he wouldn't be going any further than Twickenham.

On South Georgia, Lieutenant Keith Mills weighed up his options. For the last two and a half hours his outgunned contingent of twenty-two Royal Marines had held King Edward's Point. They'd mined the beach, dug defensive trenches and kept their attackers at bay, but without heavier weaponry there was little more they could do. While they rattled machine-gun fire at their attackers, 100mm high-explosive shells whistled in on a flat trajectory from the Argentine frigate *Guerrico*. They were beginning to find their range and only one needed to be accurate to potentially decimate the small British force. Behind them, cutting off their escape route, Argentine commandos were already ashore. One of Mills's men had already taken two bullets in the arm. If they fought on, the casualty list was sure to grow. Then there was the safety of the British Antarctic Survey scientists to consider. The twenty-two-year-old officer had made up his mind.

'That's it. We've made our point, that's enough. I've decided to surrender. Does anyone have any violent objection?' No one spoke. But forced to give themselves up after the one-sided contest for Grytviken, Mills's men *had*, at least, made the enemy's eyes water. They'd brought down a troop-carrying Puma helicopter and blown a hole in the side of the frigate *Guerrico* with a Carl Gustav anti-tank missile as well as peppering her with 1,275 rounds of small-arms fire. But the Argentine flag now flew above the island that had been the trigger for it all. The Argentinians now had their *Georgias del Sur*, a place even the commander of the Argentine soldiers on the island, Teniente de Navio Alfredo Astiz, regarded as 'the end of the world'.

By the end of the day, the only piece of good news for Britain was winning Security Council Resolution 502 at the UN. Pushed through quickly, it demanded the immediate withdrawal of all Argentine forces from the Falkland Islands.

In Argentina, people crowded the streets of Buenos Aires to celebrate the nation's triumph. There hadn't been scenes of euphoria like this since Argentina had won the World Cup in 1978. The country's new hero, General Leopoldo Galtieri, drank up the adulation from the balcony of the presidential palace. The country's delicate economic position, the brutal repression of the previous week's anti-junta demonstrations, the 'disappeared' – all had, for the moment, been put to one side. A withdrawal was the last thing on Galtieri's mind.

# Chapter 8

## 4 April 1982

By Sunday, as men and stores poured into the Navy's dock-yards on the south coast, Sir Michael Beetham was reorganizing the RAF for war. First he delegated the day-to-day running of the Air Force to his Vice-Chief of the Air Staff, Air Marshal Sir David Craig. Beetham, with his right-hand man, Air Vice-Marshal Ken Hayr, was now free to focus exclusively on the role the Air Force could play in the coming war. Next, he needed to ensure that the RAF had some influence at an operational level. In 1982, each of the services was run in almost total isolation from the others and Operation CORPORATE, the codename assigned to the campaign to retake the Falklands, was still primarily a naval affair. Air power in theatre would be the preserve of the Navy's Fleet Air Arm and any effort on the RAF's part to muscle in on that would, he knew, be resisted. The solution lay at Northwood. In the 1960s office block above the underground NATO facility, Admiral Sir John Fieldhouse, Commander in Chief of the British Fleet, had an office next door to Air Marshal Sir John Curtiss, George Chesworth's boss at 18 Group. The two men enjoyed a strong rapport. The gales of laughter that often came out of the Admiral's office during the pair's daily morning meeting set the tone for effective co-operation throughout the entire campaign. Northwood was the only place in the country where the RAF and Navy were so closely harmonized. There was genuine synergy.

The blunt, uncompromising Curtiss was a veteran of Bomber Command in the Second World War, and his forty-year career had also provided him with fighter and transport experience. When Admiral Fieldhouse was given command of the CORPORATE Task Force, Curtiss became his Air Commander.

Inside Northwood, Curtiss was at the heart of the decision-making, effectively reporting straight to Beetham, with whom he began to talk daily. Curtiss had never worked directly with Beetham before but, under huge pressure, the two men established a new, sometimes fiery, relationship. While Curtiss got to grips with his new role, though, the Chief of the Air Staff was always supportive, and insistent that Curtiss fight the Air Force's corner.

In order to streamline the chain of command further, Beetham effectively cut Curtiss's own superior at Strike Command, Air Chief Marshal Sir Keith Williamson, out of the loop. Curtiss took responsibility for all RAF assets involved in the campaign and communicated his needs directly to the Group AOCs, like his counterpart at 1 Group, Air Vice-Marshal Mike Knight, to a great extent bypassing Strike Command altogether.

As AOC 18 Group, Curtiss knew that he couldn't use his long-range Nimrods further than 1,200 miles south of Ascension. The Falkland Islands were another 2,500 miles or so beyond that. The problem he faced was what, exactly, the RAF was going to be able to do 8,000 miles from home.

In the MoD building in Whitehall, Beetham and Hayr were wrestling with the same issue. The C-130s and VC10s of the transport fleet were already establishing 'the motorway' to Ascension. Hayr, his own flying background on Harriers, also saw the potential for the RAF Harrier GR3 fleet to fly from the Navy's carriers to reinforce the Fleet Air Arm's handful of Sea Harrier FRS1s. It had never been done before, but it seemed feasible. The maritime Nimrods of the 'Kipper Fleet' were placed on alert, as were their intelligence-gathering cousins, the

Nimrod R1s of 51 Squadron, a force shrouded in secrecy. Beetham and Hayr asked their staff to look at other options. The answers weren't encouraging. The Blackburn Buccaneer S2s, the RAF's low-level strike specialists, didn't carry enough engine oil for such an extraordinarily long mission. The all-singing, all dancing Panavia Tornado GR1 on which the RAF pinned its future had only been in squadron service for a matter of weeks. Despite Beetham's enthusiasm for the new strike jet – he'd recently been quoted in a manufacturer's advertisement claiming 'it's a real pilot's plane' – it was simply too new and unproven to even be contemplated. Faced with such limited choices, Beetham considered the assets available to him and began making connections. The seed of a plan was forming.

'What can we do with air-to-air refuelling?' he asked Hayr. It was abundantly clear that extending range through in-flight refuelling was the key to the RAF's contribution. It was fortunate that few people in the RAF had greater knowledge or experience of the possibilities it offered than the Chief of the Air Staff himself. After all, he'd practically written the book on it.

'VALIANT BREAKS LONDON TO CAPE RECORD BY 54 MINS', led the 9 July 1959 edition of the *Cape Argus*. It followed with daily updates and looked back with pride to an earlier record set by two South Africans, Sir Pierre van Ryneveld and Sir Quentin Brand. 'Congratulations to the RAF,' wrote 'Loyalist' of Cape Town, 'and hats off to the memories of our own pioneers too.' That historic 1921 journey had taken the two South African adventurers over four and a half days to complete. Four years later, van Ryneveld arranged an airborne escort for the arrival of the aviator whose name became most closely identified with the iconic London–Cape Town route: Sir Alan Cobham. Cobham had flown south through Africa pioneering the route for the planned Imperial Airways service.

As Cobham had thirty-three years earlier, the latest British arrival attracted large crowds. This time, though, access was strictly controlled because much about the sleek, white-painted bomber was still classified – no civilians would be allowed on board and only a handful of press photographers were escorted anywhere near her. Still new in service, she represented the cutting edge of Britain's new airborne nuclear deterrent. During the week Beetham and his crew made their record-breaking flight, British newspapers reported '200 US H-bombers Coming to Britain', 'France to Explode H-bomb' and 'Russians Claim 2 Dogs and a Rabbit Have Gone to Space'. The two sides were squaring up to each other across the Iron Curtain.

On the face of it, the day their Valiant left its Norfolk base for Cape Town wasn't a good one for the RAF. Three airmen were killed when their Canberra bomber crashed in a wheatfield near Cambridgeshire and two others narrowly escaped when their Javelin fighter, flying through the storms that brought an end to Britain's eleven-day heatwave, was struck by lightning and exploded.

But despite the PR opportunity offered by the record-breaking flight to Cape Town, Beetham and his crew sounded measured in their reaction to their achievement.

'I'm very happy about it,' Beetham told the South African press, 'but the real object was the non-stop flight and we beat the record incidentally.'

The flight to Cape Town was no stunt. Instead it was part of a continuing RAF experimental programme into air-to-air refuelling. The man whose company was supplying the equipment to make it possible was Sir Alan Cobham, an evangelical advocate of the potential of the new technology. Beetham worked closely with Cobham on the Air Force trials and eventually came to share the same conviction. But the Operational Record Book for 1956 of 214 Valiant Squadron, Main Force, Bomber Command, records what a 'gloomy and unpopular prospect' refuelling trials were thought to be by the unfortunates assigned the role. The Squadron CO, Wing Commander Michael Beetham, stung with the same indignation. *I'm a bomber man*, he thought, *and I want to be in a bomber role.*

But the flying was good. While other V-bomber crews were stuck on the ground on QRA, the Quick Reaction Alert (at five minutes' readiness to get airborne in response to a nuclear attack on the UK), 214 Squadron were in the air, allowed to get on with it because no one on the Air Staff seemed to have the slightest understanding of what they were up to. Beetham began to enjoy the new role and relish the independence it offered. It meant 214's crews were free to explore doing things their own way, refining and adapting the techniques passed on by the test pilots, making the new role their own.

And in an environment eager for broken records and tales of derring-do they were quick to realize the publicity value it might hold. Without refuelling, the Valiant could fly for seven hours at a pinch. Soon the squadron was regularly undertaking flights of twice that duration around the UK, but it was the long-range flights to Africa that caught the public's imagination. Flying from RAF Marham, their Norfolk base, refuelling over Kano in northern Nigeria, Luqa on Malta, or El Adam in Libya, each non-stop flight to Nairobi, Salisbury or Johannesburg would capture the speed record for 214.

In October 1959, one of the Marham Valiants refuelled another of the RAF's trio of V-bombers, the Avro Vulcan, for the first time. Two years later, a Vulcan B1 flew non-stop to Sydney, refuelled all the way by 214 Squadron's Valiants.

Now Beetham remembered that twenty-hour flight. If a Vulcan could reach Sydney, it should be able to get to the Falklands and back. It wasn't quite as simple as that, however. For Sydney, tankers had been stationed along the route in Cyprus, Karachi and Singapore. Flying from Ascension, they didn't have that luxury. On top of that, the remaining Vulcans were nuclear bombers. No one was seriously counting that as an option, but it meant that their crews hadn't practised dropping conventional bombs for ten years. The last, and potentially most serious, problem was that the Vulcan force hadn't practised air-to-air refuelling for twenty years. They'd be lucky to find anyone still flying the old bombers who'd even tried it before.

There was no plan beyond seeing if it could be done – no consideration yet of possible targets on either the Falklands or the Argentine mainland. But by converting the Vulcans back to the conventional role and advertising the fact, Beetham wanted to send a message to the junta: *You are not out of range and we mean business.*

'Make some publicity out of it,' he told Hayr. 'Pass the word!'

Beetham wanted to use the V-force.

In the Operations Room at Waddington, the flying schedules for the month ahead were mapped out on a large chinagraph board fixed to the wall. On Monday morning, the day the fleet sailed from Portsmouth, crews gathered underneath and discussed the invasion, unaware of developments at the MoD. Jim Vinales was sure, at least, that Vulcans wouldn't be involved. Martin Withers agreed; he just couldn't take the whole thing seriously. Even watching the tearful scenes as sailors embarked, he thought, *well, it won't come to anything.* In an office just around the corner, a different picture was emerging.

'We're going to have to do something,' Air Vice-Marshal Mike Knight told Group Captain John Laycock, RAF Waddington's affable Station Commander. 'I don't know what's likely to happen, but if there's going to be action in South America, the Vulcans may be involved. By all means stand your station down over the bank holiday weekend. But', Knight added, 'don't let too many people go too far away.'

At this point in the Vulcan's long career, it was an unlikely turn of events. Four months earlier, Knight had phoned Laycock, then barely a month into a two-year tour as the bomber station's Commanding Officer.

'You're not going to like this,' Knight had told him, 'but we're going to close the whole operation down on the 1st of July.'

In her current guise at least, Waddo, as she was known to all her crews, was a station preparing for extinction, not war. With the Tornado's introduction to service it had been on the cards, but a date had not been mentioned. Now the rush seemed indecent. Laycock knew he'd be unlikely to get command of another station. The RAF's V-force had been his life for a quarter of a century. A promising club rugby career for Leicester had been abandoned because of the inflexible demands of the QRA, that dominated the lives of the RAF bomber crews throughout the 1960s. The camaraderie and rivalry that had existed throughout the V-force was coming to an end. A tall, bearish man who'd inevitably attracted the epithet 'Big John', Laycock was an approachable, steady and popular figure at Waddington; the least he could do was to make sure that the passing of the last four remaining Vulcan squadrons was marked with the pomp and ceremony that the station's rich history deserved.

RAF Waddington sits on Lincolnshire heights, five miles south of the county's cathedral city. Carved from flat, well-drained farmland during the First World War, it wasn't until the RAF's rapid expansion in the late 1930s that Waddington became a significant bomber base. Although operations were flown on the first day of the Second World War, it wasn't an auspicious start. The Handley Page Hampdens of 44 and 50 Squadrons failed to identify the German fleet and returned to Waddo after dropping their bombs into the North Sea. With the introduction of Lancasters in 1941, things improved dramatically and the contribution of her squadrons to the war effort was a substantial one. By 1956, with the formation of 230 Operational Conversion Unit, she became home to the RAF's first Vulcans and the piston-engined heavies were consigned to history.

Now, in 1982, it was the Vulcan's turn to go. Experienced aircrew were already beginning to drift away from the squadrons to new posts. *That might not be too good an idea*, thought Laycock after his conversation with Air Vice-Marshal Knight, and he picked up the phone to his OC Administration Wing.

'Look, we might have to get people to turn round and come straight back.'

'Don't worry,' came the reassuring reply. 'We're on top of it. Let's see what happens.'

HMS *Splendid* surfaced for only fifteen to twenty minutes every day to fix her position. For the rest of the time she kept up a punishing pace. A day and a half behind *Spartan*, sailing from Gibraltar, Lane-Nott pushed his boat through the water at a constant 26, 27, even 28 knots. But in the control room the only evidence of her speed was a small dial indicating that they were travelling at 20-plus knots. As they travelled south, sticking to the anti-metric depths they used to complicate the Soviets' efforts, Lane-Nott and his First Lieutenant worked up their attack teams. They trained the crew hard for an hour and a half, three times a day, letting them resume normal duties between sessions to keep them focused. The Captain's knowledge of Soviet submarines, Soviet surface vessels and Soviet tactics was encyclopaedic, but when it came to the Argentinians, the copy of *Jane's Fighting Ships* they carried on board represented the sum of it. The Argentinians had good, German diesel-electric submarines, but how effective were they in Argentine hands? For a while, Lane-Nott wasn't even sure what sort of torpedoes the enemy were carrying. But he did know, from his own experience, that a well-handled diesel boat will always detect a nuclear submarine before it is itself detected. There were French A-69 frigates and a carrier, but what sort of a threat did they represent? And there were the British Type 42 destroyers. At least he knew what they sounded like; the *Hercules* had been the ship on the slip at Barrow-in-Furness immediately before *Splendid* herself. For all of the crew's confidence in locking horns with the Soviets in the battleground of the North Atlantic, knowing so little about the threat they were facing made him genuinely apprehensive.

Only a slight rise in the temperature on board as they sailed into the warmer water of the tropics gave any hint to the crew of *Splendid*'s progress. But as they approached the equator, they expected problems with satellite communications. At least on this journey they actually had such a facility. When HMS *Dreadnought* had been sent south to patrol Falklands waters in 1977, Lane-Nott had been at Northwood. The only way they'd been able to get a message to her then was to send a high-frequency signal to *Endurance*, who in turn would have to turn it into a UHF signal before flying one of her helicopters at sufficient height for the message to reach the submarine over the horizon. Although the British satellite communication system, SCSYS, was yet to come on line, *Splendid* was fitted with an American system and had access to a reserved British channel on an American satellite.

It was one of the many ways that American support would prove crucial to the campaign ahead.

It took nearly a month for the Americans to come down publicly on the side of the British, but, as the US Secretary of State, Al Haig, raced between London, Washington and Buenos Aires in gruelling rounds of ultimately futile shuttle diplomacy, Beetham was relaxed about securing their help. As well as Caspar Weinberger, Ronald Reagan's anglophile Secretary of Defense, Beetham had another ally at the Pentagon in the shape of Weinberger's Chief Military Adviser, Brigadier Carl Smith. In an earlier NATO staff posting, the British Chief of the Air Staff had been lucky enough to have this talented officer as his Executive Officer. The two men had been golfing partners and remained good friends. The Pentagon, Beetham knew, would give the Royal Air Force all the help it needed, even though Weinberger's own advisers were telling him that the British objective was 'not only very formidable, but impossible'. Beetham knew through his own contacts that the American Air Force thought 'we were bonkers to even think about it', but, undeterred, he wanted fuel for his V-bombers and transport fleet. Lots of fuel.

The British Air Attaché in Washington wasn't feeling as confident. But as he walked through the Pentagon dressed in formal uniform, draped in gold braid, the slaps on the back and exhortations to 'Give 'em hell down there!' and 'Go, Brits!' were heartening. He sat down with the Admiral in charge of logistics and began to outline what was needed. First of all, he explained that the weekend flights into Ascension were just the beginning. Ascension would be the hub for all air operations against the Falklands and, he hoped, the US wouldn't object to that increased traffic. The meat of the discussion, though, was about fuel.

'How much fuel are you thinking of?' the Admiral asked.

'We'd like an eight-million-gallon tanker full of jet fuel off Georgetown within the next seven days.'

Unfazed, the Admiral drew back screens to reveal a chart pinpointing the position of every tanker supplying the US military throughout the world. After a brief telephone exchange, he pointed to the chart and said that a tanker on its way to Guantanamo could be diverted. So far, so good. Weinberger, it seemed, had already made his wishes clear.

'How are you going to store the fuel?' enquired the Admiral.

'The ship will have to lie off Georgetown with lines ashore and be used as a floating fuel station until empty.'

'How long will that take and will you need any more?'

'We'll need a similar tanker seven days after the first, and then another in seven more days, and so on.'

'You can't *use* that much fuel!' the Admiral said, finally questioning the Briton's requests.

'I can assure you we're going to try.'

Gerald Cheek had already been back to Stanley airfield once. Soon after the invasion he'd travelled back up there with the Argentine air traffic controllers. He'd half-heartedly resisted their invitation. 'You're in charge now,' he told them, but secretly he was itching to get up there and curiosity got the better of him. As they drove past soldiers lining the roads, Cheek turned to the Argentinian.

'Enrique, you want to get these troops home as that'll be the next target for Britain – Buenos Aires!'

The sign for Stanley airport had already been smashed and changed to 'Malvinas'.

For the time being, it seemed that the hopes of the architect of the invasion plan, Admiral Lombardo, that the impact of the military could be kept to a minimum, lived on in spirit. It wouldn't last long. Troop numbers in the Falklands were now growing. In response to UN Security Council Resolution 502, Galtieri had said Argentina would fight for the islands. Rather than withdrawing its forces, the junta was reinforcing the garrison. On 6 April, the Army's 8th Regiment was airlifted the 500 miles from its barracks at Comodoro Rivadavia to the islands. The seas around the Falklands were no longer believed to be safe for Argentina's transport ships. In Buenos Aires, newspapers had reported that a British nuclear submarine had been detected off the Argentine coast.

In New York, the British Air Attaché knew that neither *Spartan* nor *Splendid* was yet on station. As he talked to the French representative after a long and very boring meeting of the United Nations Staff Committee, a Soviet Admiral brushed past him.

'Are our submarines being of any help?' the old sailor asked, not stopping for an answer.

Two days after the Argentine 8th Regiment arrived, a detachment of the Marines with field and anti-aircraft artillery was flown in. Armed with 30mm Hispano-Suiza cannons and Tiger Cat optically guided surface-to-air missiles, the unit marked the beginning of the building up of Stanley's defences against air attack.

# Chapter 9

## 9 April 1982

*Spartan* reached her destination first. A day and a half later, on 9 April, Good Friday, she was joined by her sister-ship, *Splendid*. As the two attack boats had raced south, their captains, communicating directly via satellite, had agreed how to divide the water between them. *Spartan* would patrol to the east of the islands, *Splendid* to the west. Less than a week after the invasion, on the other side of the world nearly 7,000 miles from home, the British had their first forces in theatre.

On the same day that *Splendid* arrived to enforce the soon to be declared Maritime Exclusion Zone, or MEZ, around the Falklands, John Laycock received a signal from HQ 1 Group at Bawtry. Waddington, it read, was to generate ten Vulcans for a conventional bombing role and reactivate the air-to-air refuelling system. The order wasn't unexpected but its effect was dramatic. Laycock had already warned his engineers about the formidable challenge that might lie ahead. Now it was a reality.

The first task was to select the ten bombers. Each of the four squadrons at Waddington had eight Vulcans on its strength. Although built in the 1960s using what was then cutting-edge technology, they were, in many respects, hand-built. There was little of the precision and uniformity that robots and computer-aided design would later bring to aircraft manufacture. Every aircraft displayed its own unique, individual set of characteristics. Some were happy flying slowly. Others became difficult below 155 knots. One turned well to the right, but needed full outboard aileron to control the bank in a left turn. Another had stiff throttles, but handled well. XM594 was reckoned, simply, to be ''orrible'.

It wasn't just the airframes that needed to be considered either. The Navigation and Bombing System was also temperamental. Linked to the radar set, the analogue bombing computer had been a leap forward when it had been introduced. But then, it could hardly fail to have been, given the woeful inaccuracy of much of the Second World War technology it replaced. In the earliest days of that long war only three bombs in every hundred were believed to land within five miles of their target. The NBS, fed with figures for height, speed of the aircraft, wind and the ballistic properties of the bomb itself, would calculate the forward throw of the bomb and, consequently, the point of release needed for the bombs to hit the target. It had always been good *enough*. For despite the pride men like Mick Cooper and Bob Wright took in trying to achieve pinpoint accuracy, it didn't actually matter if a nuclear bomb was a couple of hundred yards off the bull's-eye. Even so, by 1982, the collection of gears, bicycle chains, valves, 35mm film and lights that whirred out of sight behind the navigator's dials really was every bit as antiquated as it seemed. There was a rumour that it had been designed during the Second World War by the astronomer Patrick Moore.

Over the years, this *gash old kit* had been tweaked and honed on the ranges and in inter-squadron competitions and the results recorded. The engineering team tried to put it all together and choose the best of them: the good bombers – the ones that flew well and dropped bombs where they were supposed to.

Then their carefully considered plans unravelled. Because one thing was certain: the bombers would be hauling a full load of over ten tons of high-explosive iron bombs. With a full fuel load, they'd be operating close to, even above, their maximum take-off weight. To take off they'd need every pound of thrust that could possibly be coaxed out of their Rolls-Royce Olympus engines. And that meant choosing the jets with the 301 series engines.

Britain had planned to maintain its nuclear deterrent throughout the late 1960s and 1970s with the American Douglas Skybolt missile. This huge ballistic nuclear missile with its 1,000-mile range would have been launched from beneath the wings of American B-52s and British Vulcans. In the expectation that Vulcans would be carrying Skybolts, more powerful Olympus 301s replaced the 201s halfway through the B2 production run. Then Skybolt was cancelled by John F. Kennedy. Instead, Britain bought the submarine-launched Polaris missile but forty Vulcan B2s still entered RAF service, each fitted with four 20,000lb Olympus 301 turbojets. Then they didn't use them. In order to keep the handling characteristics consistent throughout the whole Vulcan fleet, the more powerful engines were de-rated to just 97.5 per cent of their maximum rpm. And it was in those last few per cent of revs that you found the real power.

As the Waddington engineers went through the Vulcan fleet, trying to marry the two requirements, they soon realized that only two or three of the accurate bombers had the 301s. It was frustrating, but that extra thrust was vital. When it came to the quality of the NBS, the aircrews would have to make do with whatever could be found within the small pool of 301-engined jets. The best of the rest had their engines unharnessed. This had the unlikely effect of increasing the available power to 103% of their stated maximum.

It was another two weeks before the decision to select the 301 series jets proved to have useful unintended consequences. For the time being, the biggest headache was reactivating the air-to-air refuelling system. The plumbing, Laycock was told by his engineers, had been inhibited.

'What do you mean, "inhibited"?' Laycock queried.

'Well, basically, sir, we filled the refuelling valves,' they told him.

The fix was a permanent one. Fuel from the tanker was supposed to flow into the refuelling probe above the Vulcan's nose through 4-inch non-return valves into the jet's fuel tanks. The material used to block the valves was resistant to the corrosive effects of aviation fuel and had been set like concrete for twenty years. The Vulcan's refuelling system had effectively endured a vasectomy and now there was an order from Group to reverse it.

'What do we do about it?' Laycock asked.

'We've got to have replacement valves, sir.'

'Do any exist?'

'Don't know, sir.'

They were fortunate. Waddington had just been wired into a new computerized supply system that quickly discovered that twenty 4-inch non-return valves were sitting on a shelf at RAF Stafford, a vast RAF maintenance unit near Utoxeter. They arrived at Waddington the next morning. *Extraordinary*, thought Laycock, thrilled that a potentially show-stopping problem appeared to have been solved so easily. The engineers, meanwhile, got on with chipping the hard-set old filler away from the pipework surrounding the valves. Easter wasn't going to get much of a look-in this year, but at least *something* was being resurrected.

With the effort to prepare the aircraft up and running, Laycock turned his attention to the people who were going to fly them. He decided to talk to the charismatic Officer Commanding 44 (Rhodesia) Squadron.

There was something bohemian about Wing Commander Simon Baldwin, a pipe-smoking Navigator with a rich, baritone drawl that sounded like burnt caramel. Since assuming command in 1980, Baldwin had fostered a loose, confident and exuberant atmosphere in 44 Squadron. They were big on sport and big on drinking. But if they played hard, they also worked hard. Baldwin's laid-back style couldn't mask his competence.

After success in the 1973 Strike Command bombing competition, Baldwin was given responsibility for navigation in 1974's GIANT VOICE bombing competition in America. Under Baldwin, the British Nav teams played to their strengths, devising techniques that might counter the great technical advantages of the USAF's F-111s and B-52s. The RAF won the navigation trophy for the first time ever that year. He returned to the States in 1975 and in 1976 commanded the entire RAF detachment. In 1981, as OC 44 Squadron, he'd beaten the Americans again. Just as the AOC at 1 Group had asked him to.

John Laycock quickly saw that the bombing competitions pointed the way forward. He realized that the best way to prepare the crews for any mission south was to pull a small, dedicated cell of aircrew and engineers out of the squadrons and have them train intensively. There was never a moment's doubt in his mind that the only man to run the training was Simon Baldwin.

Turning left into Waddington, you passed rows and rows of two-storey redbrick terraces laid out in squares with names culled from the RAF's past. Laycock and Baldwin were next-door neighbours on Trenchard Square – or 'Power Drive' as the cul-de-sac that housed the base's senior officers was known. Baldwin was at home enjoying a day's leave when Laycock knocked on the door. As he was shown in, Laycock saw again the evidence of Baldwin and his wife Sheila's enthusiasm for their squadron in every corner. The 'Rhodesia' epithet had been bestowed on 44 Squadron by George VI to reflect the large numbers of aircrew it attracted from the southern African colony. The elephant on the squadron's crest acknowledged the connection, and images of the big beast on everything from tea-towels and mugs to pictures and orna-ments around the Baldwins' house celebrated it.

'We've had a signal,' Laycock told the squadron boss.

Baldwin hadn't even thought the Vulcans would be involved. The Task Force seemed to be an exclusively naval effort, but Laycock explained the order from Group.

'In-flight refuelling hadn't crossed my mind, we've never done it,' Baldwin responded equivocally, as he considered what was being planned, 'but, yeah, perhaps it'll work.'

The two men talked more. Laycock explained that he

wanted to set up what amounted to a bombing competition training cell to train for CORPORATE. And that he wanted Baldwin to head it up. It was no time for false modesty. The CO of 44 knew he had the experience to do it and he knew he could work with Laycock. The big man had once been a flight commander on 44 himself and he knew how to delegate. They talked easily and had confidence in each other. Most importantly, Baldwin knew that Laycock could provide him with the top cover he'd need to get the job done. This was going to be something that everyone would want to be part of.

Even at that stage, Baldwin, the decorated Navigator, realized he was as shaky as anyone about the whereabouts of the Falklands, their location dimly recalled as the setting for First World War naval battles. And while he'd heard of Ascension, he couldn't place it. Once Laycock had left, he pulled out an atlas to get a sense of what needed to be done. The navigational challenges that lay ahead became immediately apparent. Even assuming they could crack the air-to-air refuelling, the crews would have difficulty just knowing where they were. The Vulcans would have to fly south over 4,000 miles of open ocean. Between Ascension and any potential target, there wasn't a single surface feature that the Nav Radars could use to fix a position with their H2S scanners.

Baldwin sucked on his pipe and mulled over how they were going to pull it off.

On Easter Sunday, Rear-Admiral Sandy Woodward arrived off Ascension Island on board the 6,000 ton 'County' Class guided-missile destroyer HMS *Glamorgan*. Flag Officer of the Royal Navy's 1st Flotilla, Woodward had been diverted from fleet exercises off North Africa and ordered to sail south in the early hours of 2 April. Fed up with a job that seemed to be turning into an endless round of cocktail parties and small talk, he considered it his good fortune to have been the closest Flag Officer to the Falkland Islands when the Argentinians invaded. In a week's time he would be steaming south aboard a new flagship, the 28,000-ton aircraft-carrier HMS *Hermes*, in command of the battle group tasked with retaking the Falklands.

Transferred to the island from *Glamorgan* by helicopter, Woodward was impressed at the extent to which this sleepy American communications and tracking station had already been transformed, in just a few days, into a forward fleet- and airbase. So too, it seemed, were the Soviets. Flying from bases in the Angolan capital Luanda and Konakry in Guinea, their giant long-range Tupolev Tu-95 Bear spy planes had kept a close eye on the British fleet's progress.

Once ashore, Woodward was quickly introduced to Lieutenant Colonel Bill Bryden. The USAF base commander confided in Woodward that he'd been told to give the Brits every possible assistance. 'But not', he added, 'under any circumstances to get *caught* doing so!' Clearly the Secretary of Defense, Caspar Weinberger, was making sure that his message was getting through loud and clear, whatever fence-sitting there might have been for diplomatic consumption from the rest of the Reagan administration.

Invited by Woodward aboard *Glamorgan* for dinner as she took on stores for the journey south, Bryden smiled as he walked through the destroyer's narrow corridors and companionways past cases of Argentine corned beef stacked from floor to ceiling for the long deployment. *Can't give it away back home*, he thought wryly.

Food was just one element in a vast logistical exercise that was being staged through Ascension. Unconfirmed reports that materiel had been flown in to Ascension had appeared in British newspapers a few days earlier, but they gave no hint of the scale of the operation. When the British Task Force had cast off from the docks at Portsmouth to cheers and waving flags, its departure had been driven by the imperative to set sail immediately. It had been an astonishing achievement, but the fleet was in no sense ready for war. Weapons, consumables, ammunition and equipment all had to be flown ahead to Ascension by the RAF's round-the-clock transport operation out of bases at Brize Norton and Lyneham.

*

Ready or not, that the Navy was coming at all was what mattered to those living under the Argentine occupation in Stanley. Some felt instinctively that the Argentine presence was temporary – that the British were always going to ride to the rescue. Having felt for years that they'd been an unwanted burden to successive British governments, they knew now that Britain cared. As well as being a source of pride and comfort, this knowledge also fuelled small acts of defiance. In the telephone exchange, Hilda Perry had been persuaded to come back to work by the Argentinians, who were struggling to operate the old switchboard. On the same day as she was ordered out, she was asked to return.

'No,' she told them, 'you told me to go.'

'You must go back and then you'll be working for the Argentine government.'

'No, I won't. I'm not coming back to work for the Argentine government.'

The occupiers tried a different tack. 'For the sake of your own people, will you go back and ask the other girls to go back?'

'I'll ask them.'

Perry talked to her colleagues and the four operators decided to return to the harbour-front exchange. Surrounded by armed soldiers, the women went back to work wearing demure smiles while handing out wrong numbers, misrouting calls and cutting off Argentine conversations mid-flow. Pictures of innocence.

Gerald Cheek, meanwhile, was playing chicken with Argentine armoured cars. The new administration had ordered that, from now on, all cars would drive on the right. While they believed that this might protect islanders from careless soldiers driving on the right through habit, Cheek didn't see it quite like that. He simply refused to drive on the 'wrong' side of the road. If he met an Argentinian coming the other way he'd pull up and wait, staring out to the narrows on the other side of the harbour. And that was how he stayed, bumper to bumper, until the enemy got fed up, reversed and went round him. On one occasion, driving up to the airport he met a string of the heavy, rumbling APCs that had first brought the troops into Stanley. He saw an opportunity to drive them into the peat bog beside the road.

'You're mad!' his two passengers told him nervously as the big troop carriers bore down on him.

'Hell, I'm not getting out of the way of these idiots,' said Cheek through gritted teeth, pissed off that while all three were forced to drive around him, none got stuck in the soft ground.

Peter Biggs's defiance was tempered by concern. He still doubted the British would actually fight to liberate the islands. He'd followed similar incidents around the world and watched them descend into stalemate. Sabre-rattling, UN farce, peace-keepers, a line of control, the invading power keeping what it had seized. He was acutely aware of how the Argentine regime dealt with political dissidents. And on the Falkland Islands there were a couple of thousand of them. Two weeks earlier he'd had a new job to throw himself into and looked forward to the birth of his first child. Now he just felt helpless.

By Monday, Waddington's engineering wing reckoned they'd done it. The plumbing for the Vulcans' in-flight refuelling should be serviceable. They phoned their counterparts at RAF Marham, engineers familiar with the equipment, to ask how to test that it actually worked. They were told that they needed to attach a fuel bowser to the probes and pressurize the whole system. To make the connection, though, they had to have a specialized fitting. The experts at Marham couldn't get one to them, but they described what was needed.

'I think I know where we've got one,' said one of the 101 Squadron technicians after a moment's thought. He seemed to recall that they had one stuck in the corner of the groundcrew room, where they used it as an ashtray. They dusted it down and used it to check the results of their weekend's labour. It worked.

# Chapter 10

On 11 November 1918, aircraft took off from RAF Marham in Norfolk bound for the airfield at Narborough, just a mile and a half to the north-east. The most destructive war the world had ever seen was over and Marham's airmen were going to celebrate Armistice Day by bombarding their colleagues with bags of flour. The unprovoked attack didn't go unanswered for long. In retaliation, Marham was hit from the air with bags of soot.

It was the last offensive action launched by either base before both were closed early in 1919. Peace also ended the embryonic career of Second Lieutenant Alan Cobham. He had been an RAF flying instructor at Marham for barely five months. Marham and Cobham, however, were both destined for greater things.

In 1982, RAF tanker crews slaked their thirst with beer served at the Sir Alan Cobham bar in the RAF Marham Officers' Mess. Cobham's brief connection with Marham in the dying days of the First World War was not the reason he was so honoured at Marham. Over the sixty years since the end of the Great War, the Norfolk airbase had become one of the largest and most important stations in the Air Force, and its main role was as home to the RAF's entire fleet of Victor K2 aerial tankers. Without Cobham, the RAF might never even have had an air-to-air refuelling capability. After being demobbed, the young Second Lieutenant went on to become one of Britain's legendary aviators and the world's most passionate advocate of the potential of air-to-air refuelling. It was his persistence that culminated in Michael Beetham's record-breaking long-range Valiant flights in the late 1950s.

In contrast to its American counterparts, the RAF was slow to embrace the possibilities the new air-refuelling technology offered, dismissing it, in 1947, as an exercise that was 'not a paying proposition'.

Cobham thought they were fools. With a series of pioneering flights to India, South Africa and Australia in the 1920s he had become one of the most well-known and respected figures in British aviation. In 1934, driven by a belief that air-to-air refuelling would revolutionize commercial aviation, he registered the name of his new company: Flight Refuelling Ltd. Five years later he was proving the efficacy of his ideas with a transatlantic airmail service that was refuelled in flight. The system it used was developed by his new company at their base near the picturesque village of Tarrant Rushton in Dorset. While this nascent operation ended with the outbreak of war, trials continued and in 1944 the Air Ministry awarded him a contract to supply the in-flight refuelling equipment for the Lancasters of the RAF's TIGER FORCE then preparing to deploy east for the expected brutal, bloody and drawn-out offensive against Japan.

At an RAF bomber base in Lincolnshire, the 21-year-old Flight Lieutenant Michael Beetham, DFC, was beginning his second tour as an already experienced bomber pilot. When the American nuclear bombs dropped on Hiroshima and Nagasaki hastened the end of the war, plans for TIGER FORCE were abandoned. *Thank God*, thought Beetham, painfully well versed in the dangers faced by bomber crews, *it's not necessary*.

But while the end of the war brought relief to the country and her servicemen, it was a potentially fatal blow for Alan Cobham's Flight Refuelling operation. The contract to supply 600 sets of 'looped hose' flight-refuelling equipment for TIGER FORCE, despite being well advanced, was cancelled with Japan's surrender in 1945. Cobham, though, never wavered in his faith in the system. He simply thought the Air

Ministry lacked vision and he bought back, at scrap value, all of the equipment already supplied. Then, with typical bullishness and the fortune of the brave, he stayed in business long enough to establish a ground-breaking transatlantic air-refuelled passenger service to Bermuda that caught the eye of the Americans.

And in April 1948 a party of senior USAF officers arrived in Dorset to see if Cobham's system could improve the prospects for their vast new nuclear bomber, Convair's B-36 Peacemaker, then losing a fierce battle with the US Navy for Congressional funding. A contract with Cobham was signed soon after – the USAF were planning a surprise.

Before dawn on 7 December 1948 – the seventh anniversary of Pearl Harbor's Day of Infamy – a heavily laden Boeing B-50 bomber clawed its way into the air from Carswell Air Force Base, Fort Worth, Texas, and, using the refuelling equipment Cobham had saved from the scrapyard, flew non-stop to Hawaii to carry out an undetected mock nuclear attack on that same US Navy Pacific base before returning to Texas.

Two and a half months later, another B-50 – *Lucky Lady II* – flew non-stop around the world. She was airborne for nearly four days.

As a result, Congress cancelled the US Navy's ambitious 70,000-ton super-carrier and the 'Magnesium Overcast', the name given to the USAF's vast B-36 bomber, became the spearhead of Strategic Air Command until the arrival of the B-52 in the middle of the next decade. But in Britain, the Air Ministry and RAF remained unmoved by the Americans' success and by Cobham's 'slow bombardment of letters'. Instead, it was the winning combination of one impetuous remark and the inspiration of a Sunday morning lie-in that finally led the RAF to begin embracing the new technology.

While enjoying lunch with senior USAF officers at Wright Patterson Air Force Base in Dayton, Ohio, in 1948, Cobham heard not only of Boeing's development of its own refuelling system for Strategic Air Command's heavy bombers, but of the Tactical Air Command's interest in any new air-to-air refuelling technique it might use for its single-seat fighters. The Englishman brazenly claimed that work on a suitable system for the latter was well advanced at Tarrant Rushton. The remark was utterly without foundation, but the American generals, sensing they may have found what they were looking for, arranged to visit the small Dorset factory in the spring of 1949 – just four months later.

Until now, the 'looped hose' system, on which all Flight Refuelling Ltd's operations had been based, was literally hit or miss. The receiving aircraft had to extend a weighted hauling line behind it as it flew. A grappling hook-like projectile was then fired from a tanker aircraft at the trailing line. If the harpoon made contact, the receiver's hauling line was then wound in towards the tanker. Inside the tanker, it was attached to the end of the tanker's fuel hose before being used to wind the whole coupling back to the tail of the receiver. Only once the tanker's fuel hose was connected to the fuel coupling at the back of the receiver could fuel flow. While it may have been easier to perform than it at first sounds, it could in no way be considered a routine or straightforward manoeuvre.

The Americans, while they'd appreciated the potential of in-flight refuelling, knew that something entirely more practical than the 'looped hose' system had to be devised for it to see regular squadron service. And that is exactly what Cobham had promised them he had up his sleeve.

He now had to conceive, design and test a completely new system before they arrived in Dorset, hoping to be impressed. His designers eliminated unfeasible options until they settled on a method that looked good: a receiver aircraft would fly a probe-mounted nozzle into a funnel-shaped drogue trailed behind the tanker. It nearly never got off the drawing board, however. The problem that could have killed it was finally solved when an engineer, Peter Macgregor, lying in bed on a Sunday morning, considered the way his spring-loaded roller blinds retracted. If, he thought, a similar spring was mounted in the drum unit trailing the hose and drogue, it could keep the hose taut when contact was made, eliminating the whipping and looping that had so far made the system unworkable and dangerous. Just two days before the Generals arrived, the new system was tested for the first time using a Lancaster and Gloster Meteor 3, blagged from the RAF by the ever-resourceful Cobham. His brilliantly simple method had been produced with a typically British lack of governmental support. And with no sign whatsoever of that situation changing, a little over a year later Cobham was forced to sell the manufacturing rights to the Americans to keep his company solvent.

Not until 1954 did the Air Staff, perhaps persuaded by the USAF's operational success with Cobham's probe-and-drogue system in the Korean War, finally come to the conclusion that there was merit in giving their new V-force an air-to-air refuelling capability.

While sixty miles from Marham, on the other side of the Wash, RAF Waddington prepared for a mission that had long before ceased to be part of the Vulcan's repertoire, at the Norfolk tanker base the story was rather different. Unlike most parts of the RAF, Marham's Victor K2s of 55 and 57 Squadrons did in peacetime exactly what they would have to do in war – refuel the RAF's fighters and other fast jets, keeping them in the air, giving them the range to reach their targets. In fact, throughout the Cold War, the tankers had fought a war that felt as real as the one waged by Roger Lane-Nott's beloved submarine service.

At fighter stations like RAF Leuchars, Wattisham and Binbrook, McDonnell Douglas F4 Phantoms and English Electric Lightnings sat fuelled and armed in their hangars on Quick Reaction Alert. Their crews maintained a twenty-four hours a day, 365 days a year vigil, ready to scramble at a moment's notice to intercept intruders into UK airspace. These were invariably the Bear and Bison bombers of the Soviet Long Range and Naval Air Forces. On average there were five incursions into UK airspace a week, each testing the reaction of Britain's stretched air defences. The Soviet bombers would come in from the north, probing through the Faeroes–Iceland gap. All had to be intercepted, identified and turned back by the RAF. Without the support of the Victor K2s the fighters, particularly the notoriously short-ranged Lightning, simply couldn't have kept the Soviets at bay.

The 'tanker trash', as the Marham crews referred to themselves with pride, were doing their job for real. There was no question of them using training rounds, or checking bombing scores with cameras and computers. If they failed to deliver, in peacetime or in war, there was always potential for disaster.

As a result, Marham was a close-knit family. Many of the crews had been on the Victor K2s from day one. A number of them helped devise and refine the operating procedures that made the RAF tanker force one of the most flexible, effective and safe in the world. Safety during in-flight refuelling was always the responsibility of the 'tanker trash'. It was a mindset that was ingrained – the life or death of the receiver was paramount.

Group Captain Jeremy Price liked things to be neat – done just so. The thoughtful, well-groomed tanker man had spent much of his professional life making sure that this was as true of air-to-air refuelling as it was of the vintage Aston Martin Ulster that he'd lovingly restored. He'd devised refuelling procedures that took decisions on safety out of the hands of stubborn fighter pilots with an aversion to admitting defeat. Another opportunity to put his skills to the test was as much a reminder of a bygone age as the old Aston: the 1969 *Daily Mail* Transatlantic Air Race. Price was part of the planning cell that steered an RAF Harrier to victory and enabled a Navy F-4 Phantom to set a new New York to London speed record – only beaten five years later by the astonishing SR-71 Blackbird.

Price had done it all at Marham: Flight Lieutenant, Squadron Leader, Wing Commander and Group Captain; Flight Commander (on Michael Beetham's old squadron, 214), Squadron Commander of 57 Squadron and now, since June 1981, head of the tanker family, the Norfolk airbase's well-liked and respected Station Commander.

But the family was feeling the strain a little. Marham had been home to V-bombers since 1956. Once considered an elite, the V-force were, by 1982, no longer the newest toy in the Air Force's box – far from it. April 1982 saw the arrival at Marham of the first of the new Panavia Tornado GR1s, the swing-wing fighter-bombers of which so much was expected. This European collaboration had started life known as the MRCA, the Multi-Role Combat Aircraft. The Victor old-hands were not at all impressed with the brash new kids on the block. They didn't like the way the pilots and navigators never changed out of their flight suits – that wasn't the way the V-force did things. They didn't like the attention the new 'superjets' attracted. And the fact that it was 617 Squadron, the Dambusters, the most famous squadron in the entire Air Force, didn't help either. The 'Dim Bastards', they called them. *MRCA?* Short for 'Much-Refurbished Canberra Aircraft', they laughed, referring to the old English Electric Canberra jet bombers designed in the 1940s and now relegated to a declining role as the RAF's jack-of-all-trades.

It was the Victors, though, that the RAF needed now. Marham's shiny new residents were of no use whatsoever. Price was taken entirely by surprise. Just a few days before the invasion of the Falklands, Air Marshal Sir John Curtiss had visited Marham from 18 Group HQ at Northwood. The two men had sat around a table discussing *Endurance's* frantic efforts to contain Argentine ambitions in South Georgia. They talked broadly about the South Atlantic as a theatre of operations, but without urgency. But now, while there were no clear indications yet of how the Victors might be used, it was evident that if the RAF were going to get involved, the old tankers were the only machines in their arsenal that would allow them to do so.

Soon after Sir Michael Beetham ordered the mobilization of the RAF transport force, with the Argentinians now in control of the Falklands, Price received a signal from Air Vice-Marshal Knight at 1 Group.

The 'tanker trash' were to prepare for war.

# Chapter 11

Since handing over the reins of the nuclear deterrent to the Navy, the V-force had been run on a shoestring. The Vulcans, their crews were led to believe, wouldn't be in service for much longer. The official line was that it wasn't, therefore, cost-effective to spend good money on them. The few modifications that they'd had incorporated were hardly a great leap forward in technology either. The apparently endless upgrade programmes lavished on the USAF's B-52 force were eyed enviously by their cash-strapped British counterparts. To contest bombing competitions with Strategic Air Command, Waddington's Vulcans did have their ageing systems tweaked and enhanced. But it was little more than a bare minimum. The Heading Reference System was modified to give a smoother, more accurate feed into the Nav Plotter's Ground Position Indicator. An additional Radar Altimeter dial was installed for the co-pilot, along with triple offset boxes for the Nav Radar that allowed him to 'walk' the bomber to its target using distinctive ground features. Radar-guided join-the-dots. The big delta's ECM – Electronic Countermeasures – kit was also boosted. It didn't, perhaps, amount to much, but Simon Baldwin, unsure whether any of it would even be relevant to the demands of CORPORATE, was determined to give his crews any help he could. Crudely screwed in and sometimes rescued from scrap heaps, the extra equipment was fitted to all the airframes selected for his training cell. And it didn't stop there. Over the days and weeks that followed Easter, more would be done to enhance the old bombers' capability and, more importantly, their ability to survive.

As Commanding Officer of one of Waddington's four bomber squadrons, Baldwin had also been asked by John Laycock to put forward one of his flight crews. He had two outstanding candidates: 44's two Flight Commanders. He had to choose one of them. In the end, though, he didn't have to wrestle with the decision. One of them was, perhaps, the best pilot on the squadron. The other, though, was just back from RED FLAG.

'Now you be careful.'

Monty didn't get it. He'd just emerged from the funeral of a good friend and now his friend's widow was telling *him* to be careful.

'What do you mean?' he said, brightly. It sounded upbeat and unconcerned. 'This is me, Monty!' But she wouldn't be reassured.

'I don't like this,' she stressed, concerned about what the invasion of the Falklands was going to mean for the RAF. And for her friend Monty, in particular.

'Oh, we won't be going anywhere . . .' Monty tried again to put her mind at ease. He drove back from the funeral with no reason to dwell on the exchange. But it soon turned out to be remarkably prescient.

When he got home, Monty's wife Ingrid told him Simon Baldwin had phoned. The live-wire Scot called his squadron boss back to ask him what he was after.

'You'd better come up,' Baldwin told his Flight Commander.

Monty headed straight in to the base. And there, confusion and speculation about what might lie ahead were all around. Someone suggested they practise Vulcan on Vulcan formation flying to rehearse for refuelling.

*But none of us has done any refuelling!*

*And the system's dormant.*

*We'll load up some bombs and there'll be a firepower demonstration at Ascension Island.*

*Where's Ascension Island?*

*We'll drop some bombs to show the Argies we mean business!*

*That's just dumb. Either we're doing something or we're not . . .*

It was early days.

Baldwin told Monty that he wanted his crew to represent the squadron. 'How do you feel about that?'

'Fine, but I think we'd better start doing some training quickly!' Monty told him.

Before finally settling on Montgomery's crew though, Baldwin needed reassurance on one thing.

'What about Dave?' he asked.

Monty's Nav Radar, Dave Stenhouse, was a hugely popular member of the squadron with a rare talent for instigating mischief then being nowhere to be found when it was time to face the music. As a Radar, Monty reckoned, there was no one to touch him. *When he was good.* But he wasn't always good. The Vulcan's best defence was always to fly down low in valley floors, out of sight and shielded from search radars. Entry into the valleys needed to be finely judged by the Nav Radar. The bomber would approach the ridges surrounding the trough at a right-angle, waiting for a signal to turn from the radar operator. And during the intense work-up for RED FLAG there'd been a wobble. Monty and his crew had flown north before turning towards the Scottish Western Isles and descending to low level. They'd done it a hundred times. But then an urgent demand cut through the laconic, well-practised communication between the five crew members.

'Up the stairs. Quick!' Monty shouted to Stenhouse over the intercom.

Stenhouse quickly unbuckled and leapt up the stairs between the two pilots. As he stood, holding on, to look forward through the cockpit windows, Monty pointed out the mountain ahead. Closing at around 300 knots, they were flying straight for Mull's Ardnamurchan.

'Dave, the next time we fly this, we're in the bloody

dark. Get it wrong and we're probably going to hit that!'

But he didn't get it wrong again, and throughout RED FLAG the Montgomery crew became a confident, effective unit. Five months after the close shave in Mull, Monty didn't hesitate.

'I think we're in it as a team, boss.'

It was enough for Baldwin. 'I'm happy if you're happy.'

'It's all of us or nothing,' Monty stressed, confident that his mercurial Nav Radar would rise to the occasion. The decision made, it wouldn't be mentioned again. Not mentioned at all, though, was Monty's concern that his Air Electronics Officer, Squadron Leader John Hathaway, appeared to be going deaf. He seemed to struggle with the RT – instructions needed to be repeated. But he was a good AEO. He'd be OK. Making up the crew were the co-pilot, Bill Perrins, and Flight Lieutenant Dick Arnott, the sharp-dressing Nav Plotter. Monty still felt a twinge of guilt. *What*, he wondered, *am I getting them into?*

On the morning of Easter Monday, Baldwin joined John Laycock and the Commanding Officers of 101 and IX Squadrons in the Ops block to choose the crews. Above the door, a plastic sign read 'ROYAL AIR FORCE WADDINGTON OPERATIONS', blue lettering against a white background. Inside the front entrance were dark, polished wooden boards listing decorations, aircraft types and station commanders. Among the latter, in gold calligraphy, were names that spoke of a different era: Twistleton-Wykeham-Ffiennes, Bonham-Carter and Dado-Langlois. At the end of the list was Laycock's name. His office was down a corridor to the left of the boards, one of the few rooms in the cobbled-together building that had windows providing natural light and a view of the world outside. And there, around a conference table, was where the four senior officers met.

Laycock asked the three squadron bosses to nominate their top crews, while he spoke for 50 Squadron in the absence of their CO, Wing Commander Chris Lumb – away on leave. They looked at overall experience, experience on aircraft type, bombing competitions, RED FLAG, the reputations of the Nav teams and soon a consensus emerged. Crews were almost self-selecting. Martin Withers and Monty were just back from RED FLAG. Both were QFIs – Qualified Flying Instructors – and, as a result, had experience in flying formation – what, in essence, successful air-to-air refuelling is all about. That was 101 and 44 accounted for. Brian Gardner from IX Squadron and Chris Lumb himself had also been on the deployment. Gardner was added to the list, but Lumb was ruled out by his seniority.

'I will not have any Vulcan Wing Commanders down at Ascension throwing their weight around,' Laycock had been told by Air Vice-Marshal Knight at 1 Group. 'The most senior rank you will have in your crews is Squadron Leader.'

With his hand forced, Laycock chose Squadron Leader Neil McDougall's crew instead. McDougall hadn't been to Nevada, but he had more experience flying Vulcans than nearly anyone else on the station. Laycock knew him well and had flown with him recently. The big Scot with the tinder-dry sense of humour got Laycock's vote. But only until Chris Lumb returned to Waddington the next day. Once Lumb, with the greatest of reluctance, had removed himself from the list, he queried McDougall's presence.

'I'm surprised you selected Neil,' he told Laycock, encouraged by the Station Commander's invitation to speak his mind. 'I didn't rate him as highly as a couple of my other guys.'

'Well, who?' Laycock asked him.

'John Reeve.'

'Well, I've known Neil for fourteen years,' Laycock countered, 'and I've watched him operate in some particularly difficult conditions during the winter of '78. I've got the highest regard for his captaincy skills.'

In the end, though, it was Lumb's call. Laycock didn't know as much about Reeve himself but, aware of the experience and ability found throughout his crew, was happy to defer to the 50 Squadron boss. It soon became academic, in any case, with the news from 1 Group that Marham's stretched tanker resources wouldn't be able to support the training of more than three crews. Neil McDougall dropped down the pecking order to become the reserve captain, replaced by Squadron Leader John Reeve.

'Really?' queried Monty when Baldwin told him, unable to mask his surprise. He wasn't sure. He'd flown as Reeve's co-pilot in Cyprus years earlier. He remembered him as a decent enough pilot, but, he worried, Reeve might go at this a bit like a bull in a china shop.

Squadron Leader Bob Tuxford had been on his new squadron for barely a week. He wasn't too pleased about the move from 57 either. But with an influx of ex-Vulcan personnel, 55 was short on tanking experience. And he had plenty of that. Since joining the RAF in the late 1960s he'd become one of the youngest captains in the V-force, gaining command after just two years as a co-pilot. After a three-year exchange posting in California flying KC-135s for the USAF, he'd returned to the RAF as a QFI on Jet Provosts out of Leeming. Since 1980, Tux had been back with the 'tanker trash'. He was a tall, stylish man with dark hair that swept back from a widow's peak; his own paintings hung on the walls of a beautifully presented home. Tux's self-possession could ruffle feathers, but no one doubted his ability, least of all the Station Commander, Jerry Price, who'd known him since they'd flown together in the early 1970s.

Price summoned Tux to the Marham Ops Centre in the evening of Easter Sunday. When Marham had been ordered to prepare for CORPORATE, there was only one Victor crew with a current qualification for day and night tanking and receiving. That had to change if the Victors were going to reach the South Atlantic. They would need to take fuel from each other in a complex long-range relay to cover the distance. There followed an unprecedented, intensive effort to bring every crew on the station up to speed. All week, Victor K2s had been streaming into the refuelling areas over the North Sea and later that night it was Tux's turn. He was scheduled to head out to towline 6, a rectangular slice of airspace just off the East Anglian coast, bang in ten contacts and come home night-qualified. Up and down in less than two hours, he thought. First of all, though, he had to go and meet Jerry Price.

Inside Ops, Tux was greeted by a tangle of jagged-looking metal scattered across the floor: old F95 cameras. Wrestling with the sorry-looking pile were two technicians from RAF Wyton, home of the Air Force's reconnaissance squadrons. *What's going on here?*, wondered Tuxford, eyeing what looked like a pile of Meccano. Jerry Price explained. Marham's twenty-three Victors were the only asset the RAF could deploy as far south as the Falklands. Anything that was going to be done had to be done by them. Price, along with the two Squadron Commanders, had chosen three Captains to fly low-level photographic reconnaissance missions in the Victors: Tux, Squadron Leader Martin Todd and Squadron Leader John Elliott. As Tux was the most recently qualified QFI, with the most recent low-level experience flying the little Jet Provosts, Price wanted him to fly with both Todd and Elliott on their first sorties. Nothing was said about what they might be taking pictures of, but a shortlist seemed obvious. He and the two other captains were being singled out to spearhead Marham's effort. There was already an atmosphere of excitement and purpose on the base caused by the invasion of the Falklands, but this was going to be vastly different to the usual routine.

Then Jerry Price told him he could hand-pick his own crew. Walking into the crewroom and saying, *I want you, you and you*, Tuxford thought, was going to be worth the price of entry alone. A few names sprung immediately to mind.

Squadron Leader Ernie Wallis was a Marham institution. He'd seen it all. Now a sandy-haired 52-year-old veteran, he'd been a Nav Radar on the tanker force since the late 1950s, when Michael Beetham had been his squadron boss. He'd flown out of Nigeria in support of Beetham's record-breaking long-range flights to Africa and helped develop the three-point 'triple nipple' Victor tanker – work that had earned him an MBE. In 1979, after twenty-one years at Marham, he was awarded the 'Freedom of the Station' – although in typically self-deprecating style, he wondered aloud whether it was because he was indispensable or only because the Air Force couldn't think what else to do with him. He knew more about how the Victor's refuelling equipment worked than anyone else at Marham. When there was a problem, if Ernie couldn't either rectify it or circumvent it, no one could. He definitely deserved the accolade 'Mr Flight Refuelling'. The Nav Leader of 55 Squadron, he was first on Tuxford's list.

In return for Tux's faith in him, he viewed the self-assured pilot affectionately as 'a pain in the arse', in the same way that a teacher might regard a naughty, but likeable pupil.

On the V-force, navigators came in pairs and Wallis was part of a double-act with Flight Lieutenant John Keable. Both men were well known for their sense of humour, both always ready with a quick quip or retort. Tux knew them both well socially through the Mess and was sure he was picking the best team – their selection was a foregone conclusion.

Tux was still new to 55 and hadn't had time to see everyone at work. But the squadron boss's hard-working co-pilot, the stocky, dependable Flight Lieutenant Glyn Rees, was the most experienced co-pilot on the squadron. He looked like a good bet.

As AEO he picked his mate, the not inappropriately named Mick Beer. Squadron Leader Mick Beer was a social animal, one of a group of fellow officers who could end up back at Tux's house for Sunday lunch. Tux's wife Eileen was used to it. Whatever food there was would end up shared between sixteen of them. But if the Tuxfords were regularly eaten out of house and home, at least they were never out of drink. None of their guests would dream of arriving without booze, least of all Mick Beer. The tall, broad-shouldered AEO may not have had as much experience on the Marham tanker force as some, but he'd got time on the old Victor SR2 reconnaissance squadron. He was a good AEO and Tux knew he could rely on him. In the air *and* at the bar.

Beer, of course, was also regarded by Wallis as a 'pain in the arse'.

# Chapter 12

## 13 April 1982

On Tuesday morning, Tux, taking the place of the regular co-pilot, strode out to the Victor K2 with Martin Todd and the three members of the rear crew. Their mission was to familiarize themselves with the big four-jet tanker at low level and trial the makeshift camera fitting, mounted behind the glass panels of the visual bomb-aiming position in the nose. To do so they would be conducting simulated attacks on the sea cliffs of north Yorkshire's Flamborough Head – a feature that was going to receive a great deal more aggressive attention from the RAF over the weeks to come.

XL192 sat camouflaged and ready on the Marham pan, fussed over by a team of ground engineers and technicians, all marshalled by a crew chief – the man with responsibility for the old jet's well-being. On the Tarmac, still attached by cables to ground equipment, the Victor resembled a bird with broken wings. Her unique, once celebrated, crescent wings sloped down from the fuselage towards the ground in search of support, their clean lines broken up by underslung refuelling pods and fuel tanks. Hunched above the squat undercarriage, her white belly barely clearing the Tarmac underneath, she was all lumps and bumps and afterthoughts. But, like an albatross awkward on *terra firma*, she needed to fly. Once in the air she had a presence to rival the Vulcan. Her high dihedral T-tail and swept, tapering wings were graceful and elegant. Her distinctive nose, apparently stolen from the rocketships of Buster Crabbe-era Flash Gordon, gave her a purposeful look. A 1950s vision of the future.

Designed to the same 1940s Air Staff Requirement as the Vulcan, she was the last of the V-bombers to fly. Sir Frederick Handley Page, a giant of the British aviation industry, was stung by the superiority of the Avro Lancaster's performance over his own wartime four-engined heavy, the Halifax. The company that bore his name didn't let it happen again. The Handley Page Victor could carry nearly twice the bomb load of the Vulcan and she was faster too – in 1957, test pilots took her through Mach 1, much to the annoyance of the team developing the Vulcan. At the time she was the largest aircraft ever to have broken the sound barrier – and the Observer, sitting in one of the rear-facing crew seats, the first man to break it travelling backwards. Rivalry between Avro and Handley Page was intense. Crowds at Farnborough were the beneficiaries as the two bombers slugged it out, performing rolls, loops and high-speed Immelman turns – manoeuvres never before seen in aircraft of their great size and weight. Sir Frederick – or HP as he was known – left nothing to chance in competing for the affections of the public and the Ministry of Supply. He even chose a special colour scheme. The Victor prototype was painted in a striking matt black finish, set off with silver wings and tail. A distinctive red cheatline ran from nose to tail. His futuristic new bomber looked stunning.

The Victor was built to slice through the sky at 60,000 feet – twice the height of today's commercial airliners – untroubled by the fighters of the day. But when Gary Powers' U-2 spy plane was shot down by a Soviet SA-2 surface-to-air missile 'above 68,000 feet' over Sverdlovsk, Russia, in 1960, it was obvious that altitude alone no longer offered the V-force any security. The decision to switch to low-level operations was quickly taken, and it was a decision that would have major consequences for the Victor.

It was the first of the V-bombers, the Vickers Valiant, that suffered most as a result of the new flight regime. In 1964, a crew were lucky to escape with their lives when, during a training flight, their Valiant was rocked by a loud bang followed by a shaking throughout the aircraft. The pilots were able to bring the bomber home safely, but it was clear when the jet came to a standstill that the starboard wing was sagging. When engineers examined her, they found that the rear wing spar had cracked in flight. Urgent inspections on the rest of the RAF's Valiants showed all bar one to have signs of similar damage. The entire fleet was grounded for good, leaving the RAF without an airborne tanker barely five years after Beetham's 214 Squadron had proven the new capability.

The Victor, able to carry its own weight in fuel, was chosen to fill the breach. But the Victor's great load-carrying ability was not the only reason for the decision. Like the Valiant, the Victor's airframe stood up less well to flying in the thick, gusty air at low level, where the bomber force was now confined, than the Vulcan's more robust, rigid delta. Crews pulling the Victor into a fast, steep climb from low down – a manoeuvre designed to simulate the release of a weapon – could hear the wings crack under the strain. The Victor, with her more flexible, shock-absorbing wings, was easier on her crews at low level than her Avro rival, but stress was killing her and, had it been allowed to continue, it probably would have killed her crews too. By the end of the 1960s, the last Victor bomber squadron was disbanded. Of the three V-bomber designs, the Vulcan was left to soldier on alone. The Victor's future with her wings clipped, her bomb bay sealed and her defensive Electronic Countermeasures stripped out lay in tanking at medium altitude.

But now Tux relished the chance to take a Victor down low again. Providing they stayed inside the prescribed fatigue limits, a few flights 'in the weeds' weren't going to hurt. They may have been uncomfortable, difficult to handle and hard to see out of, but he had huge respect for the old jets. He *admired* them. The RAF needed to provide long-range reconnaissance and the Marham tankers, with their Heath Robinson collection of hastily installed cameras, were the only option available.

Ten-year-old Leona Vidal had had her heart set on it. For weeks she had been nipping into Stanley's West Store to gaze longingly at the black Raleigh Chopper with the silver lettering. The classic push-bike design with its long *Easy Rider* handlebars and stick-shift Sturmey-Archer gears made her heart beat a little faster. But she knew that her mother Eileen, the islands' radio operator, couldn't afford it. Eileen, though, had other ideas. Signing up to a hire purchase payment scheme she bought her daughter the bike she so coveted. It became her pride and joy. For two months she cleaned it every day until, kept in the yard at the front of the house, it gleamed.

On Tuesday the 13th, she woke up to a beautiful cold, calm, clear Falklands day – the kind that in years to come she would tell people helped make Stanley such a great place to grow up. Or had done.

That morning, her bike was gone from the yard; taken, during the night, by Argentine troops whose numbers seemed to grow with every passing day. *How could anyone do that to a little girl?*, she wondered. *What possible use could a kid's bike be to them?*

Squadron Leader John Reeve drove the mile or so to work on Tuesday morning and parked, as usual, outside the 50 Squadron buildings. He was unaware that he'd been the focus of such debate over the long Easter weekend, but didn't stay in the dark for long. As he walked into the squadron, the faces were all familiar, but the atmosphere was anything but. It was buzzing. Then someone explained it.

'Have you heard they're putting crews together for the Falklands?'

Reeve was immediately determined to be a part of it. Still regretting that he had missed out on the RED FLAG deployment earlier in the year, he was desperate for a slice of the action this time.

'You cannot exclude me from this!' he spluttered, hammering his fist on a desk to force his point home, unable to mask how much it mattered to him that he be involved.

Brought up near Birkenhead on the Wirral peninsula, Reeve still carried a soft trace of Merseyside in his vowels. An aviation enthusiast from a young age, even now he collected Air Force memorabilia. He won an RAF scholarship after being part of the RAF cadet force at school; then, apart from a tour on Jet Provosts as an instructor, he had been on the V-force, flying Vulcans, since 1969. He had an eagerness that was sometimes mistaken for a gung-ho attitude. And his appetite for all aspects of Air Force life didn't stop at the Mess door. At squadron dining-in nights, a box of chocolates was always handed out to mark the occasion when Reeve's wife Pat had burst into the bar, fed up that Happy Hour had ruined another Friday night.

'John Reeve, get your arse home,' she shouted through the smoke and booze-fuelled chatter. 'Your dinner's been in the oven for four hours!' Then she made to leave, before turning back a moment later with the clincher.

'And, by the way, I'm having a 1lb box of Black Magic!'

It wasn't the kind of thing that was easily lived down.

But when the 50 Squadron boss, Chris Lumb, was asked which of his crews should train for CORPORATE, it was Reeve's can-do approach to whatever was asked of him that made a difference.

'Relax, John, you've been selected,' Reeve was told quickly, and put out of his misery.

If John Reeve was desperate not to miss out, Bob Wright, Martin Withers' young Nav Radar, greeted with disbelief the news that their crew too had been put forward from 101 Squadron. Given the faltering start to his career as a bomb-aiming Navigator, he realized that his crew's performance during RED FLAG must have really turned his fortunes around.

All the chosen crews were ordered to the Main Briefing Room, a large auditorium in the Ops block. The room also served as Waddington's museum, the walls lined with black-and-white photos of long-retired aircraft like Blenheims, Hampdens, Lancasters and Washingtons. In an air of intrigued anticipation, the crews took their seats. Simon Baldwin and the other squadron bosses also sat down on the hard, straight-backed chairs.

John Laycock got to his feet at the front to address them, choosing not to speak from the stage behind him. He looked at the officers picked to do the job. Reeve had joined Mick Cooper and the rest of his crew. Monty's lot were there. And Bob Wright sat with his Captain, Martin Withers, and the other 101 Squadron men – Hugh Prior, Gordon Graham and Peter Taylor – reunited as a complete crew for the first time since RED FLAG, over two months earlier. Laycock told them all he knew: that 1 Group had asked them to prepare the Vulcan for a conventional bombing role and revive the air-craft's air-to-air refuelling capability. Had anyone, he asked, ever had any experience of in-flight refuelling? Only one hand went up, and it went up reluctantly. Neil McDougall had tried it once. In 1962. He remembered well the incident that had led to it disappearing from the Vulcan's training schedules. It had been a very close call.

Closing on the tanker too fast, McDougall's squadron boss hit the drogue hard. The refuelling probe broke off and flew back into the wing-root air intake of the number 3 engine. It was as if someone had thrown in a petrol bomb. The Olympus engine exploded. The Captain managed to bring the Vulcan home, but it was as close, McDougall thought, as you ever wanted to get to an accident.

Air-to-air refuelling in the Vulcan had been shown to be inherently dangerous. As McDougall sat and listened, he found it a little difficult to believe that, twenty years later, they were going to give it another go. Only this time, they'd be doing it without days of ground school at Marham. Instructors would be arriving from Marham the next morning. And then the flying would start.

Three months before all the remaining Vulcan squadrons were due to disappear for good, they had been asked to train for a war none of them had expected. Drawing to a close, John Laycock tried to capture the occasion's significance.

'People would give their right arms to be in your position,' he told them. For some of the men listening it struck the wrong note, but all of them knew what he meant. He finished by asking if there was anyone who didn't want to be a part of it.

There was just one. John Reeve's Nav Plotter, Dave Harthill, had leave booked. He was due to fly to the States to be with his pregnant wife, but if this thing was really going to kick off he'd cancel. There was no way he was going to miss it, so he asked Laycock where he stood. The Station Commander felt that it was unlikely; that they were just going through the motions. After all, Air Vice-Marshal Knight had told them to enjoy themselves while it lasted. No one really believed that they'd actually be sending the Vulcans to bomb Argentina or anywhere else. It seemed a bit unnecessary to insist Harthill miss the birth of his son on account of something that might never happen. Laycock told him, 'Go, Dave.'

It left him and Baldwin with a problem though. The V-force was made up of constituted crews that operated together as units. It was always the crew's collective performance that mattered rather than that of any individual member. Such was the importance attached to this that if a crew member went sick before a deployment, the likelihood was that an entirely new crew would be found instead. This time, though, they were prepared to make an exception and, fortunately, a new Nav Plotter soon presented himself, rather by accident.

'Jim will volunteer, won't you, Jim?' suggested Neil McDougall when it became clear that the Reeve crew was short of a navigator. 'You'll fill in as Nav Plotter!'

'Yeah, sure . . .' Jim Vinales answered, without really thinking about it. But it was enough. There was every chance he'd have been chosen anyway. Like Mick Cooper, Reeve's Nav Radar, Vinales was another veteran of the GIANT VOICE bombing competitions and had an impressive record against the Americans. In 1974, his crew flew to victory in the Navigation Trophy against American B-52s and FB-111s. As

Nav Plotter, it was Vinales who really took the plaudits, winning a Queen's Commendation for his performance.

On paper, he and Mick Cooper now looked to be Baldwin's outstanding Nav team. With his tall, Chelsea-supporting co-pilot, Flying Officer Don Dibbens, and his new AEO, Flight Lieutenant Barry Masefield with his years of experience on the maritime 'Kipper Fleet', Reeve's outfit looked strong.

With the crews in place, Simon Baldwin turned his thoughts to the skills and equipment they were going to need to do the job. He needed to put together a training programme for the crews, but in order to do so had to make certain assumptions. In his long, narrow office next to the Operations Room, he set to work with his Operations team. The ashtrays filled quickly and the conference table soon disappeared under a mound of maps and reference books as he drafted an outline plan for the attack. There were three priorities: reaching and finding the target; protecting the bomber from the air defences; and hitting and destroying the target. Any mission in the South Atlantic would have to be mounted from Ascension Island, and the entire route southbound would be over 4,000 miles of featureless ocean. The certainties offered by the South American coast were outside the range of the Vulcan's radar. That meant that the only way for a crew to fix their position would be to go back to the old ways and use the stars. They would have to fly through the night. The crews would need to brush up on their astro navigation, but that alone, Baldwin worried, would probably not provide the necessary navigational accuracy.

At least there was no point worrying about the refuelling plan. That would have to come from the 1 Group Tanker Planning Cell. Nobody at Waddington had even basic knowledge of tanker planning. Ensuring that the crews were qualified to refuel in flight, though, would be a vital part of the training programme.

Baldwin never considered the possibility of using anything but conventional 1,000lb bombs – the largest available in the RAF's Cold War arsenal. But he had no information at all on what the target would be. He studied an old 1:250,000 map of the islands. It was all he could get his hands on. At the east of East Falkland was the capital, Stanley, and beyond that, clearly marked right next to the coast itself, was an airfield. The 4,000-foot runway ran almost east–west. In the absence of more concrete information, the paved strip appeared to be the only viable military target for the Vulcan's bombs. To take it out, he thought, the bomber would have to fly at 300 feet down the runway to release a stick of twenty-one parachute-retarded 1,000lb bombs. That would rip it up from end to end. The Vulcan force hadn't practised lay-down attacks with conventional thousand-pounders for years. One more thing to be built into the training schedule.

Beating an enemy's air defences was dependent on three things: surprise, avoidance and suppression. But Baldwin and his team had only sketchy, published, information on Argentine air defences in general and none whatsoever on the equipment that had actually been deployed to the islands. The only assumption to make was that the air defences would be comprehensive. The Vulcan's best chance of getting through would be at night, at low level – as they would expect to go in against the Soviets. This way the bomber would be detected only at the last possible moment – surprise. The dark would reduce the chances of visual detection, and degrade any Argentine optically aimed defence systems, but the air defence radars weren't so easily side-stepped.

They needed to come in under them. To approach from the west on an easterly heading, the crew would have a difficult overland penetration in rocky terrain in the dark, and the risk of visual detection would be increased. So the obvious approach was to come in over the sea on a westerly heading. Doing this meant there was no need for a long low-level overland penetration using the TFR – Terrain Following Radar. However, it would be very useful in descending and maintaining height over the sea, and during the immediate exit from the target area over land. And while it seemed reasonable to Baldwin to regard the airfield at Stanley as the target, it would be dangerous not to allow any possibility that it was not. If the crews were going to be asked to go in overland, he was going to make sure that they were equipped with the skills they needed to do so. The training, he decided, would include some TFR flying.

The low-level approach over the sea from beyond the range of the radar cover should bring the bomber in under the radar lobes. This had implications for the navigation though. The Vulcan would have to descend before the Falkland Islands were within range of the aircraft's map-painting radar. The first opportunity to fix their position using the radar would be on the run-in to the target itself. The navigation would need to be pinpoint accurate if the crew were going to be able to position themselves over the centreline of the runway on their first approach over the sea from the east. The astro-nav was unlikely to be able to guarantee that and a second run-in through now wakened, alert air defences was out of the question. So it was clear already that navigation was going to be a problem.

But worse, even the most basic assessment of the potential Argentine air defences – modern, Western and effective – made it perfectly clear that the Vulcan's elderly electronic warfare equipment, tailored to cope with Warsaw Pact systems, just wasn't going to be up to the task of defending the aircraft. The third component of the defence penetration triangle, suppression, was almost entirely absent.

# Chapter 13

## 14 April 1982

Flight Lieutenant Dick Russell was flown to Waddington aboard a specially laid-on two-seat Canberra hack. That in itself was remarkable. It was normally just top brass who got ferried around like that. He was now a 49-year-old senior pilot, and there wasn't a lot that surprised him any more, but this was unusual – an indication of the importance attached to getting him to the Lincolnshire bombing base.

Since joining the RAF as a teenage national serviceman in the early 1950s, Russell had enjoyed a remarkable career. As a young Wireless Operator/Air Gunner, he'd flown aboard the Short Sunderland flying boats providing air cover for UN ships during the Korean War. When there was no further need for WAGs he found himself training as a pilot in Rhodesia. Over the next ten years the flying was varied and rich. He flew Canberras during the Suez Crisis then, as a Victor B1 pilot, endured life on the brink during the Cuban Missile Crisis and was deployed to the Far East, on standby to attack Jakarta International Airport, during the Indonesian Confrontation.

He reckoned he'd had a good time of it. Flying out over the North Sea on a cloud-free night, looking down at the fires from the oil rigs flaring below, it was difficult to see it any other way. Now an instructor on the Victor OCU, the small training unit at Marham, the avuncular, golf-addicted Russell didn't expect to be involved in the Falklands crisis. Much to his surprise, though, he turned out to be exactly what the Vulcan crews needed.

On Easter Monday, as he sat on the patio of his Norfolk home listening to the non-stop noise of the Victors training for CORPORATE, he took a phone call asking him to come in to the station. Jerry Price wanted to see him. Russell had been an air-to-air refuelling instructor, or AARI, for eight years until 1979. Now Price wanted him to requalify. The station commander had a surprise for him: Vulcans.

'Right, Dick, you fly tomorrow a couple of times, by day and by night,' Price told him, explaining that he'd be training Vulcan crews who were completely new to air-to-air refuelling. 'I've got a Canberra for you at eight o'clock to take you to Waddington.'

There wasn't time for the night flights. He'd have to somehow squeeze in his own night qualification before taking the Vulcan crew through it.

The aircrew feeder at Waddington was in the Ops block, separated from the locker room by double doors. On one side it smelt of athletics, on the other fried food. Russell arrived late, already wearing his flying kit, to find the three Vulcan crews finishing off a breakfast of steak and eggs. Two other AARIs from Marham, Flight Lieutenants Pete Standing and Ian Clifford, had already joined their crews. They were the only familiar faces in the room. They'd been assigned to the Reeve and Montgomery crews respectively, which meant Russell was going to be joining Martin Withers. The two men got on immediately, each recognizing the even temper of the other. Russell quickly got the impression that Withers trusted him. It was a good start and breakfast was soon wrapped up.

'We'd better get off to the simulator so you can see what the cockpit looks like,' Withers suggested.

Russell was struck by how small the cockpit felt in comparison to the Victor's. The basic layout was similar but he felt hemmed in. Avro had originally planned for the bomber to be flown by a single pilot. At the Air Force's insistence, though, a co-pilot was shoe-horned in. The result was that without lowering the ejection seat, a tall man like Russell couldn't actually hold his head up straight because of the curve of the roof. Ten minutes in the simulator was enough. Air refuelling was regarded as the 'Sport of Kings' by the fighter pilots, who practised it regularly. Withers and Russell were looking forward to flying. They signed for their Mae West life jackets and half an hour later they were walking out with the crew to Alpha Dispersal where XM597, their Vulcan B2, was waiting for them. A comparable size to a Boeing 737 airliner, the delta-winged bomber appeared to be much larger – an impression created by her height and dramatic shape.

Although she first flew just seven years after the end of the Second World War, standing on the apron, taut and purposeful on a stork-like undercarriage, the old 'tin triangle' still looked startlingly modern in 1982. Up close, however, her camouflage looked conspicuously hand-painted. The brush strokes that smoothed over banks of rivets suggested her real age. It was her cockpit, though, that really betrayed her.

Inside was a cramped, claustrophobic, matt-black confusion of wires and pipes crafted from steel, canvas and bakelite in the days before ergonomics. It now looked and felt defiantly old-fashioned. It smelt of sweat, leather and old metal. Stencilled panels warned of '200 volts', or hand-painted notes annotating the mess of dials competed for space – everything competed for space – with company names like Dunlop and Electrical and Musical Industries Ltd. Dotted on the roof towards the rear was a small blue enamel badge that read Marconi, just another of the *smörgåsbord* of old British engineering firms that contributed to the Vulcan's creation.

The five-man crew sat on two different levels; the captain and co-pilot were cocooned up front inside a small blister with barely room to squeeze in between the two ejection seats. Once in, the view was deceptive. Glazing to the front and sides gave little hint of the huge aeroplane spread out behind them.

Four or five feet below the pilots, behind a zip-up, lightproof curtain facing backwards, were three seats for the Nav Radar, Nav Plotter and AEO. Responsible for bomb-aiming,

**Right:** This contemporary magazine cover gives a sense of how futuristic the Vulcan must have seemed when it first appeared in the skies above post-war Britain.

**Below:** Sir Frederick Handley Page personally designed the striking black and silver livery for the prototype Victor, his equally ground-breaking rival to the Vulcan.

THE AEROPLANE

APRIL 15, 1955

EVERY FRIDAY
ONE SHILLING
AND SIXPENCE

**AVRO VULCAN**

**world's first**

**4-jet Delta bomber**

TOMORROW'S AIRCRAFT TODAY!

**Left:** Upside down. An extremely rare shot of a Victor rolling out at the top of a loop. Although surprisingly agile, Victors stood up less well than Vulcans to the stress of flying at low level and were eventually converted into aerial tankers – a role in which they enjoyed great success.

**Below:** 'If it looks right, it is right' went the old engineering adage. The white-painted Vulcan prototype looked right from any angle.

Just six months before the Vulcan was due to be retired, Martin Withers and his crew were chosen to train at RED FLAG.
**L to r**: Flying Officer Pete Taylor, Flight Lieutenant Bob Wright, Flight Lieutenant Martin Withers, Flight Lieutenant Hugh Prior and Flight Lieutenant Gordon Graham.

**Left:** Vulcans at Nellis AFB. This vast airbase just beyond the Las Vegas suburbs hosts RED FLAG, the most realistic training for war available to NATO crews.

The Nellis flightline. Beyond the nose of a Vulcan are USAF F-111s and FB-111s, the RAF crews' far more advanced rivals for bombing honours at RED FLAG.

Port Stanley, Falkland Islands – the world's most southerly capital city. As Martin Withers flew home from the United States in February 1982, the Argentine Navy's plans to invade 'Las Malvinas' were passed to Galtieri's ruling junta.

**Left:** 2 April 1982. The invasion forces arrived by sea and air, over the beaches and aboard a stream of transport aircraft like this Argentine Air Force C-130 Hercules.

**Below:** The islands' tiny defence force was quickly overrun as Argentine AMTRAC armoured troop carriers rumbled into town.

**Left:** Air Chief Marshal Sir Michael Beetham. When Argentina invaded, Sir Michael, a decorated Second World War Lancaster pilot and air-refuelling pioneer, was quickly able to see the potential of his ageing fleet of V-bombers so far from home.

**Below:** RAF Waddington flightline. While still declared to NATO in April 1982, the Vulcans' time was drawing to a close. Although operations continued, decommissioned Vulcans were already being torn apart for scrap on the far side of the station.

**Right:** Wing Commander Simon Baldwin. When Waddington was ordered to prepare for war, Station Commander Group Captain John Laycock went straight to Baldwin, CO of 44 (Rhodesia) Squadron. An experienced Navigator and veteran of successful bombing competition campaigns against the Americans, Baldwin had all the necessary experience.

**Above:** Work on the Victors went on around the clock. One modification explored, but not adopted, was the fitting of Martel anti-radar missiles to the tanker's wing pylons in preparation for a possible offensive role.

RAF Marham from the air. In 1982, it was home to the RAF's entire Victor tanker force. This picture was taken from a Victor flown by Squadron Leader Bob Tuxford by a side-looking camera newly installed in the jet's nose.

Vulcans trained to drop conventional 1,000lb iron bombs for the first time in many years. In this sequence, a stick of seven slams into Garvie Island off the north-west coast of Scotland.

**Above:** At low level over Spadeadam ranges, the crews tested the effectiveness of their bombers' Electronic Countermeasures kit.

Much time and effort went into reinstating and practising with the Vulcan's in-flight refuelling capability, unused since the early 1970s, but essential to success over the distances posed by the invasion of the Falklands.

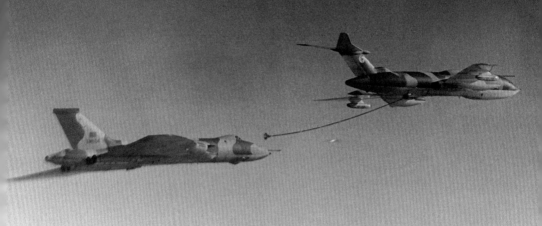

**Right:** No room for error. As the Vulcan crews got to grips with an unfamiliar role, the distances between them and the tankers could become heart-stoppingly small.

**Right:** Victors arrive at Ascension. For a while the veteran tankers based there were the only aircraft in the RAF capable of even reaching the Falklands.

**Above:** Ascension from the air. Thousands of miles from South America to the west and Africa to the east, this tiny island was crucial to any chance of British success. The airfield is clearly visible in the picture.

**Left:** Victor flight crews and engineers all mucked in to put up the tents that would serve as their operations centre for the duration of the war.

navigation and the bomber's electrical systems (including jamming the enemy's radar) respectively, their troglodyte space was brightened only by two small, high portholes that required the AEO or Nav Radar to stand in their stirrups to see through them. Three dented reading lamps snaked out of their control panel on flexible stalks to give their workspace the studious feel of an old library. Despite the dials, switches and screens it all looked engagingly low-tech – an impression cemented by grab handles that hung from the cardboard-lined flight deck ceiling. They were identical to the swinging balls used in the carriages of the London Underground District Line.

There was no toilet, and no kitchen, and there were no soft edges. It wasn't a comfortable place for a five-man crew to spend any length of time, and with Dick Russell on board there would be six of them. Flying Officer Peter Taylor, Withers' co-pilot, was condemned to the jump seat – an unwelcoming metal platform in the bottom of the cabin, just next to the crew hatch. His only cushion was his parachute.

They strapped in, snapping shut the machined-aluminium Personal Equipment Connectors, or PECs, to tubes that carried oxygen and the intercom. The fabric of the Nav Radar's PEC tube trailed down from the roof of the cockpit, like a two-inch-thick vine. Pre-flight checks complete, they taxied to the runway threshold while Withers explained to Russell how the Vulcan was steered on the ground. Sitting in the co-pilot's seat, Russell was struck by the commanding view from the Vulcan. Perched much higher than in the Victor, he felt like he was sitting at the top of a double-decker bus. Withers turned to him. 'Well,' he said, 'you might as well take off,' confirming the impression of trust that the AARI had picked up earlier. Russell opened the throttles of the Vulcan for the first time in his life, held the brakes for a moment as the turbines spooled up, then let go, surging forward, propelled by over 80,000lb of thrust from four 301 series Rolls-Royce Olympus turbojets. The big delta leapt into the air behind Reeve and Monty. With that departure, the crews had begun the most intense, demanding training programme any of them would ever endure. Over the next two weeks, they would log flying time that normally would have taken six months to accrue. Peacetime regulations were swiftly abandoned. Of the three Vulcans climbing out over the North Sea, perhaps only Withers' jet – he being the only current Vulcan QFI, or Qualified Flying Instructor – should legally have been in the air with the 'student' Victor tanker pilot in the right-hand seat. In an emergency, unfamiliar with the jet, there was little Russell, Standing or Clifford could have done to help.

The first attempts at hooking up with the Victors were demoralizing. The AARIs, unfamiliar with the position of the Vulcan's refuelling probe struggled initially. Officially, the technique was to look at neither the probe nor the drogue trailing from the tanker. Instead, the receiver had to line up on a series of black and fluorescent orange lines on the belly and wings of the tanker. Get that right and you'd make contact. Dick Russell had had twenty years to get used to the view from a Victor cockpit. Like riding a bike, refuelling in a Victor wasn't something he thought too hard about. He could just do it. In the Vulcan, though, the picture was completely different. Instead of extending forward from above and behind the pilots' heads, the Vulcan probe was mounted below them, right on the nose. It was virtually impossible to see both the probe and the tanker at the same time. Russell loosened his straps and leaned forward to look over the coaming a third time without success, then he handed over to Withers. Much to everyone's surprise, the Vulcan captain made contact on his first attempt. But the 100 per cent success rate wasn't to last long. Like the other two Vulcan captains, he was confident. *Piece of piss*, Monty had thought until his efforts to stick the probe in the basket attracted ridicule from the rest of his crew.

'Would it help if we put hair around it?' they laughed. The association was unavoidable.

Nearly three hours after taking off, the three Vulcans were back on the ground at Waddington. After shutting down and disembarking, their captains were quick to compare notes.

'He was working like a one-armed paper hanger!' As he

described his AARI's early efforts to make contact with the tanker Monty reached instinctively for an imaginary stick and throttle, his hands playing out his instructor's actions.

'So how did you get on?' Withers ventured, sounding out the others.

'Yeah, fine.' A stock answer from Monty.

'And you, John?'

'Oh, nothing to it!' he replied, sounding like he'd rather talk about something else. There was a pause before Withers tried again.

'Did you get it in the basket then?'

'Erm . . . no,' the other two pilots admitted reluctantly and all three laughed in solidarity.

'It was bloody hard actually,' confessed Monty, 'probably need a bit more practice . . .'

*Sport of Kings?*

*More like trying to stick wet spaghetti up a cat's arse!*

*Or taking a running fuck at a rolling doughnut!*

Over a beer at the debrief in the Ops block, Russell, Standing and Clifford appeared unconcerned. In fact they seemed to be enjoying their students' discomfort rather a lot.

'What are you laughing at?' asked the bomber pilots. The AARIs tried to sound reassuring. They'd seen it all before.

'Don't worry,' they told them, 'it's always like this. You'll get it next time.'

The scratched paint and bent pitot tubes suffered by the Vulcans didn't seem to support this point of view. To Mick Cooper, John Reeve's Nav Radar, who'd listened to the drogue clanging hard against the outside of the fuselage a couple of feet from his left ear, success felt a long way off. He drew heavily on a cigarette.

In London, news reached Sir Michael Beetham in his office at the MoD that the Vulcan air-to-air refuelling training was under way. His plan appeared to be coming together. At the time of its conception, no one knew whether or not it was even still possible. Now, perhaps, it was time to let the Argentinians know what the RAF was up to. Let *them* worry about what might or might not be possible. But while it was true that the Vulcans had begun formating on the Victors and the AARIs at least had made some successful prods, not a single drop of fuel had yet been transferred. When they progressed from dry contacts any hope Beetham had that things were up and running would start to look a little premature.

CFIT, Controlled Flight into Terrain, is how air crash investigators describe what happens when a completely serviceable aircraft simply flies into the ground. CFIT kills hundreds of people on commercial flights every year. It's one of aviation's biggest killers. It can happen for a variety of reasons and flying low over the sea, with atmospheric conditions conspiring to provide no visible horizon, is one of them.

Training for the camera runs in goldfish bowl conditions like this, a few hundred feet above the North Sea, Tux had a scare. He felt uncomfortable. Disorientated. He knew something wasn't right, before realizing with a shot of adrenalin that the Victor was a lot closer to the surface of the sea than he'd thought. *The pilot lost situational awareness*, they would have concluded in the accident report. At altitude, it's easier to recover from. There's time to check the instruments, to take stock of the situation and get your bearings. At altitude, loss of situational awareness rarely kills aircrew. But low and fast, spatial disorientation usually will. The aircraft will crash with its pilot knowing only that he's lost it – the final, fatal view of the mountain or sea surface perhaps providing a snapshot confirming height and heading at the very moment of catastrophe. Tux caught it this time, but the danger was real. The main problem was the jet's Radar Altimeter. Like the Victor itself, it was designed to operate at high level. Calibrated to be accurate at 50,000 feet, at 250 feet it didn't perform well. The relative scale of the instrument meant that distinguishing 250 feet from 500 feet – or sea level – just couldn't be done with any confidence.

This wasn't the only problem. The profiles of the flights Tux and the other two captains were flying meant a high-level transit before descending to take pictures. As they flew down into the relatively moist, warm air at low level, the two cameras in the nose misted up. After the first flight the engineers had to come up with a fix that prevented misting by ensuring there was air flowing over the lenses to prevent it.

As an ad-hoc solution to the long-range reconnaissance problem, the Victor had no mechanism for accurately aiming the cameras. Unless some method could be worked out the whole exercise was pointless. Tux called colleagues at Wyton, home to the Canberra PR9s of 39 Squadron, the RAF's reconnaissance specialists, and asked what they could suggest. The next morning he was sitting in a Victor on the Marham ramp drawing lines on the cockpit glass with a chinagraph pencil. Outside, two airmen moved bits of tape around the Tarmac shouting, 'Up a bit, down a bit.' The tape represented the targets. The chinagraph marks were calibrated so that, when they appeared over the target at a given height, the correct image would be captured by the port-facing camera. It was hardly high tech, but it worked.

The Victor crews honed their new skills with low-level camera runs over the airfields and coastlines of the Scottish Western Isles. The Air Force called it Area 14. In their logbooks, the pilots recorded the more evocative names of the places they photographed: Stornoway, Islay and Macrahanish. There was pride in developing this new capability in such a short space of time and, inevitably, competition developed between Elliott, Todd and Tux over the quality of the pictures they were taking. They were enjoying themselves. But while frightening the life out of the inhabitants of coastal caravan parks was fun, in the back of their minds there was a growing anxiety about the Victor's terrible vulnerability as a low-level camera platform.

In Vietnam, the US Navy had found tactical photo-reconnaissance to be the most hazardous task it could give its aircraft. The North American RA-5C Vigilante was dedicated to the role. In the late 1960s, the Vigilante was deemed to be a hot ship, one of the fastest jets in the sky. Her awesome low-level performance provided a degree of security, but still the Vigilantes suffered the highest loss rate over Vietnam of any Navy aircraft.

The Victor didn't share the Vigilante's speed advantage. In comparison she was large and lumbering. She was also defenceless. Since the Victors had been converted into tankers, all the radar-jamming equipment had been removed; so too had the chaff dispensers that might confuse radar-guided attacks and the flares that tackled heat-seeking missiles. All that was left was the RWR – Radar Warning Receiver – that could tell them when fire-control radars had locked on to them. But that was hardly a comfort. Flying down an enemy coastline or the centreline of a heavily defended airfield the Victor would be an open target. And that was assuming she'd survived the danger inherent in using the radar altimeter to descend to low level over the pre-dawn South Atlantic.

Tux relished the challenge of being singled out for such a demanding mission, but he had no desire to go out in a blaze of glory. He collared Wing Commander Ops, David Maurice-Jones, in the bar to try to find out more.

'Where's all this going?' he asked. 'What are we doing racing around at 200 feet?'

Maurice-Jones couldn't tell Tuxford much more than he already knew. High-level transit, low-level photo-reconnaissance run, high-level transit.

It was a daunting task. While Maurice-Jones and his superiors knew that the Victors could be ordered to run the gauntlet of the Falklands air defences, what might be waiting for them during that low-level run was left only to Tux's imagination.

# Chapter 14

The Argentinians had quickly begun preparing their air defences. An American Westinghouse TPS-43 search radar was rolled out of the back of an Air Force C-130 Hercules at 4.00 p.m. on the day of the invasion. The next day, the first anti-aircraft guns were deployed in the form of twin-barrelled 20mm Rheinmetall batteries. Heavier weaponry began to follow a week later, when, on 8 April, elements of the Marine Anti-Aircraft Battalion armed with their 30mm Hispano-Suiza cannons and British-made Tiger Cat wire-guided surface-to-air missiles flew in. What had been planned to be as unmilitary an operation as possible was rapidly changing its complexion. Since the dispatch of the British task force, the nature of the Argentine occupation had been transformed. But it was after Roger Lane-Nott's HMS *Splendid* and her sister-ship *Spartan* began their patrol that troops, equipment, fuel, supplies and armaments really started to flood into Stanley airfield. With the British declaration of the Maritime Exclusion Zone on 12 April, everything had to come in by air. Gerald Cheek, now redundant as the head of civil aviation on the islands, watched the constant stream of aircraft flying in: C-130s; Fokker F-27s and F-28s; BAC 1-11s and Boeing 737s, which, he thought, must have been tight on Stanley's 4,100 foot runway. But while the runway was short, skilful Argentine pilots were demonstrating its utility daily. It may not have offered much margin for error, but it didn't stop Aerolineas Argentinas, the state carrier, landing a fully laden four-engined Boeing 707 without a mishap.

Planes were turned round and sent home as quickly as possible. C-130s would leave behind fuel not needed for the return trip to the mainland and aircraft were unloaded on the taxiways, but the volume of men and materiel threatened to overwhelm the limited facilities at the small airfield. During April, over 9,000 troops and 5,000 tons of cargo were flown in. The Commander of Base Aerea Militar Malvinas, Commodore Héctor Destri, called for help.

Major Héctor Rusticinni of the Fuerza Aerea Argentina flew into Stanley on 15 April. He was boss of the training squadron at the Air Force school for non-commissioned officers in Ezeiza, south-west of Buenos Aires, and his organizational talents were what Destri needed. Rusticinni felt strong emotions as he stepped off the transport plane into the watery sunshine of BAM Malvinas. Responsibility for communications, food, clothes, shelter, armament, transport and maintenance on the base was now his. Argentina, he felt, had won back what was rightfully hers.

The change in the tone of the Argentine occupation was also showing itself to the residents of Stanley. Some were being singled out for thorough house searches. Peter Biggs and his pregnant wife Fran were visited every couple of days – perhaps because the Argentinians found plenty to interest them. A keen diver, Biggs found his scuba gear was quickly confiscated. So too was the Morse key he kept in his workshop – left over from his time working in radio. Often there'd be a thump on the door in the middle of the night. Biggs would open it up to eight armed troops who'd go through the house, even taking up the carpet. While the soldiers conducted themselves with a veneer of respectability Biggs found it hard to contain his anger, but tried to debate what was going on with any English-speaking officers.

Like Biggs, John Fowler, the islands' Superintendent of Education, had more than just his own safety to worry about. His wife Veronica had given birth to their son, Daniel, on 13 April, just two days earlier. Now as mother and child recovered from the labour back at home, the BBC World

Service reported that the US Secretary of State Al Haig's shuttle diplomacy was faltering. And Fowler, who'd already lost half a stone in weight since the invasion, could only see war ahead.

On high ground at the back of the town, anti-aircraft guns were now in place.

A full flying programme for the Vulcan training culminating in day and night bombing runs on the ranges had been written up and distributed. The crews flew twice on the 15th, persevering with the air-to-air refuelling qualification. Monty was getting it right about 50 per cent of the time. Martin Withers and Dick Russell were having a little more luck. Between them they were working out a technique that played to the strengths of each of them. Withers, unencumbered by the muscle memory accrued over years flying Victors that hampered Russell's efforts, would make the contact. From the second sortie on, that was something he was achieving with increasing and reassuring regularity. The AARIs had been right about that. Once a contact had been made Russell would take over, flying the ten, fifteen or twenty minutes of smooth formation flying that a successful fuel transfer required. He was pleased to note that the Vulcan, lacking the distinctive high T-tail of the Victor, was actually the easier of the two V-bombers to fly in the tanker's slipstream. A problem was beginning to emerge, however, and that afternoon John Reeve and his AARI, Pete Standing, were to get an indication that it could actually scupper the whole project before a single bomb was dropped. In the morning, Reeve had flown his first wet contact, transferring 2,000lb of fuel into the Vulcan's tanks. As he broke contact, fuel spilled back over the bomber's windscreen. Mick Cooper was standing on the ladder between the pilots and watched as the glass immediately turned opaque. *Like trying to look through a toilet window*, he thought. Not ideal when you're flying so close to a 70-ton tanker that you can hear the roar from its jet pipes in your own cockpit. They tried a further five contacts during the afternoon sortie, each time suffering fuel spills on disengaging. On the sixth attempt, Reeve misjudged the power and overshot. But it wasn't contact between the two big jets that was the biggest danger. As the nose of the Vulcan reached for the underside of the Victor, the trailing cone-shaped drogue scraped down the side of the bomber's fuselage and into the starboard engine intakes. Inside the cockpit there was a loud physical thump as the numbers 3 and 4 Olympus engines, starved of air, coughed and flamed out. The rpm spooled down immediately and, without power, the two engines' alternators tripped off-line, causing a red warning light to come on ahead of the pilots: *electrical failure*. Reeve yanked the handle to release the RAT to restore emergency power to the jet.

*Captain to crew, we have a failure on 3 and 4 engines*, he called and applied full power to the two remaining engines on the port side, stamping on the rudder to keep her straight.

Losing two engines on a Vulcan should be manageable. She's blessed with deep reserves of power and because of the layout of the engines, built into the wing root with all four tucked in close to the fuselage, even losing both on one side doesn't cause overwhelming asymmetry. But as Reeve gunned the throttles on the two good engines, one of them faltered. *If we're down to one*, thought Mick Cooper, *it's time to sit by the door with my parachute*. But it stayed with them. And as Barry Masefield tripped all the non-essential electrics and hit the AAPP – Auxiliary Airborne Power Pack – with his right hand, Reeve held the lame bomber in a gentle descent to begin the relight drills. In the thicker air below 30,000 feet Masefield began reading from flight reference card 25: *Altitude. Airspeed. Windmilling speed. LP cock*. From the front, Reeve provided the required responses: *HP cock shut, throttle back adjacent engine as required*.

*Relight button, press and hold in.*

*Throttle. After five seconds move very slowly towards the idling gate.*

Reeve nursed the 3 and 4 engines back into life and made sure they were stable. The alternators were switched back on and they tried to continue with the sortie, only for Masefield to report that a number of small electrical failures persisted. Reeve decided to call it a day and they turned for home.

When flying, you can only ride your luck for so long.

Only thirty-four Mk 2 Victors were ever built. Of them, twenty-four were subsequently converted into tankers. And one of these was destroyed in a take-off accident in 1976. On paper, the RAF had just twenty-three aircraft capable of flying to the Falklands and back. On paper. The reality was that on an average day there were rarely more than about four or five Victors available for normal training. Many would be undergoing servicing at Marham and couldn't be generated at short notice. Others would always be in deep servicing at RAF St Athan, the RAF's maintenance facility in South Wales. With advance notice, for a major exercise perhaps, the number of airframes flying could reach eleven or twelve. In April 1982, while the aircrews worked up, the Marham Engineering Wing laboured to bring as many Victors on line as possible. Ex-Victor personnel were drafted back to Marham to help this unprecedented effort. The chief technicians were organized into shifts so that work could go on round the clock. Such was the intensity of the work, there was little chance of getting home or even to the Sergeants' Mess. The aircrew feeder in the Ops block, they reckoned, was the only thing saving them from starving.

Servicing periods were extended. When two Victors were collected from their major overhaul at St Athan, the aircraft scheduled to replace them stayed on the flightline. Any Victor that was unserviceable was cannibalized to keep the others in the air. It was nearly a year before one of these unlucky, stripped jets was to fly again. In anticipation of the difficulties of maintaining the Victors once they'd deployed south, parts approaching the end of their life were replaced with new ones. Needing even closer attention were the airframes themselves – they were old, the first of Marham's current fleet having been delivered to the Air Force in 1960. Every time an aircraft manoeuvres, the airframe is put under a degree of stress. Over the course of its lifetime, the effect of that stress is cumulative. Aerobatics or combat will see the total fatigue index jump sharply, but any kind of manual handling, such as tight formation flying or air-to-air refuelling, will also see it rise. Unchecked it can lead to catastrophic failure like the cracked wing spars that grounded the RAF's Valiants. Research that followed the tragic losses of Comet airliners in the 1950s meant that the effect of metal fatigue was well understood. Every Victor had a finite life, measured by a fatigue counter in the bomb bay, and many were approaching the end of it. It was to be an area of critical concern for the Marham engineers.

As well as maintenance work in preparation for the deployment south there were also modifications which needed to be made – a job which was again complicated by the age of the airframes. All the Victors were originally built in 'Fred's Shed', Handley Page's huge hangar at Radlett, near St Albans. It was a facility that was infamous for its ramshackle appearance – a visiting American VIP had been impressed by the Victor, but wondered aloud 'why you had to build it in a barn'. Like the Vulcans, they were essentially hand-built. None were entirely identical, which meant that modifications couldn't be applied in an entirely consistent way throughout the fleet.

Cameras were already installed in the jets flown by Tux, Elliott and Todd. Further work was done on their radars. The RAF's dedicated maritime radar reconnaissance squadron, 27 Squadron, had disbanded just two days before the Argentine invasion. Their Vulcans, with radars designed to operate over land, had their sets tuned to enhance their performance over water. Engineers from 27 were recalled from new postings so that the Victors' radars could do the same job – hunting for surface contacts at sea.

Most important of all was the upgrading of the navigation systems. For most of their long careers, Victors had flown along well-known routes supporting deployments to North America, to the Far East or, most frequently, up and down the towlines of the North Sea. Even in unfamiliar airspace there was always the option of fixing a position by using the radar to pick out ground features. The South Atlantic, though, was going to be a very different proposition. Thousands of miles from safety, over featureless water, the Victor's ageing systems simply weren't up to the job. There were two solutions. Most of the jets were fitted with a strap-down Inertial Navigation System, or INS, known as Carousel, a piece of kit already used successfully aboard commercial airliners. Later, others were fitted with Omega, a very low-frequency, very long-range radio device designed for the US Navy's submarine fleet. Omega allowed the Americans to fix their boats' positions without forcing them to surface. It could do the same for the Victors in the air, however far they might be from home. Positioning the Omega aerial was crucial, though. Get it wrong and it didn't work. Electronic surveys of the Victor pointed to the back of the jet, underneath the tail cone. Right next to the airbrakes. These hydraulic barndoors would extend like huge 7 foot by 6 foot clamshells into the airstream to slow the aircraft. It was like dropping an anchor, but the vibration around the brakes caused by the disruption to the airflow could dislodge fillings. The Omega's sensitive electrical connections weren't robust enough to endure such savage treatment. The Marham engineers didn't muck around: they just glued up the whole installation with massive amounts of Araldite. Nothing, but nothing, was going to shake those aerials loose. Ever again.

Secrecy meant that rumour and intrigue surrounded much of what was happening at Marham. Sideways glances were cast at Tux and crews training for the reconnaissance missions. Similarly, the engineering work attracted speculation. Word went round that there were plans to fit the Victors with AIM-9 Sidewinder air-to-air missiles. *Now that*, thought excited aircrews, *would be great sport*.

Hanging Sidewinders off the wing was about the only thing, however, that the toiling engineers *hadn't* been asked to do. But they were working hard to turn the Victor into a missile carrier for the first time since it was retired from the bomber force in 1968. Developed in the 1960s, the AS37 Martel was a big 13-foot-long, 1,200lb anti-radar missile used primarily by the RAF's Buccaneers. Marham, though, was home to the Martel servicing unit. Stress and design men from British Aerospace arrived at the Norfolk base at the beginning of April and set up drawing boards in the Engineering Wing. They began work from scratch on marrying the Martel to the Victor airframe. As designs for each component were finished they were dispatched to the station workshops for manufacture. In the hangar, Victor and Martel technicians laboured together to replace a test Victor's wing refuelling pod with the new weapons pylon, then wire it to control panels in the cockpit.

The effort going on at Marham was extraordinary, and visiting from 1 Group in the first week of April, Air Vice-Marshal Mike Knight was accompanied into one of the hangars by Jerry Price to see it for himself. As they looked on, an exhausted Corporal wriggled out from inside a Victor and practically collapsed at the AOC's feet. The airman had been cramped into the stifling confines of the jet's maintenance spaces for nearly ten hours. Knight was struck hard by the dedication on display.

Another anti-aircraft battery went up in Stanley behind the town hall on the waterfront on Wednesday the 14th. In the eastern part of town towards the rubbish dump, John Smith thought Argentine troops seemed well dug in. In addition to digging effective-looking covered trenches, they'd also mocked up dummy guns made of lorry wheels, gas bottles and 6-inch fuel pipes to confuse aerial reconnaissance. But interspersed amongst the fakes were the real guns. While the young Argentine conscripts couldn't help but let their inexperience show, it was clear, Smith thought, that there were many in the professional army who knew exactly what they were doing. Smith would do what he could to get around Stanley collecting information about the military build-up. Walking the dog provided the excuse. His youngest boy, eleven-year-old Tyssen, would walk with him – always making sure to put on shorts, even with temperatures down to zero. It made him look younger and seemed to disarm the soldiers, giving him and his father more time to look around and ask questions. Peter Biggs employed a similar subterfuge. Incensed by the continual house searches, he harboured plans to petrol bomb the Argentine helicopters that sat on the open ground between the government buildings and the Governor's mansion. Frustrated in that ambition by the blanket of Argentine guards, he wandered around town discreetly taking photographs of Argentine defences. He found that if Fran joined him he was able to avoid the attentions of the soldiers. Her pregnancy seemed to provide cover. He marked their positions on a map, photographed the map, then sent the film back to the UK on one of the last planes to leave, smuggled out in the luggage of a departing Irish schoolteacher's wife.

Access to the heavily fortified room in the Ops block was strictly controlled. 'The Vault' contained RAF Waddington's target information and was where the Vulcan crews would spend hours mission-planning. Each was allocated both NATO and national targets. Such were the levels of secrecy that one crew wouldn't know the target of the next. The NATO targets tended to be more popular. The more capable American strategic bomber force tended to be allocated the more heavily defended targets. In the unlikely event that Britain found herself waging war against the Soviets alone, the national list might find crews tasked with delivering a nuclear weapon to downtown Moscow – through the most comprehensive integrated air defence network in history. The short straw. Banks of documents pertaining to particular sorties were stored in vast sliding floor-to-ceiling cabinets. The files were designed to cover any possible contingency during a flight, from engine failure to civil aviation procedures. The volume was overwhelming. With way too much to learn, the information in 'The Vault' acted as a kind of corporate memory. What was conspicuously absent was any information *at all* on the Falkland Islands.

Accurate intelligence was a huge problem – as the priority given to preparing the Victors to fly reconnaissance missions underlined. The South Atlantic was way beyond the range of 39 Squadron's high-altitude Canberra spy planes – unless a closer friendly operating base could somehow be negotiated. There was no satellite imagery from the Americans. Neither Professor Ronald Mason, the government's Chief Scientific Adviser, nor the Defence Secretary, John Nott, were able to persuade them to divert a KH11 satellite away from NATO duties – much to both men's frustration. Instead, there were rudimentary 1:25,000 and 1:50,000 maps and the detailed notes made by an ex-commander of the Falklands Marine garrison as he sailed around the islands' coast. HUMINT, or human intelligence, was also in desperately short supply. In April 1982, MI6 had one officer based in Buenos Aires. He had been responsible not just for intelligence on Argentina, but for the *whole* of South America. Those planning the campaign would take whatever they could get, although what inform-ation there was was played close to the chest. Even Air Vice-Marshal Mike Knight, as Air Officer Commanding 1 Group, the officer with ultimate responsibility for delivering jets and crews capable of doing whatever they were ordered to do, felt outside the loop. He did whatever he could to try to anticipate what would be demanded of him and his assets. Working within such a compressed time frame, anything he could do to help those working on the coalface at Marham and Waddington, *before* an official signal arrived from Northwood, he would do.

# Chapter 15

Simon Baldwin started early and finished late as he concentrated on trying to bring Sir Michael Beetham's vision to life. As he worked, he lived off a diet of bacon sandwiches, coffee and Gold Block pipe tobacco. Many of the challenges he faced were entirely new to him. The Vulcan community knew all about what they would face attacking the Warsaw Pact – fighters and missiles given names by NATO like Fishbed, Flogger, Foxbat, Guideline and Grail. The AEOs probably mumbled the frequency bands of the Soviet fire-control radars as they drifted off to sleep. But Argentina, Baldwin learnt from *Jane's* or material published by the Institute of Strategic Studies, had none of the Russian kit they were trained to counter. Most of it came from much closer to home, produced by factories in France, Germany, Switzerland, America and Britain. He was going to have to hit the books.

Within Air Vice-Marshal Knight's 1 Group planning cell at Bawtry, no possible use of the Vulcans was left unconsidered. New weapons were studied, including cluster bombs and laser-guided bombs. Suddenly, a bomber a quarter of a century old, which had been neglected for years, was the centre of attention. *What about a four-ship firepower demonstration to demonstrate Britain's resolve and capability?*, they asked themselves. *Or minelaying sorties to keep the Argentine Navy at bay? Maybe leaflet-dropping, to demoralize her conscript troops. Even*, in whispered tones, *the possibility of hitting the Argentine mainland*. All relied on an assumption that the

Vulcan's flight refuelling system would be successfully revived and that the Victors could provide the fuel to support whatever was planned. As it happened, it wasn't to be as simple as that.

None of the creative thinking in evidence affected the simplicity of the orders given to Waddington in that first week: restore the Vulcan's ability to refuel in the air and drop conventional bombs. So Baldwin's CORPORATE flight pressed ahead. Despite the fuel leaks there had been nothing lacking in the Vulcan pilots' ability to make contact. Someone needed to find out why the machinery was failing, but by Friday the 16th all three Captains completed their day receiver training. The bombing, though, also posed a challenge – it had been a long time since the Vulcans had dropped 1,000lb iron bombs.

Once again it fell to the engineers to get to grips with the problem first.

As a conventional bomber the Vulcan had been capable of carrying twenty-one 1,000lb bombs on three septuple bomb carriers attached to hardpoints in the bomb bay. The release of the bombs was controlled from a panel in the Nav Radar's station in the cockpit known as the '90-Way' that monitored electrical connections to each bomb. It was said that it provided ninety different ways of sequencing the drop, from one bomb to twenty-one and every combination in between, in quick succession or one at a time. It provided options and flexibility, meaning that differently fused weapons could be used separately as the mission demanded – air burst bombs in the front, delayed fuses in the back.

None of Waddington's Vulcans was still fitted with either the bomb carriers or the 90-Way. But they didn't just have to be reinstalled; they had to be found first. It was a good thing that the engineers seemed to have an aversion to actually getting rid of anything for good. All RAF stations had engineering dumps where the Engineering Wing stored anything that they felt might one day come in handy – anything they couldn't bear to part with. Dumps at Waddington and Scampton, the nearby base that had just drawn the curtain on twenty-one years of Vulcan operations, were scoured for the missing kit: 90-Way panels were found, refitted and tested but the septuple bomb carriers – and they needed *at least* nine of them – proved harder to find. The required number was eventually made up when someone recalled that some had been disposed of at a Newark scrapyard. Incredibly, they were still there.

Much that was once known about the Vulcan had been lost. RAF training no longer offered the kind of deep foundation that had once been deemed necessary. There was someone to turn to, though: 50 Squadron's John Williams. Williams had been through the very first Vulcan conversion course and, during a year of ground school, had practically learnt how to dismantle and rebuild the jet. If he said, 'You need to tweak the third nut on the left one quarter-turn to the right,' you did it. And it usually did the trick. Baldwin brought him into the CORPORATE flight's planning team.

If the Vulcans were going to practise bombing, they were going to need bombs too. When Simon Baldwin first enquired, he discovered that Waddington's armoury had just forty-one 1,000lb high-explosive 'iron' bombs. With three crews to train, they could be used up in one day on the ranges. He widened his search, but was alarmed to track down just 167 in the whole country – all that was left from thirty years of trying to dispose of the stockpile left at the end of the Second World War. Hundreds had simply been dropped into the sea. This was much appreciated by fishermen off Cyprus – where two Vulcan squadrons were stationed throughout the 1960s – who eagerly scooped up the dead fish as they floated to the surface. Many of the bomb cases that were left were cast rather than machined and that too was potentially problematic. Cast-iron cases shattered on impact like glass on a tile floor, dissipating the force of the blast. What were needed now were the tough machined cases that would penetrate deep into the ground before exploding. But the bombs had been disposed of in-discriminately and Baldwin had no choice but to take whatever he could get his hands on.

*

The Chief of the Air Staff knew Marham well. Visiting his old station on Friday the 16th to meet the Victor crews as they prepared to deploy to Ascension, Sir Michael Beetham felt pleased to be back. It had changed a bit since his day, but it was still recognizably the same place, still known to some of the old-timers ambivalently as 'El Adem with grass', after the RAF's now long-vacated remote, windswept desert airbase in Libya. Beetham was a man held in high regard by the 'tanker trash' – he was one of them. As Marham's Station Commander, Jerry Price, ushered Beetham around, he was struck again by the CAS's gentle manner and encouraged by his interest in what was going on. Beetham, it was clear, properly understood the value of what they were doing. After all, Price reflected, he knew as much about in-flight refuelling as anyone. Responding to this, the Marham crews appeared bullish. And Beetham returned to Whitehall, both proud and confident in his men, impressed by their mood – *Get up and go, we're going to do this.*

Most important of all was the news from Marham that the Vulcan pilots were proving to be 'good prodders'. It was time, perhaps, to make sure that the Argentinians got wind of what he had in mind. There was still a faint hope that if the mounting military pressure on the junta became overwhelming, war might be averted.

With Beetham gone, Price returned to the job of getting the first four Victors ready to fly south. Then his phone rang. The message was straightforward: an aircraft would soon be arriving to pick him up from Marham. He had a couple of hours to pack his bags. He'd had absolutely no intimation of this sudden development. Where he was going wasn't mentioned, although he had to assume it was Ascension Island. He was just told he was going to be briefed.

Price rushed home to pack and say his goodbyes to his family who, however they might have felt about the surprise news, accepted it phlegmatically. In the late afternoon he boarded the HS125 Dominie for the short flight to Northolt, on the outskirts of London. From there he was driven straight to Whitehall to be briefed in MoD Ops Room. He was, they told him, going to become the Senior RAF Officer on Ascension Island. He'd be flying out from Brize Norton the next day.

Until now, the Senior RAF Officer on Ascension had been drawn from the Nimrod force. As the Victor's crucial role began to emerge, though, Price became the obvious candidate to succeed him.

On Friday evening, as Jerry Price was ferried around the country, Martin Withers, Monty and John Reeve prepared to fly again. With their day-refuelling qualification complete, it was time to try it at night. Between two and five o'clock in the afternoon the crews sat through briefings, impatient to fly. Ground school and intelligence briefings were a permanent fixture in a packed schedule. For the time being it was limited to subjects like refuelling and the forgotten art of conventional bombing, but some of what was to come would raise eyebrows.

At eight o'clock, Martin Withers and Dick Russell pushed forward the throttles and released the brakes. The first of the Vulcans accelerated down the Waddington runway and roared into the night sky, then rolled out towards the North Sea tow-lines to rendezvous with their tanker. Reeve and Monty followed at hour-and-a-half intervals. At night, unexpectedly, refuelling seemed more straightforward. The view of the flood-lit white underside of the Victor seemed more abstract. There was less of a temptation to fly instinctively. Instead, closing on the red and black stripes and making contact could be carried out without distraction from what the seat of their pants was telling them. The Vulcan captains were gaining in confidence, making contact time after time, but still the persistent, in-explicable fuel leaks that threatened to scuttle the whole enterprise continued to undermine them.

Jerry Price spent the night in a room at Northwood Headquarters. Before leaving for Brize, he made his way to the main Ops Room for an early-morning briefing with joint planners from all three services. Conspicuous by their absence were CORPORATE's senior military commanders, all of whom were 4,000 miles away. Admiral Fieldhouse, along with Air Marshal Curtiss and Major-General Jeremy Moore, his air and land commanders respectively, had flown to Ascension to confirm the military plan to retake the Falklands. Naval helicopters flew the visitors out to HMS *Hermes*, the Task Force flagship. On board the aircraft carrier they met with Admiral Woodward, Brigadier Julian Thompson and Commodore Mike Clapp, the men responsible for implementing the plan. One factor dominated their thinking: time. It forced them to plan the campaign backwards. By the end of June, the ships of the Task Force, operating in a brutal environment, far from proper maintenance, would start to fall apart. The war would be won or lost by then. A strict timetable based solely on military, not political, imperatives was drawn up and agreed on. Two elements of the plan related directly to the job being asked of Waddington's Vulcans. First of all, Fieldhouse hoped to convince the Argentinians that Buenos Aires was under threat. If they believed – whatever the reality – that their capital city was at risk, ships and aircraft would have to be kept north, away from the battle for the Falklands, to defend it. Secondly, he wanted to pull the Argentinians on to the punch, provoking them into committing their sea and air forces in defence of their conquest against an expected British amphibious assault on 1 May. For the British plan to work, Woodward's Battle Group needed to sail by lunchtime the following day, 18 April.

Admiral Fieldhouse returned to London to tell the politicians that, if a war was to be won, it had to begin by 1 May, no later. Negotiations had until that date. Waddington had less than two weeks, and they'd yet to drop a single bomb.

In the late 1960s, in the face of a growing Soviet naval threat, the Defence Secretary, Denis Healey, made the bold claim that the British knew the position of every single Soviet ship in the Mediterranean and, should it be necessary, he added, could cope with the lot of them. His confidence came from the Victor SR2's ability, using its radar, to accurately survey 400,000 square miles of ocean in one eight-hour sortie.

With the need for the Victor to assume the tanker role, the task of maritime radar reconnaissance, MRR, had been passed to the Vulcans. But following the upgrade to their old radars by the ex-27 Squadron engineers, the Victors were being pressed back into service in their old capacity.

The British plan to retake the Falklands was built around four main objectives, the first of which – the establishment of the 200-mile MEZ by the nuclear attack submarine – had already been achieved. Next on the list was the recovery of South Georgia.

The decision to retake the remote South Atlantic island was essentially a political one. On purely military grounds it would have been preferable to focus solely on the Falklands. If not essential, however, Operation PARAQUAT, as the plan to recapture South Georgia became known, was desirable for a number of reasons. From the moment the decision was taken to put the Task Force to sea, a major consideration had been the length of time it would take to arrive in a position to conduct operations off the Falklands. What could happen militarily or politically during that hiatus was unpredictable and both the Cabinet and the defence chiefs remembered how the tide had turned against Britain during the 1956 Suez Crisis. The early recapture of South Georgia could provide momentum for Britain's military campaign and shore up the public's morale. It was hoped that a successful campaign might even persuade Argentina to abandon the Falklands themselves. Finally, the Chief of the Defence Staff, Admiral Lewin, wanted to be able to demonstrate that his forces could do what he and the service chiefs had said they could do.

Two destroyers, HMS *Antrim* and HMS *Plymouth*, had departed Ascension on 12 April, supported by the *Tidespring*, a Royal Fleet Auxiliary tanker. On board they were carrying Royal Marines from 42 Commando and troopers from D Squadron SAS. They joined up with HMS *Endurance* on 14

April and the RFA *Fort Austin*; then the five-ship Task Group sailed south, bound for South Georgia.

As it had in the 1960s when Denis Healey made his statement, the Navy once again needed to know the whereabouts of enemy ships and only the Victor could provide that information.

At RAF Marham, after a day listening to briefings on everything from the international situation to survival in the South Atlantic, Bob Tuxford was handed a will form. *Concentrates the mind*, he thought, as he filled it in.

# Chapter 16

## 18 April 1982

'VULCANS TO HIT ARGENTINA', screamed the banner headline in the *Sunday Express*. Sir Michael Beetham enjoyed it. It was exactly the kind of thing he had hoped for. He wanted to intimidate the Argentinians and sow the seeds of doubt in their minds. No one had any serious intention of bombing the mainland. *After all*, Beetham thought, *it's not the Second World War. We're not in the business of bombing capitals*. The newspapers, however, seemed to relish the idea. Follow-up reports became increasingly overheated. 'It is unlikely', one concluded, 'that any of the weapons in Argentina's arsenal would be able to stop the bombers destroying every major air-field, every port, every military centre.' On the record, the MoD merely allowed itself to admit, coyly, that they were 'extending the capabilities of a number of Vulcans' and that they were not thinking 'only in a NATO context'.

The MoD version was much closer to the truth. It was still uncertain whether it was going to be possible to get a single Vulcan as far south as the Falklands, but the publicity had been part of the Chief of the Air Staff's plan from the outset. The newspapers could speculate to their heart's content and the Air Force would do whatever it could to fan the flames.

It didn't matter to John Laycock which crew it was, because to the *Daily Express* they would all look the same. The newspaper just wanted a picture to follow up on their report that the military balance had tipped 'decisively in our favour'. Laycock hauled a crew out of flight planning. None of them were anything to do with the CORPORATE flight. In fact, they were preparing to leave on a training deployment to Treviso in Italy. That had to wait until the five of them had posed on the Waddington flightline with their helmets under their arms, staring at the camera with the intimidating stares of nightclub bouncers. Behind them, dominating the shot, was the unmistakable shape of the Avro delta.

Highly amused by the whole episode, the crew left for Italy. 'READY TO FIGHT', read the headline when the photo appeared in the next day's paper. 'A mighty Vulcan bomber sits like a Goliath on the runway and in its shadow, five men stand ready to do their duty,' the caption added. They were doing their bit, but their contribution to Waddington's effort didn't end there. Out for the night in Venice, perhaps a little the worse for wear, they became convinced that a Swiss businessman they were talking to was an Argentine spy and answered his loaded questions with the best bullshit they could muster.

John Reeve couldn't believe what he was reading. To catch the enemy unawares was the Vulcan's best defence. With news of their involvement all over the papers, there seemed little hope of that. *So much for surprise*, he thought, *now they know we're coming.*

Martin Withers was losing his appetite. He'd greeted the news that they'd be practising air-to-air refuelling with enthusiasm, but over the course of the last week the mood had changed. The plan to use the Vulcans in anger was serious. The nature of his job meant he'd thought about killing. But as a nuclear bomber pilot, his job was to keep the peace. If that failed, then, he thought, he'd have few qualms about striking back against those who threatened him and his loved ones. It had never really preyed on his mind because he never thought it would ever happen. This was different. But it wasn't the killing that fed his apprehension, it was the risk. His worry was that attacking a coastal target at the Vulcan's standard 250 knots and 300 feet then carrying out a climbing turn to avoid terrain seemed almost suicidal. Against modern, radar-laid guns an aircraft the size of a Vulcan would be a sitting duck. He was going to have to fly faster. 'The Book' – the Operating Data Manual – said that you couldn't throw a heavy Vulcan into a 400 knot full-power turn with 60 degrees of bank. But if they were going to have a chance of evading Argentine defences, that was exactly what they'd have to do. He knew that the Vulcan had been test-flown to 415 knots. He'd even been told by a pilot who'd flown the first Mk 2 Vulcan at Farnborough that, if you opened the taps and neglected to watch the speed, she'd reach 500.

As the newspapers rolled off the presses on Sunday morning, Withers was flying again. On the last of the night-refuelling qualification sorties, Withers pushed the throttles forward at 15,000 feet over RAF Leuchars on the east coast of Scotland. *If something goes wrong*, he thought, *we can always go in there. Won't help much if the wing comes off, I suppose.* At 420 knots, as Dick Russell looked on anxiously, he cranked the jet into the turn. She went round on rails, pulling 2g all the way. That settled it, if he was going in low, he was going to blast through the airfield at the lowest possible height for the bombs to fuse, then haul the Vulcan into the flattest, steepest turn of his life.

Simon Baldwin was equally concerned about his crews' chances. But the Argentine air defences were just one of the issues he was faced with. If he couldn't get them to the target the threat of the anti-aircraft guns would be academic. So the most pressing problem remained the refuelling. The AARIs had signed off the three Vulcan captains – all of them were now qualified to refuel by day and night, but still the leaking probes persisted. There wasn't anything drastically wrong with their flying, but neither did it appear to be anything mechanical. Initially, there'd been a scramble to reconstitute the system, but the engineers, using the method suggested by Marham after that first, frantic weekend, were testing the connections before every flight. In any case, there seemed to be two separate faults. During the fuel transfers themselves, leaks ran down the probe and over the cockpit glass, obliterating the view forward, but this seemed manageable compared to the second, more dramatic glitch: the huge wash of fuel that would flood back into the engines as contact was broken. Notes were circulated to everyone in the Air Force with any Vulcan refuelling experience asking them if they'd had similar difficulties and what was done to overcome them. The engineers, too, were typically creative.

Various ways of dispersing the leaking fuel were suggested and tried, from the technical – fitting lines of vortex generators to the nose between the probe and the windscreen to churn up the airflow; and the basic – bending back a metal lip that ran underneath the glass that had, at some point, for reasons no one could remember, been hammered back on itself; to the ingenious – securing a kitchen colander around the base of the probe. None worked.

A related concern was the availability of the probes themselves. Each of the Vulcans selected began the work-up with a probe fitted, but their tips, like a lizard's tail in the claws of a predator, were designed to sheer off, to prevent more substantial damage to the aircraft during a clumsy contact. A number of them had already been damaged. But it was no longer just Vulcans. The RAF effort in support of the Task Force had created an unprecedented demand. Design teams at companies like British Aerospace, Marshall's of Cambridge and Flight Refuelling Ltd were working round the clock to equip the RAF's Nimrod and Hercules fleets with probes that would enable them to operate as far south as the Falklands. By cannibalizing the rest of Waddington's Vulcan fleet the CORPORATE flight could be kept in the air, but the supply of new probes was finite. And when they were gone, they were gone.

In November 1981, a IX Squadron Vulcan had suffered a series of severe technical faults *en route* to Goose Bay in Newfoundland. She was beyond economic repair, but, rather than being scrapped, was left as a gift to commemorate the

RAF's long association with the local community. She was the first to lose her probe. Urgent calls were made to aviation museums at home and around the world. The Vulcan at the RAF Museum in Hendon was raided. The jet delivered to the Imperial War Museum at Duxford by Martin Withers lost hers too. Curators of museums at Castle Air Force Base, California, and Offut, Nebraska, turned a blind eye as teams of RAF technicians arrived in a C-130 Hercules, removed the refuelling probes from their treasured exhibits, patched the holes they left behind with blanking plates, then disappeared with their booty.

The refuelling could either be made to work or it couldn't, but Baldwin had to work on the assumption that the engineers would rectify whatever was wrong. So next on the list was navigation. The newspapers had mentioned 'pinpoint accuracy'. As things stood, though, just finding the islands over such long distances was a demanding task. Locating the actual target on a first pass attack was highly unlikely. During the Cold War, the Vulcans' routes over the Russian steppes were endlessly updated. As the reach of the Soviet air defences grew, the crews refined their flight plans to take them through the gaps. Over water, in the South Atlantic, they faced the same difficulties as the Victors: no charts, no ground features and, consequently, no way to fix a position using the radar. In fact, they had only one reliable method of checking where they were: a sextant. The Vulcan had two periscope sextants – *great big things like donkey dicks*, reckoned Reeve's plotter, Jim Vinales. They might not have looked familiar to a sailor of Nelson's day, but the principle was no different – they established the user's position relative to the known position of the stars. The Vulcan crews had always practised the technique on navigation exercises, or sorties across the Atlantic, but they never really had to *rely* on the sextants. There was a difference between keeping a skill from going rusty and having your life depend on it. The Plotters talked a confident game. Vinales reckoned it was possible, working hard at it, to be accurate to within a few miles. The other half of Reeve's Nav team, Mick

Cooper, wasn't so sure. He thought that over the kinds of distances involved, they'd be lucky to get within forty miles of where they were supposed to be going. John Laycock and Simon Baldwin were inclined to side with Cooper. Astro-nav demanded fairly long periods of smooth, straight and level flying. Flying in even loose formation with tanker aircraft would make that impossible. Astro-nav also depended on repetition. Without continual checking through further star shots, the tiniest error would grow exponentially. If they were going to send their crews to war they weren't prepared to do so with navigation equipment that was hardly more accurate than a road map that could tell you only what *county* you were in. If the Vulcan was off track by forty miles as it ran in to a coastal airfield target at low level, the first radar fix would be too late in the attack run to guarantee a successful attack. In the worst case the aircraft might have to climb into radar and missile cover to obtain a fix and then manoeuvre to make a second attempt to fly down the runway. The defenders would love that; the Vulcan crew wouldn't. Baldwin had devised astro techniques for bombing competitions that reduced the error to about seven miles or less, but it had taken weeks of training for crews to reach that level of expertise. They didn't now have that luxury.

As the Vulcans flew long sorties at night while the Plotters and Radars practised their astro-nav out over the Atlantic, Laycock and Baldwin sent a signal to HQ 1 Group: some kind of new navigational aid for old V-bombers was desperately needed.

John Smith thought they sounded like German Stukas. *Sinister*. Argentine warplanes were now flying out of Stanley airfield. The little Pucaras wheeled and dived during bombing exercises over Yorke Bay to the north of the harbour. The buzz from their turbo-prop engines rose angrily as their speed increased. Smoke and flames rose hundreds of feet into the clear, windless sky.

Families around Stanley tried to calculate the progress of the

British task force. One of Fran Biggs's little brothers cut pictures of Harriers and ships out of magazines to annotate the map her husband Peter had pinned to the wall. The nine-year-old's handiwork would earn icy stares from soldiers searching the house.

As the islanders waited, the first ships from Sandy Woodward's Battle Group weighed their anchors off Ascension and set a course to the south-west. It was lunchtime on 18 April. Admiral Woodward had, at least, met the first of his deadlines.

# Chapter 17

## 18 April 1982

It was a beautiful day on Ascension Island. Most of them were. Temperatures hovered around the mid-seventies and, despite the humidity, the constant breeze from the south-east kept it comfortable. Bill Bryden liked to watch new arrivals from Wideawake's small control tower. Over the last two weeks the USAF colonel had watched the British transport planes swarm into his normally sleepy mid-Atlantic base. Now he'd been asked to make space for four Victor K2s.

Wideawake's runway was unusual. It rose from the threshold for about 1,000 feet before peaking and sloping away. Bryden's controllers would always warn incoming traffic, but it could still catch you out. If a pilot misjudged his approach – if he failed to get his wheels down before the hump – he could end up chasing the runway as it sloped away from him and run out of Tarmac. *First-time landings*, he thought, as the first of the Victors settled into long finals for runway 14, *were always interesting*. Today, though, the surprise was on him.

The Victor touched down beautifully and quickly streamed a large white drag chute behind it. As the speed bled off, the pilot jettisoned the chute on to the middle of the runway. Standard practice. *What the hell's he going to do now?*, wondered Bryden. Ascension Auxiliary Air Force Base had just one runway with a turning head at the end. Arrivals had to taxi to the bottom, turn through 180 degrees then backtrack to the threshold to leave off a taxiway that met the runway where they had touched down. With a knot of heavy fabric sitting on the Tarmac blocking the way there was no way back. And there were three other Victors in the pattern waiting to recover. Bryden scrambled a crew of ground handlers to drive out to the runway and remove the chute. It was heavier than it looked. It was all two of them could do to bundle it into the back of a pick-up. But with the runway now clear, the stranded Victor was able to taxi back, vacate the runway and allow the second tanker in to land. Air Traffic Control radioed the second jet first to inform the captain that there was a new standard procedure. From now on, Victors would carry their chutes to the turning head before dropping them, ensuring that the runway was unobstructed.

The confusion was a clear early indication to all involved, not least the Victor pilots, of the limitations of Wideawake's facilities. If, for any reason at all, that single runway was put out of action, nothing could come in or out. And there was nowhere else to go. Not for over 1,000 miles in any direction.

The Victor crews were greeted with cold beers by the engineering team. They'd flown in separately on transport planes, bringing with them ground equipment to support RAF operations. Each Victor had carried a passenger on board: the Crew Chief. Armed with little more than expertise and experience, he had to try to keep his Victor flying when it was deployed away from home. With Tux was one of the most committed: Roger Brooks was a man devoted to the old V-bomber.

Later in the day, Jerry Price disembarked from a VC10 after an unnerving flight via Dakar in Senegal. The only other passenger on board, squeezed in with him amongst the cargo, had been an intense, taciturn SAS man, who, it appeared, had whiled away the entire flight sharpening knives at the back of the hold. Price looked around at the barren red-brown landscape of peaks and craters of his new command. Overlooking the runway from the south side, rising like giant termite mounds, were the volcanic shapes of Round Hill and South

Gannet Hill. Only Green Mountain to the north-east broke up a landscape so similar to the moon's, that NASA had actually tested their 'Moon Buggy' Lunar Roving Vehicle on the island. The mountain was a freak. When Charles Darwin stopped at Ascension in 1836 during the voyage of the HMS *Beagle*, he described it as 'entirely destitute of trees'. Barely 150 years later, following an ambitious and eclectic nineteenth-century planting scheme, a thriving tropical rainforest, inhabited by orange land crabs, graced its upper slopes. Clouds now formed around the peak, giving rise to blustery showers in the early afternoons. Without any other source of natural water, great effort had gone into trying to collect the rain that fell, but it couldn't support Ascension's 1,000-strong migrant population. Instead, fresh water came as a by-product of the island's two power stations. More than any other factor, the water supply was going to determine the numbers Ascension could support.

The USAF outsourced the management of Wideawake. The small contingent from PanAm were contracted to handle 285 aircraft movements per year. Of those, 104 – 52 landings, 52 take-offs – were accounted for by the weekly C-141 Starlifter transport that resupplied the island from America. That left one landing or one take-off every couple of days. The pace was not expected to be energetic. But that had already changed dramatically.

The task facing Price was immediately apparent. First on the agenda was to erect the tents that would become the Operations centre. Planning, engineering, briefing, tactical communications, even medical facilities would all be housed under canvas. The aircrew, engineers and planning team all rolled up their sleeves and mucked in. *Frontier stuff*, thought Tux.

For Price the one real saving grace, inflexible as it might be, was the runway. In anticipation of the Apollo moon landings, NASA built a deep-space tracking station in the 1960s. At the same time, Wideawake's runway was extended from 6,000 to 10,000 feet. Although the Apollo programme was long gone, NASA had maintained a presence on the island. And since

1981, Ascension had again become invaluable when her lengthened strip was designated as an unlikely diversion field for the Space Shuttle. The window during which, if something went wrong during a flight, *Columbia* could have used Wideawake was only minutes wide, but the runway was long enough should it have to. It was fortunate that the next shuttle flight wasn't scheduled until the end of June. Until then, the British were going to need every inch of the orbiter's runway.

In 1981, faced with rising fuel costs and increasingly stringent airport noise restrictions, British Airways put its entire fleet of fourteen Vickers Super VC10 airliners up for sale. With a number of ex-commercial VC10s already undergoing conversion into aerial tankers, and conscious of the age of its Victor force, the MoD snapped up the old jets and put them into storage. Like the Victors they were equipped with rare Rolls-Royce Conway engines and proved to be a useful and regular source of engine parts. But with the Vulcans' desperate need for a navigation system that would be accurate in the South Atlantic, in 1982 the VC10s were ransacked again.

The first wave of Victors deploying to Ascension had been fitted with the Carousel Inertial Navigation System. If it worked for them, there was no reason it couldn't also work for the Vulcans. The only problem was that it was needed yesterday. Then someone remembered the VC10s. The Super VC10s sitting outside at RAF Abingdon were fitted with twin Carousel INS.

An inertial navigation device is made up of gyroscopes and ultra-sensitive accelerometers. When it's switched on, it orientates itself to true north. Once aligned, all further movement is detected by the accelerometers and measured relative to that starting point. The beauty of the Carousel was that it was self-sufficient, needing no recourse to any further input. The disadvantage was that it needed at least fifteen minutes to warm up. It couldn't be hurried. If the warm-up was rushed or the system disturbed, small errors would creep in from the outset. Over half an hour it was probably unimportant, but over a long flight any error grew exponentially. And once an aircraft was airborne the system was impossible to reset.

A trial fit was hastily organized and a Vulcan flown to Marham, where the new navigation kit was installed. After a successful test flight the remaining CORPORATE bombers were fitted with Carousels removed from the cockpits of the neglected VC10s. The box containing the gyros was strapped down out of harm's way in the bomb-aimer's prone position in the nose of the jet under the pilots' seats. The two control panels were fitted to the Nav Plotter's station, light grey with red and yellow buttons against the scuffed black background. Then Gordon Graham, Jim Vinales and Dick Arnott were given a tutorial in how to operate it.

On Monday afternoon, the Vulcans took off to test the Carousels and further hone the refuelling skills of their Captains. They were without the AARIs for the first time. The three co-pilots, Pete Taylor, Don Dibbens and Bill Perrins, had watched their Captains' efforts to make contact from the ladder between the two ejection seats. Now all three got a chance to try it for themselves. Nearly three hours later they landed back at Waddington, taxied to Alpha Dispersal and parked in the same spots they'd left from. In Reeve's jet the two Carousels showed an error of just one nautical mile. That was good enough. The CORPORATE flight could now, at least, find its way to the Falkland Islands. But while further up the RAF chain of command this was known to be the aim, the crews, as they continued training, were still in the dark. Their target had yet to be confirmed to them. No one wanted to believe that the Argentine mainland was in their sights, but the thought preyed on their minds. And if it wasn't, they speculated, it could only be the islands themselves. And, like Beetham, Hayr and the 1 Group Planners, they knew that the only target there that made any sense at all was the hard, all-weather runway at Stanley airfield.

To much of the Argentine military, the news of the invasion was as unexpected as it was to those at Marham or

Waddington. None were quite so wrong-footed as the 2nd Escuadrilla Aeronaval de Caza y Ataque, of the Argentine Navy. The unit had only taken delivery of its French Dassault Super Étendard attack jets in November the previous year. While they trained for anti-ship operations against the British task force, the squadron's CO, Commander Jorge Colombo, explored the possibility of flying out of BAM Malvinas. Take-off and braking distances were measured and examined. It was tight, but, in the dry at least, carrying an Exocet under one wing and a fuel tank under the other, the Étendards could take off and land on Stanley's 4,100-foot runway. And it was definitely an option as a diversion if a jet was in trouble. On 19 April, satisfied that his fledgling squadron was ready for action, Colombo deployed the first of his four Super Etendards south from their base near Buenos Aires to Rio Grande, the most southerly base on the mainland, and within range of the islands.

Two piston-engined reconnaissance planes joined the 2nd Escuadrilla at the Tierra del Fuego base. The role of the elderly, barely airworthy Neptunes of the Escuadrilla de Exploración was to fly out to sea, pick up the British ships on their radars and direct the low-flying strike fighters in to their targets.

Ironically, the first Neptunes delivered to Argentina had already had one careful owner: the Royal Air Force.

It was twenty-five years since Hugh Prior had flown in RAF Coastal Command's old Lockheed Neptunes. Like Dick Russell, Prior joined as a national serviceman Wireless Operator/Air Gunner. Like Russell, he'd been commissioned, but then instead of going on to become a pilot, he'd trained as an AEO. He was exactly the kind of smart, well-educated operator that the RAF had hoped to attract when they decided that the V-bombers' AEOs needed to be officers. As the fifth member of the crew, the AEO wasn't just there to monitor electrical systems that could power a small town, look after the jet's checklists and man the radios. The AEO's job was to defend the bomber.

Unlike their American and Russian counterparts, the British bombers had never been armed with tail guns. Instead, the Vulcans relied on a comprehensive suite of electronic counter-measures, or ECM, to keep them safe from harm. With cheerful-sounding names like Red Shrimp, Blue Diver or Green Palm, the ECM kit didn't sound particularly warlike and, although it had been the best available at the time, all but the Red Shrimp jammer had been overtaken by age and Soviet technology. A more recent, and still vital, addition was the 18228 Radar Warning Receiver – RWR – that alerted the AEO to the presence of enemy radars. Visual and audio warnings kicked in simultaneously. A strobe on the screen in front of the AEO would show him the direction of the threat as well as indicating the frequency band of the enemy radar. Through his headset the sound of the Pulse Recurrence Frequency, or PRF, would confirm it. Every radar emits a number of pulses per minute, reflections from which need to travel out and return for the operator to track a target. Working over greater dis-tances, a search radar took longer to complete each sweep, resulting in a lower PRF. The higher the PRF, the greater the danger. From a slow rattle of an SA-2 Fansong fire-control radar to the angry, high-pitched buzz from the Gun Dish radar directing the fire of a ZSU-23-4's four automatic cannons, the AEOs could identify a threat from its PRF. And knowledge never stood still. Like submarines on the hunt for new sonar footprints, 51 Squadron's top-secret, intelligence-gathering Nimrod R1s were always searching for unknown frequencies. Once identified and analysed, the information was fed back to the RAF's strike squadrons and added to the list.

Hugh Prior and Barry Masefield knew the sounds well. As electronic warfare instructors they'd taught others how to recognize them. When the Vulcans switched to low-level operation, their RWR kit had been upgraded. But while the 18228 usually detected a signal before it was strong enough to provide an echo back to source, both AEOs knew that it could still only buy them time. Time was crucial, though. Radar-guided weapons can only work inside a finite box – a kill zone

– and they need time to lock and track. If the Vulcans could be in and out of the box before the system was ready to fire, they would survive.

The other tricks at Prior and Masefield's disposal were limited and designed to be used against the Soviets and the Warsaw Pact arsenal. Unfortunately the Argentinians hadn't bought their anti-aircraft weapons from the Soviets.

Simon Baldwin and his planning team had been boning up on what the Vulcan crews might expect going in against the Argentinians. Their anti-aircraft defences, it seemed, were sourced throughout the world: TPS-43 and 44 search radars from America; Oerlikon anti-aircraft guns from Switzerland – unlike Second World War pom-pom batteries, these were deadly accurate, radar-laid cannons firing high-explosive 35mm shells. It was modern NATO technology and the Vulcan's vintage ECM kit was starting to look horribly inadequate.

The AEOs didn't even *know* the PRF signature of a Swiss Superfledermaus or Skyguard gun-laying radar. That could be established easily though. The greater concern was what they were actually going to do about them when they found out. The powerful, but crude, Red Shrimp jammer might blind the Argentine search radars from a distance, but at close range they would burn through its barrage of white noise. The old jammers would actually act like beacons, their emissions doing little more than pinpoint their source. And against the frequencies used by the gun-laying radars they were useless. As things stood, the AEOs would be left with nothing to do but fly their bomb-run and fire bundles of chaff at the first sign of a lock-on from an enemy fire-control radar. It wasn't enough.

Thoughts had already turned to possible alternatives. The Buccaneers at RAF Honington carried a more modern, sophisticated ECM pod – the Westinghouse AN/ALQ-101D, or Dash 10. It would work, but the two weapons pylons under each wing of the Buccaneer meant they had somewhere to hang it. The Vulcan didn't. With a capacious internal bomb bay, it had never needed to carry stores externally. Chris Pye's engineers again saved the day when they remembered that the reason why some of the Vulcans had been delivered with the more powerful 301 series Olympus engines was because they'd been expected to be carrying two huge Skybolt missiles – one under each wing. Despite Skybolt being cancelled, those 301-engined aircraft must somewhere still have the hardpoints that would have allowed them to carry the big weapon. The problem was, no one knew where they were and any blueprints that might have shown them were long discarded. The only thing for it was trial and error. One of the CORPORATE aircraft, XL391, was unlucky enough to be in the hangar undergoing minor servicing when the need arose. The engineers prodded, tapped and drilled at the underside of the jet until they found, just behind the point where the wing's angle of sweep decreases, the missing hardpoints. They were, however, still a long way from being able to attach anything.

By the morning of Monday the 19th, a day later, they'd welded together sections of L-shaped mild-steel girders found on the engineering dump and bolted them on to the once-clean wing. The pylon itself was also built in the station workshops. With only the most basic aerodynamic fairing over the front it was equally agricultural in appearance.

Chris Pye's team were again lucky with the Vulcans they'd chosen. Cooling ducts built into the wing for the Skybolts allowed them to run the wiring for the Dash 10 back to the cockpit. The control panel was screwed into the top of the AEO's station replacing his cool-air duct. It was still stickered 'HONINGTON ONLY'.

The job just needed finishing off. One of the engineers asked if someone could tell him which one of the squadrons home-brewed its own beer.

'Someone can,' he was told, 'but we'd rather you finished this first. Then we can talk about the home brewing!'

'No,' he said, defending himself, 'you misunderstand. I've drilled through the bulkhead to take the wire in and all I want is some of those corks with the hole in the middle so that if I put the wires through the hole, push the cork into the hole in the bulkhead, shove a bit of matchstick round it, it'll be the perfect pressure tight seal . . .'

To call it make and make do was understating the ingenuity by a considerable degree.

The trial fit was a success and over the next two days the remaining CORPORATE Vulcans were rolled into the hangar to be similarly equipped. At the same time, the engineering team worked to refine the design of the hastily constructed prototype pylon.

Having the Dash 10 – the best kit available – was something at least. But it didn't put an end to Simon Baldwin's concern about those radar-laid guns. The thought of them nagged away at him. He'd seen what they could do.

Another five Victors flew in to Ascension the next day. The following morning, 20 April, they were going to send a Victor south, beyond the Antarctic convergence.

# Chapter 18

## 20 April 1982

Bob Tuxford reached up from his ejection seat to a central control panel mounted in the roof of the Victor's cockpit. He checked the power source for engine start and opened the cross feed cock before flicking the ignition isolation. Then he selected the engine and pushed the start button.

'Pressing now. One thousand . . . One.' Communicating with his crew. 'One thousand . . . Two.' Then he repeated the action for the remaining engines. He dropped the other hand down to his left and released the throttles, then eased them forward before clicking the levers back into idle, turning over at around 48 per cent of their maximum revolutions. The crew went through the long list of checks: call and response over the conference intercom that connected all the men on board. Everything up and running. Today they were flying with a sixth crew member: a radar expert from the recently disbanded 27 Squadron, the specialist maritime reconnaissance unit. He would normally have had a proper seat, bolted down and secure between the pilots and the backseaters, but with the wooden box that housed the gyros and accelerometers of the Carousel INS strapped to the middle of the floor taking its place, he'd have to sit on that instead. For fifteen hours.

It was nearly three weeks since the Falklands had been invaded and until now the Argentinians had had it nearly all their own way. Marines had put up fierce but limited resistance in Stanley and on South Georgia, but in the end they'd been overwhelmed. Today, Tux felt, was when things began to turn round. It had struck home during the briefing. As he'd looked around at his colleagues listening and taking notes from sheets of cardboard hanging from the canvas of the Victor Ops centre, he couldn't help but think of the images of the Second World War. *This is what the RAF gets paid for*, he thought.

Tux had been chosen to fly the long slot. The plan was for five Victors to fly south together. Then, like rows of cutlery used and discarded from the outside in at a banquet, the Victor formation would shrink as each wave of aircraft transferred spare fuel to those continuing, before turning for home, their usefulness at an end. Eventually, just Tux would be left, flying alone into potentially hostile skies to survey the unwelcoming seas around South Georgia. 'What intelligence do we have and where are *our* surface forces?' Tux had asked, concerned about what might be waiting for them when they descended to begin their search pattern. Knowing the location of British ships was important. Anxious, about to engage the enemy for the first time, they were as much of a cause for concern as Argentine anti-aircraft destroyers. It was all very well the Navy shooting first and asking questions later, but a beautifully worded apology wasn't going to bring back a dead Victor crew. Tux didn't really get an answer. The blank looks that greeted him suggested that nobody really knew.

Now it was time to go. Tux checked in on the RT, just a brief transmission to prove the radio. Then, as he gently nudged up the power from the four Rolls-Royce Conway engines, the Victor began to roll forward. Before going too far, he tested the brakes. The big jet bowed heavily on its nosewheel. The view from the pilots' seats was poor. Even the rear-view mirrors designed to help manoeuvring on the ground were of little use. Instead the Nav Radar and AEO would peer through their portholes on the sides of the cockpit to check the wings for clearance.

*Clear right.*

*Clear left.*

Then John Keable told them the Carousel had tripped off-line.

There was no quick fix. For the INS to find its bearings again they needed to start from scratch. It would take at least fifteen minutes to reboot and, with the rest of the formation burning precious fuel, ready to take off, they couldn't afford to delay. Keable had no idea what had happened, but there was no way they could fly the probe slot without it. Bitterly disappointed and cursing the wretched piece of new kit, Tuxford thumbed the RT again.

'We've lost our INS, we're not capable.'

And then the flexibility on which the 'tanker trash' prided themselves kept the mission on track.

Watching the Victors fly into Ascension, Bill Bryden had thought about how many of the old converted V-bombers the Brits needed to support any long-range mission. *Why,* he wondered, *can't we lend them some of the USAF's big Boeing KC-135s?* As they were nearly twice the size of the Victors it was true that fewer of the American tankers would have been needed, but that would only increase the responsibility shouldered by each one. If you're using two tankers and one fails, you're worse off than if you needed five and one then develops a fault. The other critical advantage the British tanker force had was the ability to both give and receive fuel. For all its advantages, the American Stratotanker didn't give that option. Tux knew that well – he'd spent two years flying them out of California with the USAF. It was a distinction that, in the days to come, would prove to be of vital importance.

The five Victors waiting on the Wideawake pan were interchangeable – even at this late stage. Each of the crews carried copies of the flight plans allocated to their colleagues. Swapping positions within the formation was almost as simple as turning the page and following a new flight plan. If Tux couldn't fly the long slot, then Squadron Leader John Elliott would. The Captain with whom Tuxford had trained in the Highlands the previous week seamlessly assumed the new role.

As part of the first wave, flying as far as the first refuelling bracket, Tux and his crew would be barely an hour and a half out of Ascension. Always in the company of another jet, they could do without the help of the miserable Carousel that had, on this occasion, so let them down.

The five fully loaded Victors powered down Wideawake's runway 14, streaming one after another, and disappeared into the ink-black sky. At three o'clock in the morning local time, thousands of miles from the mainland, the only lights were those shining and blinking from the jets themselves. Careful to maintain a safe distance, they tail-chased each other up in an ascending spiral – the Victor force's trademark 'snake climb'. At 32,000 feet the formation turned south, to send Squadron Leader John Elliott on the longest radar reconnaissance mission in history.

Bob Tuxford's time would come.

In the frigid waters off South Georgia, the ships of Task Group 319.9 waited to move. Soldiers from M Company 42 Commando – the 'Mighty Munch' – D Squadron SAS and No. 2 Section SBS prepared themselves for battle, packing and repacking their kit, cleaning their weapons, trying to stay fit. On board HMS *Plymouth*, Captain David Pentreath spoke to the SAS troopers he was playing host to.

'*Plymouth*', he told them, 'is about the oldest ship in the fleet. She's never been this far south. Wasn't designed to. And she's got a crack in the bow.'

The hard to impress special forces men warmed to him immediately. *Exactly what you want in a naval captain*, they thought.

While the Victors cruised south, three Vulcans took off at twenty-minute intervals from Waddington. Then their pilots, Reeve, Withers and Montgomery, flew north along Britain's east coast towards John O'Groats. Each aircraft carried seven 1,000lb high-explosive iron bombs, armed with 951 nose and tail fusing. Instant detonation on impact. They climbed to height and continued out over the North Sea before rolling on to a new heading that would take them to Garvie Island, a bleak slab of granite off Cape Wrath, mainland Scotland's most north-westerly point. Forty miles out, they began their descent into thick, murky cloud.

*Weather could have been organized by the Argentinians*, thought Monty as he emerged into the clear air below 5,000 feet. One by one, they dropped to 350 feet over the rough water to begin their bombing runs. Height, heading, airspeed, speed over the ground, wind direction and wind speed were all fed into the bomber's old analogue computers. Once settled, all control inputs were made at the direction of the Nav Radars, staring into their screens, making sure the cross-hairs stayed over the target, tuning the gain on the radar to sharpen its accuracy as they got closer. As they ran in, there were familiar, terse exchanges between the Nav Radars in the back and the pilots on the flight deck.

*Go to bomb and check the demand.*

*Left.*

*Take it out.* They had drifted to the right a little; the Nav Radar told the pilot to correct it.

*Demand zeroed.* On target. Now it was crucial they kept the wings absolutely straight and level. *Any* acceleration in *any* direction as the bombs separated from their racks and they'd be thrown off course. The margins were fine, the slightest error amplified by speed and distance.

The Nav Radars were dropping retarded bombs at low level. The bombs were standard 1,000lb bombs fitted with a tail cone that housed a small parachute. When the bomb was released from the aircraft, the tail cone opened and the small parachute deployed and slowed the descent of the bomb to ensure that it hit the ground well behind the Vulcan. Without the extra distance these devices allowed the escaping bomber to put between itself and the blast, there was the danger of scoring a disastrous own-goal.

John Reeve's AEO, Barry Masefield, watched through the rear-facing periscope as the bombs tumbled out of the bomb bay. He'd only ever seen this in archive footage of American B-52s. It was an exhilarating sight.

As the bombs slammed into Garvie in a fierce hail of iron and rock, they threw spray hundreds of feet into the air. Masefield grinned as he heard the deep, percussive bellow of the explosions they'd left in their wake. The three V-bombers stayed low, continuing west at over 400 mph, leaving oily black smoke trails drifting in the wind.

Looking out of the cockpit window to the left as he'd sped over the island, Monty couldn't help noticing that the sheep, a few hundred yards away on the mainland, seemed utterly unbothered by his efforts. *Slightly disconcerting*, he thought.

Before they returned to Waddington, the three Vulcans flew down the Scottish west coast before banking left over the English coast towards Spadeadam in the fells of east Cumberland. In the late 1950s, their destination had been the unlikely home to the Spadeadam Rocket Establishment, the largest rocket development facility outside America or the USSR; a kind of Cumbrian Cape Canaveral where Rolls-Royce had tested engines for the abandoned British Blue Streak ICBM. Now Spadeadam was a 10,000-acre electronic warfare range. Simulated Soviet radars and missiles mounted attacks on NATO aircraft as they flew through the range. It was where the RAF could test their defences. The range facilities had been hastily reprogrammed to replicate what little was known of the Argentine radars. As the Vulcans flew over, the Spadeadam systems transmitted the I and J band frequencies of Swiss Superfledermaus and Skyguard fire-control radars, and of the feared Roland surface-to-air missile. On board the bombers, the AEOs – Barry Masefield, Hugh Prior and John Hathaway – tried the new Dash 10 jamming pod for the first time. Compared to the ECM suite the Vulcans had fitted internally, the new pod, tuned to respond to the Argentine equipment, offered an altogether different measure of protection.

Hugh Prior ignored the slow pulse of the Echo band search radars. They were harmless. *Never jam until you've got to.* But when the malevolent flutter of the fire-control radars buzzed through his headset and lit up the strobe on his control panel he hit the switch for the Dash 10. The pod went to work. As well as noise jamming like the Vulcan's old Red Shrimp unit, the borrowed American-built pod was a deflection jammer. It worked on the same principle as a ventriloquist throwing his voice. It picked up the detection pulse of the enemy fire-control radar and electronically altered the radar return of the incoming jet to place it in airspace four or five miles away. So even if the noise-jamming alone failed to break the radar lock, the missile should go boring down on a phantom radar signature miles from where its would-be target really was. Over Spadeadam at least, the pods worked as advertised. And the AEOs had confirmed what they already knew: a Swiss anti-aircraft gun sounds exactly the same as a Russian one. Moreover, if either caught up with you, Swiss and Russian high-explosive cannon shells were going to do exactly the same damage.

As the crews shared a beer in the Ops block they chatted excitedly about the three-and-a-half-hour sortie. After the frustrations of the air-to-air refuelling, this was much more like it. Still high on adrenalin, the crews felt bulletproof. Monty looked at them all and tried to inject a little realism.

'I have to point out, fellows, that tomorrow we're doing it in the dark.'

*Just the ticket*, Mick Cooper thought and smiled to himself.

Continuing alone from the final refuelling bracket, John Elliott allowed his Victor to cruise-climb gently to 43,000 feet. As the first burnt orange of dawn appeared on the horizon, he pulled back on the throttles and descended to 18,000 feet and into the search area, ninety miles east of South Georgia. From this point, Elliott flew west towards the centre of the island, before turning north for 120 miles. At the top of the next leg he again turned west for ninety miles before turning on to the next southerly one. Like a groundsman mowing parallel stripes into a football field, the up-and-down search pattern was precise, ensuring that each leg met the edge of the one adjacent to it. In just under an hour and a half, after completing two of these giant doglegs, Elliott's Nav team had mapped over 150,000 square miles of sea to the north and north-west of South Georgia – an area the size of the whole of the United Kingdom. From the bridge of HMS *Antrim*, the ship leading the small naval Task Group, officers saw white contrails streaming from behind the Victor through a break in the clouds.

Progress was needed. The Defence Secretary John Nott's worry that a news vacuum would develop was shared by colleagues in the War Cabinet. The long wait while the Task Force steamed south had, from the outset, been one of Sir Michael Beetham's concerns. As long as it continued, the initiative lay with the enemy. The recapture of South Georgia could fill the void. There was still the faint hope that decisive action here would weaken Argentine resolve over the Falklands them-selves. But if it came to war, South Georgia, with its deep fjords and natural harbours, might provide safe haven for British ships – especially those merchant ships that had been pressed into action to support the military effort.

At ten o'clock in the evening, the phone rang in Michael Beetham's London flat. He picked up to hear news of the RAF contribution. Beedie and Cowling, the radar team on board Elliott's Victor, hadn't discovered a single ship or iceberg that might threaten operation PARAQUAT. It was negative intelligence, certainly, but it was good and welcome information.

Beetham acknowledged the news and placed the phone back on to its cradle, satisfied and relieved that his old V-bombers had made their first move without incident. Soon, perhaps, they would really make their presence felt.

The next morning the War Cabinet would give the order to retake South Georgia – a decision that was to provide all concerned with some of the most worrying moments of the entire South Atlantic campaign.

When they had arrived in Stanley many Argentinians had done so with high hopes. Flyers carrying a kitsch picture of Jesus and the Virgin Mary were distributed to 'The People of the Malvinas' celebrating the islands' liberation from illegal colonial rule and inviting them to 'join us in forging a great future for the islands'. Whatever some of the invaders may have imagined, it was no liberation and it was becoming increasingly clear to even the most optimistic of them that they were going to have to fight.

Two more expatriate families were flying out of the islands that morning. On a wet, grey day, a convoy of nearly ten Land-Rovers drove them and their luggage to the airfield, escorted by military vehicles carrying Argentine guards. It was the first glimpse John Smith had had of the quiet local airfield since it had been transformed into BAM Malvinas. It was now a high-security military zone, overrun by troops and stores. The windows of the passenger terminal below the control tower were blacked out with newspaper. Anti-aircraft batteries lined the perimeter of the airfield and its approach road. The Canache – the narrow isthmus linking the airfield on Cape Pembroke to the rest of the East Falkland mainland – was lined with minefields and barbed wire.

The announcement that greeted Smith on his return to town was equally depressing. The Argentine authorities, perhaps alerted by reports of the RAF bombing of Garvie Island, were issuing air raid instructions to the civilian population.

At the sound of the siren, Stanley's residents were advised to turn off the lights and hide under the table. All car headlights were to be covered up leaving only a thin two-inch letterbox for light to shine through. Only the fire brigade were allowed to be on the streets. Smith's dining table didn't look like it was up to the task. At all.

The Argentinians weren't alone in their concern about the effect of RAF bombs. The RSPB, *The Times* reported, worried about disturbances to nesting puffins, guillemots, fulmars and kittiwakes around Cape Wrath, wanted to see a moratorium on exercises with live ammunition during the April to early July breeding season. In the same edition of the paper, a cartoon depicting the unhappy birds joked, 'It's not the noise I mind so much as the droppings.'

An MoD spokesman tried to explain, tactfully, that the situation was 'critical'.

# Chapter 19

## 21 April 1982

Of the three helicopters that would make the insertion, only one was equipped to fly in the extreme South Georgia weather. 'Humphrey', as HMS *Antrim*'s ageing Westland Wessex HAS3 was affectionately known, was fitted with a Flight Control System that allowed the pilot to keep track of his movement over the ground without any other visual references. Lieutenant-Commander Ian Stanley, RN, Humphrey's pilot, could fly blind.

It therefore fell to him to act as shepherd to two, more basic, troop-carrying Wessex HU5s. Without sight of either Humphrey or the horizon, the pilots of the HU5s would become disorientated quickly. With the capriciousness of the conditions 3,000 feet high up on an Antarctic glacier, a white-out was a definite possibility.

Aboard *Endurance*, Nick Barker had tried to point out that only Shackleton and one other expedition had ever made it across the Fortuna Glacier and both had been exceptionally lucky. But the SAS had made up their minds. Before any attempt to retake South Georgia they needed to establish observation posts to gather intelligence on Argentine positions in Leith and Stromness. And they wanted to go in from the isolation of the glacier to avoid any possibility of unplanned contact with the Argentinians. Barker, the man who best knew local conditions, was sure they were making a mistake.

The signal to go arrived from Northwood during the night. From on board *Antrim* the next morning, just fifteen miles from her near 10,000-foot peaks, South Georgia couldn't be seen. And the barometer was dropping.

At 9.30, Humphrey took off from *Antrim*'s deck. Ian Stanley wanted to see for himself if it was going to be possible to fly in the SAS men. Maps hadn't prepared him or his crew for the awesome sight of South Georgia's sheer black cliffs rising intimidatingly out of the dark sea to heights of 2000 feet and more.

'Why didn't you tell us?' they asked after their return.

The truth was that *Endurance*'s officers had tried, but nothing really conveyed just how spectacular a sight it was. Stanley reported back that the Fortuna Glacier, as massive and uninviting as it looked, seemed clear of enemy troops, with conditions much as had been described by the crew of *Endurance*. Rain squalls and unpredictable winds strafed across it, but Stanley believed they could do the job.

At 1300 on the 21st, the SAS were flown in aboard the three Wessex helicopters. As Stanley descended towards the ice he focused on his instruments. Snow, ice and cloud all blended into one. White-out. The three other members of his crew craned their necks and strained their eyes to provide a running commentary on Humphrey's progress towards the glacier's surface. Stanley slowly descended into the murk as gusts of 60 knots buffeted the cab and snow whipped up from the downdraft of the main rotor.

'You are going down,' he heard through his headset. 'You are going down.' At the last moment, his Aircrewman, 'Fitz' Fitzgerald, leaning out from Humphrey's side door, shouted that one of the main wheels was coming down into a crevasse. Stanley was lucky it didn't topple them.

As the SAS men left the relative comfort of the helos, they were hit by the vicious wind and cold. One trooper noticed that the Wessex he'd just stepped off was being blown sideways across the ice. And he realized as it lifted off, taking with it his shelter from the violent squalls, just what they were all up against.

Somehow, all three helicopters managed to disgorge their special forces cargos and return safely to their ships. They had no hesitation in describing what they'd seen as a 'hellhole'. Ian Stanley was relieved to be back on the deck of *Antrim*.

'I'm glad we'll never need to go up there again,' he said to the rest of his crew.

The soldiers of the SAS 'D' Squadron, Mountain Troop, meanwhile, were in the grip of a savage Antarctic storm.

In the event of war, the Vulcans were tasked with penetrating underneath Soviet radars, at night and, preferably, in foul weather. It was impossible to train exactly as they planned to fight, however. In peacetime, to protect the crews from unacceptable levels of danger and preserve the life of elderly airframes, strict rules governed how and when the Vulcans trained. The Terrain Following Radar had been fitted when the V-force switched to operating at low level. When used in conjunction with the H2S map painting radar, TFR gave the V-force the capability to fly low level at night and in all weathers, but it had its limitations. The TFR scanner was fitted into a small pimple on the aircraft's nose. It transmitted a narrow radar beam along the aircraft's heading. The pilot selected the height above ground that he wished to fly, and the TFR would provide him with fly up/fly down indications in the cockpit. By following them he could maintain a constant height above the changing ground contours. In hilly country it was like riding a roller coaster. A swimmer trying to cross a fast flowing river to a spot directly opposite where he sets out from has to aim up river to allow for the strength of the stream. Similarly, an aircraft flies in a moving air mass, and has to head off into a crosswind to follow its desired track over the ground. The stronger the crosswind, the bigger the angle between the heading along which the aircraft's nose is pointing, and its track over the ground. If the crosswind is too strong – if that angle becomes too great – the forward-looking TFR can't cope. It might not be a problem in normal wind conditions, but rely on it in *very* strong crosswinds and you'll fly into a mountain, suffering the further indignity of accident investigators recording that you did so sideways.

The Nav Radars offered some comfort. Using the jet's main H2S map-painting radar, they provided back-up to the TFR. Eyes glued to their scopes, they issued instructions to the pilots.

*Ridge twelve o'clock, five miles ... four miles ... three miles. Any visual contact? Right, pull up.*

Get it wrong, at night, and you'll still fly into a mountain.

So, in the end, it all came down to the Mk 1 Human Eyeball. Unless visibility was sufficiently good for the non-flying pilot to see far enough ahead to act as safety pilot, TFR training wasn't happening.

There had always been another restriction on the Vulcan's low-level flying. Like the Victors at Marham, the old V-bombers were running out of fatigue life. Every hour in the bumpy air at low level accelerated the speed with which they used what was left. With the aircraft so close to retirement and now training for war, the need to prolong the airframe's fatigue life could be, if not ignored, at least put to one side. With authority from HQ 1 Group, Laycock and Baldwin lifted the restriction on the Vulcan's speed from a stately 250 knots to 300 knots and more. In a similar fashion, a minimum height of 1,000 feet for TFR training was reduced to 500 feet. An attack on a defended airfield which entailed running down the runway at 1,000 feet and 250 knots would have been close to suicide – assuming any crew could have been persuaded to attempt it.

*Go in like that*, Baldwin thought, *and the Argentine air defences will think all their Christmases have come at once.* What he had in mind was an attack at 300 feet, the lowest height from which retarded thousand-pounders could be dropped, at a speed of 350 knots. It would be a hell of an entrance.

When the training began a week earlier, all the flights had been signed off by John Laycock. Vulcan captains were usually self-authorizing, but with the addition of in-flight refuelling –

something none of the CORPORATE crews had any previous experience of – the Station Commander assumed responsibility for the first few sorties. As they grew in confidence and experience, however, Laycock recognized that authorization could revert once more to the Captains themselves. In truth, he thought, they probably now knew more about the demands of air-to-air refuelling than he did.

The weather was grim again that evening, but given that the weather in the Falklands was often atrocious, it was probably no bad thing to train in less than perfect flying conditions. Monty, Reeve and Withers were scheduled to fly north for TFR training at 500 feet followed by further night-refuelling practice, then finish with radar-offset bomb-runs on the Jurby ranges on the Isle of Man. The three Captains signed themselves out again, looking forward to another long, demanding night.

For John Reeve and his crew a particularly miserable few hours lay ahead. Mick Cooper had a problem with his radar. At night, without the Navigation and Bombing System, dropping live ordnance was out of the question. Frustrated, Reeve scrubbed the rest of the sortie and headed back to Waddington. Just to cap it all, he was forced to take avoiding action during an Instrument Landing approach and overshoot the runway in strong crosswinds.

The silver lining to Reeve's dismal night's work, perhaps, was that, in aborting, he had abandoned the opportunity to shower the Vulcan with fuel in another depressing session of air-to-air refuelling training. It was still desperately problematic. The other two crews weren't so lucky.

Bill Bryden had heard the reports on the BBC that Vulcans were practising dropping conventional weapons, and speculation that they would be launched on offensive operations from Ascension. The prospect troubled him. He and the small team of Americans and Saints who reported to him had done their utmost to accommodate the British. But with the volume of air traffic now using Wideawake, the letter of the lease agreement providing for its use by the British was becoming strained. The situation needed to be clarified. On 22 April, Bryden delivered a letter to the commander of British forces on Ascension reminding him that prior notification of all aircraft arrivals was necessary. Furthermore, he pointed out, the current agreement covered only logistical support. He could *not* support armed combat missions without authorization. The Vulcans, he made clear, could not use American fuel.

At the same time, Bryden signalled his HQ at Patrick Air Force Base, asking for direction. Early on they'd decided that all contact with Bryden from the States would be routed through Jerry Bennett, a civilian attached to the Patrick missile facility. Bryden had suddenly become the man everyone wanted to talk to and this was a way of keeping the message traffic manageable. The one secure line between Wideawake and Patrick could only handle telemetry data from the range. But with Ascension now the focus of an increasing amount of Soviet intelligence-gathering, much of Bryden's communication with Bennett had to rely on a new method. The Thursday after the invasion, a C-141 had flown in to Wideawake carrying supplies. On board, a secure courier carried a hastily drawn-up checklist covering all of Bryden's expected requirements. He and Bennett would go through the list item by item. *Question one – I need seven. Question two – four* and so on. It was basic, but impossible to crack. No one listening in could know what was being requested.

This time, the list didn't cover it. The British wanted to stage long-range bombing raids from Wideawake. *How do they want me to proceed?*, Bryden wondered.

His uncertainty reflected the differences in opinion there were at the highest levels of Ronald Reagan's administration. While the American Secretary of State, Al Haig, shuttled tirelessly, but hopelessly, between Buenos Aires and London in search of a diplomatic breakthrough, he tried to maintain, in public at least, an impartial position. From the outset the old general's efforts were doomed to failure – Argentina would not abandon her prize, but no other outcome was acceptable to Britain. At the Pentagon, the Secretary of Defense, Caspar

Weinberger, despite certainty from his own military that the difficulties faced by the British were too great and that they could not succeed, simply got on with helping them. On the day Bryden signalled his concerns about the developing British operation, the American Department of Defense announced the approach to Ascension of a US Navy Military Sealift Command tanker carrying aviation fuel to replenish supplies used by the British.

Getting the fuel to Ascension was out of Jerry Price's hands. His concern was with getting it to the aircraft. The tanks of the Victors needed to be kept filled with 109,000lb of fuel. Any less and condensation could form during the day and con-taminate the tanks' contents with water. Any more and the fuel would vent out of the tanks' overflow on to the Tarmac, attacking and degrading the surface of the pan.

There was a bottleneck in the system, though. The Bulk Fuel Installation, where jet fuel was pumped ashore from the American tankers through floating pipelines, was three and a half miles away from Wideawake near Georgetown. Twelve RAF fuel bowsers had been flown in on a HeavyLift Cargo Airlines Short Belfast to supplement the small number PanAm already had *in situ*, but the BFI could only dispense fuel to one of them at a time. With each Victor thirstily putting away the contents of two full bowsers, the noise of the heavy trucks rumbling between the airhead and the BFI was nearly constant.

Ascension's unique geography had one further spanner to throw into the effort to keep the 'ready use' tanks at the air-head supplied with fuel. The road between Wideawake and Georgetown didn't take long to shred the fuel trucks' tyres. Finished with compacted volcanic rock, the road's abrasive surface meant Price was getting barely 3,000 miles out of each set. Spare tyres for a fleet of lorries just became one more addition to the long list of equipment and materiel being flown in to Ascension by the RAF's round-the-clock transport operation.

Nearly everything had to come this way. Georgetown had no harbour, only an exposed pierhead that, in heavy Atlantic swells, could be out of action for days. In any case, anything being brought in by ship would take two weeks to arrive. However the solution arrived, though, the limitations of the endless to and fro of fuel bowsers and the small size of the 'ready use' tanks had to be addressed. Royal Engineers said they could put in a temporary steel pipe quickly and easily. To fly in three and a half miles of steel pipe, though, would tie up the transport fleet for days. Out of the question. The solution was aluminium piping at a fraction of the weight. The Engineers got to work, installing a wonky-looking pipeline that fed into new large-capacity collapsible fabric pillow tanks at the airhead. The arrangement was better than it looked. With a series of small pumps along its length and frequent leaks, the pipeline needed twenty-four-hour supervision, but it was a revelation, drastically reducing the time it took to refuel the ever-growing number of aircraft. Another problem solved. Whether or not the Vulcans were going to be allowed to use it, of course, was another matter.

John Smith didn't realize who the man was until later. Out walking the dog with his youngest son Tyssen, he'd waved at General Galtieri – in Stanley during his one and only visit to the islands he'd invested so much political capital in seizing. Had he known, he'd have been considerably less civil. Equally, as war drew closer, the temper of the Argentinians hardened and Smith wasn't the only one to notice it. It was personified by Major Patricio Dowling, an especially unpleasant intelligence officer of Irish descent who'd been sent to the islands to deal with any anti-Argentinian elements he found amongst the Falklands population. Peter Biggs reckoned that probably meant just about all of it. Dowling, perhaps, reached that conclusion too. He soon broke with the efforts of the islands' Argentine Governor, General Menendez, to treat the islanders in as decent and non-threatening a way as possible. And he quickly made himself a feared and reviled presence.

Leona Vidal's father was Chilean. That alone was enough for Dowling to regard the family with suspicion. That her mother Eileen spoke passable Spanish and operated the islands' radio station made matters worse. During the occupation, the Vidals were staying in a large three-storey town house that belonged to friends who lived for most of the time in Camp – the name given to the islands' wild countryside. While the Vidals knew their way round the house, much of what it might contain behind closed doors was a mystery to them.

Then one night, Dowling arrived with soldiers. He pushed in past Eileen and grabbed Leona's older brother, seventeen-year-old Glen. As *Tom and Jerry* played on the television, Dowling threatened to shoot the boy unless Eileen Vidal told him where the radio was hidden. There was no radio, she argued, but it wasn't her house. How could she be sure? Dowling prowled around the ground floor and found the pair of binoculars the children used to watch what was happening outside; they found it all captivating. To Dowling, though, they were just what he was looking for. He started to pull the house apart, floor by floor. Eileen was forced upstairs with him, returning moments later, the blood drained from her face. She looked terrified. On the third floor, Dowling had discovered a locked trunk.

'Open it,' he ordered.

She said she hadn't got a key. Didn't know where there was one. So Dowling smashed the lock and lifted the lid, while she looked on, scared to death of what he might find. Her heart sank. Inside was a piece of equipment wrapped in a blanket. A radio, she thought. And so did Dowling. Triumphant, he whipped off the blanket to reveal a Singer sewing machine.

Then he went berserk, tearing up the blanket, enraged at being thwarted. For the first time, ten-year-old Leona was truly frightened by the threat from this dangerous man.

The War Cabinet were to be briefed on the military options by the Defence Chiefs in the MoD that morning. The mood amongst them was indignant, however. News of Bill Bryden's letter stating that he could not supply fuel for the Vulcans had just reached them. *It was intolerable! Disgraceful!* John Nott assumed, wrongly, that the development had Al Haig's hand on the tiller. They put the problem to one side as they listened to the heads of the three services outline their plans.

The politicians tried to absorb the mass of information they were given. The Prime Minister was softer in private than she could appear in public when harangued by the opposition or hostile journalists. Except, that is, when she was dealing with the unfortunate Foreign Secretary, Francis Pym. Having been only weeks in the job, Pym appeared uncomfortable with the stark choices military action presented. Concerned about the implications of any decision, he seemed always to be trying to find a reason not to commit to one course of action or another. Margaret Thatcher could be so dismissive of his caution that Nott sometimes felt obliged to intervene. *Let's just consider the point that Francis is making,* Nott would suggest, but Pym's apparent desire not to do anything that might upset anyone just fuelled the Prime Minister's belligerence. Only Willie Whitelaw shared the Foreign Secretary's caution. And he sometimes seemed to be in the wrong century – not quite over the shock that the enemy, this time, were people we played polo with.

Sir Michael Beetham briefed the Cabinet, explaining his plan in detail. When he had ordered the Vulcans to train for air refuelling and conventional bombing he'd had no clear idea what might or might not be feasible. Discovering the capabilities of a combined Victor and Vulcan formation had been an iterative process, but the possibilities were emerging. Earlier in the week, the newspapers had claimed confidently that Argentina's mainland military bases would be destroyed on the first day of any conflict. Word came back from the planning cell at 1 Group that to take out just one would require four Vulcans. And for the bombers to reach the bases in southern Argentina that might influence the conflict, and return, would require the support of over *seventy* Victors. Even if such a mission had been politically acceptable the RAF simply didn't have the resources to do it. Of course, it did the

British cause no harm whatsoever to continue to allow the Argentinians to believe it was a possibility. Beetham continued to outline his intentions, explaining that an attack on the airfield at Port Stanley was, while extremely difficult, both technically possible and strategically desirable. Like the Americans' opening shot of the Second World War, the Doolittle Raid against Tokyo launched in retaliation for the bombing of Pearl Harbor, the effect of Beetham's plan was more than physical. It was a powerful statement of intent.

The Prime Minister and her Defence Secretary were quick to embrace it. Predictably enough, Pym and Whitelaw expressed doubts. It didn't matter. Beetham was told to go ahead and plan for the raid. While Pym, who was due to fly to Washington immediately after the briefing, was told by the Prime Minister to clarify the American attitude to launching the strike from Ascension.

Beetham left feeling satisfied with the reaction to his proposal; particularly so with the interest Margaret Thatcher had shown. Francis Pym, he'd noticed, did not look at all amused.

Before Pym had even left Heathrow, Bryden had received his answer from Jerry Bennett at Patrick AFB. He was to provide the British with whatever they wanted. *Instructions like that,* he thought, *are easy to follow!*

# Chapter 20

## 22 April 1982

'We've got a bloody firelock on us!' shouted AEO Terry Anning, the RWR alive through his headset. The pilot, Flight Lieutenant Steve 'Biggles' Biglands, mashed the power, pulled at the control wheel and booted the rudder, tipping the Victor into a steep, screaming dive. As he was thrown against his harness, John Foot, the tanker's Nav Radar, struggled to get his fingers to the switches of the control panel for the wing pods to try to break the lock.

The Victors were sitting targets for surface-to-air missiles. Engineers had tried sealing bundles of foil chaff in the tanker's airbrake, but it had got caught up in the mechanics. In a last-minute piece of improvisation, someone at Marham had realized that chaff could be kept in place in the backs of the wing pods by the retracted refuelling baskets. With the master-switch off, the baskets were gripped tight. When the Nav Radar turned the system on, they trailed slightly – relaxed a touch – before winding back in ready for the drogues to be trailed properly. It was a one-shot deal. As the Victor twisted through the air, Foot managed to reach the refuelling controls and flicked 'On'. Clouds of foil strips billowed out of the two Mk 20 pods, presenting the fire-control radar with a larger, more attractive target. It broke the lock, leaving the crew shaken, confused, but safe, wondering what the hell had happened.

As the shadow boxing that preceded the British operation to retake South Georgia played out, the Victors mounted further long-range radar reconnaissance missions, to check that the seas around the island remained clear of Argentine units and ice. Biggles' Victor K2, providing refuelling support for the second of these, had overflown Admiral Woodward's battle group as it steamed south. Tux's concern at the first briefing about the whereabouts of friendly ships had proved to be well founded.

The next day, John Smith again gave friends a lift to the airport. He drove slowly past newly arrived missiles stacked next to the terminal building. Still in the packaging in which they were delivered from the manufacturer, they were marked with instructions like 'DO NOT LIFT HERE'. *British Tiger Cats*, he thought.

The weapons of the Grupo de Artillería de Defensa Aeria 601, an army anti-aircraft unit, had begun to arrive. The GADA 601's guns, missiles and radars had been loaded on to a transport ship, the *Ciudad de Córdoba*, which, it was subsequently decided, would not run the gauntlet of the British submarines patrolling the Maritime Exclusion Zone. Now they were coming in by air to reinforce the Marine and Air Force anti-aircraft guns already in place. If they had time to work up to full strength, GADA 601 had the potential to be the most lethal unit of the lot.

But it wasn't the Tiger Cats that most worried Simon Baldwin. These old weapons were guided visually via a long trailing wire. To hit the target, the operator on the ground had to be able to see it. Going in before dawn, the Vulcans would be relatively safe from these. The radar-laid Oerlikons, on the other hand, worried him a great deal.

The Oerlikon cannons had a prodigious appetite for high-explosive ammunition. Each of the twin 35mm barrels fired shells at a rate of 500 per minute. Together they threw out over 16 rounds per second. With a muzzle velocity of over 3,000 feet per second they had enormous destructive power. Baldwin remembered witnessing it.

Faldingworth, near Scampton, had once been an RAF facility – a storage and maintenance facility for Blue Danube nuclear bombs. The scattering of low-lying buildings around the site gave little hint of its real purpose, because most of the facility was beneath the surface. When Baldwin visited in 1979, it was as a guest of the new owners, Bmarc, a subsidiary of the Swiss arms manufacturer Oerlikon-Buerhle. Bmarc were laying on a firepower demonstration at Faldingworth's underground weapons ranges. The technicians told their guests that the two-foot-thick slab of steel bulkhead they'd be firing into had come from the German battleship *Tirpitz*. Baldwin wasn't sure he believed them about that, but it certainly looked as if it could have done. What left no room for doubt was a dinner-plate-sized hole punched through it by the powerful anti-aircraft gun. And that was from a shell that, unlike those the Argentine gunners would be using, contained no high explosives.

Three years later, the mess it could make of a thin-skinned Vulcan hardly bore thinking about. He desperately needed more information on the defences they were going to face. Then he remembered Spike Jones, a retired Wing Commander whom both he and Laycock had known when he'd been working at the Department of Air Warfare, part of the RAF College at Cranwell. Baldwin reminded Laycock that he was now working at Bmarc. The Station Commander didn't need persuading.

'Let's find out what he wants to say.' Baldwin picked up the phone and dialled the number for Werner Loyk, Bmarc's managing director.

'I know why you're calling,' said the Swiss businessman.

'May I come along and see you?' Baldwin asked.

'No,' replied Loyk, and Baldwin prepared to make his case, 'but if you can send someone in civilian clothes, that might be OK. I'll get back to you.'

Spike Jones later called John Laycock and arrangements

were made for the Station Intelligence Officer, Flight Lieutenant Martin Hallam, to take a trip to the Grantham factory to meet him. The information Hallam brought back to Waddington was priceless.

Oerlikon, it turned out, had trained the Argentinians to set up and use their guns. Jones could tell them the recommended pattern of radars and gun emplacements to defend a standard airfield. And from this, Baldwin and Laycock were able to make an informed estimate of how the guns might be deployed around Port Stanley airfield. Jones told them how many shells had been sold to the Argentinians, how many they'd since had to replace and what they'd been replaced with. Some of them had been supplied by a rival company and, he said, were inferior in performance to the Oerlikon-manufactured ammunition. He told them by how much. But most important of all, he was able to provide them with details of all the Argentine anti-aircraft weapons and their respective kill zones – the range within which they were considered deadly – and confirmed the frequencies of their air defence radars.

The information from Jones was a real nugget, but, in addition, information on the Argentine defences was starting to filter through from the RAF Intelligence net. Baldwin asked the Station Intelligence Officer to mark the kill zones on to a piece of A3 graph paper. Concentric lines arced across the orange squares recording height and distance from the weapons' launch point where the $x$ and $y$ axes met. A Tiger Cat missile burnt out at 8,500 feet. It was optically aimed, which certainly reduced its effectiveness, but with the Vulcan flying down the length of the runway at 300 feet, on a clear night a lucky shot from an alert operator couldn't be ruled out entirely.

Another ring drawn on this diagram at 12,800 feet out on the face of it represented the biggest threat of all: the Franco-German Roland missile. Roland was a modern and effective radar-guided missile. Capable of supersonic speeds of up to Mach 1.6, it could be fired in all weathers, day or night, without its operator ever catching sight of the target. A Vulcan was desperately vulnerable to a weapon like Roland but, Jones had told them, the Argentinians couldn't deploy the system with its bulky launch trailer to the islands. Baldwin hoped he was right.

The third line represented the Oerlikon guns. This was the one. The heavy shells began to tumble out of control at 6,500 feet. *Go in below 6,500 though*, he thought, *and they're going to get you*. And that was exactly what Monty, Reeve and Withers were training to do. Baldwin sat back and lit his pipe as he weighed it all up. Low level wasn't looking like such a good idea.

In Argentina, meanwhile, GADA 601 had unloaded their Roland missiles from the hold of the *Ciudad de Córdoba*. It hadn't been thought possible to squeeze Roland into the hold of a C-130 Hercules, but Argentine Air Force engineers decided that if there was a way of doing so, they were going to discover it.

Regulations stated that safety altitude was the height of the highest ground within twenty-five nautical miles of the air-craft's track, plus 10 per cent of that height, plus another 1,500 feet. Unless there was visual contact with the ground, or the aircraft was under positive radar control, these limits were not to be broken. The RAF took a belt-and-braces approach to making sure that its aircraft avoided coming into unplanned contact with the ground.

Although Neil McDougall hadn't yet been day- and night-qualified for refuelling, he and his crew were shadowing the training programme of the three principal CORPORATE crews. And McDougall was following the rules; while he watched his instruments, his co-pilot, Chris Lackman, main-tained visual contact with the ground.

Flying mock night-time attacks against remote airfields scattered around the Scottish Western Isles – Stornoway, Benbecula, Tyree and Islay – McDougall dropped to 500 feet and held the aircraft there. Then, comfortable and confident at that height, he stepped it down on the TFR selector: 400 feet, 300 feet, 200 feet. It seemed fine but for the increasingly enthusiastic exclamations from Lackman in the seat next to him. As part of the drive to enhance the Vulcan's capabilities each of the co-pilots had been issued with night vision goggles, or NVGs, and instructed on how to use them. Down low they'd allow the co-pilots to provide a visual back-up to the Nav Radar during the bomb-run. Lackman couldn't contain his excitement.

'Wow! That's amazing,' he kept on until the laconic McDougall had had enough.

'Chris, what the bloody hell are you talking about?' he snapped.

'It's the sheep!'

'What about the bloody sheep?'

'I've never flown as low as this before, I'm looking them in their eyes!'

'What do you mean?' asked McDougall. 'We're at two hundred feet.'

'More like twenty . . .'

The NVG sets made objects appear closer, but that didn't make sense. McDougall checked his instruments and realized with a thump of adrenalin that he'd forgotten to turn on the TFR. He'd been flying on nothing but the hopelessly inaccurate altimeter. Through the NVGs, the young co-pilot could see they weren't going to hit anything and was enjoying the ride. It frightened the living daylights out of McDougall.

Aboard the other three jets there were other worries. As they targeted the airfields for the first time, Mick Cooper started to question the wisdom of the way they were training. If they were practising low-level attacks against coastal airfields, he assumed, not unreasonably, it was because the powers that be expected that they were going to fly a low-level attack against a coastal airfield. That was fine if they wanted him to take out hangars or a line of parked fighter jets, he thought. *We can run in as fast and low as possible, keep our arse to the blast and go like shit off a shovel.* But if it was the runway they were after, this was definitely *not* the way to go about it.

On top of Cooper's emerging doubts about the tactics, there had been further problems with the refuelling. Their first tanker went unserviceable and had to return to Marham. Then, on contact with its replacement, they suffered another massive fuel leak. Looking ahead to a long-range mission Cooper asked himself: *How many reserves are we going to have?* On the evidence so far, whatever reserves there were might quickly find themselves stretched pretty thin.

News of the difficulty Waddington was having with the fuel leaks had filtered back up the RAF chain of command. Ten days into the training programme, senior RAF staff were becoming increasingly concerned that the problem had not yet been solved. There was a fear that, having said they were going to do it, they might not actually be able to pull it off. Beetham, overseeing every aspect of the RAF build-up, didn't have time to dwell on the minutiae of Waddington's struggles.

'For God's sake,' he told Ken Hayr in exasperation, 'go and sort it out. I've already told the Cabinet we're going to do it!'

In fact, in a moment alone with the Prime Minister, Beetham had levelled with her about the challenge they faced.

'We're trying to do this in a hurry,' he explained. 'We haven't done it in a long time and we *are* having problems, but we'll get over them.'

Despite his frustration, Beetham was confident they would. Margaret Thatcher didn't seem to doubt it.

There were niggling little problems with the Victors, but on the whole they were bearing up well. While Jeremy Price concerned himself with trying to ensure that Ascension's creaking infrastructure could support them, the men from Marham were bedding in well. The CO of 57 Squadron, Alan Bowman, had been drafted in as head of the Victor detachment, while the man he replaced, Marham's cultured OC Ops, Wing Commander David Maurice-Jones – who'd once been disappointed to have to describe another officer as a man who thought Vivaldi was a drink – returned to the Norfolk base to hold the fort in Price's absence. Before going he left the detachment on Ascension with an important bequest.

Realizing the difficulty there was in reproducing complete sets of flight plans for every tanker in the growing formations, he'd sent a signal to Marham asking them to send out a photocopier. The brand-new Thermofax was flown in on one of the incoming Victors. The machine was worked hard, duplicating flight plans, frequencies, Met reports and air traffic information for diversion airfields. It was a crucial asset to the Victor Ops team under Squadron Leader Trevor Sitch.

The aircrew, too, were proving adaptable. Ignoring protests about fire regulations, they were squeezing six to a room in the American barracks. Three got beds, the other three slept on the floor. Tux's wheeling and dealing AEO, Mick Beer, had even managed to blag an old Ford Cortina from the locals. It meant the whole crew could escape their cramped billets for trips to English Bay in the north-west. Despite the crashing surf, this fine white sand beach was the only one on the island deemed sufficiently free from dangerous currents to swim from.

The close-knit atmosphere that served them so well back home paid dividends on Ascension. Planning, Engineering and aircrew had been picked up as a unit and relocated somewhere new. It made little difference to the way they approached things – they were a genuine team who worked together well.

Every morning Alan Bowman would chair the daily meeting, but it was often informally that ideas and problems were talked through. Tux sat on stacked cases of beer as he discussed with the navigators the problem of large formations joining up before flying south. With ten aircraft taking off at one-minute intervals, they realized the first would be 120 miles away by the time the last was leaving the runway. It sounded as harmless as a GCSE maths problem, but without forethought it could have serious repercussions.

In the evening, they'd offload over a beer in the Georgetown Exiles Club, the best way of shedding the pressure that, however reluctant they were to acknowledge it, was growing with each passing day.

*

As he travelled south, Admiral Woodward reflected that the loss of either of the aircraft carriers, particularly his flagship, HMS *Hermes*, would effectively end British hopes of retaking the Falkland Islands. The greatest threat to the two capital ships and the rest of the British task force came from the attack jets of the Comando Aviación Naval Argentina, the Argentine Naval Air Arm. They were the specialist ship killers. While the Super Étendards of 2 Escuadrilla Aeronaval de Caza y Ataque had rehearsed air-refuelled Exocet missions, the A-4Q Skyhawk pilots of 3 Escuadrilla had done their best to impart what they knew to their Air Force colleagues. But as they were only too aware, it was difficult to pass on years of hard-won experience in a couple of weeks. Like their colleagues, they too had explored the possibility of operating their jets out of BAM Malvinas, and, in early April, had actually flown one of their Skyhawks in and out of the islands' airport to put the theory to the test. Since 17 April, though, they'd been back where they belonged, catapulting from the deck of Argentina's only aircraft carrier, the 16,000-ton *Veinticinco de Mayo*, to refine the art of sinking enemy ships with 500lb Snakeye bombs.

The carrier steamed south towards the naval base at Ushuaia in Tierra del Fuego. She stayed close to the coast, just inside the limit of Argentina's territorial waters. Just outside the twelve-mile limit, HMS *Splendid* shadowed her. For the submarine's captain, it was going to be a long, frustrating night. For while an attack on the pride of the Argentine Navy may have been against the spirit of the Rules of Engagement, Roger Lane-Nott was sure that, as long as *he* was in international waters, it was within the letter of the law, providing, that is, he could visually identify the ship. He needed to see her with his own eyes. That day, Admiral Woodward had been given authority by Northwood to shoot down the Argentine Air Force Boeing 707 that had been flying daily reconnaissance missions to track the fleet's progress, providing it could be positively identified. There was no doubt at all in Lane-Nott's mind that he would receive the same authority. If the *Veinticinco de Mayo* was in torpedo range, he was going to sink her. But he had to wait until daybreak. Through the night, in *Splendid*'s control room, men concentrated on their individual roles, tense with anticipation. Sonar reports kept them updated.

At two o'clock in the morning, Lane-Nott told them he was going to action stations at 5.30. And then they counted the minutes. The captain never had to mention it again, it just happened, as planned, at dawn.

'Periscope depth,' Lane-Nott ordered and, with torpedoes in the tubes, the 4,000-ton attack boat rose through the water to let the captain identify his target. Nothing. He could barely see a hundred yards ahead of the boat. After days of gales and thirty mile visibility, he was gazing into thick fog. *Can't see a bloody thing*, he cursed to himself. He continued his pursuit as best he could, but it was pointless without a positive ID. *Veinticinco de Mayo* and her crew had been extremely lucky. *Splendid* had to let her go.

The number of Argentine troops in and around Stanley was now approaching 10,000 and any house which they thought was unoccupied – especially one on the outskirts of town – was likely to become a shelter to them. Liz Goss hated the thought of her home being violated. Every day she would leave her children Karina and Roger with their grandparents and return to the house she'd left on the first day of the invasion. Autumn had been mild so far and, despite the occasional snow flurry settling on the ground, the carnations growing in her garden were probably the best she'd ever had. *A welcome splash of colour.* She'd pick a fresh bunch on each visit and put them in a vase inside, replacing the flowers from the previous day. If the soldiers came in, she hoped there would at least be the appearance that the house was still occupied. This time, as she walked to the garden to pick the carnations she felt herself being watched. She tried to ignore it. Then, as she approached the flowerbed, she saw that severed ducks' heads had been scattered around the stems. *Just*, she thought, distressed at the cruelty and ugliness of such a senseless act, *to see my reaction.*

# Chapter 21

Monty was worried about his friend. During RED FLAG in January, he and Martin Withers had become close. Now, in the ten days since they'd begun training for CORPORATE, Withers had lost over half a stone in weight – his nervous loss of appetite compounded by the relentless pace of the training schedule. The friendly, unassuming glow that had made such an impression on Monty, just a few months earlier, was in danger of being worn away.

When the Vulcan crews weren't flying – they sometimes flew twice a day – or sleeping, they were in briefings: long afternoons in uncomfortable chairs in the Ops block. Much of what they were told was straightforward and no more or less than was expected. But increasingly it was starting to paint a stark picture of what lay ahead. The crews were briefed on the capabilities of Argentine fighters and anti-aircraft defences. There were lectures on South American politics which left none of them in any doubt about the bloody campaign waged by the Argentine junta on its own citizens; on the disputed history of the Falkland Islands; on the Geneva Convention – and on survival. All of them had some training in that. Week-long courses were held during deployments to Goose Bay, its bleak landscape chosen to simulate the Russian tundra. There was a bit of cooking on the campfire and shelter building, but nothing too severe. For that you had to volunteer. Then you got escape and evasion and resisting interrogation too. It was the interrogation that put Withers off. *It's just not the sort of thing*, he thought, *that you'd want to volunteer for!* Others on his crew had been through it. Posted to Singapore in 1963, Hugh Prior had been chased by one of the Highland regiments through dense jungles and rivers that seemed more like open sewers. He'd been caught, stripped and hooded, before a female voice told him, 'That's a very small prick you've got there.' He only discovered later that the tape recording didn't discriminate. Gordon Graham *had* volunteered for winter training. The Scot was a keen skier and that was the carrot. It didn't do it for Withers, but at least he understood the motive: *A week's skiing, a week's torture. But it's free!*

If they were forced to bail out over the Falklands, they were to make their way to designated safehouses, the locations of which they'd be given before the mission. Photocopied sheets explaining the 'PW One Hand Mute Code' – a Vietnam-era sign language that provided for silent communication while on the run – were distributed. When they reached the rendezvous they were to stay put until they were pulled out by special forces. If they weren't found by the Argentinians first. This was also covered. A typed sheet explained how to conceal a secret message in a letter:

```
CONCEALMENT OF INFORMATION IN LETTERS/
MESSAGES — SAMPLE TEXT
(Writer's daughter was born on 6th October —
read every 6th and 10th word alternately of
text.)
                                   1st May 1980
              (= Contains concealed message)


My darling (= Safety check — not under duress)
You will (= 3 x 4 = 12 words concealed in
text) feel after the hours waiting that the
three of you can now relax. Time passes, and
the best news is always worth waiting the (=
ignore rest of sentence) extra few days for.
Your memory and the childrens' lights my way
```

```
forward. No problems now but perhaps the end
will be for western people some way off.
There's room I'm sure for highest level talks
which should be kept going on although the
(= ignore rest of sentence) chance of doing
anything to help things from here is small.
                    Best wishes dearest, Your loving
                                              Alex
```

```
Message reads (in reverse order) KEPT HIGHEST
ROOM WESTERN END. NO LIGHTS. BEST TIME THREE
(= 0300) HOURS.
```

It would have been fiendishly difficult to compose, especially under the strain of captivity. Most of the crews simply remembered that if, while being filmed, they scratched their nose, those watching at home would know that they were lying.

Each of the AEOs was given a cassette tape that carried a hissing recording of a message in Spanish. Designed to confuse the enemy air defences, it claimed to be from an Argentine maritime patrol aircraft that had lost an engine and wanted to put down at Port Stanley. *No puedo oirle. Usted no esta muy claro* ('I can't hear you. You're not very clear'), repeated the coda at the end of the message, precluding further debate. Barry Masefield took the tape to Gibraltarian Nav Plotter, Jim Vinales, the only man on any of the crews who actually understood what was being said. Despite its not using the appropriate Catalan dialect, Vinales thought it was a reasonable attempt – even if the intonation did sound a bit like a 'Learn Spanish the Easy Way' course. Broadcast on a long-wave frequency, crackling with static, he told his colleagues, it might buy them time. On the other hand, they all knew, it would alert whoever was listening to the fact that *someone* was out there. The AEO's defence of the aircraft was driven by one rule above all others: you never gave anyone anything for nothing; you never showed your hand unless you had to. The tapes got quietly tucked away. Things would have to get pretty desperate for them to come out again.

Some of what was said at the briefings was taken with a pinch of salt by crews looking to relieve the pressure of the work-up. It didn't do to dwell too much on what could go wrong. Despite efforts to remain in high spirits, though, they were all getting tired. The concentration demanded by the training sorties was intense. Their sleep was curtailed. And underpinning it all was a draining, insidious unease about the mission itself.

But however reluctant the crews themselves might have been to acknowledge the fatigue and stress, others were keeping an eye on them. All of them, eventually, were ordered to visit Squadron Leader Warwick Pike, Waddington's station doctor. None of them wanted to – it was more time out of an already full schedule – and none of them accepted his offer of Temazepam to help them sleep.

'I've never taken pills, Warwick . . . sir' – Monty added a little deference to soften his rejection – 'and I'm not taking them now!'

'You will,' Pike said wearily as Monty turned and left his office, 'you will . . .'

On Saturday the 24th, Martin Withers took advantage of a single day's break in the flying programme to visit his parents in Fakenham in Norfolk. Throughout the day, in the background, was the prospect of war. Nothing was said, but when it was time for Withers to leave his mother and father, their parting felt loaded with significance. *A last goodbye.* Driving home through the Fens after dark, Withers stopped the Ford Capri behind a queue of traffic to wait for a boat to pass through a raised bridge. When he woke up, the boat was far away, the bridge had been lowered, and the cars in front of him were long gone.

While Simon Baldwin's aircrew trained for war, supported by a small clique of engineers and operations staff, life for everyone else at Waddington continued much as it always had. The difference now, of course, was that they knew they were being closed down in July. John Laycock did his best to straddle the two concerns, dividing his time between CORPORATE flights and the business of the ceremonials that would mark the rundown of the station and disbandment of its squadrons. The timing was far from ideal, but plans were too far advanced.

As Martin Withers had been with his parents, men and women from four Waddington squadrons and their support Wings, twenty-four Alsatians and their handlers, and the 1 Group Pipe Band marched down Lincoln's main street to commemorate the anniversary of the base being given the Freedom of the City. As four Vulcans flew low overhead, spontaneous applause broke out. It continued long after the roar of the engines had receded into the distance. The historical reason for the parade was lost. The crowd were angry and proud. It was clear to Laycock that they would not be persuaded that this was anything but a display of military might; a demonstration of the country's determination to win back the Falkland Islands.

That evening, when those who'd been on parade earlier in the day had settled down with their families to watch *The Val Doonican Music Show* or ITV's popular quiz show *3-2-1* over dinner, Monty and Reeve and McDougall rumbled out for another four-hour night-time sortie.

After a clear day, cloud had settled over Lincolnshire at 300 feet. As the power came on and the bomber began its take-off roll, Monty tried to relax. While he'd been strapping himself in he'd felt disengaged, absent. He sensed that the rest of the crew's minds weren't really on the task in hand either. He needed to get on top of things. At about 100 knots, the jet veered violently to the left. Monty caught her quickly and straightened her up to continue down the runway.

'What the fuck was that?' came the inevitable question from the back. He laughed it off, but it was another warning.

The Vulcan was lightly loaded. Like this, it had bootfuls of excess power and an agility in the air that belied its imposing size and shape. Monty rocketed up through the low clouds into a beautifully clear sky above.

He continued his climb out east to the rendezvous, trying to shake himself out of his torpor. *Right*, he told himself, *snap out of it.* Up over the North Sea he spotted the tanker easily. Then he closed in on the Victor's trailing fuel hose. Gently playing tunes with the four throttle levers as he made contact, he drove the refuelling probe into the basket. *Too fast.*

With a visceral 'whumph', the sky around him exploded and the tanker disappeared from view.

A sheet of fuel from his broken probe flushed into the engine intakes, simultaneously blowing 1 and 2 out and torching the unburnt fuel that had cascaded straight through to produce an angry, billowing fireball. The dusk sky flared and the Vulcan dropped away – *down like a B-17*, thought John Reeve as he looked on, recalling images of American heavy bombers shot down in flames over Germany forty years earlier.

As the Vulcan fell, Monty realized he'd lost the engines. But the bomber wasn't on fire. They had altitude and they had time.

'John, get the checklist,' he told his AEO over the RT. With two engines gone, so too were two-thirds of the jet's electrics. Hathaway was already running through his blue book.

'Engine failure number 1 . . .' Hathaway began initiating the call-and-response drills to shut down both engines correctly. Once that was done it was safe to relight them.

'Restart drill number 1 engine . . .' Both ignited again without drama, but Monty had had enough. He pointed the nose back towards Waddington, their evening's work brought to an abrupt, unnerving conclusion.

Monty's collision with the Victor's drogue hadn't just ripped the tip off the Vulcan's refuelling probe; it had also damaged the drogue itself. Unable to transfer any further fuel to Reeve, the Victor returned to Marham. A second tanker was scrambled, but that too was unserviceable. A third also had problems with trailing its hose. Reeve managed to take on just 2,000lb of fuel – barely enough to taxi down the runway and back – before a massive fuel leak sluiced over him too. And he'd been perfectly positioned behind the Victor. The air-to-air refuelling was still a lottery.

The uncomfortable truth was that the V-force was no closer

to being confident that they could make this work than they were when they started. There were too many opportunities for things to go wrong. One thing was certain, though: unless Waddington came up with an immediate solution to the refuelling problem there was no hope of success; the South Atlantic was simply out of their reach.

Difficulties had been expected. But it was clear now that this was more than just teething trouble. Something essential was being overlooked, they just couldn't pinpoint what it was. The Air-to-Air Refuelling Instructors said there was nothing wrong with the way the Vulcan Captains were flying. And the engineers were scratching their heads too. Laycock had seen clusters of them gathered in the hangars under hot lights, poring over books.

He and Baldwin decided it was time to bring together everyone involved to thrash out a solution. With the night's training sortie scrubbed, they wasted no time. The aircrews and engineers were there, as well as Baldwin's Ops Team. The AARIs were back from Marham and AOC 1 Group. Air Vice-Marshal Mike Knight was driven down from Bawtry with Keith Filbey, a member of his Victor planning team.

As they examined the evidence, two separate problems emerged. And, as it turned out, Monty's flame-out didn't appear to have been caused by either of them.

When, during the Easter weekend, the engineers called Marham to ask how to test the reconstituted refuelling plumbing they did as they were told: they plugged a fuel hose from a bowser on to the end of the refuelling probe and pumped. It was what they weren't doing that was important. At Marham, the fuel hose, with its contents, was supported by a cherry-picker parked next to the aircraft's nose. If that information had been passed on, its importance hadn't been realized. At Waddington the probe itself was left to take the weight. And it hadn't been built to. In the act of actually proving the system, they were leaving it ever so slightly crooked. The damage wasn't obvious, but in the air the bent valves were unable to form a proper seal inside the drogue. This allowed a steady stream of fuel to flow down the probe and up over the cockpit windows. Any leak at all would always be felt acutely in a Vulcan because of the position of the probe, but if using a cherry-picker was going to help reduce the number of leaks, it would be an important step forward.

The more alarming problem was the flood of unburnt fuel that could wash over the jet as the probe was withdrawn – as if the valve was somehow remaining open. When any aircraft pulled away from a tanker there was always a fine white puff of fuel as the probe disconnected, but it was little more than vapour. The Vulcans suffered from a wave that threatened to wash out the engines. The solution lay with the Engineering Wing, frustrated that the fault just made no sense. Apparently identical probes that had worked for years fitted to the Victors didn't work on the Vulcans. To try to solve the puzzle, a Victor probe was quickly dispatched from Marham to Waddington and both were systematically stripped down on the bench. It was a *eureka!* moment. For something so small, the satisfaction was immense. The Vulcan probes, redundant since the late 1960s, were missing a shim in the valve assembly. All of Waddington's probes were modified to include it. For want of a nail . . .

There was reason for guarded optimism now, but the engineers wouldn't know whether or not they'd cracked it until someone flew again. Only if the next refuelling was successful would they know if this was do-able.

And ironically, given that it provoked such urgent action, Monty's violent loss of his 1 and 2 engines looked like nothing more than 'finger trouble'. Exhausted, he'd just hit the drogue too hard.

Air Vice-Marshal Mike Knight had made up his mind that the AARIs had to fly any mission as part of the bomber crew. As he'd travelled to Waddington that evening, he considered the reaction his decision might provoke. With such store attached to V-bomber crews as cohesive units, he didn't think it was going to be a popular move. Not only was there the possibly dented pride of the Vulcan crews to hurdle, but also

**Below:** 'Fuel flows'. Victors staged long-range radar reconnaissance missions in advance of Operation PARAQUAT, the retaking of South Georgia. This picture of a Victor refuelling was taken through the rear-facing periscope of another Victor.

**Right:** Cursed with notoriously unreliable brakes, Victors returning from the missions south would let the drag chute take the strain on landing.

The Victor's ageing, temperamental refuelling equipment was responsible for a high percentage of aborted missions. This Victor was lucky to survive when a catastrophic failure punched shrapnel out through the fuselage in all directions.

**Above:** Apart from a small force of Royal Marines based on the Falklands themselves, HMS *Endurance* was Britain's only presence in the South Atlantic when the Argentinians invaded. Her Wasp helicopters were eventually to play their part in the recapture of South Georgia.

**Below:** Operation PARAQUAT nearly ended in tragedy when an effort to extract the SAS from a high glacier in horrendous conditions led to the crashing and loss of two Wessex helicopters.

**Right:** Only some remarkable flying from Lieutenant Commander Ian Stanley RN in the one remaining Wessex saved the day. He's seen here climbing to height, up over South Georgia's dramatic and unforgiving landscape.

VIEW SW

SKYGUARD Radar

Area contains either 3 or 6 poss AAA guns

Poss PACK HOWITZER - type

Defensive Position

Intelligence on the Argentine air defences was scarce. These two pictures, smuggled out by residents leaving the islands after the invasion, were annotated by British planners as they prepared to hit back.

VIEW WEST

Poss TIGERCAT Launcher

Poss Cmd Veh/Trailer (with whip antenna)

Prob 105mm GUN/HOWITZER.

TIGERCAT Launcher

Trench

**Above:** 29 April 1982. The Vulcans took off from RAF Waddington bound for Ascension. This picture, taken from just beyond the airfield's perimeter fence, clearly shows the newly fitted jamming pod beneath the starboard wing. In the bomb bay, each aircraft was carrying twenty-one 1,000lb bombs.

**Above:** Nine hours later they arrived at Ascension's Wideawake airfield.

**Left:** After backtracking down the runway, the two Vulcans taxied to the dispersal in the shadow of Ascension's Green Mountain and shut down their engines. The next time they spooled up would be on Operation BLACK BUCK itself.

**Above:** BLACK BUCK planning. Captain of the Vulcan Ops crew, Squadron Leader Alastair Montgomery, seated on the left with a hat hanging off the back of the chair, joins the Victor planning cell on Ascension.

The Reeve crew on Ascension. Nominated as the Primary Crew by Waddington Station Commander John Laycock, they *should* have been the ones flying BLACK BUCK 1.
**L to r:** Navigator Radar Mick Cooper, John Reeve, Air Electronics Officer Barry Masefield, Co-pilot Don Dibbens, Navigator Plotter Jim Vinales and Air-to-Air Refuelling Instructor Pete Standing.

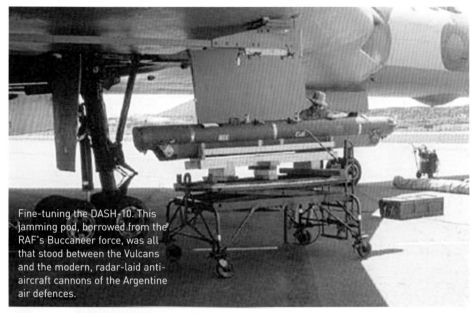

Fine-tuning the DASH-10. This jamming pod, borrowed from the RAF's Buccaneer force, was all that stood between the Vulcans and the modern, radar-laid anti-aircraft cannons of the Argentine air defences.

**Left:** The business end. Looking up into the Vulcan's bomb bay. The yellow bands around the bombs' noses indicate that they are live weapons.

**Below:** Dusk at Wideawake airfield, Ascension Island.

**Below:** Flight planning. Martin Withers, standing in the foreground, and Gordon Graham, his Navigator Plotter, seated at the table, plan the mission in detail.

**Right:** A map showing alternative attack plans. The first, coming in from the west, would have been the low-level route, flying overland, down the runway centreline, then escaping out to sea. The second, coming in from the north-east, shows the route flown: cutting the runway at 35 degrees from medium level.

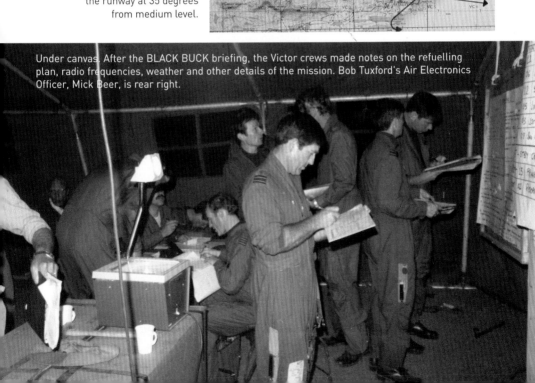

Under canvas. After the BLACK BUCK briefing, the Victor crews made notes on the refuelling plan, radio frequencies, weather and other details of the mission. Bob Tuxford's Air Electronics Officer, Mick Beer, is rear right.

**Above:** After dark. A rare night-time shot of a bombed-up Vulcan being pre-flighted at Wideawake shortly before taxiing out to fly BLACK BUCK.

**Right:** Minutes to go. John Reeve's Air Electronics Officer, Barry Masefield, was always first on board. The familiar environment and the distraction of running through his checks calmed his nerves.

the understandable surprise of the AARIs when they discovered that they'd be going in at the sharp end. Stealing
himself to broach the subject, he was completely disarmed
when, without prompting, John Reeve spoke up to make the
suggestion himself. Knight paused, as if considering the idea,
then he leaned over to Filbey and asked, 'Is that a possibility
do you think?' Job done, Knight returned to Bawtry. He'd let
John Laycock have the pleasure of telling the men from
Marham.

# Chapter 22

## 22 April 1982

'You messy bastard, you've left your wiper running!' It was all Ian Stanley could think of to lighten the situation. What do you say to a pilot who's just scrambled clear of his crashed helicopter?

The conditions endured by the SAS dropped on Fortuna Glacier had been horrific. The troopers were able to cover barely 500 yards over the treacherous crevasses and ice bridges, all the time assaulted by the biting, bruising wind. At nightfall, they tried to put up their tents only to have poles and fabric ripped from their hands. Instead, they chopped into the compacted ice to try to find some protection from the wind and snow. They made it through the night, but another one would surely bring hypothermia and frostbite. Wet, locked in a huddle and beaten by the weather, they were unable to perform any kind of military function.

*Antrim* received the signal asking for an evacuation at ten o'clock that morning. Humphrey and the two HU5s were going to have to run the gauntlet again.

The first attempt failed. While the two Wessex troop carriers remained in calmer conditions at low level, Ian Stanley spent half an hour searching for a route through the thick cloud to the waiting soldiers. With intermittent tail rotor control, ice building on the fuselage and a wildly fluctuating altimeter, he was forced to turn back.

Two hours later, taking advantage of a break in the cloud over the glacier, they tried again. The sky was clear and Stanley led the loose formation up over the crawling river of ice towards orange smoke grenades triggered by the stranded SAS party. The wind, though, was still ferocious. Their engines straining against it, the helicopters put down and the troops bundled in.

From the right-hand pilot's seat of one of the HU5s, Lieutenant Mike Tidd watched anxiously as another squall of cloud and snow gusted towards him. In the back of the Wessex, his Aircrewman, Sergeant 'Tug' Wilson, was already pouring hot coffee for his grateful cargo. Tidd thumbed the RT, requesting immediate clearance from Stanley. Stanley let him go. The pilot increased the revs, pulled up on the cyclic and, nose down, scudded north. Then the squall overtook him. White-out. Tidd couldn't see the rocks, but banked to avoid them. He couldn't see *anything*. The altimeter spun down. Instinctively, Tidd applied full power a moment before the helicopter's tail and main rotor clipped the ice, ripping the whole aircraft round on to its side. The Wessex scraped along the glacier before coming to a final rest eighty yards away in a bank of soft snow. Tidd went through the drills, shutting down the fuel and electrics before, along with his passengers, abandoning the wrecked helicopter. For some reason, a single wiper blade continued to sweep pathetically to and fro across the windscreen.

The unravelling of PARAQUAT provided the most acute cause of concern for the Defence Chiefs so far. After Tidd's crash the second Wessex HU5 was also caught in a white-out and destroyed. Only Humphrey survived the appalling conditions. The operation to retake South Georgia – the much-hoped-for boost to the country's morale – had got off to a truly disastrous start. Had it not been for some remarkable, brave flying by Stanley the situation might have been catastrophic. Wondering privately how long his luck was going to hold out, the Fleet Air Arm pilot had taken Humphrey up on to the glacier for a sixth time and had squeezed the remaining troops and marooned helicopter crews into the cramped hold. Dangerously over-loaded, the old single-engined helicopter returned to *Antrim*. Too heavy to hover, she'd slammed into the deck in a one-chance-to-pull-it-off controlled crash landing.

On Whitehall, at a table dominated by a high-backed wooden chair that had once belonged to Mountbatten, the First Chief of the Defence Staff, Sir Michael Beetham, chaired a meeting of the current Chiefs. They chewed over the disaster on Fortuna Glacier and subsequent attempts by special forces to infiltrate by inflatable boat, which had also ended in failure. While they'd been exceptionally lucky that there'd been no loss of life so far, the bottom line was that British forces had made no progress towards retaking the island. And worse, there were now intelligence reports that an Argentine diesel-electric sub-marine was in the area. They were at an impasse. And there seemed to be no clear way of forcing the situation forward.

The long-range missions to South Georgia had helped orientate the Victor force to operating over the huge distances involved. What had been planned in theory was working in practice. The more the Victors were flown, the more reliable they seemed to become. In reality, though, this did little to lighten the load on the shoulders of Squadron Leader Bill Lloyd, the head of the engineering detachment. The most obvious difficulty on Wideawake's exposed pan was the abrasive volcanic dust. It was kicked up every time the wind blew. So when four Rolls-Royce Conway engines spooled up, the effect was predictable. Every effort was made to protect the jets. They were parked as far back as possible, often the entire empennage hung over the dust beyond the hardstanding. This saved limited space, but it also meant that when dirt and debris was thrown up by the jet exhausts, it was blown off the hardstanding, away from engine intakes of the other aircraft. The Tarmac, too, caused un-foreseen problems. It was softened by the heat and the degrading effects of spilt Avtur, so the heavy, fuelled-up Victors would sink into it. Freeing themselves from these ruts used extra power, which blew up extra dust. So before engine start, the ground crew would tow the Victors forward a few feet so that their wheels could roll unhindered.

Despite all the precautions, the metal compressor blades of the Victors' four turbojets soon acquired the polished appearance of mirrors.

The main headache, though, remained the HDU, the hose-drum unit. Mounted in the belly of the Victor, the HDU, pronounced 'hoodoo', was an old piece of kit with a reputation for being temperamental. In contrast to the airframes themselves, the more it was used, the more worn out it seemed to become. And that was a big problem.

The principle was simple: the fuel hose unfurled from the drum unit like a thread from a cotton reel. There were powerful forces at work on the mechanism, though, and these needed to be balanced. Gravity and drag would ensure that the hose trailed. Once it was in position, hydraulic motors were kept on, poised to wind in the slack caused by the impact of the receiving aircraft. Without them, when a receiver made contact with the drogue, a loop caused by even a gentle impact could travel up and down the hose like a wave, damaging either the receiver's probe or the tanker itself. The condition of the HDU was monitored intently by the Victor's Nav Radar. The strength of the electrical current drawn by the hydraulic motor was the main indicator of the HDU's health. If it didn't function, they couldn't tank.

The last part of the refuelling system was the fuel pump. Powered by a turbine driven with compressed air from the engines, it operated at enormously high speeds. If it broke up, it did so explosively. Unrestrained kinetic energy would throw out slices of broken metal in all directions. It was like a bomb going off inside the aircraft. At the very least, it could create a ring of jagged holes around the circumference of the fuselage, weakening it like the perforations on a sheet of stamps. If you were unlucky, it would take out fuel lines and hydraulics too. A catastrophic failure of the fuel pump meant that losing the ability to refuel would be the least of the unfortunate crew's problems.

Underneath the khaki canvas of the Ascension Ops centre, some of the Victor captains considered the possibility of the HDU failing. Could they, *in extremis*, use either of the Mk 20 wingpods? Tux talked it through with the two 57 Squadron Flight Commanders, Martin Todd and Barry Neal. Even if it was the only chance of saving the jet it seemed unlikely. When they placed plan drawings of the Victors next to each other it became clear just how difficult it would be. It was one thing for a small jet fighter like a Lightning to hold station behind the wing of a Victor, but to try it in another Victor was a recipe for disaster. The eighty-foot hose on the centreline was nearly twice the length of those that trailed out of the wingpods. Making contact with the baskets trailing from the pods would bring the receiving Victor's wing dangerously close to the tail of the tanker. On top of this, the receiver's own high tail would sit right in the turbulent vortices spinning off the tanker's wingtip. When it was needed most, control would be near impossible.

Even if the wingpods had been able to transfer enough fuel to make the effort worthwhile – which was, at best, marginal – it was a non-starter. If the Mk 20s were all that could save you, you were shafted either way.

Simon Baldwin sat alone at his desk with a cup of coffee and his pipe. He shared Mick Cooper's doubts about how they were training to go in. As a clearer picture of the Argentine air defences had emerged his own concerns had grown. The previous night the 44 Squadron boss hadn't been able to sleep. As he'd lain in bed, different ideas and possibilities raced through his mind. Assuming the Victors could get the Vulcan to the right place, he had to take care of two things: he had to try to ensure his crew survived and he had to maximize their chances of destroying the target, which, although yet to be confirmed, seemed certain to be a runway. An enthusiast like Cooper could talk for Britain about the different bombing options available. He'd hoarded official Air Ministry publi-cations on bombs dating back to 1948. From practice bombs to the 22,000lb Grand Slam, he could tell you what sort of impact to expect. Of course, he'd tell you, it also depended on whether you used cast or machined cases; what fusing and detonator combination you chose. You could have instantaneous explosions or anything else up to a 144-hour delay (should you decide to ignore the Geneva Convention). And you could mix it all up within one bombload if you liked.

Baldwin knew that with more definitive information on the Argentine defences he had to reconsider the attack options. The Argentine low-level defences now looked extremely strong, and if the troops were on the ball, the Vulcan making a low-level attack could be exposed to an appalling barrage of anti-aircraft fire as it flew all the way down the runway at 300 feet. On top of this, the laydown attack was also by no means guaranteed to hit the target. The normal procedure was for the Nav Radar to issue directions until the pilot could make a positive identification of the target, and take over to make the final corrections visually. This approach was hard to fault in good visibility, and the Night Navigation Goggles meant that it remained an option in darkness. However, with the imminent onset of the Falklands winter, there was every possibility that the weather would be diabolical. In snow or fog the pilots would be all but blind, meaning that the attack would have to be carried out using the NBS and its antique computers. The runway was only about forty yards wide and radar bomb attacks were not always that accurate. There would be a strong probability that the Vulcan would end up decorating the airfield with a neat line of craters running parallel to the runway. Miss with one and you'd miss with them all.

And yet this wasn't the clincher. Baldwin knew that from 300 feet, even if they got the bombs on target, there was a danger that they just wouldn't do the necessary damage. On a laydown attack the 1,000lb bombs slowed down by their small parachutes wouldn't hit the runway at sufficient velocity, or at a steep enough angle, to do the job. There would be insufficient penetration for them to do more than pockmark the hard surface of the strip.

Baldwin's mind began to turn to the possibility of using a bombing technique he'd practised as a young Navigator during his first tour in the Air Force on Canberras in Singapore in the mid 1960s. The bombers would run in towards the target at low level, and shortly before the target, pop up to a height of 7,000 feet, and level off for a short run-in to the release point. Back then, the reason for using the tactic had been self-preservation. The potential targets at that time were Indonesian airfields and a pop-up to 7,000 feet put the Canberra out of range of the Indonesian anti-aircraft batteries. But the pop-up brought with it another crucial advantage: they could use ballistic bombs instead of retarded thousand-pounders.

To properly break up a Tarmac runway, these needed to be falling nearly vertically – at an aerodynamic terminal velocity of over 1,000 feet per second. They would then penetrate deep underneath the Tarmac into the substrata and destroy the strip from below, exploding upwards to rip out its foundations and leave a huge crater. Baldwin wasn't sure of the exact dimensions but he knew it would be big – big enough for any aircraft trying to take off to fall into. The effect wouldn't simply be more spectacular; it would also be more permanent. Like a test match wicket, a runway, once damaged, is unlikely to be quite the same again. Even if it was patched up efficiently, a deep hole would always be liable to subside, ensuring that it was out of action as far as fast jets were concerned. A very comprehensive repair was possible, but it would take days rather than hours, and that was assuming the Argentinians had the equipment, material and expertise on the islands to even contemplate it.

Baldwin now turned his attention to how he was going to keep the bomber safe. Soviet long-range ground-to-air missiles, supplemented by fighters with air-to-air missiles, had forced the V-force to low level. The Argentine fighters on the mainland were too far away to interfere. Word from Intelligence was that there were no fighters based at Port Stanley. Even if there were, though, at low level the Vulcan would retain a large measure of surprise. In the short time it would be exposed to the Argentine search radars – from early in the pop-up climb to bomb release – the Argentinians would struggle to get a fighter airborne.

Baldwin checked against his graph of the Argentine air defences. At 2,000 feet – the minimum from which the bombs could be dropped and reach terminal velocity – the bomber's chances of survival were slim . . . *Roland: kill zone – 12,800 feet*. He asked the Station Intelligence Officer to check again with his Intelligence community whether or not Roland was deployed on the islands. The answer he got was the same. Roland, Baldwin was told, had not been deployed. He moved on. *Tiger Cat burns out at 8,500 feet, but it's visually aimed . . . so barely threat at all at medium level at night. Oerlikon –* that was what he was really worried about *– 6,400 feet. Give it a bit for the wife and kids . . . 8,000 feet.* That *should* put them above the kill zone.

Keeping out of the kill zone was the critical step, but it didn't completely remove the aircraft from danger. The Argentine high-explosive cannon shells would continue to heights well above the kill zone and explode automatically at the end of their upward flight. That they were travelling relatively aim-lessly at this stage would be no consolation to the crew if they happened to fly into one. He could raise the height of the bomb-run to, say, 20,000 feet, which would put the aircraft well above everything the Argentinians had, deployed or otherwise, but this was likely to have a hopelessly detrimental effect on bombing accuracy. And Baldwin knew from his Canberra days that there were no data or formulae to give him a clue to the rate at which accuracy degraded with height. He sought opinions from some of the Nav Radars, but none felt confident of hitting the small runway from 20,000 feet. This came as no surprise; he knew that to hit the runway, the lower the better.

To reassure himself, he again turned to kill-zone graphs. The kill zones and burn-out zones are roughly hemispherical. He imagined half a grapefruit placed flat side down over a map of the target. Providing the attacking Vulcan stayed outside the grapefruit it was reasonably safe. At 8,000 feet plus it would always be above the apex of the hemisphere – above the vertical limit of the Oerlikon kill zone. On a flatter trajectory, though, the cannon's range was greater – perhaps two and a quarter miles. But the guns weren't going to find the Vulcan down low. She'd be running in at 8,000 feet, releasing the bombs two miles from the target and relying on their forward throw to carry them the rest of the way to the target as they fell. At worst, the Vulcan wouldn't do much more than pierce the skin of the grapefruit.

So above the kill zone, with the added insurance of the Dash 10 jamming pod, 8,000 feet plus looked a realistic, acceptably safe attack height. But it meant that the crews would have to aim the bombs using the H2S radar alone. And with the inherent inaccuracies of the old NBS computer, they didn't have a hope in hell of sticking a line of bombs along the centreline of a runway that was only forty yards wide.

During the Second World War, it had been calculated that the optimum angle at which to attack a runway was not at 90 degrees to the centreline but at about 35 degrees. The experience and calculations had stood the test of time. The Nav Radar's bomb control unit, the 90-Way, allowed him to adjust the stick spacing – the distance between the bombs as they hit the ground – by setting different time intervals between bomb releases. He would need to calculate the stick spacing necessary to ensure that even if successive bombs straddled the runway, they were close enough for the resulting craters still to bite deep into both edges of the runway. Nothing could ever be for certain with NBS, but they did have a good *chance* of getting a bomb on the runway.

So Baldwin had a plan: low-level approach under the search radars; pop up to 8,000 feet or a little above; jam the gun radars – if necessary – with the Dash 10 pod; drop free-fall thousand-pounders, with an appropriate stick spacing, in a classic 35 degree runway cut. The bombs should hit the target and do the necessary damage. The element of surprise would count in their favour by giving the Argentinians very little time to react, and the Vulcan should be safe from the anti-aircraft defences. It was obviously not without risk, but as he sat back and considered the plan, Baldwin thought: *Nobody has ever designed a war without risk*. And, in any case, he felt he had another trump card. He knew his crews were very good.

He took his work to John Laycock and the two men talked through every point. The Station Commander didn't need to be persuaded.

'Send a signal to 1 Group,' he told Baldwin, happy that they'd got it right. At two in the morning, the exhausted Navigator sent a 'Personal For' signal to Air Vice-Marshal Mike Knight at Bawtry outlining their intentions. Then he headed home to Trenchard Square to try to get some sleep.

Bob Wright, Martin Withers' young Nav Radar, and the man who might be responsible for hitting the target, had never flown a 'pop-up' in his life. For that matter, until a few days earlier, he'd never dropped a 1,000lb bomb either.

# Chapter 23

## 24 April 1982

The chilling wail of an air-raid siren echoed through Stanley at eleven o'clock the next morning – the Argentinians testing their newly installed system. They were confident of providing forty minutes' warning of any incoming attack. Plenty of time to make it to safehouses and shelters, they said. Many of the islanders weren't so sure. A civil defence committee was quickly pulled together which issued its own typewritten instructions to the 545 residents who remained in town.

John Smith carried food and bedding down into his shelter under the porch, while in the west of the town the walls and roof of the King Edward VII Memorial Hospital were painted with red crosses, designed to be visible from the air. Sandbags were filled and piled high around the exposed windows of the operating theatre.

Air Vice-Marshal Mike Knight returned to Waddington on Sunday. Simon Baldwin was eager to hear his reaction to the plan he'd sent to Bawtry the previous night.

'What do you think of it?' Baldwin asked, confident that had Knight had any doubts, he would not have been backward in sharing them.

'It looks OK to me,' replied the AOC, 'but you'll be able to ask the Chief of the Air Staff yourself. He's coming up here tomorrow . . .'

*

Force 7 winds, snow and sleet couldn't dampen the mood in Stanley. At five o'clock in the afternoon, the BBC had reported news of the Argentine surrender on South Georgia. After the dreadful setbacks on Fortuna Glacier, the recapture itself had turned out to be an anti-climax.

With a single sweep of the radar, Humphrey's Observer picked up a faint radar contact north of Grytviken. Checking against the known positions of icebergs, he gave his pilot, Ian Stanley, a new heading and the Wessex set course to investigate. It was the source of the intelligence reports from the previous day that had so rattled the *Antrim* group: the Argentine submarine *Santa Fé*. She'd been caught on the surface. Humphrey dived to attack her from behind with two Mk 11 depth charges. Her stern was lifted out of the water by the explosions. Lucky to have survived the first attack, the hunted boat turned back towards South Georgia, trailing oil. Helicopters from the rest of the small British task group then joined the attack, assaulting the lame submarine with Mk 46 torpedoes, AS12 wire-guided missiles and general purpose machine-guns fired from the cabin doors. One of the Fleet Air Arm pilots even unclipped his Browning 9mm automatic to take potshots at the submarine's black hull, before thinking better of it and replacing the pistol in its holster.

After days of phoney war, the attack on the *Santa Fé* became the trigger for British action. Her chaotic arrival back at the British Antarctic Survey jetty, hounded all the way by the swarm of helicopters, caused confusion amongst the Argentine forces on the ground. Rather than wait for the Royal Marines of the 'Mighty Munch' holding off 200 miles away onboard RFA *Tidespring*, the British command decided to take advantage of the confusion using the seventy-four soldiers who could be mustered from the ships already standing off the island. While the 4.5-inch guns of *Antrim* and *Plymouth* provided naval gunfire support, the *ad hoc* force of Marines and special forces troopers was shuttled in by helicopter. As they gathered themselves to launch an assault on the Argentine defenders, the white flags went up. If there had ever been any will to fight amongst the occupiers, it was undone by an intimidating barrage of fire so unrelenting that the heat generated caused the grey paint on *Antrim*'s gun barrels to flake off and expose the metal below. South Georgia had, after setbacks which threatened the momentum of the whole British campaign in the South Atlantic, been retaken without loss of life.

In Buenos Aires, the junta took it badly, protesting indignantly to the UN Security Council that the British had 'perpetrated an act of armed aggression against the South Georgia islands, which form part of Argentine territory'.

And on the Falklands, the military build-up continued. But the occupiers were jumpier now. Less certain, thought the islanders. More aggressive. The influence of men like Dowling was in the ascendant.

The *Río del Plata* set sail from Bilbao in north-west Spain on 15 April and headed south into the Atlantic. At 10.45 on 26 April, as the Argentine freighter closed on Ascension, a signal arrived on the island from Northwood telling them she was on her way and that, while in Spain, it was possible that she had taken on a force of Argentine Commandos.

If South Georgia was important for political reasons, the vital strategic importance of Ascension Island was of a different measure altogether. While Jerry Price's concern was inevitably less acute than Woodward's fear of losing a carrier, he knew that Ascension's security was equally crucial to success. Should anything happen to the airhead, the British campaign would come to an ignominious halt. The Argentinians, he thought, must see that too. Despite the colony's extreme geographical isolation, what they might be able to do to threaten Wideawake was a subject taken very seriously indeed. A 200-mile terminal exclusion zone, patrolled by the Nimrods, was established around the island. The boundary carried no legal force, however. It was little more than a tripwire. Since early in April, the *Zaporozhive*, a Soviet 'Primorye' Class spy trawler, had sat within it, just eighty miles to the north. Listening. A British helicopter was sent out to wave a bottle of whisky at its deprived crew, but neither that, nor an accidentally-on-purpose attempt to blow down its aerials with the rotor downwash put them off. And the huge silver-winged Tupolev Tu-95 Bears operating out of Africa continued to fly close to the island. Unsure whether or not Soviet intelligence might be finding its way into the hands of the Argentinians, or whether a high-flying radar contact or approaching ship was friend or foe, the British on Ascension had always to assume the worst.

Northwood authorized the use of Task Group 317 – the British amphibious force on board HMS *Fearless*, still lying off the coast – to defend Ascension against the potential threat of the *Río del Plata*. As a result, Marines were posted as lookouts on vantage points across the island, while a joint Royal Navy and Marine team swept the boundary to the north-west and the SBS checked the beaches. While the island was secured, all incoming transport flights were stopped. The only thing airborne was the Nimrod MR2 combing the seas around Ascension.

The RAF contingent were given daily intelligence briefings. GCHQ had always maintained a presence on Ascension and the Victor detachment looked forward to the arrival of the man from Britain's signals intelligence agency arriving at Wideawake on his bicycle. It was always the potential threats to Ascension that most held Jeremy Price's attention. Two more Victors had flown in today. Half of the RAF's entire tanker fleet was now tesselated around the small Wideawake pan.

Faced with the difficulties of operating its frontline attack jets out of BAM Malvinas, in early April the Comando Aviación Naval Argentina decided to deploy its Aermacchi MB339s. These little Italian-built weapons trainers didn't carry the punch of the Skyhawks and Super Étendards, but armed with 30mm cannons and 5-inch Zuni rockets, the unit's CO, Capitan de Corbeta Carlos Molteni, believed 1 Escuadrilla

Aeronaval de Ataque could pose a genuine threat to British ships. By 26 April, four of the single-engined jets were in place, parked on improvised wooden planking near the eastern threshold of the runway. The Argentinians now had an aircraft capable of mounting offensive air operations flying out of the Falklands themselves. The need to disable the airfield was even more pressing.

# Chapter 24

## 26 April 1982

It quickly became known as the 'Star Chamber', the day the RAF's top brass arrived at Waddington for a targeting conference. Led by the Chief of the Air Staff, Sir Michael Beetham, some of the service's most senior officers were ushered into John Laycock's office and settled around the table. Laycock and Simon Baldwin then set out their stall.

The Station Commander sat down opposite Beetham. To his left was Simon Baldwin. Beyond him, almost out of Laycock's view was the Commander-in-Chief Strike Command, Air Marshal Sir Keith Williamson. AOC 1 Group, Air Vice-Marshal Mike Knight, was back down from Bawtry and Air Marshal Sir John Curtiss, the CORPORATE Air Commander, had joined them from Northwood. There were a lot of stripes in the room. John Laycock opened the debate by simply asking exactly what it was the Chief of the Air Staff wanted the Vulcan crews to do. Beetham's reply was straightforward and unequivocal: 'To prevent the Argentine Air Force from using the runway at Stanley airport.'

Now Laycock and Baldwin felt they were on safe ground. Even though it was not what the crews had so far been training for, they now knew that it had to be a medium-level attack with ballistic 1,000lb iron bombs. It was the only way to put deep craters in the ground. Laycock described their plan, explaining how and why they'd reached their conclusions. They knew that Beetham and Curtiss, both ex-Second World War heavy-bomber crew, would see their logic. And Knight had already discussed the attack profile with Baldwin the previous day. But it didn't seem to be what C-in-C Strike was expecting to hear. The only man in the room with a background flying fighters, Sir Keith Williamson wouldn't have had any personal experience of what the two Waddington men were describing. As a consequence, he appeared reluctant to accept that what Baldwin and Laycock were suggesting could be the best way. And it did fly in the face of what had almost become a sacred cow for the RAF: that going in low over the target was the only way for the bombers to do their work. The RAF's entire attack force of Buccaneers, Jaguars, Harriers and now Tornados – all under Williamson's command – was built on that foundation. Wrong-footed, he questioned the wisdom of the return to such a classic attack profile. Laycock turned to Beetham for support, frustrated that what he knew made sense was being undermined.

'It sounds very sensible to me,' Beetham said quietly. 'Carry on.'

'Thank you, CAS,' said Laycock, reassured.

Beetham asked about the size of the craters they could expect, but Baldwin, his career spent training to drop nuclear, not conventional bombs, struggled to give him detail on that. He felt fortunate the CAS was an ex-bomber man.

'Can we do it?' asked Beetham, finally. Since Monty's broken probe two days earlier, Martin Withers and Dick Russell had flown with the modification to the valve – with a probe that hadn't carried the weight of a full fuel hose on the ground. It had gone without incident, but it would have been rash to dismiss the difficulties of the past two weeks on the strength of one sortie. Laycock and Baldwin sounded confident, but realistic.

'If everything works, we've got a chance, sir. If the gods are with us, yes.'

The four senior officers retreated into conference to discuss what they'd been told. Keith Williamson wanted his staff at Strike Command to examine the plan. Beetham and Knight supported that and suggested that the Air Warfare College at Cranwell might also take a look. The target had been confirmed. Laycock and Baldwin had explained the only effective way to attack it using the resources available to them, but the plan still needed to be rubber-stamped.

'Don't worry,' Baldwin encouraged Laycock, 'I *know* the guys at Cranwell will come through.'

It was time for 'their air-ships' to meet the crews.

Monty was trying to get some sleep when the phone rang. It was Simon Baldwin.

'Monty, could you come over to the Ops block?'

'Simon, I'm in bed. I'm tired,' Monty complained.

'No you're not, Mont. Now!' Baldwin insisted.

Monty hauled himself out of bed and headed over. All the CORPORATE crews had been mustered in the main briefing room for the occasion.

As Beetham was introduced to the crew members in turn, John Reeve tried to engage him.

'I told him there'd be a promotion in all of this,' he joked, indicating his co-pilot, Don Dibbens. Reeve was making light of Dibbens' recent, routine promotion, which just happened to have come through since the training had begun. Dibbens cringed. Beetham greeted the remark with a thin smile, but, when introduced to Reeve himself, looked as if he had been about to say something before stopping himself.

The Vulcan crews took their seats for the briefing. As they got settled, not all of them had their minds on the briefing to follow. Martin Withers' co-pilot, Pete Taylor, couldn't help puzzling about the Chief of the Air Staff's blue socks. *Shouldn't they be black?*, he pondered.

Then Beetham began to speak. He knew the way aircrews' minds worked, knew that however lofty his own rank, they were a tough audience. Their hard-to-impress self-confidence was a vital part of what they did. But Beetham also understood the way they might be feeling now, as combat drew nearer. The veteran of Bomber Harris's Second World War strategic bombing campaign had been there himself, nearly forty years earlier.

Now he was addressing a new generation of bomber crews. Their target, he told them, was the runway at Port Stanley airport. Furthermore, he told them, the raid was a powerful political statement. 'We *cannot* be seen to be losing,' he stressed. Beetham didn't need to wait for confirmation from Cranwell. He explained that they would be going in low, before a pop-up to 8,000 feet for the bomb-run. They'd be supported on the journey south by a fleet of Victors, then one of them would be on their own.

Monty didn't like it. *We're the boys for low level*, he thought. They'd been to RED FLAG. They'd spent the last two weeks taking the jets down as low as they dared. And now they were going in at medium level. Reeve shared his irritation. First they'd needed new navigation equipment. Then they learnt that the jamming equipment they'd depended on probably wasn't up to the job. Now, he was being told that the bombs wouldn't work if they were dropped at low level. Why had this all been discovered in the last two weeks? It seemed to him that no one had taken the Vulcans seriously for ten years or more. But Reeve was pragmatic. He certainly wasn't going to waste time worrying about it. *If you want me to be ready*, he thought, *I'll be ready*.

When they were asked at the end if there were any volunteers, Reeve stuck up his hand.

Martin Withers was surprised about the decision to go in at medium level, too, but he felt less like challenging it than making sure of it. The news came as an almost overwhelming relief. Since speculation about their target had begun, he'd been burdened by a huge sense of vulnerability. Flying straight and level at a few hundred feet down the length of a heavily defended runway had always felt to him like a one-way ticket. A few words from Beetham had changed everything.

'Are there any problems?' Beetham finished. A question to which there was only one answer.

Monty hesitated. Unlike Withers, he hadn't flown since breaking his probe and losing the engines. He didn't know that things were looking more hopeful. So he stood up, and the room turned to watch.

'We're all keen to get on with it,' Monty began, his frustration finding a voice, 'but until we've solved the problem of the probes, we're not going anywhere, because we can't refuel in the dark for more than five or six minutes.'

The look he received from Air Vice-Marshal Mike Knight was chilling. He realized immediately that he had played it all wrong. He should have said something to John Laycock privately. Not here, not in front of the Chief of the Air Staff. All of the senior men knew about the refuelling problems. They'd also just been reassured by Laycock and Baldwin that, hopefully, the worst was behind them. Monty's contribution was unnecessary and unwelcome. He felt he'd done the right thing, but he also couldn't help feeling that it was the sort of *faux pas* that would be remembered. As the crews shuffled out of the Main Briefing Room, Martin Withers leaned over.

'That's you buggered, Mont,' he joked, trying to make light of it, but Monty was inclined to agree. His gloom wasn't helped by John Reeve's evident enthusiasm. Beetham's words seemed to have had a stirring effect on him. At this point, Monty thought, *John would flap his wings down to the South Atlantic.*

In the end, Monty's pessimism didn't greatly affect the mood of the meeting. Beetham had the reassurances he needed to brief the War Cabinet in detail and the crews, if tired, were, he felt, in good heart. Before the Chief of the Air Staff returned to London, there was just one more thing Laycock hoped to get a steer on. He was still working on the assumption that a big disbandment ceremony for the remaining Vulcan squadrons was expected on 1 July. Already frustrated by the distractions of the parade through Lincoln and IX Squadron's imminent transformation into a Tornado squadron, Laycock asked if it was really necessary.

'I wouldn't expend too much energy on it, if I were you . . .' Beetham told him.

Just the reply the genial Station Commander had hoped for.

As soon as the Air Marshals had departed, Simon Baldwin gathered his Ops team and described the new plan. They would need to completely revise the work they'd done so far, changing the attack profile to the medium-level pop-up, the attack track to 35 degrees off the runway heading, look again at the radar offsets now that the Vulcan would be approaching the target from the north-east and work out new stick-spacings that would ensure they could take out the runway from 8,000 feet.

The crews took off from Waddington again late that evening to fly another training sortie, a composite profile putting together all the elements of what they'd rehearsed so far – air-to-air refuelling, low-level flying, radar bombing, Carousel navigation and electronic countermeasures. On top of this they added the 'pop-up' manoeuvre they'd be using to drop their bombs from medium level. Twice, over Leuchars and Flamborough Head, they climbed steeply from low level for their bomb run before diving back down to the deck again. For the first time the sortie was properly representative of the mission they were being ordered to fly. Bob Wright and Pete Taylor now both had a grand total of two 'pop-ups' under their belts.

Reeve, Withers and Monty finally got their heads down just after 2 a.m. They all expected to be able to sleep late the next morning, though. Monty had checked: they weren't flying the next day.

'Definitely not,' Laycock told him.

As they drifted off to sleep that night, none of them was aware that they'd trained for the last time. The next time they flew they'd be heading to war.

# Chapter 25

## 27 April 1982

Monty was woken from a deep sleep by persistent knocking on his window. As he got out of bed to find out what was going on, he noticed his wife Ingrid was already up. He pulled back the curtains and light streamed in past the silhouette of a policeman, standing on a ladder to reach the first-floor bedroom.

'Is your name Montgomery?' he asked, getting straight to the point.

Monty, blinking, nodded his assent.

'I've got a Flight Lieutenant here to take you to Waddington.'

Monty asked for time. Now wide awake, he knew what was happening. Unable to rouse him by phone, and with Ingrid out of the house, Waddington had been forced to employ a less than conventional alarm. His bag was packed, he was ready to go, but he wanted to see his wife. He guessed she'd be round the corner with her friend Marjorie and called her. Right first time.

'Marjorie, could you ask Ingrid to pop home.'

The wives had barely seen their husbands for three weeks. Some had talked amongst themselves, pooling the snippets of information their husbands had felt able to share, speculating on what was being planned. A support network of sorts had grown up. The squadron commanders' wives tried to look after those of the squadron officers. The men were told that what they were training for was top secret, but most tried to prepare their wives as best they could. It was all over the newspapers, after all. It didn't take a genius to work out what was going on.

The strangest thing was saying goodbye. Monty just couldn't shake off a nagging feeling that he might never see Ingrid again. As he turned to walk to the car, he thought of his father going to fight in the Second World War. The old man must have felt the same sensations as he left to join his warship. *He was going to war.* Monty pulled the car door shut and headed into the station to join his crew.

'We have a 90 per cent chance of getting one bomb on the runway and a 60 per cent chance of two,' began Michael Beetham. To help explain the art of runway cutting and ballistic bombs to the Prime Minister and her War Cabinet, he illustrated his briefing with a flip chart and maps, carefully explaining why trying to fly a bomber along the length of the runway would be a mistake. The Chief of the Air Staff told them that in an ideal world he'd like ten or a hundred Vulcans over Stanley, but it couldn't be done. One Vulcan, he stressed to them, was all that resources allowed. And even that depended on the success of a hugely complicated series of in-flight refuellings. It was vital that the politicians' expectations were realistic.

'That's all we can do, but it's worth doing,' he concluded.

Like the Prime Minister, John Nott was supportive of the effort, all for giving it a go, but the prospect of success, he thought, sounded rather touch and go.

Beetham left with the authority to deploy the Vulcans to Ascension, 4,000 miles closer to their target, but still only halfway there.

Monty's crew was waiting for him in the Ops Room.

'Right, boys,' he greeted them.

'What exactly are we doing?' asked Nav Plotter Dick Arnott, speaking for all of them.

'D'know, Dick, I'm waiting to see the Station Commander.'

There was no time to speculate further, before the hyperactive Scotsman was sitting in Laycock's office with Air Commodore Tony Carver, Air Vice-Marshal Mike Knight's chief of staff from Bawtry. Carver came straight to the point, while Laycock listened in. His brain whirring, Monty tried to force himself to listen.

'Your crew has *not* been selected for the first mission.'

That got Monty's attention. *Shit*, he thought. The disappointment was instant. He didn't think he'd ever get another chance. *And I'm flying the Vulcan better than I ever have in my life*. He couldn't just let it go.

'Come on, sir, we're as good as the rest of them,' he argued.

'Maybe, but because of the nature of your personality—'

Monty cut him off. 'Is this another way of saying I'm a stroppy bastard, sir?' he asked, sure somehow that his ill-judged intervention the previous evening had influenced the decision.

'Yes,' Carver told him, which didn't exactly put the bomber pilot's mind at rest. The truth was, though, that Monty was the right man for the job long before he'd stood up for himself and the rest of the crews in front of the Chief of the Air Staff. A 'stroppy bastard' was exactly what Carver and Laycock were after. Monty was like a terrier. Throw him a problem, Laycock had told 1 Group, and he won't let go. He'll keep fighting until it's sorted out.

'We want you to go down and get everything ready to go,' Carver explained.

'All right,' Monty accepted, coming to terms with the idea. 'You mean we're going to run the set-up? What authority have I got?'

'My authority,' Carver replied. 'You've got to get yourselves to Brize Norton. They're holding an aeroplane for you and your crew. You'll be in Ascension tonight.'

As he left, Monty put to Carver the question that really mattered to him: 'Will we be flying later on, sir?' he asked, still hoping that he'd get a chance to fly the Vulcan in anger.

'I don't know.'

It didn't offer much ground for optimism.

John Reeve and Martin Withers were discussing Monty's departure when they were called in to the Station Commander's office. Both of them assumed that Monty had been chosen to fly the mission. They stood side by side in front of John Laycock's desk, the window to their right providing wide views of the north side of the airfield. Laycock told them that the mission was on. Waddington had been asked to forward-deploy two Vulcans to Ascension. Monty's crew were already on their way to Brize. The Vulcans would be launching one raid on Stanley airfield in the near future. He told them there might also be more to follow. And then he surprised them both.

'One or other of you two will do the attack.'

It was not what either of them was expecting to hear.

Laycock continued: 'Would either of you like to volunteer?'

Withers, expecting Reeve to snatch the opportunity, attempted to make the whole process more straightforward: 'My father told me never to volunteer for anything, so . . .' he joked, sidestepped and turned to face Reeve, gesturing towards him with open palms, 'over to you, John!'

Reeve, to Withers' surprise, given his raised arm the previous night, said that he couldn't volunteer without talking to his crew. But he wasn't given that chance. In the absence of a volunteer, Laycock gave them his decision. He and Simon Baldwin had already made up their minds. In Mick Cooper and Jim Vinales, Reeve's crew had the most experienced navigation and bombing team, and in Reeve himself it had a captain whose unsinkable confidence and 'can do' attitude had been manifest throughout training. He'd been unfazed by whatever was thrown at him. Mistaken for a gung-ho attitude in some quarters, Reeve's no-nonsense temperament had, initially, given some around Waddington pause for thought about his suitability, but Laycock was in no doubt now. In any case, Reeve was the senior of the two captains. The Reeve crew was Primary. Martin Withers would be flying reserve.

As the decision was absorbed, Monty's men were boarding

a Hawker-Siddeley Andover CC2 of the RAF's Queen's Flight. With them was Squadron Leader Mel James, flying out as boss of the Vulcan engineering detachment with five of his advance guard of technicians. This felt *important*, thought Monty. It was a short hop to Brize, the hub of the RAF's epic logistic operation to and from Ascension. From there, they'd be flown to Wideawake. Nav Plotter Dick Arnott boarded the elegantly liveried red and blue VIP transport with a dangerous look on his face – one only too familiar to the rest of the crew. As he cast an eye around the twin-turboprop's bespoke interior, he caught the attention of the steward.

'Is this the plane that Margaret Thatcher flies on?' he asked.
'Yes.'

Monty felt a sense of dread at what might come next.

'Where does she sit then?' Arnott carried on.

The steward innocently pointed out the seat and Arnott walked over to it.

'Dick, you're not going to do this!' Monty tried to stop him. 'You're not!' But it was hopeless.

As he got close, Arnott stooped down towards the Prime Minister's chair, then performed an unpleasantly close inspection of the seat's fabric before claiming it as his own. Next they were served tea and sandwiches. *Surreal*, thought Monty. It was going to be a very strange day.

One of the reasons Dick Russell was first chosen to work with the Vulcan crews was the size of his waistband. As the Vulcan was originally designed to be flown by a single pilot, its flight deck was cramped. Before either pilot could take to his Martin Baker ejection seat, he had to slide away the large fuel management tray that sat centrally, extending backwards at ankle level from the mess of dials of the instrument panel. Negotiating his way through the narrow gap between the pilots' seats to swap places with the co-pilot was a job the tall, slim Russell was expected to accomplish with less palaver than his more rotund colleagues.

John Laycock walked around to the Ops Room from his

office to find Russell and the two other AARIs. It had been confirmed by 1 Group that they would be joining the Vulcan crews on the mission itself. Laycock bumped into Russell first. The two men knew each other well from shared time on a Victor bomber squadron in the 1960s.

'Dick,' Laycock opened, with no hint of the bombshell to come, 'I'm going to have to send you to fly with the Vulcan crews.'

'I don't think I can do that,' Russell answered instinctively, not initially taking on board the importance of what was being said.

'I can't think of a single reason why not!' Laycock persisted affably, knowing it hadn't quite sunk in.

'It's my birthday party on Friday! My fiftieth! Muriel and I have got all these people coming. We can't cancel it now . . .'

Russell's wife had spent weeks making plans for friends and family to join them. Laycock explained the thinking behind the decision: the length of the planned mission; the necessary complexity of any refuelling plan; the inexperience of the Vulcan pilots as prodders. However unappealing the idea, on the face of it, might seem to Russell and the two other AARIs, Pete Standing and Ian Clifford, they'd be a valuable addition to each of the bomber crews. Russell's protests evaporated. In truth, serious doubts had never entered his head; it had just taken him rather by surprise. Poor Muriel would just have to rearrange the party for when this was all over.

For now, there was just time to get back to Marham, break the news to her, pick up his kit, and return to the bomber station.

Jim Vinales was in the garden when John Reeve arrived to tell him that their crew were flying Primary. Monty and the rest had already left for Ascension as Ops crew, he told his Navigator. They'd be following him tomorrow.

Vinales and his wife Jean were worried about their son, Edward. Two years old, he suffered from recurring earaches, which were sometimes so severe that the boy would bang his head on the floor to try to relieve the pain. They felt they were making progress when the condition had recently been diagnosed as glue ear. After Reeve had left, Vinales took a phone call from the consultant, hoping to arrange another appointment.

'Can you come in tomorrow?' he asked.

'No, I . . . erm . . . I've got another engagement,' Vinales told the doctor apologetically.

Withers, who had no burning desire to fly into harm's way, was philosophical about leading the reserve crew. He discussed the merits of the decision with them all. It cut both ways: Reeve might be the guinea pig, but he would at least enjoy an element of surprise. The co-pilot, Pete Taylor, agreed with his Captain – if they didn't go on this one, at least they were *guaranteed* to live to fight another day. There might not, after all, even be a second mission. Hugh Prior, Withers' tough, experienced AEO, disagreed. He rather wished his Captain had volunteered. All things considered, the first raid was, he was sure, the one that would give them their best chances of survival.

The VC10 was routed to Ascension via Banjul and Dakar. On board the packed transport jet, Monty sat next to Mel James. The two men took a notebook and tried to plan for their arrival. Since leaving Waddington they'd barely had time to think. After two weeks completely absorbed by the Vulcan work-up, the organized chaos at Brize had been eye-opening. A WRAF had asked Monty if the kit he was requesting was for Op CORPORATE.

'You can't say that, it's secret!' Monty hissed.

She patiently explained that *everyone and everything* at Brize was part of CORPORATE. Monty's head was spinning from the pace of it and, once on board the VC10, he and Mel James found it difficult to know where to begin.

'What do you think we should do?' Monty ventured.

'No idea . . .' James told him.

They struggled on briefly before Monty put his notebook away and tried to get some sleep on the aircraft's cabin floor.

# Chapter 26

## 27 April 1982

A small team of armed police arrived at Gerald Cheek's house early in the afternoon of Tuesday the 27th. They were, they said, going to take the family away to the airport 'for their own safety'.

'Are we *all* going to go?' Cheek asked them, thinking of his two young daughters and his elderly parents.

The policemen said they were.

Fourteen people around Stanley had suffered similar visits that day – including two other families with young children. They were a mixed bunch that had in common a pro-British outlook matched in intensity by the strength of their anti-Argentinian feelings. Apparently they were upsetting the authorities – that was something at least – who wanted to remove them before anything really ugly happened.

Cheek called Carlos Bloomer-Reeve, the ex-head of the Stanley LADE office, the operation running the pre-invasion passenger service between the islands and Argentina. The unfortunate Air Force officer had been hurriedly recalled from a new posting in Germany to act as the friendly face of the occupation. Bloomer-Reeve told Cheek that they didn't all have to go, but that he did. He could take his family with him to whatever lay ahead, or leave them behind. It was an appalling choice. Cheek had no idea what lay in store, but he did know what happened to people when armed police took you away in Argentina. He asked, hopefully, if he needed a passport. Alarmingly, he didn't. He fought a corrosive, not entirely irrational, fear that he was just going to be thrown out of whatever flew him out of the airfield. The goodbyes he shared with his parents, wife and daughters were traumatic and, as he was driven away by an armed escort, thoughts of them all raced through his mind. At BAM Malvinas, a green-and-brown camouflaged C-130 Hercules stood waiting on the pan with all four engines turning. *Hell*, he thought, *that's my next transport*. Over on the eastern side of the airfield he noticed a battery of anti-aircraft guns.

In The Vault at Waddington, the two Nav Radars, Mick Cooper and Bob Wright, bent over desks studying maps of East Falkland. They made an odd pair: Cooper, the untidy, red-haired veteran; Wright, the neat, earnest first tourist. They were in The Vault to be briefed by Simon Baldwin's Ops Team and to do their target study. Used to the beautifully prepared comprehensive target information, including photographs, from JARIC, the Joint Air Reconnaissance Intelligence Centre at RAF Brampton in Huntingdonshire, they were now provided with little more than a few old maps.

As far as they could, Simon Baldwin's Ops Team had tried to replicate the nuclear-training system the crews were familiar with, preparing go-bags for each crew member that contained all the information they needed to fly the mission. The flight plan had been hastily revised to an attack track that cut the runway and pop-up was at thirty miles from the target. While the Nav Plotter's charts were less than ideal, it was still the Nav Radar's planning that was made most difficult by the lack of detailed information.

The Vulcan's offset-bombing facility allowed the Nav Radar to release the bombs accurately without ever having to put the radar cross-hairs on the target itself. This was particularly useful at low level, where targets such as runways would not paint on the radar because they had no vertical extent. At the pre-flight planning stage, the Nav Radar would identify a feature on the map which he was confident *would* show on his radar. Then, by inputting the distance and location of these to the relative target into the NBS computer, he could aim at the offset and leave the machine to do the rest.

To do the offset planning, Waddington had been crying out for large-scale maps and photographs of the target area, but none was available. The Falklands had never featured on JARIC's list of concerns. The Ops Team had to make do with copies of an elderly 1:250,000 map, and these were not of a sufficiently large scale to show potentially good offsets like air traffic control towers. Two jetties were marked on the maps around Cape Pembroke, but were they wood, steel or concrete? That would affect their radar return. Given the age of the maps, were they even still there?

The Ops Team were forced to go back to basics, and use geographical features like Mengeary Point, Cape Pembroke, Ordnance Point and Eagle Headland – where land and sea meet. And even these apparently reliable features were less than ideal as bomb release offsets because they moved with the changing tides. With luck, given the medium altitude of the bomb-run, the Nav Radars would be able to paint the runway itself and place their cross-hairs over the target. That, though, was no more than a possibility and certainly not something upon which they could hang the success of the mission.

The Nav Radar would also have to set the stick spacing for the bombs. Since the targeting conference in the Station Commander's office, the Ops Team had discovered that the optimum setting on the 90-Way bomb control unit was 0.24 seconds between bombs. This translated at ground level into fifty-four yards between each bomb. But although the runway was only forty yards wide, there was no danger of missing completely because the Vulcan wouldn't be flying at 90 degrees to it. Rather than having a target forty yards across, the 35-degree angle of the cut meant the potential target increased to seventy-six yards. If two bombs straddled the runway perfectly, each would land well within the opposite edges of the paved surface. The craters, plus heave, would rip out each side of the runway. Baldwin's planners were fortunate; they had a 90-Way setting that meant they didn't have to hit the centreline to put the strip out of action.

In the normal scheme of things crews weren't allowed even to discuss their targets with other crews. The restricted access to The Vault was absolute. As the CORPORATE crews refined their attack plans, the target planning room continued to be where the rest of the Vulcan force planned the nuclear mission that was, for the next few months at least, still declared to NATO. The AARIs, although now joining the Vulcan crews on the attack itself, weren't cleared to enter. It didn't seem right, and Pete Standing, attached to John Reeve's crew, was quietly taken aside and filled in on the details of the discussions taking place on the other side of the door.

Throughout the day, other preparations were made for the deployment to Ascension. Careful not to miss a trick, John Reeve and his crew looked into whether they were entitled to some sort of tropical allowance. The Falklands might be on the edge of the Antarctic Circle, but Ascension looked promising. Reeve himself qualified for a pittance to re-rank his KDs, khaki drill tropical kit, but Mick Cooper struck gold. Having left the Air Force before rejoining, he was entitled to hundreds of pounds to renew the whole lot. That sort of cash, he baited his crewmates, was going to pay for a fantastic new TV and video.

Reeve ran round the station seeing what he could cadge out of different departments to make the deployment more comfortable. The sports centre were happy to send them down to Ascension with whatever they could spare. He had less success at the library.

'You'll have to sign the books out individually and each of you can only have two.'

Reeve was incredulous. 'Let's get this right. The station's going to war and you're telling me you can't help?' He didn't have the time or energy to argue and turned on his heel, muttering darkly about the librarian being a stickler for rules.

*

'Who the fuck are you?'

'Squadron Leader Montgomery, sir.'

'What the fuck are you doing here?'

'Vulcans, sir.'

'Sort yourselves out, son. I haven't got time for you. I don't know why the fucking hell you're here and I don't know what you're fucking well going to do, but get on with it.' Captain Bob McQueen, RN, greeted all new arrivals to Wideawake with equal warmth and Monty was no exception. But for all the cultivated prickliness that quickly had him labelled 'The Admiral' by the RAF contingent, there was method in his madness. While Jerry Price was the Senior RAF Officer, McQueen ran the British show on Ascension. It was McQueen to whom Bill Bryden had handed his letter raising doubts about whether Wideawake could supply the Vulcans with fuel. Since early April, Bryden had watched him keep the entire operation together, deftly winning the trust and support of the large St Helenian work force already on the island. But with even basic requirements like water and sanitation just a breakdown away from collapse, it was understandable if strangers weren't exactly welcomed with open arms. He needed to be relentless and ruthless in trying to keep numbers down. One unfortunate padre, flown in on more than one occasion to provide spiritual support, was each time deemed surplus to requirements and sent straight home on the next flight.

Monty was struck by just how well set up the Victor contingent seemed to be. He'd only been on the island for a couple of hours, but the desk he'd been allocated in the corner of the tent still seemed rather unimpressive by comparison. While Mel James' technicians made contact with their counterparts from Bill Lloyd's Victor engineering detachment, a Sherpa van drove him and his co-pilot, Bill Perrins, north to Two Boats to their accommodation.

Named after the two wooden boats upended in the nineteenth century to provide shade for those traipsing up and down Green Mountain, the village was no more than a handful of buildings put up in the 1960s to house BBC families.

From the settlement, perched 850 feet above sea level, three miles east of Georgetown, the two Vulcan pilots could see beyond hard black rivers of lava to English Bay, where the 'Great White Whale', P&O's flagship *Canberra*, sat at anchor alongside a few stray warships. The accommodation was as spartan as the views were spectacular. One half of the dormitory block already housed RAF Hercules crews, off duty, drinking and noisy. Monty and Perrins got to work sweeping out the other half. *Twenty people with one toilet and two sinks – this is going to be bloody awful,* he thought. No windows – at least there'd be fresh air. The two of them did their best to make it presentable, before Perrins finished it off with a hand-drawn sign of a man with his arm chopped off. If they were doing something those stuck at Waddington would give their right arm for, their hovel, it seemed only fitting, should become 'The Right Arm Hotel'.

The Flight Planning room at RAF Waddington lay in the heart of the Ops block. Electrical cabling inside metal pipes ran across the walls and ineffective air-conditioning vents hung from the high ceilings. Below them, eight wide wooden desks faced each other. Each redecoration was simply layered on top of what had been there before. The thick magnolia paint smothered what had once been a brass loudspeaker grill in a wooden box fixed above the main entrance.

But the fact that each member of the three Vulcan crews had just been issued with a Browning 9mm automatic pistol meant that the comfortable familiarity of the scene was skewed. This was something none of them had really considered. It brought into sharp focus that the training was over. Although each had an annual proficiency check to make sure he knew his way round the weapon, carrying one outside the range was a different feeling altogether. Most of them reckoned that they were more likely to be a danger to themselves than anyone else. And while Hugh Prior thought he saw a flash of excitement on the face of his co-pilot, Pete Taylor, the gun offered him no comfort at all. With a thousand angry Argentinians running towards you, he thought, a few rounds in a sidearm were unlikely to calm them down – *especially* if you'd just tried to bomb them. He wondered whether it might be of some use trying to kill food, but that was bordering on the ridiculous. After all, it was difficult to actually hit *anything* with a Browning 9mm . . .

The crews spent the afternoon preparing for the nine-hour flight to Ascension. With two hours to go until their scheduled departure, John Reeve was becoming concerned that they had an intelligence briefing to sit through and they hadn't yet even begun flight-planning. It wasn't as if it was straightforward. Three fully laden Vulcans were leaving Waddington, joining up with the Victor tankers and only when the first refuelling was successful would the third Vulcan, included as an airborne reserve, return.

'Don't worry, John,' he was appeased, 'you don't need to, it's all been done by computer by Group.'

*Wow . . . computers*, he thought wearily, *that's a new one.* After the pre-flight brief, Reeve left Don Dibbens to check the figures and joined his backseaters in aircrew feeder.

The Catering Squadron had pulled out all the stops. Nothing was too much trouble. No formica this time: all the tables were laid with white tablecloths. Reeve sat down with Mick Cooper and Barry Masefield. Cooper had already signed for the bombs. He'd been out to the jet with the armourers to check that the fusing and arming wires were all connected and the safety pins in place. The bombs had been properly decorated with messages like 'A present from Waddington' and 'If found, return to Port Stanley'. Now he was tucking hungrily into a fillet steak, served blue, just the way he liked it. Cooper's eating habits were well known, but at least watching him devour raw meat was better than having to inhale the stench from his cheese and onion sandwiches in a cramped cockpit. Back in the Ops Room, the co-pilots had finally been given the flight plans.

The bombers stood ready to go on the dispersal pans: XM598, XM607 and McDougall's reserve, XM597. Each was fully fuelled and each modified to bombing competition standard. They had the Twin Carousel INS that would keep them on track over thousands of miles of featureless ocean. The Dash 10 ECM pod hung from the wing on its newly fashioned pylon. As a final measure to reduce their vulnerability, individual squadron markings had been painted over, and the entire underside of the bombers had been resprayed in dark sea grey to camouflage them against the murky South Atlantic skies. In their cavernous bomb bays, they carried twenty-one 1,000lb high-explosive iron bombs armed with 487 fuses and 117 ballistic tails, each one capable of smashing a crater sixty feet wide and thirty feet deep in whatever was unlucky enough to be underneath it when it landed.

But in the Ops block, the flight planning was coming badly unstuck. Fuel management and planning were the responsibility of the co-pilots, Pete Taylor and Don Dibbens. Each of them worked on the figures separately, and each kept hitting the same brick wall. Taylor worked on the fuel plan with his crew's AARI, Dick Russell. Whichever way they ran them they kept getting the same result. Taylor and Russell called over their Captain, Martin Withers.

'We've got a big problem,' Russell told him.

Withers went through it himself and reached the same conclusion: *This isn't going to happen.*

Barry Masefield came in from the feeder. Reeve had suggested his AEO go and see where their co-pilot had got to. It was immediately clear to him that something was up. By now the crews were comparing notes. And Don Dibbens looked ashen.

'What's the problem?' Masefield asked.

'We can't get there.'

'What are you talking about, we can't get there?'

'The refuelling plan we've got – we're going to fall out of the sky before we get to Ascension. You'd better go and tell John . . .'

Dick Russell went through it again with Pete Standing, the other AARI, but the calculations remained stubbornly unworkable. After a nine-hour flight they were going to be landing with a reserve of barely 4,000lb, 10,000lb short of what they should have. Such a tiny amount spread throughout the Vulcan's fourteen tanks counted as vapours. With relatively inaccurate fuel gauges and Ascension lying at least a thousand miles from the nearest diversion field, they were setting themselves up for disaster before they'd even started. Questions began bouncing around the Ops Room: *Can we get another Victor in? Can we move the tanker bracket up or down?*

They were clutching at straws.

The bulk of the thinly stretched Victor tanker force had already deployed to Wideawake along with the most frontline crews. The two Vulcans would be flying south to Ascension supported by inexperienced tanker crews. The possibilities for shuffling things around at this late stage were severely limited, to say the least.

*Great*, thought Simon Baldwin as he'd watched the plan unravel. John Laycock was in his office, talking with AOC 1 Group Air Vice-Marshal Mike Knight, oblivious to it all. *Now I've got to go and tell them . . .*

Baldwin walked around the corridors to the office; the Station Commander's door was ajar. He knocked and went in.

'Please don't shoot the messenger,' he said, 'but the Victors can't give us enough fuel to get to Ascension. In fact, the Vulcans are likely to fall into the sea several hundred miles short of Ascension.'

When John Laycock was told he looked like he'd rather have been anywhere else on earth than standing next to his boss, the AOC, hearing the news that his Vulcans were going nowhere that night.

'How could we have possibly overlooked something like this?' Knight flared – he, after all, was the one who was going to have to pick up the telephone and tell Northwood – but it was momentary. There was no mileage in apportioning blame. Knight quickly realized that everyone was too busy to bear the brunt. It was a cock-up, certainly, but nothing could be done other than postpone the deployment until the following day.

He passed the message up through the chain of command through gritted teeth. The launch had been scrubbed.

Once the decision was made people speculated about who'd been at fault and where it had arisen, but it wasn't easy to pin down. What *was* clear was that the planners at Bawtry had been working with completely fanciful fuel consumption figures for the Vulcan. They'd certainly asked the question: how much fuel does a Vulcan burn? And someone had answered it. But the whole exchange had been too vague. The answer is that it depends. The fuel plan had been worked out using the average fuel consumption of a Vulcan cruising at high level – about 10,000lb an hour. And that bore very little relation to what the three heavily laden bombers taking off from Waddington were going to use.

The difficulties of organizing large mixed formations with complex air-to-air refuelling plans had revealed themselves. And had hinted that at the heart of the planning was a problem which, while it had caused little more than delay and annoyance today, might have far more serious repercussions in the days to come.

*Holy cow!*, thought Monty when he saw the first draft of the refuelling plan for the mission itself. To get one Vulcan to the Falklands and back was, it was first thought, going to take *twelve* Victors. The RAF had never done anything like this before. Jerry Price had received the Op Order from Northwood earlier in the day and immediately got Trevor Sitch's planning team to work. They'd produced a model that worked like an inverted pyramid. A large formation would take off together from Wideawake and turn south. At four points along the route, the formation would split into two groups: those continuing south and those returning to Ascension. Before the latter turned for home, they would fill the tanks of those continuing. From each of these refuelling brackets, a reduced total of fully fuelled jets would fly on towards the target. The Vulcan was at the pyramid's apex. And key to the success of the whole exercise was the Vulcan's fuel consumption. The Victor planners knew the capabilities of their aircraft inside out. They needed watertight information from someone with comparable knowledge of the Vulcan. So they asked Monty: 'What do you expect the Vulcan fuel consumption to be?' Monty and Bill Perrins got to work. Using the new photocopier, they copied and enlarged the fuel graphs from the Vulcan Operating Data Manual. The big delta's normal maximum take-off weight was 204,000lb. With full tanks, the bombs and the Dash 10 pod, the weight was going to be a lot higher than that. Off the graph. The ODM simply didn't include the figure they needed – a Vulcan wasn't supposed to try to take off at that weight. The curve on the fuel consumption graph they had was exponential, rather than linear. Monty and his co-pilot tried to extrapolate a figure from where the curve on the graph ended, and estimated 13,500lb per hour. They passed this figure on to the Victor planning team to weave into their refuelling plan and wondered why it had fallen to them to figure it out. *What*, thought Monty, *about the resources available at HQ 1 Group?*

Then, just after midnight, news came through that the Vulcans weren't leaving Waddington that night.

'Monty, it's off,' Jerry Price told them. None of them was entirely clear on the reasons for the change in plan.

'What the bloody hell are you doing here?'

Sharon Cooper's reaction to her husband's unexpected reappearance reflected that of all the wives. The goodbyes hadn't been at all easy either. All the couples had held each other a little tighter. Many of them had babies and small children. Don Dibbens' wife Janice was five months pregnant – and had her leg in plaster after dislocating her knee. She knew her husband was flying into danger. Saying goodbye once had been upsetting. To have to do it again was going to be much worse. Barry Masefield's wife Gwyneth was distraught when he arrived back at their house in Hayington. Gareth, their young son, had persistent, serious health problems. The whole family had been under an enormous amount of emotional strain already, but over the two weeks he'd been training Masefield had retreated into himself, had even stopped interrupting during *Coronation Street*. It was obvious something was wrong, but he couldn't tell Gwyneth what was causing his anxiety. Now she had her husband back, but she knew she was going to have to go through it all again the next morning.

'This is silly,' announced Hugh Prior, 'we've all said our goodbyes.' He'd already told his wife Caroline, 'Don't you worry, it will be all right,' and kissed his baby daughter, Tara. He lived on the station, a few hundred yards from the Ops block, but he couldn't face going through it all again. He joined Pete Taylor and Dick Russell in the Mess. And, with his wife in Australia, there was no reason for Martin Withers not to join them. He, too, opted to sleep in the Mess, deciding to forsake the lonely charms of his Lincoln maisonette. The four of them stayed up drinking, putting the world to rights.

Mick Cooper shuffled in to his house, trying to explain himself to Sharon. 'Small foul-up,' he said sheepishly, 'only temporary . . .' Then he closed the door behind him.

# Chapter 27

## 29 April 1982

Television camera crews were there for the occasion. Inside Waddington's number 3 hangar IX Squadron was finally disbanding as a Vulcan squadron. Almost exactly twenty years earlier, at RAF Coningsby, they had become the first operator of the then ground-breaking new Avro delta. The building holding the parade had an industrial age feel. Thick layers of dark-green paint tarted up the exposed ironwork. Behind enormous sliding doors, a large audience sat under bunting and flags to watch the ceremony. Any sadness at the famous unit's passing was tempered by its immediate rebirth as a Tornado squadron. The squadron standard was being passed straight on to a new team, flying the state-of-the-art new pan-European strike jet. There were speeches and reminiscences. Afterwards, the throng would move to number 2 hangar for a reception followed by lunch in the Officers' Mess. No one could accuse them of not properly marking the occasion. John Laycock sat watching proceedings. A little before ten o'clock, though, he managed to slip away to the control tower to oversee the departure of his three Vulcans.

It wasn't straightforward. They were leaving in strict radio silence. And although their 301 series Rolls-Royce Olympus engines had been uprated to run at 103 per cent rather than the usual 97.5 restriction, the jets were overloaded with fuel and bombs for the first time. A green Verey flare was fired to signal engine start. Either side of the Runway Two One threshold, on Alpha and Bravo dispersals, the Vulcans came to life. The weather was fine, but the wind was tricky. Every extra knot of wind speed down the runway would make the take-off safer and now its direction was marginal, not really favouring either runway. Any tailwind would only make it harder to get off the ground. Laycock had to make a decision but, as the three bombers waited, he was caught in two minds. Should he have the jets taxi the entire length of the runway and take off down Runway Zero Three, or should he stick with the plan, Runway Two One. He remembered a calculation made when he was flying Victors in the 1960s. Taxi too far, too heavy, and main tyres were going to blow. If it happened now the consequences didn't bear thinking about. He stuck with Two One and another Verey flare signalled to the Captains that they could take off at their discretion.

Cleared to depart, Martin Withers pushed the four throttles forward, increasing the engine rpm to 80 per cent. He checked the engine instruments and released the brakes. Once rolling he wound up to maximum power and 598 accelerated down the runway, while Nav Plotter Gordon Graham, eyes fixed to the air speed indicator, called the speeds: '60 . . . 80 . . . 100 . . . 110 . . .'

The Waddington runway isn't flat. It features a hump beyond which, seen from the tower, it slopes away out of view. Laycock had never seen a Vulcan travel so far down the runway without leaving the ground. They were always away by the time they reached the hump. He watched as 598 disappeared down the slope, still, it seemed, glued to the ground.

'120 . . . 130 . . . 140 . . . 150,' Graham continued in the cockpit. 'Decision speed . . . Rotate.'

Withers pulled back on the big jet's fighter-style joystick, lifting the nose.

Despite its imposing bulk, a lightly loaded Vulcan leapt into the air like a giant balsa wood model caught in a gust of wind. No sooner had the nosewheel left the ground than the whole machine pointed skywards at 45 degrees to the ground. It was a trick that never failed to impress an audience.

This time, though, they staggered into the air, looking as if the sky could barely carry their weight. As well as fuel and bombs Reeve and Withers had a couple of other small disadvantages. Alongside the seven men crammed into the crew compartment – as well as the AARI, each aircraft also had a crew chief on board – both jets, like the Victors, carried one necessary last piece of new equipment: a chemical toilet. Then, in what little space was left, Martin Withers, worried about possible deprivation on Ascension, had squeezed in a large plastic homebrew bin filled with cans of McEwan's Export and bottles of whisky. John Reeve was also carrying extra weight. After getting wind of the pilot's fruitless visit to the station library, Waddington's Education Officer had made amends by dropping off a box of books with Reeve's ground crew. Without asking questions, they'd dutifully secreted them away in the Vulcan's nosewheel bay. Then didn't think to tell anyone.

John Laycock relaxed a little as he saw XM598 claw her way into the air, followed a minute later by Reeve in 607 then Neil McDougall's reserve XM597.

In number 3 hangar, some of the guests frowned as their ceremonial was disturbed by the distinctive howl and thunder of three Vulcans taking off in quick succession. The television cameras completely missed the real story: on the other side of the hangar wall, that distracting roar was the sound of heavily armed bombers leaving Britain to strike the first blow of the campaign to recapture the Falkland Islands.

Overhead Bedford, the Vulcans picked up their five Victor tankers and formed a loose 'Balbo' heading south-west towards Cornwall. As they flew high and radio-silent into the controlled airspace of London's Air Traffic Zone they caused a panic. Faced with an unidentified formation of eight aircraft appearing unannounced on their radar screens, controllers at London Air Traffic Control Centre in West Drayton hit the emergency button. The supervisor arrived quickly to soothe nerves, telling them not to worry about it, but didn't leave them any wiser as to what was going on. He'd been the only person warned that they were coming through.

A couple of hours later, the first refuelling was completed without incident. Reeve and Withers were safely on their way south past the Bay of Biscay towards the Azores and Neil McDougall turned for home. On the return flight, in an effort to disguise the deployment, he was forced to pretend to be a Victor and route back to Waddington via Marham's overhead – a complication he didn't think would fool anyone.

Simon Baldwin had done all he could. Relieved that they were finally on their way, he tried not to dwell on the possibility of something going wrong because of an oversight on his part. Had he missed something? He had confidence in the crews, but the planning, the modifications, the tactics . . . However, the Vulcans now belonged to Northwood HQ. The order to go would come from them. All he could do was try to follow developments as best he could.

At BAM Malvinas, engineers of the Argentine Army were working to improve the runway. Two hundred feet of steel matting was put down at the western end, which provided a marginally greater safety margin for the aircraft operating from the strip. Of greater significance was the effort to install arrestor gear at the same end. When the work was finished, wires would lie across the runway and could be caught by a hook trailed from the back of a landing aircraft, bringing it to a safe stop before the end of the Tarmac. The equipment worked in exactly the same way as the arrestor wires on the Argentine carrier *Veinticinco de Mayo* and would allow the Super Étendards and A-4Q Skyhawks of the Comando Aviación Naval Argentina to land at BAM Malvinas carrying stores in all weather conditions.

Near the Cable and Wireless building along the road between Stanley and the airfield, Grupo de Artillería de Defensa Aerea 601 sited their single Roland anti-aircraft missile unit. Because of its imposing, awkward size the Roland launch vehicle had been christened 'Incredible Hulk' or '*La*

*Chancha*' – 'The Pig' – by its operators. It hadn't been thought possible to transport it aboard an Air Force C-130, but somehow it had been done. The big transport's Captain had nothing but admiration for the men who'd managed to find a way of loading the missile system on board his plane. Their lateral thinking and commitment, he thought, reflected the incredible effort being made by the entire Fuerza Aérea Argentina.

The commander of the 601st, Lieutenant-Colonel Arias, knew that the Franco-German radar-guided twin launcher was the most capable weapon he had under his control. And by 29 April, despite the piecemeal, week-long deployment of his regiment's weapons systems, Roland was fully operational.

On this last, lethal component of the Argentine air defences the intelligence received by Simon Baldwin had been wrong.

# PART TWO

Ascension

*Major Campbell was succeeded [as Commandant of Ascension Island] by Lieutenant Colonel Nicolls. Upon the peculiar difficulties, the privations, the horrors with which they had to contend in the early formation, on such a spot, of an Establishment for civilised beings – and to Colonel Nicolls particularly – is praise due, for the untiring ardour with which he laboured to overcome the Hydra-headed obstacles he had to grapple with at every step. But his well-known energy achieved so much that the due chaos was beginning to take shape when . . . he gave over command to Captain Bate. This officer, after a brief illness, died in command. He was a kind-hearted, amiable man, who strove to do all the good in his power. While the island wore, unmitigated, its own native hideous aspect, – with all its disheartening privations, and the physical obstacles to improvement which every where met the eye, making improvement as it were hopeless, none appeared to envy the ruler such a scene of desolation, or to covet his place . . . The next appointed to the Command was Captain Tincklar. An active, upright Officer, very zealous – perhaps too much so, for his constitution, it would seem, did not long resist the pressure of the anxieties, or the responsibilities of his situation. He was soon taken ill, and, after a short illness, he died.*

From *Ascension Island: A Partial Military History*,
thought to be written by Captain Thomas Dwyer, RM,
Commandant of Ascension Island 1842–4

# Chapter 28

## 29 April 1982

No one actually briefed Bill Bryden on British plans, but at noon on the 29th, when Air Vice-Marshal George Chesworth arrived by VC10 on top of a cargo of cans of Coca-Cola and beer, the American was sure this signalled a change in tempo. Air Commander Sir John Curtiss had sent his number two from Northwood to make sure those running the bombing operation had, as he put it, *their ducks in line*. Bryden's suspicions were confirmed that evening when he watched as the two Vulcans of Reeve and Withers landed on Wideawake's Runway One Four. He'd seen pictures of them in magazines, but this was the first time he'd seen them up close. *Beautiful aeroplanes*, he thought, *and it looks like they can do a job too*.

Monty watched them come in from the tower, then hurried down to the pan to meet the crews as they disembarked into the evening warmth.

'Couldn't have lasted another minute,' Mick Cooper gasped as he lit his first cigarette in nine hours. One hour or nine, it didn't matter: that first lungful of smoke was always just in the nick of time. Unlike the good old days, when captains had been known to flick on the autopilot at 500 feet and light a cigar, the V-force had been a non-smoking airline for a number of years now and Cooper bore the burden stoically.

The crews were struck immediately by the buzz of activity around them, by hills, tucked close to the airfield, that rose like sandcastles into the dark, and by the tents. There were olive green military tents everywhere, pitched straight on to the dust. The entire RAF operation, they realized, was run from under canvas. John Reeve liked it immediately. *No admin, no bullshit*, he thought, *just aircrews and engineers*. Barry Masefield looked around at the dozen RAF Victors packed close to each other around the airfield. It was an impressive, reassuring sight. *With this lot we're going to win*, he thought, feeding his confidence with the spectacle. The two Victor squadrons, 55 and 57, had already customized the entrance to their Ops tent with a board that read '5557 MASH Air Battle Fleet' in a nod to Hawkeye *et al*. Visually, at any rate, the collection of tents meant that the comparison was a good one. The Vulcan detachment would have to find a legend of their own.

Monty said he'd take them up to where they were sleeping after a short debrief. Before leaving the airfield, John Reeve needed to find Engineering Chief Mel James. He thought there was a problem with 607's fuel system. The number 1 tank didn't seem to be topping off. It would need looking at. Reeve didn't want any nagging worries about the jet he'd be flying. If there were any doubts, he'd elect to fly Primary in 598, the Vulcan Martin Withers had flown in. Since coming in on the VC10, James had been joined by the rest of his thirty-strong engineering team, who were transported with their equipment, in rather less comfort, aboard two C-130s. Included in their number was a technician from Honington in case anything happened to the unfamiliar Dash 10 ECM pod. James had tried to come prepared for all eventualities. When Reeve spoke to him, he was already casting an eye over his two new charges. As the bomb bay doors swung open he checked their contents. Condensation from the cold-soaked bomb casings – formed as the Vulcans had descended rapidly from the sub-zero air above 40,000 feet into the humid, tropical atmosphere on Ascension – splashed on to the warm Tarmac.

As James got to work on the two Vulcans, the aircrews climbed into a Sherpa van for the short journey to Two Boats to check in to the Right Arm Hotel. Sadly, there was no real evidence of the effort Monty and Bill Perrins had put into trying to make it look presentable and the reaction was predictable.

'What a shitheap!' someone goaded.

'I've just spent two fucking days sweeping this out, you arsehole!' retorted Perrins.

But even Monty thought, looking around: *This looks terrible*. And it smelt like a Gents. The sleeping bags seemed to have been made under an MoD contract by prisoners who had relieved themselves into the finished product before rolling it up and sending it on its way. It wasn't going to be a problem in any case. Two Boats was only a degree or so cooler than sea level and, in the scramble to get the kit to Ascension, the crews had been issued with Arctic bags. As they milled around deciding who was going to sleep where, the Reeve crew turned on their co-pilot.

'Don, you'll sleep in the kitchen next to the fridge because you're such a noisy bastard.' Dibbens' snoring was well known and only taking bold action was going to make sure that the sleeping arrangements didn't become any more unpleasant than they already were. With Dibbens safely stuck out of earshot, it was time to get something to eat. They barrelled out of the dusty dormitory to get some food at an outdoor field kitchen set up in the village. Mick Cooper had said the food must be really good.

'*Why?*' they asked him.

'Because a thousand flies can't be wrong . . .'

Martin Withers and his crew were noticeably more relaxed than their counterparts on the Primary crew. They, after all, were going to get a good night's sleep, then fly as far as the first refuelling bracket before returning for another good night's sleep while Reeve and his crew flew south to launch their attack. Unconcerned about the next day they dumped their stuff, changed out of their flightsuits and headed off in search of a drink. After the disappointment of the accommodation and food – and his fears that Ascension might be dry – Martin

Withers was cheered to discover that at least there was somewhere they could finish off the evening with a beer. There was, after all, something to celebrate. Tomorrow was AARI Dick Russell's birthday. They ended up in a bar called The Seniors' Mess. None of them had any idea who 'The Seniors' were, but their hospitality was outstanding and the Vulcan crew drank enthusiastically – fuelled by a belief that, if it took their bodies an hour to deal with each drink, they had nothing whatsoever to worry about. The SAS were there too, keeping themselves to themselves. The RAF officers were impressed to note that the troopers would return from the bar carrying whole slabs of beer and that each one appeared to be for personal consumption. At midnight the celebrations for Russell's fiftieth began. The six men found what they imagined were the last few bottles of South African white wine and loudly toasted their new crew member's health. Drunk and happy, they finally got their heads down at 2 a.m.

As the aircrews drank and slept through the night, Mel James and his team worked to ensure the two bombers were ready to go the following day. Just after midnight they sent a message estimating they'd be ready by 0500. By 0300, both 598 and 607 were accepted as functional, fuelled to 90 per cent and left, watched over by a guard of Royal Marines grateful to be off the crowded *Canberra* for a few days.

Despite fine weather, the atmosphere in Stanley had darkened since the town's gymnasium had been commandeered by Argentine special forces. When pressed, Carlos Bloomer-Reeve admitted that the authority of these hard, professional-looking troops superseded all other. After dark, between the hours of 5 p.m. and 7 a.m., a strict curfew was imposed on the civilian population, who also now had to carry ID papers whenever they went outside. And these, it was announced, would be replaced by new documents issued by the military government. Telephone lines were disconnected to any household who were members of the FIDF and orders were issued that the windows of all homes were to be blacked out. The soldiers took to cruising malevolently around the streets of the little capital on brand-new Kawasaki motorbikes, short-barrelled sub-machine guns strapped loosely across their backs.

# Chapter 29

## 30 April 1982

The US government came down publicly on the side of the British on Friday 30th. After weeks and thousands of miles of shuttle diplomacy, Ronald Reagan's Secretary of State, General Al Haig, finally conceded defeat. The decision to abandon a neutral stance, let alone impose economic sanctions against Argentina, hadn't been a foregone conclusion. But by suggesting that Haig's final peace plan be put first to the junta, Margaret Thatcher's War Cabinet shrewdly assumed the moral high ground at the death of America's efforts to broker a settlement. While Haig's proposals were totally unacceptable to the British, by giving Argentina the opportunity – which she took – to reject them first, the British were able to claim good faith. Because of the Argentine rejection, there was no need for the British to reveal their hand. As a result, they could legitimately claim that they bore no responsibility for the breakdown of negotiations.

With what seemed to be the final restraint on British military action removed, Argentine forces on the Falklands expected the first British attacks to arrive at any time. Also waiting, steaming less than a hundred miles outside the 200-mile Maritime Exclusion Zone around the islands, were two Argentine naval Task Groups: to the north-west, the *Vienticinco de Mayo* with her squadron of A-4Q Skyhawks, escorted by four destroyers; to the south-west was the cruiser

*General Belgrano*, accompanied by two ex-US Navy 'Allen M. Sumner' Class destroyers armed with MM38 Exocet missiles.

Flight Lieutenant Dick Russell woke on his birthday with a hangover. Nearby, on another of the metal camp beds in the Two Boats accommodation, Bob Wright was also awake. He really could have done without being shaken from his slumber, only to be told he needed to go back to sleep: *Get some rest.* Along with Russell and the rest of the men from the two Vulcan crews, he closed his eyes and tried to get back to sleep.

Tonight was the night.

At ten to nine, down at Wideawake, Jerry Price received the Air Tasking message for Operation BLACK BUCK, the code-name given to the mission to bomb Stanley airfield. The message added detail to the Op Order of the previous day, but it was still only a statement of intent, not yet an order to go. All being well, that would follow. Between now and then, Price had to make sure that there was nothing that would prevent them carrying out their orders. Half an hour later, two more Victors arrived from the UK, turning off the long runway towards the crowded pan to complete the force he needed for BLACK BUCK. Fourteen. More than half of the RAF's entire tanker fleet. He was going to need every one of them.

Seated on canvas-backed chairs around folding wood and metal tables, the Victor Ops team, Trevor Sitch, Barry Ireland, David Davenall and Colin Haigh, laboured with Jerry Price over the refuelling plan. The first draft of the previous day provided the template. Now they needed to make it as accurate and predictable as it could be. It was a fiendishly complicated task that relied on pens, paper, performance tables and slide rules. Their only digital assistance was from a £3.99 pocket calculator bought from Swaffham market.

Using tried and tested procedures evolved over many years at Marham, recently enhanced by the experience of the reconnaissance missions to South Georgia, they constructed an elaborate plan with one simple goal: to move as much fuel as far south as possible.

Eleven Victors and two Vulcans would take off together, each jet part of a White, Red or Blue section. The White and Red sections were Victor four-ships; the Blue section, three Victors and two Vulcans. Two of the Victors and one of the Vulcans in the Blue section were airborne reserves. If anything went wrong with any of the other jets, the reserves would simply take their place in the formation. At designated lines of latitude along the route south known as brackets, fuel would be transferred from those returning to Ascension to those continuing south. At the first bracket, four Victors, having passed on their fuel, would return, along with the two airborne reserve Victors and the reserve Vulcan. A short while later, another Victor would again top up the Vulcan before returning to Wideawake. At the next bracket two more Victors would turn back after filling the tanks of the three remaining aircraft: two Victors and the Vulcan. There would be one further Victor–Victor transfer before just one Victor and the Vulcan were left flying south together. Less than a thousand miles from the Falklands, that long-slot Victor would refuel the Vulcan then turn north. After the bomb-run, at a rendezvous about 300 miles east of Rio de Janeiro, the returning Vulcan would be met by two waiting Victors that would transfer enough fuel for the bomber to make it back to Ascension. One of these Victors was, again, an airborne reserve in case for any reason the primary Victor couldn't refuel the Vulcan. Given the frequency with which the HDU equipment failed, it was a necessary precaution.

Thought was given to the composition of each section. Working with the head of the Victor detachment, Alan Bowman, the Ops Team spread age and experience throughout the formation. The longer-range slots were allocated to those with experience on the maritime radar reconnaissance missions and White, Red and Blue were each assigned a section leader: a squadron Flight Commander or CO. It was their responsibility to make decisions once the jets were out of effective radio range of Red Rag Control, the name adopted by the Ops Team. It hadn't been the tag they'd wanted. Marham's station crest featured a black bull and that had been their first choice. Discovering the mission was codenamed BLACK BUCK put paid to that. So, with a satisfying display of lateral thinking, Black Bull became Red Rag.

Over three hours, they had produced what was, on paper, a masterpiece of elegant, detailed planning that meant the Vulcan, as it ran in on its target, would be burning fuel that had already passed through five other aircraft. The amount of fuel transferred at each of fourteen planned contacts was calculated precisely. But, as Waddington had discovered two days earlier, the plan was only as good as the figures on which those calculations were based.

At one o'clock, Tux and his crew gathered with another fifty Victor pilots, Navigators and AEOs to be briefed on the re-fuelling plan. Jerry Price joined them alongside Air Vice-Marshal Chesworth. As Trevor Sitch spoke, using an overhead projector sitting on a large cardboard box to illustrate his words, Tux took copious notes – the first to confess that he'd never been blessed with the best of memories, this wasn't unusual for him. But he was struck by the complexity of the operation. He knew it was uncharted territory. Others ate from packed lunch boxes while they listened. At the end of the forty-minute briefing, they took down the details from sheets of A1 paper pinned to wooden boards then suspended from the frame of the tent by white rope. They learnt which section they'd be flying as part of and where they fitted in within that. Each crew had a specific role: long-slot, short-out, long-out, first reserve, second reserve, standby crew.

They filled their notebooks, each man trying to illustrate the mass of detail in the way that best made sense of it. The safety of the whole formation depended on them recording it faith-fully, then being able to interpret their own notes without confusion. While Tux scribbled, his AEO, Mick Beer, took down radio frequencies and call signs. Each jet had two: one to communicate with other aircraft in formation, one for Red Rag Control.

The one, vital missing ingredient was the weather. So that it was as up to date as it could be, the Met report wouldn't arrive until as late in the day as possible. But without accurate information on wind speed and direction a final flight plan was impossible. Until they had that, they couldn't lock it down.

For the rest of the day the Victor crews tried to prepare for the night that would follow: looking over the detail of the BLACK BUCK plan; checking their equipment; eating; sleeping.

At 14.42, an hour after the Victor briefing had broken up, George Chesworth received a message from Sir John Curtiss at Northwood: *Take-off to be 2300 hours Zulu tonight, subject to refined timing with receipt of updated weather forecasting. Execute will be sent flash.* Half an hour later the order came through.

```
From Air Commander
Operation BLACK BUCK
Execute op BLACK BUCK 1 AW HQ 18Gp AAAA/19F/KAA
300853Z APR 82
Time on target 010700Z May repeat 010700Z May.
Delays in mission launch are acceptable
providing that TOT is not later than 010900Z
May 1982
```

The mission to bomb the runway at Port Stanley airfield was on. A fleet of V-bombers would launch from Ascension late that night to deliver a Vulcan over East Falkland inside the window specified by Curtiss: 0700 to 0900 Zulu, or GMT. BAM Malvinas was going to be hit before dawn, between 0400 and 0600 local time.

The metal skins of the Vulcans and Victors were hot to the touch. Their dull green and grey camouflage, useless against the scorched brown and rust of Ascension's landscape, soaked up the heat of the equatorial sun. Throughout the afternoon, ground crew in khaki shorts and desert boots swarmed around them, checking and rechecking the airframes. When the temperature dropped later in the day, all of the jets had their tanks filled. Those of them parked on the Tarmac side of the pan were towed forward out of their ruts ready to be checked by reserve flight crews.

During the 1950s and 1960s, when the V-force represented the front line of Britain's nuclear deterrent, the bombers would be kept 'combat-ready'. Price, familiar with it from his own time spent on the Victor QRA, reverted to the old approach. All the pre-flight checks had been done up to the point where the aircraft was made live for engine start. Crews could be airborne fifteen minutes from the time they arrived at the jet. Tonight, with the success of the operation dependent on the serviceability of the whole formation, it made sense to adopt the old Cold War technique. Any problems, Price hoped, could be discovered and dealt with early. He ordered all the jets to be 'combat-readied' in the hours before crew-in, scheduled for 2100 that evening. Monty and the Ops crew took responsibility for the two Vulcans. They started up the engines on both and ran through the checklist: no problems. Dave Stenhouse, Monty's Nav Radar, checked the bombs, removing the safety pins from the thousand-pounders hanging in both bomb bays: five per bomb, 210 pins in total. Vulcans 598 and 607 were 'combat-ready'.

All the time, Price and the Ops Team continued to examine and refine the refuelling plan. The last fuel transfers, those taking place barely 300 miles off the Argentine coast, they decided, would be done in strict radio silence. RT needed to be kept to a minimum throughout, but so close to the operational area it was essential. Their main worry, though, remained fuel. Especially where the Vulcan was concerned.

Monty and Bill Perrins had been checking the refuelling plan against their own figures. By their calculations, if the refuelling failed at the third or fourth bracket – and their own experience in training showed that there was every possibility it would – the Vulcan couldn't make it back to Ascension and would have to try for the Rio diversion. To ignore this would mean breaking the cardinal rule of air-to-air refuelling: that the receiver should never be dependent on the success of a fuel transfer for survival. Frustration at the imprecision that seemed to surround the Vulcan's fuel burn was growing amongst the Victor contingent trying to plan BLACK BUCK. While Monty and Perrins were struggling to fill the gaps, Price realized that the Vulcan figures were overly optimistic and took action. The plan's success couldn't be dependent on carefully measuring out only that fuel Monty and Perrins deemed was necessary. To compensate for the uncertainty, the planning team decided to fill the Vulcan's tanks at every transfer. But the unchangeable constant in any recalculation was that there was only a finite amount of fuel within the formation. Every decision they made regarding the fuel had repercussions elsewhere. And this one meant that the two long-slot Victors flown by Bob Tuxford and Steve Biglands – the two tankers responsible for the most distant refuellings – might not make it back to Wideawake. So Price introduced another detail: a terminal airborne tanker, or TAT, a Victor that would hold station one hour out from Ascension on the long-slots' inbound track. The TAT would wait there for three-quarters of an hour at 29,000 feet ready to relay the gasping long-slot jets home.

After re-examining the figures, Monty told Price that the Vulcans *could* recover to Ascension if transfer three failed after all. This didn't fill Price with confidence. The whole refuelling plan felt perilously like a house of cards. And there were now just four and a half hours until they launched.

The Vulcan crews themselves were unaware of the debate raging within the planning cell. Instead, they prepared themselves for the night ahead. They were too precious now to risk being poisoned by fish and salad from the field kitchens tonight. Instead they enjoyed the hospitality of the American commissary down near the airfield. It took the welcome form of New York steak, prime American beef, air-lifted in by the USAF. *I could get used to this*, thought Mick Cooper.

Martin Withers' crew were relaxed. They'd managed to sleep for most of the day without recourse to the Temazepam recommended by the Waddington doctor. Withers had never had a problem sleeping. Stress may have caused him to lose his appetite, but he could fall asleep on a log. Among Primary crew, only Cooper really seemed to be his old self. The others now, even the irrepressible John Reeve, were a little more subdued. By seven o'clock, both crews were down at the Wideawake airhead.

'THIS IS A SECRET BRIEFING,' announced the planner Trevor Sitch through a handheld megaphone at a volume that could be heard out at sea.

*It's not secret any more*, thought John Reeve, enjoying the irony.

'Right, gentlemen,' Sitch continued, 'the purpose of the exercise is to put a stick of bombs across Port Stanley airfield.'

Despite the volume, secrecy *was* an absolute priority. Because of the presence of the Soviet spy trawler *Zaporozhive* off the coast, RT traffic had been kept to a minimum all day. At 9 p.m. a telephone and telex blackout would be imposed. Even the weather was treated with suspicion. The flash signal handed out to the Vulcan crews providing details of the wind around the Falklands – light, south-west, becoming variable – was classified 'SECRET UK EYES BRAVO'.

Following the Victor crews' briefing on the fuel plan earlier in the day, the tent was littered with coffee cups, food wrappers and cigarette butts. Now, upwards of seventy V-bomber pilots, navigators and AEOs were sitting and listening, the legs of their folding chairs digging into the red cinder underneath them. Strengthening katabatic winds rolled down from Green Mountain whipping past the flapping canvas. Bare lightbulbs flickered above them. Monty looked around the packed tent. *It's like the Second World War*, he thought, *like El Alamein*. He wasn't the only one struck by the sense of history. There was also anticipation. Bob Tuxford relished the prospect of being part of an offensive force for the first time, a feeling sharpened by uncertainty. The tanker trash had long experience working together. Tux knew his own limitations, the Victor's and those of his colleagues. Waddington's *tin triangles* were an unknown element.

Martin Withers was mystified. Much of the refuelling briefing might as well have been in a foreign language. He just couldn't picture, in his mind's eye, how it would all work. Trevor Sitch explained the shape of the formation. It would be split into three sections, Red, White and Blue. To avoid the likelihood of a mid-air collision, the join-up plans were necessarily complex. As each section ferried out to the first refuelling bracket, it would be separated from the next by a 2,000-foot height interval. White formed up at 36,000 feet, Red at 34,000 feet and Blue at 32,000 feet. Within each section, 500-foot intervals separated the jets. Withers had understood that, but as the shape of the formation changed after the first wave of tankers returned home, then changed again after the second bracket, it became increasingly hard to follow. He wondered how, in radio silence, you were supposed to know who was refuelling whom. Withers leaned over to Dick Russell.

'Do you understand that?' he asked his AARI.

'I've got it,' Russell told him as he made notes on a piece of paper.

'OK, if you understand it – I don't – it's all yours . . .'

Happy to defer to the tanker man's expertise, Withers relaxed. He wasn't going all the way and there didn't seem any point in him trying to wrap his head around it.

The crews synchronized their watches.

After the refuelling plan was briefed, the Met Officer got up to speak. South-westerlies would mean headwinds of up to 70 knots on the way down. The Nav Plotters took down the weather information. The wind speed and direction were a crucial part of their calculations of speed, distance and track. But the most potentially significant information was that, at around 20 and 40 degrees south, two cold fronts meant that thunderstorm activity was probable and that at the height refuelling was to take place turbulence was likely.

Air Vice-Marshal George Chesworth had, he felt, a duty to say something. As the briefing came to an end, he got up to speak. Careful not to go on too long, he tried to find the right words: *This has never been done before; the eyes of the world are on you; there's a lot riding on this.* But he knew they didn't want to hear him. He wished them all luck and left them to it.

# Chapter 30

## 30 April 1982

The Vulcan crews worked in teams, each of them talking through the mission with his opposite number from the other crew and supported by their counterpart from Monty's Ops crew. The AEO's Hugh Prior and Barry Masefield discussed their tactics with John Hathaway. They agreed not to use the Vulcan's own Red Shrimp jammer, but rely instead on the Dash 10 pod. Prior and Masefield marked their flight logs with AVF, HF, VHF and UHF radio frequencies, including those for the approach and tower at Rio, their closest diversion. There were local and international call signs and codes for all occasions: the maritime code, a short-term security code with which any information could be transmitted securely; and the two-letter authentication codes which changed every thirty minutes to confirm to their own side that they were who they said they were. The IFF – Identification Friend or Foe – transponder settings changed with the same frequency. Get it wrong and they'd be seen as fair game by nervous Royal Navy air defences. Lastly there were 'Superfuse' and 'Rhomboid'. The former was to be transmitted after a successful bomb run; the latter if they failed.

Dick Russell had been thinking about the threat from the guns around Stanley. During the bomb-run, he would be no more than a passenger. Once the refuelling was done, the co-pilot, Pete Taylor, would swap places with him and he would sit, plugged into the RT, with absolutely no control over his destiny. It made him feel vulnerable.

'What difference does it make,' he asked Withers, 'if we drop from 8,000 feet or 10,000 feet?'

Withers considered this briefly before checking with his Navigators. Graham and Wright agreed that it was relatively insignificant and a late decision was made to pop up to the higher altitude and fly the bomb run at 10,000 feet. It was a small extra measure of safety.

In another corner of the tent, the co-pilots and AARIs checked and rechecked the fuel, while Mick Cooper and Bob Wright went through the switching and fuses with Dave Stenhouse. They and the Nav Plotters, Jim Vinales and Gordon Graham, updated their flight plans with the latest Met reports. Ironically, given the decision to switch to Red Rag Control, Vinales had got the name of the operation wrong, scribbling BLACK BULL at the top of his flight plan. He crossed out the word 'Exercise' and replaced it with 'Operation'. Next to it, in the box meant to record the time they expected to 'End Night Flying' he wrote 'Good Question.' They looked at the slim pickings available for diversions: Rio was the only realistic bet, the rest were in Chile: Punta Arenas, Balmaceda and Puerto Monte. They were unlikely at best. And they considered their options in case they had to ditch. Tristan da Cunha was mentioned as a possibility. This tiny South Atlantic colony had no airstrip, but there was a friendly British population of about 300. And it was closer to the Falklands than Ascension. Worth a try as a last resort, maybe. Both men were having to improvise, charting their course on an upside-down map of the northern hemisphere. It was all there was. Gordon Graham scribbled out the Azores and pencilled in the Falkland Islands at the appropriate latitude and longitude. X marked the spot.

As if they were blind to the realities of the situation, a last, random signal arrived from the MoD authorizing the Vulcans to exceed 250 knots at low level. And if it hadn't arrived in the nick of time, Monty wondered, who would have stopped them doing it anyway? And while they were at it, where was the authorization for flying the Vulcans at way above their maximum take-off weight? *Ridiculous*, he thought. Then it was time for the intelligence briefing.

The nicest name the crews gave the beefy-looking Intelligence Officer with the thick moustache was 'Nick the Knowledge'. With barely an hour to go until crew-in, trying to get intelligence out of him felt like trying to get a straight answer out of a politician.

'I can't reveal my sources,' he protested as the anxious bomber crews probed him for information. In the eyes of the listening Vulcan crews, 'Nick the Knowledge' seemed to be almost *trying* to give unsatisfactory answers. Monty became increasingly angry at his stonewalling, then John Hathaway snapped. He'd had enough and tore into the man.

'You fucking well tell us what we need to know because we're the ones who are going in.'

It did no one's nerves any good. The next five minutes passed uncomfortably as the big man, aided by a Captain from the SAS, revealed the locations of remote safehouses with studied politeness. Each of them was handed a piece of a 1:50,000 map of East Falkland, cut from a larger sheet. It was laminated with Fablon sticky-back plastic to give it a degree of water resistance. They were not, he told them, to mark the co-ordinates of the RVs on the maps. *Memorize them.* If they were shot down, he told them, they were to find their way to these locations and wait to be picked up. On three consecutive nights, a Sea King helicopter from 846 Naval Air Squadron would come looking. He pointed out known Argentine troop positions and he ran through the anti-aircraft defences again: Oerlikon, Tiger Cat, Skyguard, Superfledermaus. Just as Simon Baldwin had briefed them before they left Waddington. There was no mention of Roland.

What, Monty was asked, should happen to classified documents if a crew had to abandon their aircraft? Thinking on his feet the little Scotsman suggested they load all the paperwork into the tin ration box they'd be carrying in the cockpit then just throw the whole thing out of the crew hatch into the sea.

The reality of ejection, safehouses, disposal of secrets and late-night pick-ups had a sobering effect on Martin Withers. He should have expected it, of course, but somehow he'd managed to tuck away the reality of what they were about to do and not dwell on it. Being tossed a box of 9mm bullets for the Browning did nothing to comfort him. No time to worry about it now.

'You happy about things?' Monty asked the two Captains. Silence. Earlier in the afternoon, Monty had picked up the same problem with 607's number 1 tank as John Reeve had the previous day. Mel James had explained that it was only the gauge. The tank was fine, but the seed of doubt had been sown in Reeve's mind. He decided to go with 598. Withers would fly reserve in 607. 'Nothing at all, fellows?' Reeve and Withers checked the Form 700s – the jets' detailed service histories – then signed. Vulcans 598 and 607 were now their responsibility. It was time to go.

In the Officers' Mess, RAF Waddington, IX Squadron were enjoying a final dining-in night. They were always full-blooded affairs, and under normal circumstances the sociable, hearty Station Commander would have enjoyed himself thoroughly. Tonight, though, was anything but normal. John Laycock may have looked the part, dressed impressively in full mess-kit, but his appearance was misleading. He didn't taste his food, savour his wine, or listen much to what was being said. He was just going through the motions, waiting for an opportunity to make his excuses and join Simon Baldwin in the Ops block for news of BLACK BUCK's progress.

The scene looked familiar enough, as the Vulcan crews pulled on their flying kit. But as each man went through his own routine, surrounded by neatly arranged rails of flightsuits and equipment, the mood was different. In the locker room at Waddington there would be irreverent talk of cars, girls and sport; the kind of merciless ribbing found in a rugby club. Thick skins and quick wits were essentials. But not this time.

As they slowly pulled on layers of clothing, trying not to rush because of the 80-degree heat, each of them was lost in his own thoughts. The temperature was a struggle. They were going to be flying over a distance equal to about a third of the earth's circumference: a journey from the tropics to a few hundred miles north of the Antarctic circle and back. They had to prepare to come down in the freezing seas around the Falklands. Some wore long johns under their flying suits. Then there was the 'bunny suit', one-piece overalls made out of thick acrilan pile. On top of it all they eased into a cumbersome, tough rubber immersion suit, sealed tight at the cuffs and neck. Heavy-duty zips running up the front and back further restricted free movement. If they had to ditch or abandon the aircraft, the immersion suit would buy them some time at least. Once they got plugged into the jet's oxygen system they could circulate cool air through the suit. For now, though, they had to stew. Wearing it was definitely the lesser of two evils. Only Bob Wright chose not to put on the immersion suit before boarding the bomber. If he came down in cold water without having put it on, he wouldn't have a chance. In sea temperatures around 10 degrees Celsius, his survival time would have been about three hours. The seas around the Falkland Islands in April could drop below 2 degrees Celsius. Sudden immersion in seas below 5 degrees induces vagal shock. Wright would have gasped involuntarily, perhaps inhaling a lungful of frigid saltwater as a result. He'd have begun shivering uncontrollably, then his muscles would have contracted, preventing him from swimming. A heart attack would have been a possibility, but without that quick release, acute accidental hypothermia would probably kill him just minutes later anyway. Wright knew all this. If, for any reason, the Withers crew found themselves flying south beyond the first fuel transfer, he decided, he would struggle to pull on his immersion suit inside 607's cabin. For now, at least, he was more comfortable than his colleagues.

While the two flight crews prepared themselves, Monty and his men returned to the Vulcans. His Nav Plotter, Dick Arnott, climbed into the stifling-hot cockpit of 598 and switched on the Carousel INS to give it the time it needed to align before crew-in. The tiny triangular direct-vision window on the flight deck was open and a mobile air conditioner blew cool air in through the crew hatch, fighting a losing battle to keep the temperature down. All around, ground crews scurried about the fleet of V-bombers. The machines were beginning to come to life. And the noise was coming up. Arnott moved on to get 607 ready for Martin Withers' crew.

Mick Cooper took himself away to clear his head and gather his thoughts. He lit a cigarette and pulled on the smoke. The others knew to leave him alone. It was only Mick Cooper psyching himself up, just as he did before the bombing competition. As he had then, he returned to the fold radiating confidence. And one or two of the others drew strength from that.

They all filtered out from under the canvas. Before boarding the two Vulcans there was just time to relieve themselves in the dry dirt behind the tents. After this, though, they'd be using the pee-tubes on board and wrestling with the layers of protective clothing. Wearing harnesses and Mae West life-jackets over their thick rubber immersion suits both crews walked out past a line of Victors towards the bombers. Another line of K2s on the far side of the pan pointed towards them, their five-man crews also beginning to climb on board through the hatches on the port sides of the cabins.

Jim Vinales had been shaken by the complexity of the refuelling plan. He couldn't see how such a baroque undertaking could succeed. There were so many opportunities for it to go wrong. And if anything did go wrong, he thought, there was every chance it would do so with fatal consequences. He'd been lucky to survive bailing out of a crashing Vulcan once, ten years earlier. He didn't fancy his chances of doing so again.

Vinales kept his feelings to himself. It simply wasn't the kind of thing you shared. Doubt spread fast.

Barry Masefield just wanted to get in. He was always first in. He worried until he was able to actually touch the jet. That calmed him, up to a point. So did the familiar metallic smell of the cockpit. But for the little AEO, always claustrophobic, the cramped cabin of the Vulcan was far from an ideal environment. He climbed on board 598, took his seat and started his checks, pulling the blue book out of his flight bag, double-checking the AEO log and Met reports. Displacement activity.

Before joining the rest of the crew on board 607, Martin Withers' Nav team, Gordon Graham and Bob Wright, disappeared underneath the dark shape of the Vulcan's imposing silhouette to have a look at the warload. They chinned up using both hands to peer inside the bomb bay through the two access panels at its front. The full load of twenty-one thousand-pounders hung there, yellow rings painted around their noses to indicate that they were live. The old bombs had seen better days. One or two even seemed to be oozing some unidentifiable liquid out of the front. Curiosity satisfied, they dropped down, then climbed the ladder into the aircraft's nose to take their seats alongside AEO Hugh Prior. Prior began to work through his checklist. The jets were combat-readied, but just because something's worked once, that doesn't mean it's going to work next time.

The Dash 10 pod wouldn't run up. He tried it again. No good. Vulcan 607 might only be the reserve jet, but it *had* to be fixed. Without the effective new ECM pod, they wouldn't be exactly defenceless, but going in without it wasn't a prospect he relished. He thumbed the RT and spoke to the crew chief over the closed-circuit landline. Word was passed straight up the line to the Engineering Detachment boss, Mel James, who sent immediately for the corporal he'd taken from Honington. This was exactly why they'd brought him. The specialist quickly diagnosed and fixed the snag: a tripped fuse on the X-band circuit board. They were still on.

Before the crew hatches were sealed shut for take-off, Monty wanted to wish the two other Captains well. He jumped up 598's yellow entry ladder, past the tangle of 1950s wiring and hand-painted fuseboxes, past the tin box containing sandwiches, coffee and soft drinks, and stood between the two ejection seats on the flight deck. He rapped on Reeve's Bone Dome flying helmet. Reeve and AARI Pete Standing turned to acknowledge him.

'You two all right?' he asked.

'Yup,' Reeve answered. Nothing more to say now.

'Right, see you tomorrow. Do good,' he encouraged, and left them, taking the crew ladder with him. They wouldn't need it until they got back and, until then, it would just be more clutter. Monty skitted across to 607, and pulled himself up to send them on their way. The intercom on Withers' Bone Dome had packed up on the flight out to Ascension so, much to his annoyance, he was stuck with one of the soft green fabric caps that tended only to be worn by the backseaters. He wasn't at all happy about the timing of the fault, but at least he only needed to go as far as the first refuelling bracket. Monty tapped him on the head to get his attention.

'I'll see you back here for a beer in five or six hours,' Monty said and smiled.

Withers grinned back and nodded his approval of the plan.

'See you, Mont.'

As the crew doors on the two bombers were sealed shut, the occupants were cut off from the noise and movement outside.

In Admiralty House, two hundred yards from the Operations Room at Northwood HQ, Air Marshal Sir John Curtiss sat down with the Task Force Commander, Admiral Sir John Fieldhouse. Over a glass of whisky, the two men talked about the war to come, knowing it might be a long time until they had a similar opportunity for reflection. Curtiss liked the thoughtful, astute Yorkshireman enormously, believed him to be perhaps the most impressive person he'd ever served under. The Admiral asked about the prospect of civilian casualties. Curtiss was able to reassure him. There would be none, he told him, unless they were actually on the airfield during the raid. Fieldhouse fully appreciated the immensity of the task being asked of the Victor and Vulcan crews. Curtiss couldn't help but wonder if they would succeed. Whatever the outcome of BLACK BUCK, though, both these senior officers knew that come morning, Britain would be committed.

# PART THREE

V-Force

*'Bring back, bring back, Oh, bring back my bomber and me, and me. Bring back, bring back, Oh, bring back my bomber and me.'*

Sung by Second World War Bomber Command crews
(to the tune of 'My Bonny Lies over the Ocean')

# Chapter 31

There was a lull. Then the first of the Victors broke the expectant calm as her engines fired up at 22.30. Just one of the four powerful turbines to begin with: run up to 90 per cent rpm in order to feed power through to the other three to start them in sequence. The whine grew to a roar as, one by one, the remaining Rolls-Royce Conway RCo17 turbojets spooled up. They were joined by the noise from the engines of the next Victor in line. Then the next, and the next. Eleven in all. Forty-four engines. A million pounds of potential thrust. Red dust was already being churned into the air, caught in the arc lights along the south side of the Wideawake pan. The view rippled with heat. The wind carried the tang of burnt aviation fuel.

A background hum played through the conference intercom aboard Vulcan 607 – the sound of electricity – punctuated by clicks, pops and breathing. Through it, the crew's voices sounded brittle and dry as they ran through the challenge and response checklist, called out by Hugh Prior. Martin Withers moved the stick and rudder pedals through their full range of travel, while outside the Crew Chief stood watching, reporting back to the cockpit. Without him, the checks couldn't be completed.

*Bomb door normal operation.*

*And you're clear.*

*Three, two, one . . . now.*

The two long doors slowly unfolded from 607's dark-grey belly to reveal the warload of 1,000lb bombs racked inside.

*Travelling . . . Open.*
*Less than eight seconds . . . Fine.*
*Closing now.*
*Travelling . . . Bomb doors close and flush.*

The Crew Chief disconnected the external power and Hugh Prior checked the transformer rectifier units.

*Serviceable and on.* Time to light the engines.

*Clear start.*

*Starting now.* Withers reached down to his left, almost behind him, to a panel of switches, bathed in orange light, running low along the side of the flight deck. There were four separate buttons, one for each engine. Each needed to be pushed and held, before being released.

*Pressing now. One thousand . . . One.* Withers checked the engine gauges as the power came up. Small white needles flickered and rose on the panel of dials in the centre of the instrument panel.

*RPM's turning, fuel's coming on. Ten per cent . . . fourteen . . . fifteen. Oil temperature and JPT. No fire warnings.* His voice, two-dimensional and sibilant.

The eight Rolls-Royce Olympus 301s of the two Vulcans turned faster, building, joining a rasping, thunderous wall of noise.

As Red One, the first Victor, edged out of its spot at 22.50, the roar from its Conways flared and the extra thrust kicked up dust and debris. As they rolled forward, her pilot turned towards Runway One Four. Around them the ghostly silhouettes of ground crewmen were swallowed up by the swirling cloud. Five places behind him, following his own section leader, Bob Tuxford in White Two opened the throttles up to nearly 50 per cent to overcome the heavy tanker's inertia. Once she began to roll he pulled them back to idle, but, like the three Victors ahead of him, the initial burst of power had whipped up a storm. He touched the toe-pedals to test the brakes and the jet dipped low on to the squat nosewheel as over 100 tons tried to maintain its forward momentum. The backseaters were pushed into their high-backed green-steel seats. Then Tux powered up again and taxied slowly towards the runway, turning on to it before the aircraft ahead of him in the stream had left the ground. After the disappointment of the first MRR mission, he was back flying one of two long-slot positions. He'd be escorting the Vulcan a long way south, flying for twelve hours or more.

Feet on the brakes, he wound up the engines at the threshold, released the toe-pedals and pushed the four throttles to the gate with his left hand. As White Two accelerated down the strip, the ride became progressively more comfortable as the wings took the weight off the undercarriage.

*Decision, rotate.*

*Rotating.*

As Tux's jet hauled itself into the air, the next Victor was already turning on the runway. Ahead of them, White Two was climbing away.

*Gear up, please.*

*Selected, three reds and travelling.*

Jerry Price was nervous. He'd already been forced to use the ground reserve aircraft when one of the Primary Victors couldn't maintain engine revolutions. If any of the departing aircraft had to abort their take-off that was the end of the night's work. He watched each one that safely took to the air with a sigh of relief.

'OK, there's another one away.'

On board 598, the Primary Vulcan, John Reeve was counting them out too, making sure he slotted in at the right time. The rest of the crew could hear the thunderous crackle of the Victor's engines through the fuselage. A sound to stir the blood. Number eleven in the stream, Reeve nudged 598 along, careful to control the speed. Even idling, the Olympus engines had the power to let the jet get ahead of you. As they taxied out behind the Victor leading the Blue section, the perspective from the co-pilot's seat was still unfamiliar to AARI Pete Standing. Unlike the low cockpit of the Victor, the Vulcan flight deck seems to hang high in the air, projecting forward over ten feet ahead of the nosewheel. It provided a great vantage point. Reeve leaned forwards against his straps to close the little triangular direct-vision window.

'There's a problem here,' he said over the intercom. 'I can't get this thing shut . . . I'll give it another go.' In the back, the rest of the crew could hear the banging from flight deck as Reeve struggled to close it. *Come on, get the bloody thing closed*, thought Mick Cooper as he heard the Captain hammering at the window, *it can't be that difficult*.

'Calm down, John,' urged Don Dibbens from the sixth seat as Reeve got more agitated by it. 'Just work at it.'

'I think I've got it.'

They were set. Dibbens sat back for take-off as Reeve swung round on to the runway centreline. Then he released the brakes and opened up the throttles and 598 produced an astonishing noise that cut through the night for the first time. The blistering, grating roar of the engines was flattened out by the intake resonance to create a ghostly howl. And the bomber quickly gathered speed along the Tarmac.

A minute later, the eleventh Victor followed them. Then, barely twenty minutes after the first of the V-bomber fleet had begun her take-off roll, the last of them, 607 with Martin Withers at the controls, got airborne. Vulcan 607 hadn't wanted to leave the ground. At rotation speed Withers had pulled back on the stick, expecting the familiar eagerness to fly, and she'd just continued barrelling along the runway. Filled with fuel and loaded with bombs, both Vulcans were well over their maximum take-off weight of 204,000lb. Add to that two new weapons pylons made of reinforced steel joists, the Dash 10 pod, a sixth crew member, even fresh layers of paint and it was probably over two tons. The excess alone was greater than the entire normal bomb load of an old American B-17 Flying Fortress four-engined heavy. But as the Olympus 301s powered her faster and faster down the runway, the big delta wings had eventually found purchase. Now airborne, she felt familiar again. As they climbed out of the rough cradle of mountains around the airfield, the undercarriage locked up with a comforting clunk and 607 accelerated away into the black sky.

As the crew ran through their post-take-off checks, Withers climbed straight along the track of the runway centreline of 140 degrees for fifteen miles before turning south on to a heading of 230 degrees. Two minutes ahead of him on board 598, the scene was very different.

At Wideawake, the rumble subsided to leave in its wake an eerie stillness. Those who'd witnessed the departure were still transfixed, moved even, by the overwhelming, visceral power of the armada going to work. The hot scent of jet engines lingered in the air a while longer, but after the intensity of the last few hours, Ascension seemed once again to have become a tiny isolated rock in the middle of the Atlantic.

Jerry Price didn't have long to savour the satisfaction of getting the formation into the air safely. A few minutes at most. Then things started to go wrong.

Vulcan crews were used to the red pressure-warning light coming on. Sometimes a depressurization horn too. They usually ignored them. The big delta could climb too fast for the cabin pressurization system to keep up with it. This time, though, they knew it was the DV window Reeve had been wrestling with before take-off. As soon as the bomber had started gathering speed the air had begun whistling around its edges. When they passed through 10,000 feet and the cabin began trying to pressurize, the air just bled out. While the noise of the wind rose alarmingly, Reeve was trying to work out a solution. *Not a problem*, he thought at first, *it's perfectly logical: seal it.* In the back they pulled sandwiches out of the ration tin and Reeve tried to stuff their cellophane wrapping in the gap. No good. Cursing, he tried to plug the hole with his flying jacket without success. Vulcan 598 continued to climb and the spiteful sound of the rushing air was becoming overpowering. And it was getting cold too. Approaching 20,000 feet, keeping their place in the stream of jets flying south, the outside air temperature was dropping to minus 30 Celsius. Barry Masefield turned to Jim Vinales to his left. Despite the oxygen mask, Vinales could see the colour had drained from the AEO's face.

'Oh my God,' Masefield said, speaking for all of them, 'this is going horribly, horribly wrong.'

It was really just a matter of time now. Masefield pointed out that by breathing 100 per cent oxygen through the masks, as they'd have to, their supply wouldn't last. On top of that they needed to cruise above 30,000 feet, where the air was even colder than at their current altitude. Despite the layers of insulating, protective clothing they all wore, the six of them would freeze to death if they continued. There was no way they could go on.

Just four minutes after taking off, Reeve reluctantly pressed the RT button to transmit.

'Blue Two unserviceable. Returning to base. Blue Four, you're on.'

On board 607, the message was greeted with silence. Martin Withers had been looking forward to a beer with Monty in the Exiles Club. After the initial drumbeat of adrenalin subsided, he sat at the controls, rapidly adjusting to the new reality. A sixteen-hour operational mission now lay ahead. He gathered his thoughts for a moment then spoke to his crew: 'Looks like we've got a job of work to do, fellas . . .'

Dick Russell immediately started thinking about the tanker plan – what he was there for. It was one thing sitting off until the Primary had refuelled successfully, then returning home. But now *they* were the Primary. The success of the operation depended on flying formation in the dark for the next seven hours and, just two weeks earlier, Withers had never really done any night formation flying.

*Here we go again*, thought Hugh Prior at the new development, practising the aircrew's studied indifference to adverse circumstances. But this time his resignation was tinged with satisfaction. *We've got it!*, he thought smiling to himself as he picked up Reeve's transmission.

Minutes later, as his co-pilot, Pete Taylor, reorganized the Vulcan's cramped cabin after take-off, he began to realize that something was up. Condemned to the jump seat, he had been disconnected from the intercom when the news came through. He reattached his PEC to speak.

'Have I missed something?' he asked brightly.

Meanwhile, Bob Wright started to think about how he was going to squirm into his immersion suit.

Twenty minutes later, Red Rag Control received another unscheduled RT message from the formation. As soon as the Victors were settled into the climb the Nav Radars tested the refuelling equipment. In the back of White Four, XL163, Alan Bowman, 57 Squadron's boss and head of the Victor detachment on Ascension, watched with a sinking feeling. As the Nav Radar played with the HDU controls in an effort to trail the hose, it was clear that nothing he tried was working. White Four had been tasked with the ultimate long-slot position. After a final Victor–Victor transfer from Tux, they would fly on with the Vulcan for the final refuelling before the bomb-run. That knowledge only made their disappointment more acute as they reported that they were unserviceable and turned back towards Wideawake estimating that they'd be on the ground again at 0006. With RT communication stripped to the bare essentials, no further direction was necessary. Steve 'Biggles' Biglands in Blue Three, one of the two Victor airborne reserves, smoothly took their place.

Of fourteen Victors on Ascension, two had now failed. Two had replaced them. A minimum of ten Victors were needed to make the refuelling plan work. Jerry Price had run out of options. If there was another failure they'd have to abort the mission. But, for the time being, while it might be delicately balanced, they were still on top of it. Price sent a flash signal to Northwood HQ informing them that the formation was airborne.

Once again, the flexibility of the Victor force – and the margins built into the mission plan – was keeping the thing on the rails. But only just.

# Chapter 32

Airborne for less than half an hour, John Reeve's Vulcan had used little of the 74,000lb of fuel in her tanks. Unlike the Victor, the Vulcan can't jettison fuel. Still above the big jet's maximum weight for even an emergency landing, Reeve had no choice but to stay in the air to burn it. The technique was straightforward. They could climb at maximum power in a tight spiral, or descend in corkscrew with the airbrakes out and even the landing gear down to increase the rate of fuel burn. Distressed, angry and strapped into a cold, noisy cabin, the crew of the lame bomber faced a bleak prospect. As they coiled upwards Reeve started having trouble with his communication equipment.

'I'm just going off intercom,' he told the crew before disconnecting his PEC.

AARI Pete Standing pulled back on the stick, holding the delta in a steeply banked ascending turn, while Reeve concentrated on trying to sort out the problem with his comms. Unnoticed by Standing, though, the bomber's nose was creeping up and vital speed bleeding off. Tucked away in the jump seat, Don Dibbens sensed something wasn't quite right. *Feels mushy*, he thought for a moment before the full force of what that meant hit him. *Oh shit! This bloody aircraft's going to stall!* Close to losing lift from the wings, 598 was on the verge of tumbling out of the sky. Dibbens leapt up from his seat and vaulted up the ladder to the flight deck.

'Get the fucking power up,' he shouted as he threw himself

forward over the fuel tray to grab the four throttles. 'Lower the nose!'

Pete Standing reacted immediately to bring the Vulcan back from the brink. The airspeed rose again. Caught by surprise at first, Reeve took control from the startled AARI.

'OK, we're all OK . . .' calmed Reeve. Drama over. Dibbens returned, sweating, to his seat and the six of them settled again. After the scare, Reeve decided to bring her in, over-weight or not. It was time to call it a day.

Around a hundred miles separated 607 from the first Victor of the BLACK BUCK formation. That was the distance Red One had flown at the point when Withers' Vulcan was leaving Runway One Four. As the stream turned on to the southerly heading, the neat line-astern formation became muddled. With each jet covering around half a mile every ten seconds, even small variations in the point at which they initiated their turns had a major effect on their relationship to each other in the night sky. As 607 closed on the fleet of Victors, Dick Russell gave Martin Withers directions.

'Right, at the first bracket we refuel off Blue One.'

The Captain looked out ahead at the long front of blinking navigation lights stretching across the sky in front of them.

'And which one of all those aircraft out there is that?' he asked.

While the organization of the three sections, Red, White and Blue, was clear on paper, in radio silence, darkness and three dimensions it was less straightforward. They weren't hard to see. Each Victor's white underside was illuminated by its own floodlights and red anti-collision lights pulsed. Each of the V-bombers had three anti-collision beacons above and below the fuselage that revolved like mini-lighthouses, flashing red and out of sequence with their neighbours. But scattered around the sky at different heights and distances, they all looked exactly the same. Rather than continue on his heading, Withers banked towards what, ahead and to the side, he assumed was the section they needed to join. But even the experienced Dick Russell was struggling to figure out which of the three sections they needed to refuel from, let alone which of the tankers within that section was theirs. On board 607 they had reams of paper with radio and TACAN frequencies, aircraft positions, Captains' names and call signs. But trying to operate in radio silence meant that, right now, much of this was academic. Unhappily, Russell realized they were going to have to get on the RT and ask their tanker to identify itself. Over a discrete channel, Hugh Prior asked the section leader for a flare. Mounted in the roof of each Victor above the AEO's station was a signal pistol. Aboard Blue One, the AEO loaded a cartridge and pulled the trigger, firing a green Verey flare into the night.

Withers and Russell craned their necks scanning the skies around them for the signal, expecting to see the glowing flare out ahead. Nothing.

'Ask him for another one.'

Prior again pressed the transmit button, all the time scanning from side to side through his rear-facing periscope. Then he caught it at eight o'clock, behind and below them. Withers pulled back on the power and dropped down into the formation in anticipation of the first refuelling bracket, still over an hour away, over 800 miles south of Ascension.

At RAF Waddington, John Laycock finally managed to slip away from the IX Squadron dinner near midnight. He drove straight from the Officers' Mess to the Ops block and walked briskly through to the Ops Room. A handful of staff sat at desks, surrounded by communication equipment.

'What's going on?' he asked, hungry for news.

'Absolutely nothing, boss.'

All they could tell him was that BLACK BUCK had got under way on schedule. Starved of information by radio silence and a chain of command that, now the bombers had deployed south, excluded him, he knew they faced a long, anxious night. There was absolutely nothing to be done but wait until a message filtered back indicating success or otherwise. The room was silent and tense. He decided to leave them for the night and try to get some sleep.

'Right, I'm heading home,' he told the Ops staff. 'If there is *anything* at all, call me.'

About an hour and three-quarters into the mission, the tip of Vulcan 607's refuelling probe locked into the drogue trailed by Blue One, and fuel flushed into her tanks.

Ahead of the first refuelling bracket, the three sections had descended 6,000 feet from their cruising altitude while the pilots carefully maintained the vertical separation between the jets. Ahead of the Vulcan, White section was refuelling at 28,000 feet and Red section at 30,000 feet. At 26,000 feet, Dick Russell gently held station below the brightly lit underside of his Blue section Victor. They were flying at around 15,000 feet below the delta-winged bomber's optimum cruising altitude. Over the next twenty minutes, 37,000lb of fuel flowed from Blue One through her heavy eighty-foot hose to the Vulcan – *4,500lb more than expected.*

At the first refuelling bracket, Bob Tuxford was going to take on 48,000lb of fuel – over 24 tons. This meant tailgating John Elliott's Victor, White One, at over 250 knots for nearly half an hour. Over the course of transfer, while the co-pilot Glyn Rees worked hard to distribute the fuel evenly throughout the Victor's tanks, the big jet's centre of gravity inevitably crept forward. Unchecked, this could have a powerful effect on its handling, forcing the nose down. As the effort of keeping the Victor in formation increased, Tux tried to relieve the pressure on the controls using the thumb-mounted trim switch. The longer the transfer continued the more strength was needed to overcome growing heaviness of the controls. Hands and feet made continual adjustments as Tux maintained a finely honed balance between stick, pedals and throttles. The darkness made its own demands. By day, peripheral vision helped an experienced pilot keep station almost subconsciously. At night, without a horizon, that touchstone was gone. The intensity with which it was necessary to focus on those visual cues that remained further sapped a pilot's energy. It was easy to become tired and disorientated. It was gruelling physical work for all concerned.

With his tanks filled to their maximum capacity of 123,000lb, Bob Tuxford notched back the throttles and allowed the Victor to lose ground slowly on White One. At the limit of its travel, the drogue pulled apart from the probe with a soft jerk. Ahead of him Tux saw the fluorescent studs that ringed the basket recede into the night above him. Three other Victors refuelled at this first bracket. All now carried more fuel than they'd taken off with, more than the weight of the aircraft itself. With the Vulcan now safely in formation things appeared to be going without a hitch. But operating in radio silence, Tux and the other three Captains were unaware that just a couple of hours into the mission, things were starting to come badly unstuck. The first four Victors to turn back for Ascension had cut deep into their own reserves to supply the combat formation with the fuel it needed to continue south. They barely had what they needed to get home safely.

As they embarked on their uncertain return journey, Blue One, the Vulcan's tanker, continued with the attack formation a little while longer. At the furthest extent of the first refuelling bracket she would give the Vulcan an additional top-up then turn for home herself. After 607 had taken an extra 4,500lb to fill her tanks at the first transfer, the Victor Captain, Wing Commander Colin Seymour, could see that she was thirstier than expected. The next transfer, taking place after half an hour of flying straight and level, would show him exactly how much more fuel she was burning than they'd bargained on. At 23°00' south and 24°08' west, Seymour spoke to his Nav Radar. *Clear to trail.*

Vulcan 598 crossed the Runway One Four threshold much faster than normal. The higher the landing weight, the higher the speed of the approach. John Reeve tried to put the heavy bomber down on to the main-wheel bogies as gently as possible. But, as if this wretched sortie hadn't gone badly enough, as he guided her down the runway, keeping the nose high to use the barn-door expanse of the Vulcan's delta plan-form to slow them down, he scraped her tail down the Tarmac, kicking up a flash of orange sparks in her wake. It was insult to injury.

Monty watched them taxi back to the dispersal area. Travelling fast, he noticed. He hadn't returned to the Ops tent for over an hour after the formation flew out of Wideawake. And when he'd been told that John Reeve was flying the returning Vulcan he thought it must be a mistake. After running through the shutdown checks, Reeve reached forward and opened the DV window – the source of their failure. As it swung open, a perished seal fell limply out of the frame. *All that bloody work*, he thought, unable to adequately capture his bitter disappointment. Monty waited for the crew door to open, then fixed the ladder and ran up into the cockpit.

'What the hell's wrong?' he asked as he looked round at the crew's faces. He'd never seen Reeve look so angry. 'Let's calm down,' he said, trying to sound soothing. 'We'll get everyone out and have a beer. You can tell me what happened.'

Despite the best of intentions, Monty needed to be careful. Mick Cooper wanted to lash out. Barry Masefield found it hard even to look anyone in the eye, unable to shake a corrosive feeling that they were going to be accused of LMF – Lack of Moral Fibre. The AEO was walked away by his counterpart, John Hathaway, to sign all his codes back in. Cooper, holding a bag carrying all the safety pins for the bombs, found an armourer.

'Do you need me to put them back?' he asked. The airman wisely shook his head. Cooper handed over the bag and his mind turned enviously to Bob Wright on board 607. *How good are you going to be?*, he wondered. *You've only got twenty-one; for Christ's sake don't waste them.*

'Seal on the DV window,' Reeve explained tersely as they left the bomber behind on the pan.

Monty drove them up to Two Boats where they all chatted miserably and haltingly over beer.

'John,' Monty began, in an effort to help him rationalize, 'there's nothing I can say that'll make you feel any better. It's happened . . .' But he realized it was still too soon for that. Reeve was inconsolable and, Monty thought, looked close to tears.

Along with the rest of Reeve's crew, Monty eventually turned in, leaving 598's forlorn Captain sitting alone out on the veranda, nursing a can of beer. AARI Pete Standing came outside briefly to say that he couldn't sleep with the light on. Reeve switched it off, opened another beer, and continued to stare out into the night.

Nav Plotter Jim Vinales was the only member of the crew who didn't return to Two Boats. Instead, he stayed at Wideawake. He'd expected to be up all night anyway and thought he'd discreetly watch events unfold from inside the Ops tent. Jerry Price, he noticed, was chain-smoking.

At the controls of Red Three, one of the four Victors returning to Ascension from the first refuelling bracket, Squadron Leader Barry Neal was starting to feel concerned about his fuel state. Things should have been fairly healthy after that first transfer, but he was well down. He was just about to break radio silence when a voice from one of the other three jets crackled through his headset.

'This is White Three. Are you guys short of fuel?'

Neal and the other two Victors said they were, but none of the four crews were sure what they could do about it. They all re-examined their fuel and compared notes, estimating where each would be at Top of Descent into Ascension. All would be well below minimum. The AEOs tried to raise Red Rag Control on the HF radio, but they knew that there was nothing Ascension could do. They were out of tankers. In any case, it would have taken longer to scramble one at short notice than any of the four inbound Victors now had. They considered their options and quickly realized that there wasn't going to be time for each of them to land, roll to the turnaround pad, change direction, backtrack nearly two miles and vacate the strip before the next one had to come in. They were going to have to land one after another. They got a message through to Jerry Price asking him to approve the plan. It had to be their decision, he told them. *Right, OK*, Neal thought, knowing they were all committed to it, *I'm happy with that. That's the way we're going to do it.* Then they asked Price to make sure there was a Victor pilot in the Wideawake tower and agreed the sequence in which they were going to come in, based on their relative fuel states. Barry Neal was to come in last.

In the tower, Bill Bryden and the PanAm controllers were joined by David Davenall from the Victor Ops team. Between them, they decided that the only way to recover the approaching tankers would be for the first three to land, hold on to their drag chutes, taxi to the turnaround pad at the end of the runway and position themselves right, left and straight-on like a *fleur-de-lys*. They would completely block the end of the runway. If the brakes or chute of the fourth jet failed – or if Barry Neal simply misjudged his one approach – the destruction at the end of the runway would be catastrophic. In the event of a brake failure, they suggested Neal pull off the Tarmac into the volcanic cinder field to the left of the strip. His jet would be wrecked but, they believed, the crew would survive and it might save the airfield and the other three Victors. From the tower, they asked the four Victor captains to try to allow as much of a gap between each landing as they felt they could. They alerted the fire crews and waited anxiously for the first of the big tankers to descend out of the darkness.

Ten minutes separated White Three from White One; Red One followed five minutes after that; Red Three was coming in barely two minutes behind her. As Barry Neal intercepted the glidepath, he prepared the tanker for landing. *Gear down and landing checks, please.*

*Down, three greens*, came confirmation. After setting the flap to 'take-off', he settled into long finals. With the four Conway engines set at 84–85 per cent rpm, he controlled his speed on the approach with the big clamshell airbrake underneath the Victor's high dihedral tailplane. While he adjusted the airbrake with his left hand and flew with his right, his co-pilot controlled the throttles, tweaking the power a couple of percentage points as Neal called for it. He could see the runway lights ahead and, at the point where the line ended, the other three Victors, their anti-collision beacons blinking redundantly in the distance. He had one chance to get it right. And he knew that the Handley Page Victor K2 had notoriously bad brakes. He was dependent on the brake chute deploying. Descending towards the One Four threshold he passed through 200 feet. Decision height. He set full flap and committed to the landing. Then, as if offering a psychological helping hand at the vital moment, the long, high hump in the Wideawake runway obscured his view of the three waiting Victors. Neal flared over the threshold and his co-pilot cut the power. The moment the mainwheels squealed against the Tarmac he streamed the chute, brought the nosewheel down fast and applied the brakes. He had no qualms this time about hitting them early and hard. The Victor barrelled along the runway like a runaway train, but, as she crested the rise in the runway and the flashing red lights and camouflaged shapes of the other three Victors came into view again, Neal knew the speed was coming off. The brakes had held.

As the big jet decelerated to taxi speed, Neal swung her round tightly through 180 degrees and dumped the chute – trying, as he gunned the throttles to roll back to the dispersal, to blow the discarded heap of fabric and rope off the runway with the jet wash.

In the little red and white control tower, Bill Bryden took a few deep breaths and watched the ground crew's pick-ups kick up dust as they sped away to recover the four drag chutes.

Barry Neal's crew was the only one of the four who'd just landed who were going up again that night. In less than two hours, they had to be ready to take off again in order to arrive at Rio RV in time to meet the returning Vulcan. Between briefing and planning, there would just be time to have a drink and grab a sandwich before crew-in.

# Chapter 33

John Smith joked that he used religion like one of the emergency services. But the strength and frequency of his prayer now bore comparison with that of his wife Ileen, whose Catholic faith had always been strong. As April had passed, others of all faiths, looking for succour and the practical assistance Monsignor Spraggon could provide in dealing with their God-fearing occupiers, had joined them for mass at Stanley's Catholic church, St Mary's. Some of the Argentine officers, General Menendez included, had actually worshipped with them. But as he retired for bed on the night of the 30th, thoughts of loving thine enemy were far from Smith's mind. Television was new to the Falklands and a gift of the invaders. Like many of his fellow residents, Smith had taken advantage of the Argentine subsidy to acquire a new set. Tonight he watched with rising anger scenes of General Galtieri in Stanley handing his rosary beads to young conscripts and telling them that the Blessed Virgin Mary was on their side.

Two hundred miles away to the north-west, Admiral Woodward's Royal Navy battle group plunged through the swell across an imaginary line in the sea and into the Total Exclusion Zone.

Wing Commander Colin Seymour's return to Wideawake provided Jerry Price and Red Rag Control with a nasty shock – hard evidence of how much fuel the Vulcan was burning. Half an hour after the four first-wave Victors had shown how little margin for error there was, the 55 Squadron boss's figures underlined it. In the thirty-four minutes between the first and second fuel transfers, 607 had burnt 9,200lb of fuel. During that time, the overloaded bomber's weight had never even dropped to its theoretical maximum, let alone below it. They were flying outside the aircraft's notional limits and the fuel burn reflected it: 16,250lb an hour. The BLACK BUCK fuel plan was going to the dogs. But while he could see big trouble ahead, there was little Price could actually do other than try to be ready for it when it happened.

Subsisting on tea and cigarettes, wearing the khaki short-sleeved shirts of the RAF's tropical kit, the Ops team hunched over trestle tables and tried to prepare contingency plans. They worked through different scenarios, factored in potential *ifs* and *buts*. As soon as the returning Victors were back at dispersal, the ground crew turned them round, checking the engines and refuelling them before reserve aircrew combat-readied them again. Barry Neal's aircraft needed to be ready to go by 0520 along with the three others flying west to the Rio RV. That was less than two hours away. With such an urgent demand on the ground crew's resources, preparing the rest of the waiting Victor fleet for as yet unknown, but virtually certain, emergencies had to take a back seat. Extra Victors would take three hours to turn round. The engineering teams were doing what they could, but it still seemed to Price a frustratingly long time. He was going to need those jets. The crews could stand down briefly, but after that he wanted them camped out by their jets, ready when he needed them. They could sleep under the wings, if they had to.

While the planners at Ascension crunched the numbers, the 'Balbo' continued south, unaware of the developing problem. Aboard the three remaining Victors, all seemed well – according to the Nav Plotters and their flight plans they were on time and on target. But the effects of the physical exertion of flying each fuel transfer and the intense concentration of nearly three hours' night flying in formation were beginning to show. Unnoticed by Bob Tuxford or his co-pilot Glyn Rees, his

Victor, XL189, was developing a slow, potentially dangerous roll to port.

Disaster doesn't give much warning when flight refuelling goes wrong. Seven years earlier, Flight Lieutenant Keith Handscomb, one of Tux's fellow 55 Squadron Captains, was flying a routine daylight air-to-air refuelling exercise with two Buccaneer S2 strike bombers over the North Sea, 170 miles north-east of Newcastle. Through the rear-view periscope, Handscomb's Nav Radar saw that the second Buccaneer was approaching too fast. His probe clipped the edge of the trailing drogue, sending it snaking in towards the Victor's fuselage. The Nav Radar lost sight of the Bucc as it settled again, above and a little behind the tanker's wing. The bomber pilot throttled back a touch and started to drop down again to tuck in behind the Victor for another approach. Then he flew into the powerful jetwash from the Victor's Conway engines. The Buccaneer was rolled quickly, his starboard wing smashing into the port side of the Victor's high T-tail and ripping it off.

'I think this is going to be a Mayday,' observed the pilot of the other Buccaneer over the RT as he watched the catastrophe unfold.

At the same time as his tail was struck, Handscomb felt a slight change in pitch before the control yoke went completely slack. Behind him, structurally unsound and unable to withstand the huge stresses imposed on it, the starboard side of the tailplane also sheered off. His Victor, bunting forward into an outside loop that guaranteed it would break up, was finished. Handscomb immediately lost all control. He ordered his crew to abandon the aircraft but he knew that without ejection seats his backseaters had little hope. As the dying tanker accelerated into a terminal negative 'g' loop, the conditions could not have been more unfavourable for them to try to make their escape. Even if they had managed to unstrap from their seats they would only have been thrown and pinned to the roof of the cabin; forced against the outside wall of a fatal centrifuge. Less than 2,000 feet above the sea, with the jet already inverted, Handscomb's ejection seat fired. Straps around his shins and shoulders tightened immediately as his Martin-Baker Mk 3 seat began its launch sequence. He was dimly aware that the cockpit was collapsing around him as five explosive cartridges fired in quick succession, catapulting the heavy seat through the roof at a speed of 80 feet per second. Within a second of the seat being triggered he was free, while behind him the doomed Victor was consumed by a fireball from the ruptured fuel tanks. Two hours later, through the combined efforts of a German freighter, SS *Hoheburgh*, and a bright-yellow RAF Whirlwind search and rescue helicopter, he was finally pulled from the North Sea, freezing cold and unable to recall the moment of his escape. It was six months before he'd recovered sufficiently from severe back injuries to strap himself back in to the ejection seat of another Victor. The rest of his five-man crew all lost their lives.

'White Two, you're rolling left.'

The warning from Steve Biglands, terse and crackling over a discrete radio channel, punctured Tuxford's inattention. If he and Rees had momentarily taken their eye off the ball, at least Biglands, flying to their right in starboard echelon, hadn't. As Tux checked the controls, he felt himself flush, a mixture of adrenalin and embarrassment. He shook off his drowsiness and gently rolled the Victor's crescent wings back straight and level. As he stretched and rolled his shoulders, he chastised himself, determined not to lose concentration again. And he thought of the hours ahead.

Still nearly five hours away from the moment he could strap himself into the co-pilot's seat, Pete Taylor tried to make himself useful. After the first refuelling he stepped up on to the ladder to the flightdeck to help check the Vulcan's fuel tray, but mostly he was simply doing a good job keeping his colleagues supplied with cups of orange juice from the ration tin. They, in turn, maintained their vigil on the walls of dials, magnetic doll's-eyes and flickering needles that surrounded them. Each man went through well-rehearsed routines that had, over many hours of training, become second nature.

On the flight deck, Withers and Russell held the bomber's

place in the formation with an eye on the lights from the four Victors and small instinctive corrections to the stick. Every half-hour Hugh Prior ran through checks on the Vulcan's crucial electrical systems and asked for a fuel check from the pilots. Bob Wright was underemployed. His H2S radar scanner would stay switched off until the bomb-run. During the long transit over the sea it was no good to them, but as they approached the islands, if switched on prematurely, its emissions would give them away. Instead he rehearsed the bomb-run in his mind's eye, playing it through, step-by-step, making sure that he was comfortable with it. But there was too much time to dwell on what lay ahead if he allowed himself to. He tried to keep his mind occupied. He unstrapped and stood on the ladder between the two pilots to look out ahead. He even tried reading, but despite being stuck into John Ralston Saul's appropriately named political thriller *Birds of Prey*, Wright found it difficult to concentrate on it. He couldn't help it, his thoughts kept turning to that bomb-run. Sitting next to him, Gordon Graham was monitoring the aircraft's position. In front of him, the GPI6 provided continuous read-outs of latitude and longitude. A small discrepancy between the Vulcan's automatic dead-reckoning equipment and what the INS was telling him was developing. And he didn't yet entirely trust the twin Carousels. While there was no *reason* to doubt them, he felt uncomfortable putting all his eggs in one basket. Furthermore, if there *was* a problem with either, having two was not much better than having one. Like clocks telling different times, if one of the Carousels went awry, it was impossible to know which was right. As they reached the top of a cruise climb to 33,000 feet after the first refuelling bracket, Graham asked Bob Wright to take a star shot with the sextant so he could check their position against the night sky. Wright only managed to take one reading before they reached the next refuelling bracket. Flying in formation and frequently interrupted by the need to refuel, Graham and Wright realized they'd have to abandon their efforts at astro-navigation. It took too long. It needed relatively long periods of undisturbed, straight and level flying. In formation, leap-frogging from one refuelling bracket to the next, it just wasn't going to work. Graham had no choice but to accept what the Carousels were telling him. On the flight deck, the two pilots prepared to refuel for the third time, initiating the checks for what, Dick Russell knew, was a complicated bracket. Withers initiated the pre-refuelling checks, keeping 607 back to the rear and starboard of the formation as the Victors began their intricate aerial dance.

First of all, Red Two refuelled Red Four. Ten minutes later, the transfer complete, Red Two banked gently across the sky to the right and took up a position ahead of 607, ready to refuel the Vulcan. Martin Withers watched to his left as Tux in White Two drifted across the sky to the left and dropped in behind Red Four to take on fuel. Twenty minutes later, tanks full to 123,000lb again, Tux fell back and the coupling was broken. Then, as planned by Red Rag Control, he moved across to the right as Steve Biglands in White Four slotted in behind the tanker to take on the 14 tons of fuel that would carry him south. Framed by the ironwork of the Vulcan canopy Withers saw the floodlit undersides of the three Victors rise and fall and move forward and back together against the tar black sky; a careful three-dimensional ballet. Despite the appearance of grace and calm, 33,000 feet below the sea was speeding past at over 500 miles an hour.

Four hours into the mission and nearly 2,000 miles south of Ascension, Withers nosed the Vulcan towards Red Two. As 607 approached from dead astern, the bright-white shape of the Victor's planform grew until it filled the cockpit windows. Withers focused on it, barely blinking. Gloved in soft, pale-grey pig-skin, one hand kept a light grip on the pistol-grip stick while the other spread across the four central throttle levers. Using the heel of his hand he carefully nudged them forward and pulled them back, maintaining settings between 80 and 90 per cent, where the Rolls-Royce engines were at their most responsive. Next to him, Dick Russell kept a watchful eye on Withers' approach, ready to react to any developments before

*40 Degrees South*. An artist's impression of the turbulent electrical storm that made refuelling nearly impossible and threatened the success of the mission, the safety of the aircraft and the lives of the crews.

RONALD WON

The cramped, comfortless Vulcan cockpit was no place to spend sixteen hours.

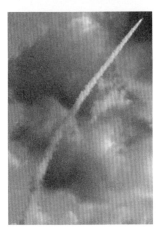

**Above:** The hornets' nest. **Clockwise from top right:** radar-laid, twin-barrelled 35mm Oerlikon anti-aircraft cannons; a Roland surface-to-air missile streaking to height at one and a half times the speed of sound; the radar-guided Franco-German Roland was, perhaps, the most lethal anti-aircraft weapon in the Argentine arsenal; belt-fed 20mm Rheinmetall shells.

**Above:** Splash One. A Vulcan caught in the gunsights of a Mirage fighter. The threat of interception by the Argentine Air Force was one further possibility the BLACK BUCK planners and Vulcan crews needed to consider.

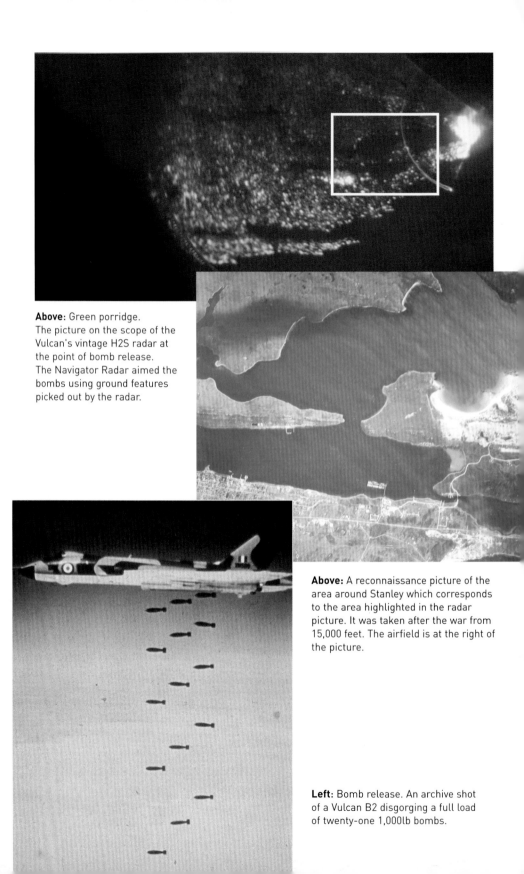

**Above:** Green porridge.
The picture on the scope of the
Vulcan's vintage H2S radar at
the point of bomb release.
The Navigator Radar aimed the
bombs using ground features
picked out by the radar.

**Above:** A reconnaissance picture of the
area around Stanley which corresponds
to the area highlighted in the radar
picture. It was taken after the war from
15,000 feet. The airfield is at the right of
the picture.

**Left:** Bomb release. An archive shot
of a Vulcan B2 disgorging a full load
of twenty-one 1,000lb bombs.

**Above:** Battle Damage Assessment. This shot, taken by a Fleet Air Arm Sea Harrier, was the first visual confirmation that Vulcan 607 had cratered the runway. The damage caused by her stick of bombs can be seen cutting across the airfield.

**Left:** A picture taken from the western end of the runway, looking east, which clearly shows 607's 1,000lb bomb crater just beyond the halfway point. Martin Withers's crew had effectively cut the strip in half and ended any lingering hope the Argentinians had that they might operate fast jets out of Stanley.

Viewing one of the craters close up underlines the destructive power of a single thousand-pounder. At the top right of the picture is an Aermacchi MB-339 light attack jet of the Argentine Navy's 1 Escuadrilla de Ataque – an air threat grounded by 607's attack.

**Above:** Martin Withers had never been airborne in a Vulcan carrying less fuel than he was as 607 closed in on the final refuelling rendezvous. He described his first glimpse of the Victor tanker as 'the most beautiful sight in the world'.

**Right:** V-force. A rare, striking picture of the Vulcan and Victor refuelling.

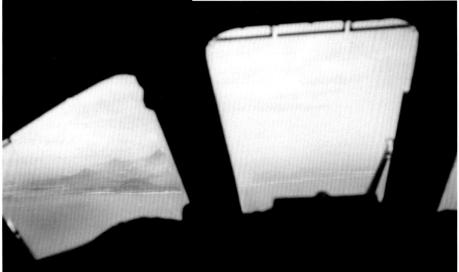

On Final Approach to Wideawake. From the Captain's seat.

**Above:** Bob Tuxford's crew celebrate BLACK BUCK's success and their safe return to Ascension in the traditional way. **L to r**: Navigator Radar Ernie Wallis, Air Electronics Officer Mick Beer, Bob Tuxford, Co-pilot Glyn Rees and Navigator Plotter John Keeble.

**Right:** With airbrakes out and undercarriage down, seconds from touchdown.

**Below:** After fifteen hours and forty-five minutes in the air, Vulcan 607 sends up puffs of smoke as she touches down to complete what was the longest bombing mission in history.

**Right:** Still wearing his thick rubber immersion suit, Martin Withers enjoys a post-sortie beer with Group Captain Jeremy Price, Senior RAF Officer on Ascension (**centre**), and Air Vice-Marshal George Chesworth of 18 Group.

**Left:** After waiting a month for the campaign to retake the Falklands to begin, news of the successful Vulcan raid was greeted with euphoria in London and Stanley. The tone of the reporting became more sober as the brutal realities of the war that followed unfolded.

The Avro Vulcan B2 – one of the crowning achievements of the post-war British aviation industry. In the twilight of her distinguished career an unlikely war on the other side of the world proved to be her finest hour.

they became dangerous. The tip of the probe felt for the drogue as 607 closed at around 2 or 3 knots – slow enough to be safe, fast enough to push the hose back into the HDU with enough force to trigger the fuel flow. Through their headsets, the rest of Withers' crew heard the sound of their captain breathing in and out. Aboard the Victor, the Nav Radar watched 607 through his periscope and relayed the bomber's progress to the rest of the tanker crew over the intercom.

As the red lights on either side of the Victor's HDU winked out, Withers flew forward through the mild buffeting that always accompanied the last few feet before contact. The drogue seemed to hover ahead of him, almost still, but gently responding to the imperfections of the fluid air in which it was being trailed. When the tip of the probe hit target, rollers inside the basket rode over it and gripped it to create a secure, water-tight coupling. The Victor's Nav Radar continued his commentary.

Aboard 607, Withers and Russell watched the two green lights come on, and, through the probe, non-return valves and four-inch-thick bifurcated pipes that ran underneath their feet, Avtur began to flush into the number 1 and 2 tanks behind them at over a ton a minute. Contact made, Withers passed control to Russell in the right-hand seat, and for the next fifteen minutes the experienced AARI comfortably held the big delta in close formation behind the Victor – less than twenty yards from her tailcone.

At the end of the second refuelling bracket, two more Victors peeled away from the formation to head home to Ascension. As they settled on to a north-westerly heading they would begin to enjoy the assistance of a 60-knot tailwind. Flying into the same wind, the attack formation pressed on towards the Falklands. There were now just three of them: Bob Tuxford, Steve Biglands flying the long-slot, and the Vulcan. The V-bomber three-ship formation cruised on south at 33,000 feet, still unaware of the biting fuel problems that jeopardized the success of their mission. Neither did they know that one of the two Victors that had just rolled away from them was now in serious trouble. Aboard Red Four, the AEO was trying to raise Wideawake on the HF radio: *Three Tango Foxtrot Niner, this is Quebec Five Charlie, over ... Three Tango Foxtrot Niner, this is Quebec Five Charlie, over ...*

# Chapter 34

At 0520, an hour and a half before sunrise and six and a half hours after the first thirteen aircraft had departed, the first of four Victors accelerated with a buzzsaw roar down Ascension's long runway and climbed away over the sea. As they left the Wideawake circuit they set course for the Rio RV, an agreed lat/long point above the South Atlantic over three hours' flying time to the south-west. Barry Neal and his crew had been on the ground for less than two hours. Two of the other crews had also already flown that night. For one of them, Frank Milligan's crew, which included the Victor detachment boss, Alan Bowman, as its Nav Plotter, it was a chance to make up for their disappointment earlier on. They'd been forced to return within an hour of BLACK BUCK's launch with a faulty HDU. They were flying the same Victor now. XL163 had her chance to make amends. The departing formation had just one task: to bring the Vulcan home.

Three minutes after the departure of the recovery wave, Red Rag Control began picking up transmissions through the static on the HF. Somebody was trying to make contact.

High-frequency – or shortwave – radio had long been used as a method of long-range communication by the RAF. It works through radio transmissions being reflected by the ionosphere and bounced back towards the earth's surface, hundreds of miles below. But while communication over great distances is possible, HF is vulnerable to the effects of changing atmospheric conditions. Night or day, summer or winter,

287

even the eleven-year solar cycle and sunspots affect the ionosphere's ability to reflect radio waves and, as a result, the performance of HF radio communications. As listeners to the BBC's World Service know only too well, frequencies can strengthen and fade away through the course of a single night.

The variable quality of HF reception in the Ops tent at Wideawake meant that following the mission's progress involved guesswork, intuition and anticipation. Little could be entirely relied on and much of what was picked up made no sense at all. This confusion was compounded by the changes that had necessarily taken place within the formation. But as Jeremy Price and the rest of the Red Rag team tried to piece together the mission's progress from talking to returning crews and the fragments of clear radio traffic, they tried to be prepared. So when, at 0523, Quebec Five Charlie crackled through the HF reporting a fuel leak, Price was able to scramble a jet to meet him. With John Elliott's crew ready to go, the Victor was airborne just eight minutes after the request came in. Elliott had been one of the four jets that had returned on vapours from the first refuelling bracket. So as he took to the air, he and the rest of his crew understood all too well the tension they were feeling aboard Quebec Five Charlie.

As the rumble of Elliott's engines receded into the distance, Price allowed himself the briefest of moments to reflect. His foresight in having a TAT on standby might just have saved the lives of one of his crews. If the jet hadn't been made ready to go it would never have been airborne quickly enough to meet the damaged inbound Victor in time. *Nice one, Cyril*, he thought, and lit another cigarette.

They'd already flown as far as London is from Timbuktu. And on board 607, Gordon Graham was becoming concerned about the flight plan. There was a discrepancy emerging between what the Carousels were telling him and where his flight plan and slide rule told him they should be. As far as he could tell, six hours from Ascension, they were nearly half an hour out. On top of this he'd noticed that they seemed to be burning fuel at a far higher rate than had been expected. What that might mean, he didn't know, but it was unlikely to be good news. Potentially more alarming was the slight but definite difference in what the two Carousels were telling him, a discrepancy that seemed to be increasing.

There was normally a healthy trade in chicken legs as the crew bartered with the contents of the ration tin. This time, though, the food on board remained untouched. Only the orange juice doled out by Pete Taylor was accepted gratefully, but they gulped it down at a price. It was running straight through them. With the third fuel bracket looming and beyond that the run-in to the target, Martin Withers knew he couldn't put it off any longer. He had to take a leak. If he went now, at least he could take advantage of the relative quiet to overcome the rigmarole of immersion suits and pee-tubes. He handed control of the bomber to Dick Russell and got to work. After loosening the straps on his seat harness, he'd just managed to unzip the heavy rubber suit when patches of cloud obscured Russell's view of the formation to the left. Withers though still had visual contact with the Victors so, with perfect comic timing, Russell handed the jet back to her captain.

'You have control,' he said with a grin, and Withers, with his one free hand, was forced to take over from his smiling AARI.

Martin Withers throttled back a little as they began their descent from the 33,000-foot cruising height to the refuelling height 4,000 feet below. During contact, with two large aircraft flying in close formation, the extra power and control that came in the lower, thicker air was welcome. Tonight it would be crucial. At night, with their radars switched off, they had no way of seeing what lay ahead. But, on what had been a gin-clear night lit only by bright stars, those first smudges of cloud warned of heavy weather ahead.

The numbers in the Ops tent had thinned out a little. Monty had gone to bed in the early hours, leaving his AEO, John Hathaway, to hold the fort. They'd agreed to swap shifts in the morning. Air Vice-Marshal Chesworth had also turned in. It made sense: there was nothing either of them could add to the work being done by Price and his Ops team.

At 0600, another message made it through to Red Rag Control on the HF. *Red Rag Control, this is Quebec Five Charlie. Request RV at 13°30' south, 17°48' west at 0622, over.* Red Rag read the message back to them to confirm it, then tried to raise Elliott in the outbound TAT to tell him of the inbound Victor's suspected fuel leak. They passed him a bearing and distance and confirmed the RV on channel 15. And, they stressed, he should make his best possible speed to the struggling jet.

Only soldiers were out on the streets of Stanley at night. As the civilian population slept behind blacked-out windows, the occasional Argentine military vehicle moved around with masked headlights. A light wind blew from the south-west. Once again, residents of the wooden houses on the hill at the back of town had sought comfort and safety in the centre. Hilda Perry and her husband had their chairs and sofas full with sleeping guests. In Sparrowhawk House, John and Ileen Smith were putting up their friends Duffy and Jeannie with the kids Eli and Maxwell as well as their own four children. Joe King had been forced into a pair of pyjamas. The seven people staying with him and his wife may have been friends, but that didn't mean they deserved to see him wandering around in a vest and Jockey Y-fronts. Leona Vidal and her brother Glen slept soundly. On the night of the invasion, their mother had made them sleep fully clothed with their shoes next to the bed. Things had settled down, but to Leona, too young to fully appreciate the anger and anguish caused by the occupation, much of what was going on still seemed exciting and different. Elsewhere, Liz Goss and her young family were staying with her in-laws and Peter Biggs and his wife Fran, despite advice, were defiantly sleeping on the first floor of the two-storey house. If they were going to die, they decided, they'd rather die in the comfort of their own bed.

On Sapper Hill, to the south-west of Stanley, the powerful Argentine AN/TPS 43 search radar of the FAA Vigilancia y Control Aereo scanned the skies. Since 13 April, when the crews and their equipment had moved during the night from near the airfield to this new location, they'd trained hard. They followed the comings and goings of the streams of aircraft supplying the islands from Argentina. They marked fixed echoes from ground features and they tried to determine the possible lines of approach by jets from the British aircraft carriers. And as FAA Mirages, Daggers and Skyhawks staged practice attacks from mainland bases, they honed their skills by tracking the low-flying strike fighters.

Fourteen anti-aircraft batteries manned by crews from the Air Force, Army and Marines ringed BAM Malvinas. Similarly dispersed around the airfield were the Four Superfledermaus and Skyguard fire-control radars that directed the barrels of the 30mm Hispano-Suiza and 35mm Oerlikon cannons. And on the outskirts of Stanley, looking east across the harbour, over the three-masted silhouette of the rusting wreck of an old cargo ship, *Lady Elizabeth*, was the twin Aerospatiale/MBB Roland surface-to-air missile launcher: deployed, ready and lethal way above the 10,000 feet at which the crew of Vulcan 607 planned to fly their bomb-run. The Roland fire unit was the pride of Grupo de Artilleria de Defensa Aerea 601. Despite his confidence in the system, the men who operated it and their training, their commander, Hector Lubin Arias, regretted not being able to field more of them. *Very sad*, he thought. Along with the radar-laid Oerlikons, it was a weapon that he knew had the potential to influence the course of a war.

*Green on, fuel flows*, reported Ernie Wallis as he saw the flashing navigation lights of the Vulcan through his rear-view periscope for the first time. Bob Tuxford and his crew were nearly done. Finish topping up 607's tanks then do the same for Steve Biglands in the long-slot Victor and they'd be on their way home. Job done. With its tanks full, the Vulcan dropped back, pulling the drogue with it until the tip of the probe tugged free of its grip. As the Vulcan slowly lost ground on the big tanker, the two red lights on either side of the HDU blinked on and 607 rolled gently away to the right. Withers and Russell soon checked their drift to the right to take up station a couple of hundred feet behind in a loose starboard echelon formation. Then they watched as the two Victors drew together.

As Biglands closed on the trailing basket, Tux started to lose sight of the stars for the first time that night. Withers and Russell watched as the two floodlit tankers began to flick in and out of the cloud tops. At 31,000 feet, the three-ship attack formation was flying directly into the path of a raging electrical storm, at 40 degrees south, just as the Met officer had warned.

The crews felt their stomachs lurch as they dropped through the first pockets of turbulent air. Wrapped in dense arms of cumulonimbus, the jets began to buck violently, smacked around by rising, twisting air that jolted and juddered the air-frames like heavy seas pummelling the hull of a ship.

While a receiver manoeuvred behind to make contact, the Victor tanker would normally engage the autopilot. It was less tiring for both crews. Any mild turbulence would affect both jets in the same way and they would ride it together, rising and falling as one. But this time the sky was too violent. Tux flicked off the autopilot to try to keep his jet stable manually. As he gripped the throttles and stick, his gloved hands working hard, he was thrown against the straps of his harness. His seat bucketed out on the bottom of its rails whenever the nose of the Victor was thrown upwards. The thuds and bangs of the aircraft's sharp movements were more visceral than audible. Instead, heard through thickly padded Bone Domes, the wind-ing up and slowing down of the jet engines' spinning turbines provided the urgent soundtrack to Tux's struggle to keep the Victor where he wanted it.

In the Vulcan, the physical discomfort was, if anything, even worse. The Victor's long, slender wings flexed up and down like shock absorbers to disperse some of the storm's ferocity, but the Vulcan's more rigid construction transmitted it to the men flying her with the same bone-jarring directness of a cartwheel on a cobbled street. Always sensitive to sudden changes in pitch, the autopilot quickly tripped out under the onslaught. Instead, Withers flew the jet manually – always confident that the power and the responsiveness of the Olympus engines would keep him out of trouble.

The dazzling white flashes of lightning destroyed Tux's night vision. For a split second he could see everything with blinding intensity before being left blinking, straining even to see the instrument panel two feet ahead of him. Lightning didn't just pose a threat to his view forward though. Great efforts were made by aircraft manufacturers to ensure that any strike was conducted directly from the extremity, like a wingtip, where it was likely to hit, to another extremity, like the tail, where it would exit. Particular attention was given to protecting an aircraft's fuel system. Thick skin around the tanks was designed to prevent burn through and structural joins were tight to prevent sparks. Every critical component had to be capable of withstanding a direct strike. But while lightning damage was rare, it could be catastrophic. In 1963, eighty-one people were killed when lightning brought down a Boeing 707 airliner. And Tux himself had already once had a close call. While he was crossing the Atlantic, a lightning bolt had punched a hole through the metal of his Victor's wing, taking out the whole of his compass system. Only a skilful talk-down through a 200-foot cloud-base by Goose Bay's air traffic controllers saved the jet on that occasion.

The best defence against lightning was simply to avoid it. So flying through a powerful electrical storm while trying to pass fuel from one aircraft to another had little to recommend it. As they flew, St Elmo's fire crackled blue, white and purple in the hot, ionized air outside the flight deck windows to give a constant, insidious reminder of the electrical threat. They all knew that the plasma only appeared when there were very high voltages in the air.

It was Steve Biglands, though, who was suffering most. While trying to make contact with the trailing hose, his view ahead was strobing like a drug-fuelled rock video. The sky burnt white for an instant, then Tux's Victor would be almost completely obscured by cloud before emerging briefly into clear skies. The unpredictable sequence was relentless. But whatever the visual challenges, it remained the punishing turbulence that made it nearly impossible for Biglands to make contact. The basket, which normally appeared to sit nearly still in the air, was jerking up and down by ten feet and more. Any attempt to connect by formating on the fluorescent lines on the tanker's belly was doomed to failure. Somehow Biglands was going to have to try to anticipate the drogue's movements and intercept it. On board the tanker, Ernie Wallis watched astern as Biglands tried in vain to stab the elusive basket. *Red out, maintaining astern*, he reported over the intercom. But however dispassionate his commentary, the old Nav Radar – Mr Flight Refuelling – didn't think 'Biggles' was going to be able to do it. In a twenty-five-year career he'd been witness to every kind of attempt to make contact, good, bad, hopeless and dangerous, but he'd never seen anything like what he was watching now.

*Closing up . . . miss . . . dropping back*, Wallis continued, describing another effort by Biglands to trap the basket. Each of the refuelling brackets covered a great enough distance to accommodate refuelling difficulties. But each also had a geographical limit. If the transfer wasn't complete by then, dictated tanker lore, then you scrubbed it and returned home. As the three jets pushed south through the storm, they were now closer to the end of the bracket than to the beginning. Biglands was running out of airspace.

*Closing up . . . contact!* When Wallis shared the news of Biglands' success, his voice betrayed a hint of his relief and Tuxford's entire crew couldn't help but relax just a fraction. An instinctive reaction. The Nav Radar continued to stare into his scope as Biglands flew his Victor forward to trigger the HDU's pump and get the fuel flowing.

*Green on, fuel flows*, Wallis told them, and kept watching behind. He knew that Biglands' making contact was a battle won but not a war. Now Biggles had to maintain formation while the two jets continued to be hurled around the volatile skies. While the co-pilot, Glyn Rees, called out the quantities of fuel being dispensed, Wallis kept Tuxford up to date with their receiver's uncertain progress.

'He's getting very unstable . . .' Wallis warned.

As the tanker was bounced around the sky, the trailing hose started to oscillate dangerously. While the motors governing the hose's travel were designed to prevent waves and ripples kicking up and down its length, there were limits to their ability to absorb extremes of movement. Wallis watched with mounting alarm until, perhaps, the inevitable happened.

Inside the cockpit of Biglands' jet there was a heart-stopping crack felt by all five of the crew as the tip of the Victor's four-inch thick refuelling probe sheered off under the strain – unable to cope with the enormous lateral forces imposed on it. Ernie Wallis' instruments told him immediately that the fuel flow had been interrupted. He sagged as he watched through the periscope.

'He's broken his probe,' Wallis confirmed to his own crew over the intercom.

Biglands called it in over the RT a moment later. Tux could hear the anguish in his voice. He'd received just 8,000lb of fuel, half what he needed to fly south with the Vulcan as long-slot. And he could take on no more fuel in any circumstances. Whatever he had on board had to get him home to Ascension, 3,000 miles away.

Tuxford quickly thought through what had happened. If, as well as the damage to Biglands' Victor, his own jet's refuelling basket had been wrecked – or if the broken tip of Biggles' refuelling probe was still jammed into the coupling valve – it meant the end of the road.

If Biglands couldn't fly the long-slot role, the only possible option was for him and Tuxford to swap places. For the Vulcan to press home her attack, Tux was going to have to take on the fuel to fly the long-slot while at the same time carefully making sure that Biggles' crippled jet had enough to get back to Wideawake without *any possibility* of needing further refuelling. He broke radio silence to talk to Biglands.

'White Four, have you left your probe in the basket?'

'I don't know,' came the reply.

There was only one way of finding out, but for the time being Tuxford had to assume his own drogue was going to work.

'If we're going to get away with this,' he told Biglands, 'the only solution is for me to take the fuel back. Can you get the hose out?' Then he spoke to his Nav Radar: 'Right, Ernie, get the hose in, let's tidy it up . . .'

# Chapter 35

'White Four, we're going to have to go for a formation change.'

As Tux explained his plan to Biglands, his own crew were preparing their jet to swap roles: tanker to receiver. Ernie Wallis checked the view behind them. *Clear to wind*, he said, before reeling in the Victor's eighty-foot-long hose. *Winding.*

After they'd cleaned up the airframe, the co-pilot, Glyn Rees, prepared the wide fuel tray that folded down between the pilots' ejection seats. Moving fuel around the tanks in preparation to take on fuel would normally take anything up to fifteen minutes, but there was no time for that. They continued through the checklist until hearing *Checks are complete* from AEO Mick Beer. Tux thumbed the transmit button and cleared Steve Biglands in White Four to overtake. Forced together by the vital need to maintain visual contact as they darted through the turbulent banks of cloud, the three V-bombers were in unusually close formation. As they changed places, in boiling air and uncomfortably close proximity, Biglands and Tuxford *had* to keep sight of one another.

Biggles drifted across to the left. With the Vulcan maintaining her position to their right, the three jets' formation took on the shape of an arrowhead. Then Biglands pushed forward his throttles to increase the engine rpm and his Victor started to gain on Tuxford's. As Biggles' broken jet nosed forward, Tux caught sight of her overtaking through the thick glass beyond his left shoulder. The electric sky raged as the three-ship streaked south in and out of the cumulus. Inside each of the

V-bombers the seats creaked and complained as they resisted the forces trying to oust their occupants from them.

'I have your visual, White Four,' Tux told Biglands, 'you have the lead.'

Tux then manoeuvred his jet into position behind the damaged Victor, his senses heightened by the adrenalin coursing through him. Fired up and worried that the whole mission was falling apart, he was in a dangerous mood. Too aggressive, too hot-headed, and he would make mistakes. Tuxford tried to force himself to stay calm. But he knew if he overcooked it he could rely on experienced men like Ernie Wallis to rein him in: *Cool it, Bob, slow down.* Around him, the rest of the crew were working. With the master switch on their own HDU now turned off, Wallis backed up Nav Plotter John Keable as he replanned the flight ahead. At the end of the fuel transfer they'd become formation leader down to bracket four, barely an hour north of the Falklands. Mick Beer monitored the old V-bomber's hydraulics and electrics while up front Glyn Rees performed heroics rearranging the fuel tray in a fraction of the time required. Tuxford composed himself, waiting for the word from Biglands' Nav Radar. Then his headset crackled into life.

*You're clear astern.*

Tuxford reduced the power and dropped back from a loose echelon into line astern.

*Clear for contact.*

He nudged the throttles forward with his left hand and began to close on the flailing basket.

Making contact by the book – following the line of the hose to the tanker's belly – could never work in these conditions, whatever was taught back in ground school at Marham. Tuxford had to go for the basket, but with the distances it was thrashing up and down that needed careful handling. If he tried to fly the Victor in pursuit of the flailing drogue, too many deliberate, opposing inputs on the control yoke would cause a PIO, a Pilot-Induced Oscillation. Each correction would become an over-correction and, like a speeding car fishtailing down an icy road, its driver wrestling the wheel from side to side, the big jet would begin to porpoise wildly. It was a difficult situation to recover from. Especially so when you were flying thirty feet behind the tail of another aircraft. Instead, Tuxford tried to pick his moment, to anticipate the path of the basket and nail it with a burst of power from the engines or a kick of the rudder pedals.

A hundred and fifty yards to the right of him, hail rattled like grapeshot against the toughened glass of the Vulcan's windscreen as Dick Russell watched the scene unfold. The green and grey camouflage of Tuxford's Victor was picked out by the floodlights lighting the underside of the tanker ahead. Russell didn't like the look of what he was seeing at all; he had never seen an effort to make a transfer in turbulence like this.

And then Tux made contact with a clunk. Relief. Fuel began to flow through the unstable hose that joined the two jets like an umbilical cord. But with barely half the transfer complete, as Tux fought to remain tucked in behind the tanker, the heavy, fuel-filled hose began to whip violently again as powerful waves travelled up and down its length. Tuxford knew the danger it posed. Forced to make a quick, agonizing decision, he throttled back to sever the contact and preserve the probe. If the force of the hose's fierce movement ripped off the tip of his probe too, BLACK BUCK would be over.

He'd saved the integrity of the airframe, but the formation was still flying south, away from the haven of Ascension. They were way past the bracket limit, he didn't have the fuel he needed to take the long-slot and still wasn't sure he could transfer fuel to the Vulcan anyway: *Put that one to the back of my mind, at least*, he told himself. His pulse was racing and his breathing uneven. Physically and mentally drained, he knew he was on the edge of what he was capable of, the limit of his flying ability. But if this was going to work, there was no choice other than to make contact with the tanker again. A flash of lightning revealed the silhouette of the Vulcan in his peripheral vision to the right. Tuxford flew the bucking jet back into position behind Biglands' Victor and, with his gloved hands on the throttles and control yoke, focused on the unsteady circle of fluorescent lights around the rim of the basket. He began to lunge for them, cursing each failure to connect. As they were thrown around in their chairs, in the back of Tux's Victor, Ernie Wallis looked across at John Keable. The look between the two Navigators, only their eyes visible above oxygen masks, shared their recognition of the severity of the conditions.

*Something's going to break*, thought Dick Russell as he watched Tuxford try to strike for the centre of the basket. Minutes passed as the Victor surged forward and dropped back hunting in vain for the basket. Throttle response from the Conways wasn't instantaneous and sometimes Tux missed by eight or nine feet as his jet lunged in underneath the tanker's tail before dropping back to try again. The stirring spectacle gripped Russell. *True grit*, he thought, as he watched Tuxford's struggle. Russell wasn't sure many of his fellow pilots could or would have done it, but as the hose twisted and reared around the sky, Tuxford rammed the throttles and locked the probe into the drogue. *Yes!* Russell reacted instantly, the tension as he had watched ending as surely as if he'd just seen a penalty hammered home in a cup final.

At the moment the fuel began pumping through the long hose into the Victor's tanks, Tuxford began to see stars twinkling around the edges of the tanker filling his view forward. The storm released its grip on the formation as quickly as it had enveloped them. The turbulence subsided and, for the first time in over twenty minutes, the three V-bombers began to settle in the air while the hose connecting the two Victors smoothed out. As a sense of the natural horizon returned, Tux was able to loosen his white-knuckle grasp on the flying. But with the intensity of flying through the storm behind them, his attention turned to the fuel within the formation. Acutely conscious that with a broken probe Biglands couldn't take on any more fuel, he asked his own crew how much they could expect from the damaged tanker. And, in case there was any confusion, he contacted Biglands directly over the RT.

'White Four, you *must* leave extra reserves to get back.'

The fuel plan was in tatters. Tux had been supposed to turn for home before the end of the refuelling bracket with 64,000lb of fuel on board, leaving Biglands to fly on with the Vulcan. But that was before the probe tip had sheered off; before they swapped places; before Tux had spent precious minutes trying to make contact, burning extra fuel with every stab at the throttles; and before all three jets had flown way beyond the southern limit of the refuelling bracket. Now over six hours out of Ascension, it was Biglands turning for home and he was going to need more than 64,000lb to get there. A rough calculation showed that around 70,000lb offered the slimmest of margins. But without any means of refuelling he had to arrive at the Wideawake overhead with more than a bare minimum. At this point there wasn't even the possibility of informing Red Rag Control. Jerry Price was in the dark about what was unfolding thousands of miles from Ascension.

The amber lights around the tanker's HDU flashed to tell Tux he'd had all the fuel that could be spared. He throttled back, breaking contact. Then he watched as the floodlights underneath the tanker flicked off before she peeled away to the north to begin cruise-climbing to an economical altitude for the long drag home.

The attack formation was down to just two jets: one Victor and the Vulcan. And between them they were carrying around 20,000lb less fuel than they were supposed to have: nearly two hours' flying time; about 600 nautical miles. *Woefully short*, thought Tuxford, *of what's needed*. It was of academic concern, though, if his Victor's drogue had been damaged in the storm. Until working out how they could continue, they had to discover whether or not they could continue at all. They decided to attempt a token fuel transfer to the Vulcan to prove the system worked.

*Pre-tanking checks*, ordered Tuxford to initiate the refuelling sequence.

While Ernie Wallis trailed the hose, Martin Withers dropped into position behind the Victor. Behind the Vulcan Captain,

AEO Hugh Prior pulled a heavy torch out of a compartment in his flight bag and passed it up the ladder to Dick Russell in the co-pilot's seat. As Withers tried to formate on the drogue, Russell shone the torch through the flight-deck window. Reflections from the glass confused the view ahead, but he was able to pick up the basket in the beam of the powerful torch.

'I can't really see anything,' Russell confessed, 'but I can't see the probe tip in there.' There was no obvious problem, but there was only one way to be certain. Dick Russell stowed the torch and Withers closed in on the basket. In the cold, clear air the contact presented no difficulties. Withers clunked home the probe for proving contact and fuel began to flow freely. It was still on. 5,000lb later they were satisfied that the refuelling equipment, at least, wouldn't provide cause to abort the mission. For the time being, they could continue south.

As far as the crew of the Vulcan were concerned, the fuel drama was now over. The mood aboard the Victor was rather different. The fuel plan was a bust, but having proved that the refuelling system was still working they now had a crucial decision to make. If they turned back now, if Withers jettisoned his bombs, they had the fuel to get both jets back to Ascension. If they pressed on, the future was uncertain. They would be placing themselves in a situation where they could no longer depend solely on their own efforts to survive. But having got this far – and hung off the end of a refuelling hose in appalling, draining conditions to do so – Tux felt a strong compulsion to carry on, but he couldn't simply follow his own gut instinct to support the Vulcan. His crew had to feel the same way. He put it to them.

'Right, we either turn back now, or pretty sharpish at least, or we press on in the knowledge that we've got to come up with an alternative plan. We may need to abandon or ditch. Say what's on your mind. I need you all to speak up.'

One by one, and quickly, the answers came back through the intercom.

*Well we've come this far . . .*
*Keep going.*

*Got to go on with the mission.*

Unanimous.

'Then let's see how far we can go with this without making too much of a mess of it . . .'

In truth Tux hadn't expected anything less from any of them, but ultimate responsibility for their safety lay with him. Their support wouldn't make their predicament any less precarious, but it was a comfort to him as he made the single most difficult decision he'd ever had to make as an aircraft captain: choosing danger over safety. Now they had to work out how they were going to do it.

'John,' Tux called out to his Nav Plotter, 'how much fuel do we need to get back from the fourth bracket?'

Keable immediately got to work, his calculations double-checked by Ernie Wallis at the Nav Radar's station to his left. He needed to factor in the winds they'd encountered on the way down, examine the Operating Data Manual that could tell them the fuel burn of the four Conway engines at different weights and altitudes. The five men aboard discussed how low on fuel they were prepared to go; how close they needed to get to Ascension to have any hope of meeting a tanker scrambled from Wideawake to bring them home; and, ultimately, as a result of Keable's rapid number-crunching, how much fuel they could afford to pass to the Vulcan at the fourth transfer. Over an intense half hour's discussion the crew focused on the ramifications of sharing the fuel available between the Victor and Vulcan in different proportions. In the end, they felt, the best they could do was to pass 607 just 8,000lb, nearly 4,000lb short of what, after the proving contact, was still required. It would still, Tux thought, give the bomber a reasonable shot at doing the job and making it back to the Rio RV. But it would leave him and his Victor crew at least 20,000lb short of what they required to reach Ascension. Unless they successfully rendezvous'd with a TAT scrambled from Wideawake, they would run out of fuel 600 miles south of the island, well beyond the range of rescue helicopters. And the worst part was, they couldn't tell anyone.

The refuellings at brackets three and four were supposed to be conducted in strict radio silence. Because of the difficulties they'd had to contend with, that hadn't happened at the third bracket, but it was one thing communicating with another Victor a few hundred yards away on a discrete VHF channel, quite another to try to reach Red Rag Control over 3,000 miles away on the HF radio. Any long-range transmission by AEO Mick Beer could compromise the strike itself by alerting the Argentinians to the imminent arrival of the Vulcan. Beer agreed with the rest of the crew's logic. If they were going to put themselves at risk by passing the Vulcan the fuel, it didn't make sense to threaten her chances of success by broadcasting their presence. They chose to suffer in silence.

Aboard the Vulcan, thoughts began to turn to what lay beyond the final refuelling. As a veteran Victor instructor, Dick Russell hadn't expected to be flying into harm's way again – and certainly not in his fifties. That was bad enough, but before the bomb-run he was going to have to swap places with Withers' co-pilot, Pete Taylor. Naturally enough, Russell's mind lingered on the safety of the aircraft at a time when, sitting below the flight deck in the jump seat, he'd be powerless to influence events. He turned to Martin Withers.

'We don't want to forget our navigation lights,' he reminded the Captain. While in the formation they'd tried to make themselves as visible as possible, but the last thing they wanted to do was run in to Stanley with lights blazing. 'Let's turn them off now, while we can.'

It seemed sensible enough to act now, rather than regret it later, Withers agreed. Russell reached down to his right and killed the lights. The black shape of the bomber was now invisible against the dark sky.

# Chapter 36

The new day came quickly so close to the equator and, hidden behind the volcanic hills that crowd Wideawake, the first orange glow of dawn grew quickly into the flat light of early morning. Jerry Price and the Red Rag team had made it through the night and forestalled disaster, but an accurate picture of BLACK BUCK's progress was still elusive.

*X-ray Four Lima.* In the dust and fug of the Ops tent, call signs ebbed and flowed over the HF, but while they could be ascribed to a particular crew and aircraft, their meaning was often impossible to interpret.

*Charlie Five Tango.* That was Skelton.

*Seven Echo Foxtrot, authenticate*: Milligan, being asked to provide the one-letter code that would prove he was who he said he was. Did it mean there was a problem?

Price could only try to second-guess what was going on further south. While fractured transmissions were coming in from the tankers closest to Ascension, there was nothing from beyond the second fuel bracket, as the attack formation pushed south in strict HF radio silence. Although unaware of the pasting the attack formation had taken from the storm Price drew his own conclusions about the shape they were in. He wasn't sure *how* desperate they might be on their return flight, but, after the close calls earlier, he was sure that their situation would be precarious. They would not have the fuel they needed. He wanted TATs airborne and ready to bring home his two long-slots: Tuxford and Biglands. At 6.15, Price ordered two further Victors to prepare to get airborne at 7.30. And while the measured, thoughtful tones in which he spoke barely betrayed the strain, the restless smoking left no doubt.

Minutes later, Milligan's presence on the airwaves became clear. Victor 163's HDU had failed again. As the sky outside the tent turned from black to blue, Frank Milligan's AEO called Red Rag Control to say they were on their way home early for the second time that night. They hadn't even been airborne an hour. Price couldn't help but feel for them. *Poor old Milligan*, he thought, knowing the unfortunate crew, including his friend Alan Bowman, would be in for a ribbing in some quarters. It was just the way of things. But aside from the blushes and frustration of the crew, their return meant that the redundancy in the recovery formation was now gone. Two of the remaining three Victors would instead fill the tanks of Barry Neal's Victor as close to the Rio RV as possible. They would then leave him to fly on alone to the holding point, a few hundred miles out over the Atlantic, abeam the Brazilian capital. The plan had called for two Victors to wait there. Now there was no redundancy. If there was any problem with Neal's jet that prevented him from transferring fuel to the Vulcan, the bomber wouldn't make it back to Ascension. Not for the first or last time this night, their eggs were, once more, in one basket.

Passing across an imaginary boundary into the fourth refuelling bracket, Ernie Wallis flashed the floodlights underneath the Victor. Flying in radio silence, this was the signal to tell the Vulcan crew they were cleared to refuel. For the last time, Martin Withers eased his aircraft into position behind the tanker with gentle, fluid precision. Once settled in the wake of the tanker, he and Dick Russell watched the red lights shining alongside the root of the trailing fuel hose, waiting for them to change; waiting for the go-ahead to make contact. And nothing happened. Then the floodlights flashed off and on again. They were cleared to move in behind the Victor. But they knew that, they were already *there*. Confused, Russell turned to Withers.

'I don't know what's up with him . . .'

The Vulcan Captain didn't answer. Instead, a voice from the Victor came over the RT: 'You're clear astern.'

'We *are* astern!' Russell replied, puzzled. And then it dawned on him: the Victor couldn't see them. With their anti-collision beacons and navigation lights already turned off, Ernie Wallis, peering through his periscope inside the Victor, couldn't make out 90 tons and 3,500 square feet of delta-winged bomber flying just a few yards away. A little sheepishly, Dick Russell flicked the switch alongside his ejection seat to bring them on again. Contact followed smoothly and easily. Fuel began to flush into the Vulcan's tanks as Russell, relaxed and comfortable flying in close formation, kept her tucked in close. Some impressive flying and the flexibility of the Victor force had overcome all the storm had thrown at them and, it seemed, things were back on track. He and the rest of 607's crew were about to discover how wrong that assumption was.

Tux knew he couldn't pass them the fuel they needed. As fuel pumped out of the back of his jet, Ernie Wallis and the co-pilot, Glyn Rees, watched the numbers spin, poised to end the transfer, when they hit the bingo figure.

*Seven five . . . six . . . seven . . . eight . . . nine . . .*

Wallis flashed the amber lights on the HDU to tell the Vulcan crew that they'd had all the tanker could spare. They had to withdraw.

Still 7,000lb short of what they needed the news was greeted on board the Vulcan with surprise and bafflement. They'd taken on a little over half what they'd been expecting. And although the Victor hadn't actually cut the fuel flow, the instruction was clear. Surprise began to turn to anger. *What's he doing?*, Withers thought. *How dare they?* Completely unaware of the knife-edge on which the Victor crew had already placed themselves, Withers was furious that with a job to do, he was being left in the lurch barely 300 miles north of the target. He wasn't going to break contact until he knew what was going on.

So, ignoring the amber lights, the Vulcan remained in

contact with the drogue. Fuel was still flowing. And the Victor was paying double for every mile further south they flew. Any fuel burnt beyond the point at which the tanker crew had planned to turn north would have to be burnt again just to return to that same point.

'What's going on?' crackled a pinched voice from the Vulcan.

'Come on,' Tuxford said to Ernie Wallis, 'we've got to call a halt to this. We can't keep on giving him fuel and abandon the plan we've just worked out.'

Wallis couldn't simply cut the fuel flow as that would empty the hose, lightening it, causing it to display different flying characteristics. Tuxford thumbed the RT.

'Blue Two, you've got to break contact,' he told them, angry that Dick Russell, the refuelling specialist in the right-hand seat of the Vulcan, wasn't putting it all together; that he'd failed to appreciate their predicament. But through the eyepiece of the rear-facing periscope, Ernie Wallis could see that he was, at least, listening.

*He's dropping back*, Wallis reported, *he's free.*

'We're 7,000lb short,' Hugh Prior radioed from the AEO station in the back of the Vulcan. 'We don't have the fuel to carry out the mission.'

Tuxford could hear the anxiety being caused, but had to hope that Dick Russell would work out what was happening and explain. Tux's own crew had been to the limit, but now, he felt, it was time they tried to save themselves.

'We *have* to turn off.'

'Why?'

'I'm sorry, that's it; I have no more fuel to give you,' Tux emphasized, frustrated by the apparent ignorance aboard the Vulcan of how marginal his position had become. It remained in formation, tucked in close behind them, its presence there questioning and accusatory.

Any understanding between the two crews had broken down.

'For Christ's sake, Ernie,' said Bob Tuxford to his Nav

Radar, 'we'll offer him more fuel.' His heart was ruling his head. He decided to gamble on one last throw of the dice to send the bomber on her way. Tuxford pressed the transmit button on his control yoke.

'I'm rolling out on to a heading of 040. Going north, if you follow us round, we might be able to give you more . . .' Then he banked into a wide, left turn towards the north, trailing the hose behind him.

Ernie Wallis, his view behind confined by the periscope's narrow field of vision, continued to watch the Vulcan's lights blink out of the dark at him.

'He's following us!' Wallis reported, unable to conceal his surprise that the delta was following them round, turning away from her target to the south. None of the Victor crew had really believed that the bomber would take up an offer made more in hope than expectation.

And Martin Withers would never have followed the Victor into the turn if it hadn't held the prospect of more fuel. But, in contrast to the view aboard the Victor, he quickly became sure that far from receiving the fuel to make 607's reverse worthwhile, he'd been given all he was going to get. And he was livid about it. Following the tanker round in the hope of an unknown quantity of fuel had been a wild goose chase. A *complete* waste of their time and precious fuel. They had a time over target to meet, they were flying in the wrong direction and, Gordon Graham had told them, they were already thirty-seven minutes behind plan.

'We can't keep going north,' Withers told his crew over the intercom and thumbed the RT to tell the Victor crew they were leaving them.

'We're off,' he transmitted before standing the bomber on her ear to bring her back on to a southerly track. He rolled out on to a heading of 237 degrees. Vulcan 607 was heading back towards the Falklands again.

Withers' transmission was greeted with stunned silence in the cockpit of Tuxford's Victor. What did they mean? *We're off to Ascension or we're off to the Falklands?*, Tuxford wondered. The bomber had rolled away. Ernie Wallis could confirm that, but they'd have had to do that even if they were climbing north on a parallel course. The exhausted Victor crew sank into their seats, despondent at the thought that the Vulcan could have abandoned the mission after all they'd put themselves through to ensure its success.

'Right,' Tuxford cut into their thoughts without enthusiasm, 'Ernie, let's get the hose in; get her cleaned up and we'll climb to altitude. Post-tanking checks, please . . .'

As the five men ran through the checklist, Tuxford trimmed the hard-worked old V-bomber into a lazy cruise-climb to 43,000 feet. And towards her uncertain future to the north.

Martin Withers was completely unaware of the tanker's predicament. Eleven tankers and fifteen fuel transfers had brought them to within an hour of their target and now he was being sold short. He felt bitterly let down – so did Dick Russell. The veteran AARI was making quick mental calculations. They were supposed to reach the RV 400 miles off Rio with 14,000lb of fuel in the tanks. Take 7,000lb away from that and it didn't leave much in reserve. *Dear, oh dear*, he thought. Russell knew the failsafe operating procedures of the tanker force inside out. If they were going to do it by the book, he told Withers, they *had* to turn back. As the only man on board with any genuine air-to-air refuelling experience, he had a duty to point out that to guarantee the safety of the aircraft, they should abort. If they were to succeed, only then to lose the bomber as the contents of the tanks turned to vapour, it would be a disaster, not just for them but for the entire British war effort.

Dick Russell had said what he had to say, but however uncomfortable he was with the prospect of pressing on towards the target, he knew that the decision wasn't his to make. The thought of aborting never crossed Martin Withers' mind. He'd barely taken in what Russell had said about Standard Operating Procedure and he certainly wasn't going to put it to the vote. Like Russell, Withers was making rough calculations about their fuel situation. But in contrast to his

AARI, he knew the Vulcan well; knew that he could move the remaining fuel around the bomber's fourteen tanks to eke it out as long as possible. He also figured that they could make their escape from the Stanley air defences at altitude instead of dropping back down to sea level. That might save another two or three thousand pounds too. They could worry about the detail of the low-fuel handling drills later. For now, he thought, *we can do this.*

'We're short of fuel, but we've come this far,' Withers said to his crew, 'I'm not turning back now.'

And while he invited their opinion on his decision, the edge in his voice precluded debate. He was determined to succeed. For all his easy affability and democratic approach to captaincy, Withers was displaying the steel that those back at Waddington knew he possessed. He never doubted that his close-knit crew would back his decision. And not one of them had a moment's hesitation in doing so. *We'll sort something out*, thought the co-pilot, Pete Taylor, from the isolation of the sixth seat.

# Chapter 37

For the first time in nearly eight hours, 607 was on her own. And, 3,500 miles from home, she was off the V-force maps. With less than 300 miles to run, everything now depended on the accuracy of the twin Carousel INS. The two Navigators had been forced to abandon astro-navigation and the bomber's GPI6 computer told them they were miles away from where Nav Plotter Gordon Graham's own dead reckoning told them they were supposed to be. And that relied on little more than compasses, stop-watches and slide rules.

'Plotting the Two . . .' said Graham in his Scottish west coast burr, as he marked the latitude and longitude readings from the two Carousels on to his improvised northern-hemisphere map. The two positions were now thirty miles apart. There was no way of knowing which one was correct or even whether either was correct; they could both be wrong.

'What shall we do?' Graham asked Bob Wright, drawing him into the problem. Although Graham was the senior man, it made sense to agree a plan of action with the radar operator – who, like Graham, was a trained Navigator. There was no certain answer. The decision they reached would always reflect whatever assumptions it was based on. Between them, they agreed to split the difference. Graham drew a line between the two conflicting positions and marked its median point. Graham input their new position into the GPI6. It meant that when Wright turned on his radar before the bomb-run, the picture he expected to see on his cathode ray screen would be dictated by an arbitrarily agreed plot on an upside down chart. It wasn't an ideal starting point.

With the Top of Descent just minutes away, it was time for Dick Russell, having helped get the thirsty jet this far, to give the right-hand seat back to Pete Taylor for the bomb-run. Although he'd felt some sympathy for the young co-pilot as he languished below during the long flight down, the veteran tanker captain didn't look forward to the move with any relish. *Let's get it over with,* he thought as he folded up the fuel tray to allow him and Taylor to manoeuvre around the cramped flight deck. Bob Wright got up from his seat in the back to help them swap places. First of all he disarmed the co-pilot's ejection seat to prevent any danger of it being triggered accidentally, by slotting safety pins back into the top and bottom of the Martin-Baker chair. Then Russell unstrapped himself and, stooping, eased sideways between the seats and down the ladder. From his new position on the jump seat, he was no longer able to see what was going on and equally no longer able to eject in an emergency. To cap it all, his leg had gone to sleep. As Bob Wright helped plug him into the intercom, Pete Taylor got up from his own spot on the starboard side of the cabin and climbed up the ladder to join his Captain.

*What a bloody awful crew compartment it is compared to the Victor,* thought Russell, and buckled up in the gloom.

In contrast, Pete Taylor felt he was back where he belonged. As his eyes adjusted to the brighter light on the flight deck, he got settled next to Martin Withers. He strapped into the harness, clipped the ejection seat's leg restraint lines to his shins and attached his PEC to the side of the chair. Then he removed the safety pins from the two yellow and black striped firing handles and pushed them into a specially designed storage block on the side of the flight deck. It was a simple system: if the pins were stowed in their slots, the seat was live. Ready now, he and Withers acknowledged each other. The Captain was quick to hand over control to his co-pilot. It wasn't just altruism. The bomber was going to slip in underneath the sweep of the enemy search radars, giving them as little notice of her arrival as possible; giving her and her crew their best chance of success and survival. He didn't want his co-pilot coming to it cold.

*Pre-descent checks, please . . .*

The crew paid particular attention to their pressure settings and altimeters. All the Met information they had was forecast and they couldn't absolutely rely on its accuracy. There were no updates from Air Traffic; no local weather stations to rely on. A descent to low level over the sea at night was an unforgiving undertaking and for every millibar of pressure the forecast was wrong, they would be another thirty feet higher or lower than they thought they were. As 607 closed on the Descent Point, Hugh Prior, preparing himself to combat the Argentine air defences, spoke up.

'Once we start running in, keep the intercom on; turn all the radios off – everything, particularly the RWR, because you won't hear the noises. If we get locked up or illuminated, you won't get distracted. Concentrate on what you're doing, like being in the simulator; just go through normal procedures.'

It was good advice and the rest of the crew followed it. All except Dick Russell, who, stuck in the sixth seat, didn't have any choice but to listen to whatever came through his headset.

When they were 290 miles from the target, Pete Taylor pulled back on the four throttle levers and relaxed his grip on the stick. The engine note fell away and all on board felt a subtle change in the bomber's pitch as she nosed over into a shallow descent.

The small hours were always the worst, when every problem seemed more intense. Since the invasion, John Fowler had frequently found himself lying awake at night in his house on the Stanley harbour front, worrying about what the weeks ahead held in store for him and his young family. On the morning of 1 May though, Fowler had been sleeping, only to be woken just after four o'clock by the sound of one of his children crying. He got up, leaving his wife Veronica in bed behind him. He settled the child but he knew he'd never get to sleep again. He padded through to the kitchen to make a cup of tea.

As John Fowler's kettle boiled, a couple of hundred miles to the north the Vulcan was descending towards the sea at a rate of 2,000 feet a minute. As they sank through the air, Bob Wright and Gordon Graham checked the bombing offsets – the distinctive features over which Wright planned to place his markers: Mengeary Point to the north-east, Cape Pembroke at the eastern extremity of the hammerhead of land on which the airfield was built, and Ordnance Point, just over one and a half miles to the north-west. Wright also hoped that a hangar he could see marked on the Public Works map might break out of the 'green porridge' too.

'Watch your speed,' Withers called out to Pete Taylor as he noticed the airspeed starting to drop off. Taylor lowered the nose. In the back, Gordon Graham was also watching his air-speed indicator, or ASI. His warning appeared to echo the one from Withers.

'Watch your speed . . .'

'I know, I know. I'm watching it,' Taylor told him, lowering the nose still further.

The jet was gathering speed in a dive, but as Withers watched, waiting for the needle on his ASI to respond, it was telling him they were about to stall. 'Watch it!' he called again to his co-pilot, his voice urgent now. Aircrew are trained to believe what their instruments tell them. Ignoring them, trying to fly by the seat of the pants in the wrong conditions, had killed a lot of pilots. But on board 607, the instruments *were* wrong. It was the roar of the wind around the cockpit that told the truth this time, and Withers was the first to realize what was happening. The pitot tube had iced up in the cold, humid air. This insignificant-looking protrusion held the key to measuring the aircraft's speed through recording and com-paring changes in air pressure; if ice seals the pitot's opening, the ASI in the cockpit will no longer work. Once the problem had been identified, it was easily contained, but it was another reminder of how far away from safety they were. A wake-up call. Taylor raised the nose and the excess speed bled off.

At 2,000 feet above sea level, a safe height even if their forecast pressure settings were wildly inaccurate, they levelled off, before descending more gently down to 300 feet above sea level. Below the radar. Dropping through a scattered cloudbase towards the sea, Withers was surprised by what he could pick out. Despite the darkness there was enough light from the moon to catch the moving planes of the sea's surface, although its distance below them was impossible to judge. He asked Wright for a height find on the Radio Altimeter, a device which worked by bouncing radio waves back and forth from the jet. Once 300 feet was confirmed, the NBS was updated again. Assuming Graham and Wright's bisection of the two Carousel readings was accurate, the old ballistic computer was now loaded with the information it needed for Wright to get the bombs on target. But until they switched on the radar they wouldn't know for sure that they were where they thought they were. Both Navigators' greatest concern was that, after flying nearly 4,000 miles, they would miss the islands altogether. It remained an unsettling possibility.

Gordon Graham called the distances to run until the pop-up as the bomber streaked towards her target, low above the uninviting sea. Now Withers took back control from Pete Taylor. Hugh Prior's eyes were fixed on his banks of numbers, screens and dials. He made sure the chaff and infrared decoy flares were set up, satisfied himself that the Dash 10 pod that had tripped at Wideawake was ready to go and checked that the transponder telling the British fleet who they were was squawking on the right frequency. And he listened. For the same reason he and Barry Masefield had decided not to use the 'Spanish Tape' he did nothing that might give away their position. Through his headset he picked up the faint sound of his crew breathing and he strained to hear the tell-tale pulse of British and Argentine search radars. The Royal Navy were supposed to be operating a 'weapons tight' during the Vulcan's approach, but it only needed one nervous mistake under pressure to cause a tragic accident. There were less than a hundred miles to go. Twenty minutes.

'Have a good trip, and don't shoot the Vulcan down!' joked pilot Steve Thomas as he handed his fighter over to his boss, 801 Naval Air Squadron's CO, Commander Nigel 'Sharkey' Ward. Sea Harrier 003 sat on the deck of HMS *Invincible* – a calmer place now that days of storms had abated. Thomas had been sitting on alert in the cramped cockpit of the little jet for hours, ready to launch at a moment's notice in response to any airborne threat to the Task Force. Bearded and charismatic, Ward was a self-styled maverick, the epitome of the swashbuckling naval fighter pilot. A few minutes later, after realigning the navigation system, he checked his engine, pushed the throttles forward to 55 per cent and rode the brakes. As the Flight Deck Officer whipped his glowing green wand down to touch the deck, Ward opened the throttle, accelerated down the deck and was forced into his seat as the jet was thrown into a ballistic curve by the ski jump over the bows. As his speed increased, the V/STOL fighter's wings bit the air and he rotated the jet nozzles backwards. Armed with twin 30mm Aden cannons and a pair of AIM-9L Sidewinder all-aspect heat-seeking missiles, he was flying Combat Air Patrol for the Vulcan, tasked with keeping her safe from any marauding Argentine fighters. And he was pretty pissed off about the whole affair. Only the RAF, he thought, would have the gall to insist on a weapons-tight procedure in a war zone. Ward was incensed by what he saw as the RAF poking their noses in where they weren't wanted. He could see no merit in a mission he thought his Sea Harriers should be performing. In his righteous indignation he stubbornly overlooked the fact that to carry the same weight of bombs as the single Vulcan would put nearly his entire squadron of precious air defence fighters in harm's way. Still, he thought, watching the RAF's back got him into the air, and if he was lucky he might get to see some explosions. He switched his Blue Fox radar to standby, levelled off 200 feet above the South Atlantic and set course for the islands.

*

Gordon Graham waited anxiously for confirmation of his position while, as the estimated range to the target dropped below sixty miles, Bob Wright reached forward to switch on the old H2S radar. Although dependable and familiar, by 1982 it was a relic that, in an earlier incarnation, had been used by the Lancasters of RAF's elite Pathfinder force as they fought the Battle for Berlin in the autumn of 1943 and early 1944. Its results were, to say the least, open to interpretation, its effectiveness largely dependent on the skill of the operator. During the Second World War, Air Vice-Marshal Don Bennett, the commander of the Pathfinders, had been so unimpressed by the sight of an indecipherable H2S map of Berlin that he simply screwed it up and threw it in the wastepaper basket. The Mark 9A version of the H2S in the nose of 607 was a vast improvement on its predecessors, but a lot now depended on Wright's dexterity with it. As he'd flown south the young Navigator had played out his role in his mind, mentally rehearsing the procedures which, at the long mission's furthest reach, he'd have one chance to get right.

The H2S scanner in the Vulcan's nose was over six and a half feet across. Switched off during the flight from Ascension, it had hung, face down, from its mountings. When Wright switched the power on from the crew compartment, the black tangle of machinery supporting it whirred into life. Wright glanced to his right to check that the power supply indicator was on then focused on the cathode ray display that dominated his work station. Random, phantom returns flickered green against the black background like static but there was no clear image. As Withers kept the jet low, on track towards Stanley, the distance to run towards the target ran down. Another mile every ten seconds. Wright's eyes darted around the radar set's control panels, looking for the problem. To his left he noticed the Scanner Position Indicator dancing restlessly.

In discussing the Vulcan raid, the overriding concern of the politicians and Defence Chiefs in Whitehall had been the safety of the islanders. Without absolute reassurance that the runway could be attacked at no risk whatsoever to the civilian population, they would not have approved the operation. Wright knew it. Unless he could bring up a reliable picture on the green porridge, they'd have to throw away the mission. Without a functioning bomb-aiming radar, at night, trying to hit the target would literally be a shot in the dark. Irrespective of whether or not they hit the runway, dropping the bombs without it would be a gamble that threatened the safety of the very people they were trying to protect.

Wright reset the controls, resisting the temptation to switch the scanner off altogether to avoid letting it drop again. He retuned the display, willing the circular image in front of him to settle down. Around him, the five other members of the crew waited anxiously for confirmation.

With fifty miles to run, the picture stabilized. The ageing radar had come good but, ahead of them, where he should have been picking up an echo from the 2,313-foot peak of Mount Usborne, thirty-three miles to the west of Stanley, there was nothing. He passed on the news over the intercom.

Ahead of him, Withers considered the situation for a moment. They had to find the islands before climbing for the bomb-run. Unless they knew they were in the right place, it didn't matter how well the radar and NBS were working. Totally out of the question was the possibility of loitering at altitude before getting established on the bomb-run, or worse, running in twice. Both would hand a decisive advantage to the Argentine air defences. All surprise would be lost. Neither would amount to anything more than a straightforward request to be shot down. Perhaps, he thought, they were just too low for the H2S to pick up the mountain's summit. If they could just gain a couple of hundred feet of altitude, it might allow the scanner enough of a view forward to confirm their position. There was a danger that in doing so they would climb into the view of the Argentine search radars, but Withers, suffering from a disconcerting feeling that they didn't actually know where they were, felt it was a risk worth taking. *It's got to be worth a quick preview*, he thought, and gently pulled back a touch on the joystick to raise the bomber's nose.

The elusive peak immediately hove into view on Wright's screen. *I've got it*, he told the crew. After over eight hours aloft, without a single opportunity to check or confirm their position, they were just a mile away from where Gordon Graham had calculated they should be. A combination of skilful dead-reckoning and the new twin Carousels had worked as advertised. Bob Wright moved his joystick a fraction to bring the green glow of Mount Usborne's radar reflection under the cross-hair markers on his screen. Withers relaxed his grip on the Vulcan's stick to take her down to 300 feet again. And Dick Russell flinched as he heard a menacing pulse through his headphones. Hugh Prior's voice cut through the background of the intercom.

'Echo-band radar, twelve o'clock. Possible Argentine search radar.'

Listening intently to the Passive Warning Receiver for threats to the jet, Prior had heard the slow ticking of an AN/TPS-43 radar at the same time as Russell, its tell-tale PRF beating at ten-second intervals. On a 3-inch display ahead of him an unbroken green line told him the radar was sweeping from the south-west, right in front of them.

'No threat at this time,' he told the crew.

Russell, sitting in the dark, wasn't as reassured as he wanted to be. He sat on his hands in a comforting, but clearly hopeless attempt to protect himself.

On Sapper Hill, just over a mile to the south-west of Stanley, the men of Colonel Arias's GADA 601 anti-aircraft unit maintained a twenty-four-hour watch for intruders as their powerful American-built radar swept the skies around East Falkland. For weeks they'd trained, gaining confidence and skill by tracking the movements of their country's own Air Force. Now, just before 4.30 in the morning local time, they briefly picked up an unidentified contact to the north-east. She was low, coming in on a heading of 245 degrees, travelling over the water at around 300 knots. Then she disappeared.

# Chapter 38

'Sharkey' Ward pushed forward the throttle lever with his left hand and pulled the SHAR into a climb. At 20,000 feet, he dimmed the cockpit lights of the little fighter. Above him, the southern-hemisphere stars shone brightly, but cloud obscured his view below. He doubted there would be any trade for him tonight, but he still hoped he'd get lucky. With his own Blue Fox radar on standby, he listened out for surprises reported by the naval escorts on radar picket duty. Twenty minutes after getting airborne, he pressed the RT transmission button to welcome the Vulcan to the Falklands.

'Morning!' he offered cheerily, but heard nothing from the bomber in reply. They weren't playing, so he left them to it. He'd wait for her to broadcast news of the attack and depart the area in one piece, then he'd head back to the blacked-out flight deck of HMS *Invincible*.

Forty miles out, low over the water on a heading of 245 degrees, 607 accelerated to 350 knots in preparation for the pop-up. As the big delta powered south-west, Gordon Graham counted down.

*Five, four, three, two.* On one, Martin Withers spooled the four Olympus engines up to maximum revs and pulled her smoothly into a 15-degree climb to altitude. The roar of the engines in the back of the crew compartment signalled the arrival of the critical part of the mission.

As she left the cover of low level, 607 flew straight into

view of the Argentine search radars. Every ten seconds the sweep of their scanners provoked a beat from the bomber's Radar Warning Receiver. As before, Hugh Prior reported the radar to his crew, finishing the same way: 'No threat at this time.'

It didn't feel like that to Dick Russell, the only man on board with nothing to do to displace his anxiety. Now the enemy could be in no doubt about their presence nearby, Prior switched on his IFF transponder. At Wideawake, he'd been given settings that simulated an Argentine maritime-patrol aircraft. Like the rest of the tricks at the AEO's disposal, the principal value of the bogus call and response of the transponder was that it might buy them time. But, with the Vulcan's own bombing radar now painting every Argentine RWR in its path, he knew that, ultimately, well-drilled air defence crews would see through their deception.

Among the radar operators of GADA 601, perched on their rock-strewn hill, 400 feet above sea level, there was uncertainty. They could see the incoming bomber on their screens, but what was it? One of their own, perhaps – likely even. This had not, so far, been a shooting war after all. The young crew's first reaction was to check whether or not there were any Argentine aircraft in the area. It was only minutes, though, before the air defences took on a more threatening posture. Around BAM Malvinas, Skyguard fire-control radars were getting ready to search the sky for targets, their operators preparing 35mm Oerlikon batteries to defend what they passionately and proudly believed was theirs.

At 9,500 feet, Martin Withers eased the power back, the bomber's upward momentum carrying her the final 500 feet to 10,000-foot altitude for the bomb-run. Twenty miles to run. Three minutes. As the Vulcan levelled off on a heading of 240 degrees, Withers trimmed her to settle into the bomb-run. Speed was good: 330 knots indicated air speed, a speed over the ground of nearly 440 mph; not so fast as to unsettle the bomber's equilibrium. An altitude of 10,000 feet: as well as stability, height was crucial too – if it wasn't exact, the bombing computer couldn't calculate the forward throw of the bombs or even measure the plan range to the target. Withers pulled down the smoked-glass sun visors around the cockpit windows to prevent exploding flak and bright lines of tracer destroying his night vision. Next to him, Pete Taylor pulled down the visor on his Bone Dome. Withers again cursed the failure of his own helmet's intercom at Ascension. The thin cloth cap he was wearing made him feel intensely vulnerable.

At the Nav Radar's station, Bob Wright was setting up the NBS for the bomb-run, making live the switches. He talked to the crew as he tuned and retuned the old radar to get his cross-hair markers as fine on his offsets as possible: Ordnance Point, Cape Pembroke and Mengeary Point. The three headlands were distinct on his display, green illuminations returning from solid ground meeting the blackness of the sea.

'I've got the offsets. Everything looks fine.'

With the offsets' positions relative to the target fed into it, the NBS had everything it needed to get the bombs on target: the bearing and slant range to the target; the aircraft's height and true airspeed; a wind component; and the forward throw of the bombs. Now Wright could let the old computing machine begin directing them to the release point. From here on, this was Bob Wright's show. Everything that happened aboard 607 was designed to position or keep the bomber where he said it needed to be to get the bombs on target.

*Go to bomb*, he said over the intercom. Ahead of him, a meter began to indicate the range to target. The NBS was working. And from it, a steer signal was sent to Martin Withers on the flight deck. A left–right needle displayed on the bomber Captain's instrument panel told him whether or not he needed to adjust his heading.

*Check demand*, Wright asked his Captain. Withers reported back the correction his indicator was asking for. Without taking his eyes off the green porridge, Wright responded.

*Take it out*, he asked and Withers gently brought the nose into line. *Demand zeroed*, he confirmed to his Nav Radar.

'Tell me when the last bomb's gone,' Withers continued, aware that because of the fuel shortage, they wouldn't be out of the woods just because they might make it through the bomb-run unscathed. 'We're not going to run out at low level. I'll climb straight out.' For now, the Captain just had to concentrate on nothing else but keeping the wings absolutely straight and level and the speed on the button. Stability meant accuracy.

With ten miles to run, less than two minutes, to the target, Withers dropped a hand to the console to his left and flicked the bomb door control to 'Open'. Selecting 'Auto' could have left the job of opening them to the NBS, but if there was going to be a problem with them, he wanted to know now in time to try to do something about it, not in the final seconds before the bomb release point.

*Open bomb doors*, he told the crew, ready to catch any disruption to the bomber's balance as they swung down into the airflow. As they travelled slowly through their 90-degree arc, the disturbance to the bomber's smooth progress through the sky could be felt slightly in the cockpit. The doors locked into position either side of the rows of bombs like a dog baring its teeth and a magnetic doll's-eye indicator in the cockpit flicked from black to white.

*Bomb doors open*, confirmed Withers. Vulcan 607 was settled perfectly into her final run-in to the target. Then Hugh Prior's headphones erupted in a high-pitched, angry rattle as the 228 RWR picked up a short-range fire-control radar. A quick PRF, one pulse running into another like the buzz from a malevolent insect. Skyguard. A fire-control radar looking for a lock-on, guiding the twin barrels of the Oerlikon cannons through smooth but sharp, decisive movements in search of a target. Three bright dashes cut across the indicator on Prior's control panel to tell him the radar emissions were coming from a point off to the left of the Vulcan's nose.

'Gunnery control radar. Medium threat. Ten o'clock.

Jamming,' Prior reported to the crew. He'd resisted the opportunity to react until now for fear of doing no more than confirming the Vulcan's presence. There was nothing more to be gained by doing so. They *had* been discovered. He *had* to act. Prior reached up to the newly installed control panel for the Dash 10 pod and switched it on, hoping that, despite the tripped fuse at Ascension, it would work as advertised. Of the rest of the crew, only Dick Russell, still sitting on his hands in the bowels of the crew compartment, heard the raw noise of the 228 through his headphones – and he wouldn't have chosen to. The rest of them couldn't afford to be distracted now. To Prior's left, Bob Wright was locked in concentration, his face buried in the H2S radar scope. Next to him, Gordon Graham monitored the NBS, backing up the Nav Radar's efforts. Ahead of them, Withers remained focused on keeping the bomber on track. Any effort to jink and turn to break a radar lock would wreck their bomb run. Over the 10,000 feet the bombs had to fall, even minor movement would be amplified, ensuring that, without any doubt, they would miss the thin strip of the runway. From this height, had they been flying in daylight, it would have looked no bigger than a match placed on an Ordnance Survey map. Like the bomber crews of the Second World War, they had to hold their nerve, not deviating at all as they pressed home their attack.

Powerful white noise emanated from the pod under the Vulcan's right wing to obscure the view of the Skyguard radar, at the same time throwing the Vulcan's radar detection pulse out to one side – telling air defence crews that the jet was miles from the point where it was actually flying. Ten seconds later, the urgent tone from the 228 broke off. The Dash 10, it appeared, had defeated the Skyguard radar and without it the 35mm cannons it controlled were blind. Relieved, Hugh Prior crossed his fingers under the desk, willing the Argentine gunners not to come back at them again.

Ahead of the bomber, a little to the right of their track, Martin Withers and Pete Taylor saw lights from Stanley flickering in the moist air through gaps in the broken cloud.

And in the back, the distance to target dial between the two Navigators was decreasing steadily towards the point – two miles from the target – where the NBS computer would release the first bomb. Gordon Graham called out the distances.

Four miles to run.

# Chapter 39

Elizabeth Goss woke up early, not quite understanding why. The young mother who as a little girl had surprised her parents with early predictions of the arrival of visiting cars just knew something was different. In the distance she could hear the barely perceptible drone of an aircraft. But that in itself wasn't unusual, these days. Since the invasion there had been a constant stream of Argentine aircraft of all types coming in and out of the airfield. Day and night. But some instinct told her this wasn't the same. The engine note was heavier and more substantial. More threatening even. She lay in bed, unable to move and hardly daring to breathe as the unfamiliar sound grew in intensity. Stock-still in the dark, with her husband fast asleep beside her, she held her breath and listened.

*Three miles to run*, Gordon Graham continued – one mile to bomb release – then began counting down, *five, four, three, two, one . . .*

Still two miles away from the airfield itself, at the point that the ballistic computer calculated the middle bomb of the stick would hit the middle of the runway, the first of the thousand-pounders fell away from the bomber's cavernous open belly. Just under a quarter of a second later it was followed by the second. From 607's height of 10,000 feet and with her speed over the ground of just over 320 knots – nearly 400 mph – the bombs' forward throw would carry them to the target while they gathered massive, destructive vertical speed. To his left,

Bob Wright watched the little mechanical counter clicking up. It appeared to be ticking over in slow motion, each bomb taking what felt like an age to follow the one before. Behind him, though, the heavy bombs dropped from their racks with relentless, metronomic efficiency.

On the flight deck, Martin Withers steadily increased his forward pressure on the stick. As the Vulcan disgorged a 10-ton payload, she tried to climb. Relieved of her burden, she wanted to soar, but until the last bomb was gone Withers had to keep her steady. Next to him, Pete Taylor was struck by an omission. He felt like he was in a movie, but one that was missing its soundtrack. Accompanying the bomb-run, he thought, should be the sound of a swirling crescendo from a symphony orchestra. Something suitably dramatic, at least. Instead there was just the soulless, metallic scratch and crackle of the intercom and a tight feeling of anticipation.

Just over five long seconds after the first bomb fell, Bob Wright's bomb counter finally clicked on to twenty-one and an amber light to his side flicked on.

'Bombs gone,' he called and immediately flicked the switch to close the bomb bay. Without waiting for the doors to shut on the empty bomb bay Martin Withers pushed the throttle levers all the way to the gate and poured on the power. The four Olympus engines assaulted the night with 80,000lb of dry thrust as they drove the jet forward. Withers pulled the stick across to his left and the big delta bit into a 60-degree bank to the left. Lighter now than at any time since leaving Waddington, she felt agile and responsive again. As he wound her round in a steep 2g turn, the whole crew was pushed deep into their seats. After the insidious, consuming uncertainty about what would await them at the end of their journey south, Withers felt an overwhelming sense of relief as he turned away from Stanley. Away from the wasps' nest of Argentine anti-aircraft defences. And away from the Roland missile battery that, still waiting for confirmation that the Vulcan was even hostile, was yet to join the battle. But there was still nearly half a minute to go until 607 would once more be outside their reach, beyond the kill zone.

From the right-hand seat, Pete Taylor looked across his Captain towards the ground. As Withers held the bomber in the turn, careful to control any sideslip with his rudder pedals, Taylor once again caught sight of Stanley's lights about seven miles to the west. Then three miles closer, he saw the milky, cotton wool shapes of the clouds around the airfield flare like cumulus in an electrical storm as, eighteen seconds after it had left the Vulcan, the first thousand-pounder bored deep into the centre of the runway and detonated. At the Nav Radar's station behind him, Bob Wright felt the distant crump of the bombs resonate through the skin of the bomber as it turned.

A plug of Tarmac, concrete and hardcore over sixty feet wide and half as deep was vaporized by the explosion as the earth below was heaved over the lip of the new crater. One hundred feet on and a quarter of a second later, the next bomb hit the ground, gouging out and destroying another superheated chunk of the airfield's surface. From the epicentre of each blast, shockwaves struck out in concentric rings. From the supersonic heart of each blast, steep walls of pressure, density and temperature were thrown out, driven from behind like the bow-wave of a super tanker. But these invisible, unstoppable, waves of boiling overpressure pushed out from the blast at the speed of sound. Huge kinetic energy turned to heat as they swept irresistibly across the flat ground against the still night air. The delay by the GADA 601 AN/TPS-43 operators in confirming the identity of the British intruder meant that when the first bomb exploded on the runway, it did so utterly without warning. Major Alberto Iannariello had been sitting in an armchair in the control tower, lost in his thoughts, when the deafening explosion ripped him out of his reverie. Almost instantaneously, a scorching red pressure wave swept violently into the building, punching out the windows and shaking the walls to their foundations. Iannariello was thrown from his chair and passed out. The rest of the stick of thousand-pounders slammed into the ground, opening up a line of wreckage that walked relentlessly across the airfield. For five seconds one heavy, percussive boom followed another, the massive sound of each explosion running into the next.

Angry, billowing clouds of heat and shrapnel rolled across the exposed airfield, mauling anything in their path. The hangar was flayed, stripped of its corrugated iron walls. Stores and equipment were smashed. And vehicles and machinery caught in the path of the fierce ripples of overpressure lost their hydraulic systems, their fluid-filled pipes bursting under the intensity of kinetic energy pulsing through the air. Only the effective dispersal of accommodation, combustibles and ammunition by Major Héctor Rusticinni protected some of the airfield's most vital assets.

Rusticinni himself had been asleep on the floor of his shelter as the bombs hammered into the ground. Close to the explosions, the terrible noise was overwhelming. He was pitched into the air, stunned awake with the rest of the men in the hideout. With each successive eruption, they were tumbled and churned together, all of them alarmed, confused and frightened by the sudden, unknown force of the attack.

And inside the foxholes sheltering the conscripts, the sound of screaming augmented the thunderous noise from the British bombs. Some screamed because they'd been told to. These unfortunates had been taught, at the first sign of bombardment, to open their mouths and yell at the top of their voices to protect their hearing. Yet still their eardrums felt like they would rupture. Those that forgot their training cried out through fear.

Sitting in his living room with a cup of tea, John Fowler noticed that his fire was dying out. He got up and bent over it with a poker. As he jabbed at the glowing peat, the ground-shaking noise from 607's stick of bombs shook the house. Desperately unsettled, he began to work out that it had come from the direction of the airport, and he knew that war had arrived.

The first explosion came almost as a relief to Elizabeth Goss – an end to the agonizing tension of anticipation that had followed the sound of the Vulcan's engines. She lay still as the hollow, heavy crump, crump, crump of the bombs rolled across the harbour to Stanley. The house rattled in the dark. And still her husband didn't stir.

Joe King leapt out of bed as the sound and shock first reverberated through Stanley. He rushed to the east window of the first-floor bedroom to try to see what was going on.

'What is it?' his wife asked urgently.

'I can't see. There's an awful lot of noise, but I can't see anything. Either somebody's bombing the airport or something's exploded down there.'

Then the force of the pressure wave slammed shut the window and King jumped back from it. As he stumbled, the old pyjamas he'd taken to wearing while he and his wife housed so many guests slipped down around his ankles.

'Look at that,' he said, turning back to his wife, 'they've blown my pyjamas off!'

Across town, other islanders were also woken abruptly from their sleep and, as they shook themselves awake, confusion and panic gave way to smiles as they began to realize that the *boomboomboomboom* from the airport meant that the British were fighting back. Peter Biggs tried to reassure his wife Fran, explaining to her what he thought was happening. Then he heard the crisper, machine-gun rattle of the flak crackle through the night.

Alberto Iannariello was underneath his armchair when he regained consciousness. He could hear the sound of a man in pain from the ground floor. Iannariello freed himself, grabbed his helmet and rifle and ran down two flights of stairs towards the baggage-handling area. At the foot of the stairs he found Captain Dovichi, his face pale and strained from the agony of a badly injured back. Iannariello continued outside to witness scenes of carnage and chaos. Soldiers and airmen were running around without apparent purpose. Wounded, shell-shocked men staggered or lay moaning. And three men were already dead. *This*, he thought, *is our baptism of fire.*

As he looked across the shattered airfield, the muzzles of the anti-aircraft guns flashed red, illuminating their immediate surroundings, as they spat out ammunition at over 500 rounds per minute. Tracer streaked into the air accompanied by the furious clatter from the gun barrels. Hundreds of high-explosive shells pumped into the air, each blown into the sky from the Oerlikon and Rheinmetall cannons at over 3,000 feet per second, lashing out at their unseen attacker. Behind him from south of the airfield, Iannariello saw surface-to-air missiles explode into the sky, burning white-orange through the dark in hopeful pursuit.

The defiant, chaotic onslaught didn't let up for nearly half an hour.

Fortunately, Pete Taylor never saw the flak open up behind them, because at 10,000 feet the Vulcan had never been immune from it. Now nearly 14,000 feet away from the guns, the bomber was beyond the *effective* range of the Oerlikons, but the shells could tumble onwards beyond that for another 6,000 feet. During that time they remained lethal, if inaccurate. And without finding a target, they exploded anyway. The bright, neat little explosions were more deadly than they appeared. Beyond the neat puff of smoke, each detonation threw twisted chunks of shrapnel across the sky. Vulcan 607's safety had been relative, but the angry Argentine hail of ammunition had been too late to touch them. Surprise, avoidance and suppression: the attack plan had worked. The invaders had been caught by a determined, British reaction that few of them, least of all the hapless conscripts, had thought would ever come.

# Chapter 40

Withers rolled out of the turn to climb away to the north. He was still on edge. In his mind's eye he'd anticipated flak; he'd even expected fighters; and so far, apart from interest from the Skyguard fire-control radar, they'd got through unscathed. For over eight hours he'd drawn deeply on reserves of nervous energy, pushing his anxiety aside, and his tiredness was now starting to make itself felt. Then, as he levelled the wings, a bright light caught his eye.

*Bloody hell* – he jumped, suddenly sharp again – *a fighter.* But as he studied what at first glance had been an Argentine Mirage bearing down on them, he realized it was a planet. *Probably Venus*, he reckoned. He'd seen only what he had been looking for. He shook himself out of it; they needed to report news of their attack. Withers had kept his feelings to himself, but Pete Taylor couldn't help notice that Withers seemed saddened by the hurt he might have inflicted. In fact, the Captain thought it had all seemed rather cold-blooded. Sneaking in before dawn using false codes and dropping bombs. *Not much gallantry in that*, he thought. The way he saw it, he'd just started a shooting war and he took no pleasure from that. None at all.

As they gained height, putting distance between themselves and the islands, an Argentine search radar continued to sweep over them. Every ten seconds, its forlorn pulse was relayed into Hugh Prior's headset by the 228. *No threat at this time.*

*

Resignation had replaced the uncertainty and gloom felt aboard Bob Tuxford's Victor when the Vulcan left them. Travelling at 43,000 feet they were still seven hours' flying time south of Ascension, but they had less than five hours' fuel in the tanks. Tuxford briefly considered shutting down one of the four Rolls-Royce Conway engines to eke a little more range out of the remaining fuel, but abandoned the idea. It would have got them further, but it still wouldn't get them home. Ultimately, all Tux had to reassure himself that his jet wasn't going to fall out of the sky was his faith in the experience and judgement of the 'tanker trash' at Wideawake. He tried to relax and recuperate a little after the exertions of the previous two hours. *It's not a hopeless situation,* he told himself, *certainly not a foregone conclusion.*

Behind him, AEO Mick Beer monitored the Vulcan's frequency on the HF radio.

Under the canvas at Ascension, Jeremy Price was still guessing. He'd dispatched two TATs for Biglands and Tuxford. The two tankers were heading south on an *assumption* that they'd be needed. He'd heard nothing from either of the long-slot Victors. He could only do what he could do, though, and they had, at least, just brought Alan Skelton home. After reporting a fuel leak when he turned north from the third refuelling bracket his jet had taken on 20,000lb of fuel 400 miles south of Ascension. After sunrise, Monty returned to the Ops tent. Price immediately explained what he knew of the night's developments. Beyond the fact that the mission appeared to be nearly an hour behind schedule, there was little Price could tell them. BLACK BUCK's progress was unknown.

'What's going on, Monty?' he asked. 'How could all the aeroplanes be an hour out?' Monty didn't have any answers.

'All we can do is wait,' Price told him.

They were soon joined in the Ops tent by George Chesworth. The Air Vice-Marshal too was quickly brought up to speed.

*

The 228 went wild, lighting up with gunnery threats, missile threats and search radars. As 607 flew north, the Task Force locked on to them with every weapon they had, Hugh Prior was as worried about being shot down by the Navy as he had been about the Argentine defences. The entire 60-degree sector ahead of the bomber was filled with menace. So much so that Prior – the electronic-warfare instructor – found it impossible to differentiate the sound of one from another. He just had to trust that he was broadcasting the IFF frequency the fleet was expecting to hear. And make the post-attack transmission as soon as possible.

'Did it seem all right to you?' asked Withers, wanting his Nav Radar's verdict on the bomb-run.

'I've seen the offsets,' Wright told him. 'As far as I can tell it was fine.'

None of them could be any more certain than that. Wright was as sure as he could be that his bombs were on target. Withers asked Hugh Prior to transmit the codeword. There were three options: silence, if the attack had had to be abandoned without alerting the enemy; 'Rhomboid', if the attack had failed but had alerted defences; and 'Superfuse', if the attack had been a success.

'This is One Quebec Delta, over,' Prior said over the VHF.

*One Quebec Delta, pass your message.*

'Good morning, this is One Quebec Delta.' Prior paused. 'Superfuse.'

*Roger, out.*

At the same time as Prior transmitted the message to the fleet, Wright set to scan his H2S radar as further confirmation of 607's presence. Rather than sweeping from side to side, he focused the scanner directly at the fleet, channelling a narrow beam of energy towards the Task Force which, he hoped, would be picked up and identified by the ships' own Radar Warning Receivers.

Prior immediately got to work on the HF radio in an effort to get through to Red Rag Control. As well as confirming the success of the attack, he needed to get the final refuelling moved 200 miles further south. Their margins for reaching the planned Rio RV off the coast of Brazil didn't look good.

*Three Foxtrot Tango Niner, this is One Quebec Delta, do you read?*

As they cruise-climbed Pete Taylor and Gordon Graham began routine fuel checks, until it struck Graham that they were pointless.

'It's not worth it,' he announced. 'We're not going to get any fuel from anywhere, so why are we doing fuel checks?'

They continued north, while Prior kept working the HF. A hundred and fifty miles from Stanley, the slow pulse of the Argentine search radar slipped into the distance behind them.

Then, at 0757, Prior made contact with Red Rag Control. And while the news of their success was greeted with relief and satisfaction at Wideawake, anything more enthusiastic was tempered by their knowledge that they still had to bring the Vulcan and two Victors home.

The grim waiting game aboard Tux's Victor came to an abrupt end.

'Superfuse,' Mick Beer announced emphatically over the intercom, unable to keep the smile out of his voice. The rest of the crew erupted, yelling and screaming with relief and excitement.

'Fuck, he's done it!' someone shouted. There was an intimacy possible in the cockpit of the Victor that the decked layout of the Vulcan didn't allow. And now, all five of the tanker's crewmen craned and swivelled in their seats to look each other in the eyes; to share the elation and satisfaction of pulling off the job they'd been sent to do under the most testing of conditions. Until the Vulcan's transmission, a nagging feeling that the bomber crew had let them down had been hard to shake. It had been dispelled in an instant. But as the euphoria died down, thoughts turned to their own desperate situation. Their fuel state hadn't been improved by the news of the raid's success, but they could, at least, now throw themselves into trying to sort it out.

'Right,' Tux said, 'let's look at all of this and try to refine it;

see where we stand; how far we're going to get; where we can reasonably expect an RV.'

Mick Beer tried to raise Ascension, but he struggled. In the early morning over this patch of the South Atlantic, the HF characteristics didn't help his efforts. As the big AEO laboured with his radio set, the rest of the Victor crew began to discuss their options. They could only fly north for another four hours at most. If a TAT out of Ascension wasn't at that point by the time they reached it, their jet was going down. As far as any of them was aware, there was absolutely no guarantee that Beer would get through in time.

In passing the 'Superfuse' message to Northwood, a mistake was somehow made. It led to an anxious delay while the Ops Team there waited for clarification of the signal. It was nearly 8.30 before a staff officer confirmed BLACK BUCK's success to the Air Commander. In the rabbit warren corridors of the state-of-the-art NATO headquarters, Air Marshal Curtiss smiled with relief. Like so many who'd been committed to the operation's success, he'd harboured private doubts about whether they would pull it off. At the very least, he'd thought, *it's pretty nip and tuck.*

From the suburbs of north-west London, news was relayed to Whitehall.

Sir Michael Beetham was sitting at his desk on the sixth floor of the Ministry of Defence. At 9.30, Air Vice-Marshal Ken Hayr came bursting into his office. The Assistant Chief of the Air Staff had run up the stairs from his Ops staff on the floor below. As the elegant New Zealander strode across the carpet towards Beetham, his hand was outstretched, his face a picture of happiness.

'We've done it!' he told Beetham, whose own grin quickly matched that of his deputy. Between them, they'd conceived and instigated the Vulcan operation. While Beetham had been its advocate within Whitehall, Hayr had monitored the developing plan's progress at Waddington. The two men shook hands, before reining in their celebration. As Hayr explained, the bombs might have gone, but Vulcan 607 was still on its own out over the South Atlantic. There were thousands of miles and a further refuelling to go before anyone could finally consider the mission accomplished.

At 41,000 feet, Martin Withers engaged the autopilot and 607 settled into her long cruise north. The first hints of marmalade orange were visible on the horizon as the sun began to come up – half an hour earlier at height than at ground level. Withers was shattered. Dick Russell was just thinking that he was probably condemned to his seat in the back until the final refuelling when Withers spoke to him over the conference intercom.

'Are you coming up, Dick?'

Withers wanted him to sit on the right after Pete Standing had moved across to fly the bomber from the Captain's seat. The bomber's Captain was going to get his head down. The fuel tray was pushed smoothly back into the instrument panel like a filing cabinet draw, and safety pins were slotted back into the triggers of both ejection seats. The three pilots shuffled around the hemmed-in spaces of the flight deck, while the ever-phlegmatic Taylor and a slightly nonplussed Russell strapped themselves into their harnesses. Bob Wright made the most of the hiatus to take care of a little housekeeping. He unclipped the five full pee-tubes from next to their owners and drained them into the chemical toilet that sat, unused till now, down in the bomb-aimer's prone position. After hanging them back up, he returned to his chair and, for the first time, began to reflect on what the mission had achieved so far. Up front, Dick Russell settled on to the sheepskin-covered, uncushioned co-pilot's seat and pulled out the fuel tray. A quick glance over the gauges immediately rekindled his earlier anxiety about the Vulcan's lack of fuel. They weren't out of the woods yet. Not by any means.

Behind him, Withers curled up on the jump seat and closed his eyes. Sleep came quickly.

*

Simon Baldwin hadn't slept well. But he was still in bed when Air Vice-Marshal Mike Knight telephoned from HQ 1 Group at Bawtry. Half awake, Baldwin was confused by the message.

'What are you talking about, sir?' he asked.

The AOC had to repeat himself to make himself understood. While Baldwin hurriedly pulled on his clothes before racing down to the Ops block, Knight's efforts to coolly and efficiently pass news to the Waddington Ops Room there were similarly frustrated.

When John Laycock had returned in the morning, there'd been no news on BLACK BUCK from any source. The silence around the room was striking. People pushed paper around, chewed their pens and waited. Occasional, routine phone calls would be dealt with swiftly and sparely – once it was realized that the voice on the line had nothing of interest to offer. Just before ten o'clock, the phone rang again. The whole room turned to look. One of the Ops clerks picked up, listened and turned to Laycock.

'It's for you, sir,' he said. 'It's the AOC.'

Laycock took the handset and announced himself: 'Station Commander.'

'Superfuse,' was all Air Vice-Marshal Knight said. Laycock considered it for a moment, then realized the word meant nothing to him.

'Superfuse,' Knight repeated impatiently.

'I'm sorry, sir, I haven't the faintest idea what you're talking about!'

'For God's sake! It's the codeword in your Operation Order!'

'Don't have one, sir. We haven't received an Op Order.'

The line turned blue as Knight digested the news.

'We'd only be an "Information" address here anyway, sir,' Laycock explained.

Each Op Order was classified 'Action' or 'Information'. Since the Vulcans had deployed to Ascension, Waddington had been downgraded to 'Information'. With the bombers under Northwood's control, they no longer *needed* to know.

'Never mind that,' Knight stopped him. ' "Superfuse" *means* that they've dropped the bloody bombs!'

'Oh, right!' Laycock exclaimed. 'Thank you, sir. Very good news!'

'I'll talk to you later.'

And the line clicked off.

Laycock put down the phone and, with all eyes on him, told the expectant crowd that the raid had been a success. The room erupted from the tense silence that had gripped it all night into a welter of relief, excitement and pride. When Baldwin came hurtling in soon afterwards, it felt like winning the World Cup – the strain of a month's intense focus and concern evaporated in an instant.

Elation was in short supply on Ascension. Since catching 'Superfuse' over the HF, the frequency had come alive, but it was virtually impossible to decipher. Each call sign needed to be checked and authenticated. But the changes there'd been within the formation and the flurry of concurrent messages, often relayed from one distant aircraft via another, meant that only confusion emerged.

*Charlie Five Tango* – that was Biglands – *affirm request TAT to fly that route to make an earlier RV. Request you pass this to Red Rag Control. I will TAT on frequency and sub one seven.*

'Lima Charlie, may I relay? Over.'

*Confirm message, Charlie Five Tango, and read back.*

*Two Mike Mike* – Tuxford – *returning with technical defect and does not require TAT. ETA Ascension One One Two Zero.*

It sounded as if Tuxford was on his way back carrying a problem, didn't need fuel and was expected into Wideawake at 11.20. But all of this applied not to Tuxford, but to Biglands. Because of the broken probe, Tuxford and Biglands had changed places, but Price didn't know that. The confirmation only served to underline how little he or anyone else at Red Rag Control really understood about what was taking place in the skies to the south-west. It was all guesswork. At 11.20,

Tuxford would still be nearly two hours from Ascension and flying on fumes.

All the Ops Team could do was make sure they had a tanker as far south on inbound track as they could and hope that the two jets would find each other. Wing Commander Colin Seymour, 55 Squadron's CO, was already on his way. *Someone*, Price knew, was going to need the fuel.

With one of Ascension's two Nimrods heading south-west to assist the Vulcan's RV off Rio with Barry Neal's Victor, Price kept the other at an hour's readiness on the Wideawake pan. In the event of a catastrophe, she could at least provide search and rescue cover up to 2,000 miles from the island. The Nimrod carried Lindhome Gear consisting of a large nine-man MS9 life raft linked by floating ropes to two containers full of stores, but it could do no more than find the survivors, mark their position and drop survival equipment. It couldn't actually fish anyone out of the sea; couldn't bring them home.

# Chapter 41

While the Vulcan headed north towards the Rio RV, staying within striking distance of the South American mainland, Tuxford's Victor was heading out to sea, *away* from any safe haven except Wideawake's 10,000-foot runway. For nearly an hour, Mick Beer tried in vain to satisfy himself that the Victor's desperate situation had been communicated and understood. As Beer persevered, talk on board turned to what would happen if he failed to confirm a rendezvous with a tanker. Tuxford was clear that they couldn't ditch the jet. Each aircraft has specific ditching characteristics and, unlike the Vulcan, the Victor was believed to be unsuited to landing on water safely. Trials had shown that the forward bulkhead immediately behind the H2S radar scanner would catch the water like a bulldozer, dragging the nose under the surface and forcing the whole jet to dive deep underwater. Its crew would, almost inevitably, be lost.

Instead, they worked out an alternative. It would mean abandoning the jet before the fuel tanks were really sucked dry. In order to have any hope of keeping his crew together, Tuxford had to be sure he could maintain control. Two hours from now, they decided, and still at least 800 miles from Ascension, they would set up in a slow cruise at 5,000 feet above the ocean. The height allowed plenty of time for the rear crew's parachutes' static lines to work. They would open the crew hatch on the port side of the cabin, then the three back-seaters would jump from the Victor in rapid sequence. It *should* ensure that they weren't too widely scattered. Tuxford and the co-pilot Glyn Rees would then stay with the Victor and try to bring her back over the point where the rest of the crew had bailed out, before pulling the yellow and black striped handles between their legs to fire their ejection seats. The hope was that they'd come down in the same patch of water. It wasn't much to look forward to.

They all then went through their abandonment drills. Every connection was physically checked: oxygen, static lines, lanyards, dinghies and the rest of their survival equipment. Each was wearing a Mae West lifejacket that carried an EPIRB locator beacon, a knife strapped to his leg, a heliograph to reflect the sun towards Search and Rescue crews, and a whistle. They had time, so it made sense to be thorough. On reaching the end of the checklist, they went back to the beginning and ran through the whole thing again.

*Right*, thought Tuxford, while Beer kept working the HF, *now it's in the lap of the gods.*

The news on the BBC World Service was astonishing. The huge, booming explosions that John Smith thought might be the sound of an Argentine ammunition dump going up had been the result of an attack by an RAF Vulcan bomber. The shock of the bombing had caused a panicked tangle of naked limbs on the landing of Sparrowhawk House. Once dignity had been restored they made tea and sat around the radio while a barrage of Argentine anti-aircraft fire raged outside. There was nothing on the five o'clock or 5.30 news, but at six o'clock Stanley time the BBC reported the raid. By the time they heard the bulletin, the newscaster explained, the Vulcan would be over the South Atlantic on its way home.

As a fourteen-year-old boy, Smith had watched the first Vulcan prototype, then still known only as the Avro 698, fly at the 1952 Farnborough Air Show. It was only the fourth time the revolutionary new aircraft had ever flown. At the time it had seemed like science fiction, but what had happened an hour and a half earlier was just bizarre. *How could we be bombed by this old aeroplane?*, he wondered. And a little part of him noted with satisfaction that he was probably a member of a pretty exclusive club: the only person watching the 698 at Farnborough that day to have subsequently been bombed by the thing.

Tuxford and his crew could have done without it. Hearing the BBC announcing the successful bombing of Port Stanley seemed, at best, surreal and definitely premature. They were still four hours from home – assuming they made a rendezvous with a TAT and were able to take on fuel. There was good news though. Mick Beer had at last had his HF transmissions acknowledged by Red Rag Control. And that long-range conversation revealed that the tanker they so desperately needed was already in the air. While Tuxford and Rees concentrated on flying the aircraft, they pooled the fuel in the central bomb bay tanks to make sure that every drop they had on board was available to them. Beer relayed lat/long co-ordinates worked out by Nav Plotter John Keable to Wideawake. The RV was as far north as they dared go along a direct track between the Falkland Islands and Ascension.

Bob Wright shook his Captain awake.
'They want you up front,' he told him as Withers opened his eyes and found his bearings. Vulcan 607 was closing on the final refuelling rendezvous and he needed to take back control of the bomber. Withers had been asleep for nearly two hours and it had done him good. It had been dark as he bedded down and, as he climbed the ladder up to the flight deck, the bright daylight was slightly disorientating. The anxiety he'd felt as they climbed away from the bomb-run was behind him, though. He clipped back into his harness and leg restraints and smiled at Dick Russell to his right. Then he looked at the gauges and realized that they were carrying less fuel than he'd ever seen aboard an airborne Vulcan. Russell was clearly uncomfortable with it. For the last hour, he and Taylor had been experimenting with the jet's altitude, gently climbing

between 38,000 and 41,000 feet in search of a tailwind that might give them a few extra knots of ground speed. They'd found nothing to help them. Vulcan 607 needed fuel within the next hour.

The refuelling window had long been and gone. Jeremy Price wanted the Nimrod at the Rio RV using its state-of-the-art navigation suite and Searchwater radar to bring the Vulcan and Victor together. The first time they'd trialled the technique with the new Mk 2 Nimrod out over the North Sea from Marham it had failed completely. But then, as one of the Nimrod crew had mentioned to a Victor pilot, someone *hadn't turned the bloody radar on properly*. Subsequent trials had shown the big, long-legged maritime-patrol jet could be of huge assistance in helping two old V-bombers find each other in a vast empty sky. But the Nimrod was only supposed to be holding station off Rio between 0915 and 1030. Unlike the Victor and Vulcan its air-to-air refuelling capability wasn't yet operational – in fact the first-ever successful transfer of fuel to a modified Nimrod had only taken place two days earlier. If the big jet handling the RV hit bingo fuel, it had to head back to Wideawake. And it was already starting to eat into its reserves.

It wasn't just the returning Vulcan and Victor that were low on fuel. They could now add the Nimrod to that list. In the Ops tent, George Chesworth, sent from Northwood to oversee the success of BLACK BUCK, was worried about the possibility of none of the three jets making it back to Ascension. Unknown to Jerry Price, he drafted a signal to Sir John Curtiss that said just that. Then he kept it clasped in his hand, holding his nerve and resisting the temptation to send it to the fiery Air Commander unless it became absolutely necessary to do so.

Converging from the north and south, the two Victors closed on each other at a speed of over 600 mph, both heading for the patch of sky chosen for the RV by Tuxford's Nav Plotter, John Keable. Tux brought his jet down from its 41,000-foot cruise to make contact with the TAT. Flown by his squadron boss, the heavy tanker needed to transfer fuel at a lower level to give the pilot an acceptable level of controllability. The engines were less responsive in the thin air and the stall speed was higher. The one and a half feet clipped from the Victor's slender wingtips to reduce fatigue when they were converted from bombers to tankers didn't help either. At a range of 150 miles Mick Beer had established good radio contact on the VHF. Ernie Wallis could see them on the radar. The tanker called the shots. They would come together with an RV Bravo – a head-on join. The two jets continued directly towards each other at the same altitude. In a continuous two-way dialogue, the two Captains counted down the range between them, all the time confirming and refining the headings. At a separation of twenty miles, the tanker broke into a wide arcing turn through 180 degrees to U-turn on to the same heading as Tuxford's Victor. If it all went according to plan he'd roll out directly ahead of them.

In beautiful, pale-blue skies, decorated by the odd patch of thin cloud, Tuxford scanned ahead for the tanker. Conditions for refuelling were ideal; for the first time on BLACK BUCK a clear horizon was visible. The basket was stable. Tuxford tried to relax for the most critical refuelling of his career.

*Don't want to make a mess of things at this point,* he told himself. Tanker captains took great pride in making contact first time and without drama. And took a fair amount of bar-room abuse if they started missing. He saw the tanker level off ahead of them, trailing its hose. Colin Seymour's crew hadn't been prepared to gamble on the HDU working when they needed it. They'd flown most of the way from Ascension with the drogue towed behind them. Through his helmet, Tux heard a radio click that signalled a transmission from the tanker.

*You're clear to join.*

Smoothly, even tentatively, Tuxford nudged the throttles to set up the overtake and his Victor began slowly reeling in the tanker to move into position behind it.

The rest of his crew listened to the sound of him breathing

in and out as he closed on the basket. Navigators and AEOs became adept at gauging the pilot's state of mind from the speed and regularity of his breathing as he jockeyed the Victor towards the contact. Sometimes they'd even had to intervene. *For God's sake take a breath*, one pilot had been told, *or we'll all be dead!*

With gloved hands on the throttles and control yoke, Tux edged the Victor's refuelling probe towards the basket. Then, at the point where a relieving clunk from a safe contact should have been heard, he watched as the tip of the probe gently slid past the basket.

*Christ, he's missed it!*, thought Ernie Wallis as he watched from the back more in frustrated expectation than concern. But Tuxford kept his composure, satisfied that as far as such a thing was possible, it was a perfect missed contact. He hadn't snatched at it. He still had the Victor exactly where he wanted her. He lowered the engine revs and calmly dropped back from the tanker to set himself up for another approach.

This time he nailed it. The end of the probe speared straight into the centre of the reception coupling without touching the guiding cone of the basket. It locked home and the green lights on the tanker's belly flicked on. For a moment, Tux continued to close on the underside of the jet ahead of him to trigger the fuel pump. Then, over the RT, came confirmation from the tanker's Nav Radar.

*Fuel flows.*

The claustrophobic little crew compartment of Tuxford's Victor erupted into a backslapping celebration of joy and relief. Underneath the black oxygen mask that covered his face as he held formation behind the tanker, Tuxford was smiling.

Twenty minutes later, Red Rag Control received a message through the static. 'Three Foxtrot Tango Nine from Lima Six Whiskey. Three Foxtrot Tango Nine from Lima Six Whiskey. Be advised that transfer to Charlie Five Tango, Charlie Five Tango is complete.'

'Roger, out.'

The HF transmission was from Colin Seymour's tanker. Charlie Five Tango, Tuxford's Victor, was safe. In the pressure-cooker of the Ops tent, the suffocating tension lifted a little. And George Chesworth, holding the signal to Sir John Curtiss, dared hope that he wouldn't have to send it. But there were still the Vulcan and Nimrod to worry about. And the Nimrod should have turned for home nearly an hour earlier.

On board Barry Neal's Victor, heading south-west on a bearing of 220 to recover the bomber, they shared the same concern.

'If the Vulcan's much later, there won't be a Nimrod!'

They weren't far wide of the mark. Their Nimrod that had loitered off Rio to shepherd the two V-bombers together was already flying for home, throwing help over its shoulder as it tracked north-east to Ascension. Both Neal's Victor and the Vulcan were now using local call signs – Zero Five and Two One, respectively. To the north of them, the Nimrod issued instructions.

'Make your heading Two Zero Zero. Tell him to go on to Zero Two Zero.'

The message was relayed south to the Vulcan by Neal's AEO, John Ingham.

'Two One, make your heading Zero Two Zero.'

'Zero Two Zero.'

They recognized Dick Russell's Hampshire burr. Nav Radar Del Padbury trailed the refuelling hose. Without the reserve, which had had to turn back to Wideawake with an unserviceable HDU, all on board knew that everything depended on their own working perfectly. Padbury followed through the periscope as the line reeled out behind them.

'She's going out quite steadily . . . looking good, going out nicely . . .'

'Keep an eye on it,' Neal interrupted.

'I am . . . stable . . . and stable.' They were in business, listening to the Nimrod's regular updates on the position of the Vulcan.

'Zero One Four, range Eight Six.'

'Zero One Four, range Seven Seven.' Heading and distance.

Aboard the Vulcan, Dick Russell was cursing 607's hopeless TACAN – an air-to-air range finder. They were only forty miles apart and he couldn't get a lock on. His headset crackled with another instruction from the Victor.

'Two One, make your heading Zero Three Zero.'

'Zero Three Zero,' he confirmed while, next to him, Withers gently rolled into the turn.

'Two One, transmit for bearing.'

'Two One transmitting.'

The transmission from the Vulcan was locked on to aboard the Victor, pointing to the bomber's direction, but Russell and Withers were picking up nothing in return. On a crisp clear morning at 27,000 feet, but for the reassurance over the RT they could have been utterly alone. Then Victor announced the turn that should bring them together. Russell could only keep his fingers crossed. He had to assume they were twenty miles away – in the right place – but for all he knew it could have been fifty.

'Seven India Echo, ceasing transmissions unless requested.' The sound of the Nimrod leaving them behind.

Withers and Russell were still scouring the sky ahead of them when, like deliverance, the Victor rolled out of its turn directly in front. Russell could barely believe it. The chances of that happening in training were one in fifteen, one in twenty even. And now, when they needed it most, the Victor was right on their nose with its hose trailing.

*Most beautiful sight in the world*, thought Withers, while Russell thumbed the RT button.

'Contact One, dead ahead. Zero Five reduce speed . . . Zero Five, you have a playmate!'

'Negative,' came the reply. The Victor couldn't see them – at least, it hadn't spotted them. The tanker asked them to transmit for bearing again.

'Two One transmitting,' Russell answered, but his voice betrayed his exasperation. 'Look, I'm right behind you – about three or four miles!' Then finally a flash of recognition. They were all set.

'You happy?'

'Yes, I'm happy now,' Russell replied. It didn't take much more than the sight of the tanker for that.

'You're clear to join, Dick. As you like. Can I check your fuel requirements, please?'

'As much as you can give me . . . but the first priority is to plug in.'

'Yeah, I know,' replied Neal soothingly. He just didn't want any surprises. He knew he had 70,000lb of fuel on board, but he had no idea what the Vulcan needed. Given the progress of BLACK BUCK so far, nothing could be taken for granted. 'But just give me some idea . . .' he pushed.

'About thirty-six?'

'Okay, we'll manage that nicely,' Neal reassured him. 'You wouldn't believe the ructions we've had already tonight . . .'

# Chapter 42

'Half a mile in your five o'clock,' reported Del Padbury to his pilot as he watched the Vulcan close in. 'There's no doubt about what that aeroplane is!'

The most distinctive shape in the RAF was usually a stranger to the Victor crews. Those Nav Radars that *had* seen the Vulcan through their periscopes had last done so twenty years earlier. Padbury was enjoying the novelty.

'HDU's looking good, radar's ready and the red light is on.'

At the first attempt, the Vulcan missed the basket and dropped back to wait for the hose to stabilize before trying again. Padbury continued his commentary.

'Here he comes again . . . still closing. Better approach this time . . .'

Then the tip of the probe glanced the rim of the basket, knocking it out of its steady flight through the air.

'No damage . . . closing up . . . Contact! And fuel is flowing. Like it's going out of fashion! He's taking it at nearly 5,000lb a minute.'

Padbury was transfixed by the view of the mean-looking delta filling his scope.

'I bet they're feeling absolutely shagged in there . . .'

'Yeah . . . I bet they're feeling fucking good though!'

Bob Wright had got up from his seat in the back and was standing on the ladder between the two pilots, ready to enjoy the final refuelling. He watched as Martin Withers, at his third attempt, made contact with the basket with a satisfying clunk. With the solid connection made, Withers and Russell couldn't help but relax a little. It was too soon. The green lights flashed on and, as if to taunt them, fuel immediately flushed over the windscreen of the jet, completely destroying their view forward.

'I can't see,' Withers said over the intercom, trying to keep his flying steady while he held formation on little more than the green lights on either side of the Victor's HDU. The wipers rocked inadequately to and fro across the glass but made little impression. Dick Russell was sure it was a soft contact – that the probe hadn't properly engaged with the drogue. Standard Operational Procedure, he argued, dictated that they should break the contact and try again. But as they followed the Victor out to sea, Withers wasn't prepared to take the risk. As things stood, they had a contact of sorts. Fuel was washing into their empty tanks, albeit at a reduced rate. If they broke off now, there was no guarantee that the next attempt wouldn't fail completely. And if that happened, with the RV already 200 miles further south than planned, they were unlikely to make it to Brazil, their only possible diversion. As Captain, it was Withers' decision. They stuck with it, but shared the job of maintaining contact in testing conditions. Control of the jet passed between Withers and Russell, the AARI finding that while the blurred outline of the Victor was enough to keep him from drifting left or right, maintaining his distance behind the tanker was nearly impossible. In the back, Hugh Prior said a little prayer to himself.

The struggle going on inside the Vulcan wasn't fully appreciated on board the Victor. Padbury could see that they were a little unsteady and noticed that 607 kept dropping back.

'I think he's having to work at it a bit,' he told his crew, sounding relaxed. He could see the fuel leak too, but didn't realize how much it was obscuring the Vulcan pilots' visibility.

Instead his concern was the fuel flowing backwards into the jet's number 2 engine. Not enough to cause a flame-out, though, he thought. And when the bomber dropped back far enough for him to have to reset his fuel pump, he assumed it was a deliberate attempt to try to stop the fuel seepage. Even though the contact was less than perfect, the fuel was still flowing out of the Victor at 4,600lb a minute.

The situation on the Vulcan's flight deck was more alarming. If he stooped, Bob Wright could see a small swatch of glass that had somehow escaped the path of the fuel streaking down the jet's fuselage. Without invitation, from his position on the ladder between the pilots' ejection seats, the Nav Radar began a commentary on what he could see. He expected to be told, sharply, to shut up. But for ten minutes he peered up at the Victor through the clear patch at the bottom of the windscreen giving instructions to Withers.

*Up a bit . . . In a bit*, he directed, and Withers and Russell listened. Wright thought that what he was telling them was probably rubbish, but it wasn't. They were managing, just, to maintain contact, and they were taking on fuel.

*Thirty-three thousand pounds.*
*Thirty-four thousand.*
*Thirty-five.*
*Thirty-five and a half, six, seven, eight, nine . . .*

As the numbers passed through 36,000lb, the Vulcan's dark shape began to drop backwards out of Padbury's view.

'He's going back smoothly . . . and he's free.'

With the fuel transfer complete, Barry Neal raised the Vulcan over the RT.

'Clear the position as you wish.'

'Going to starboard,' Martin Withers answered, back at the controls of his jet.

'Well done. Right, we'll take you home.' Neal left it a moment then, almost as an afterthought, he asked how it had all gone. 'Did you have a successful mission?'

There was a long pause, filled with static, as Withers thought about how to respond. Then the RT clicked.

'Not so bad.' He sounded utterly exhausted.

# Chapter 43

Bob Tuxford and his crew touched down on Runway One Four just after one o'clock in the afternoon. Over the previous fourteen hours, sufficient fuel had transferred in and out of his Victor's tanks to power a fleet of *ten* family saloon cars around the entire circumference of the planet. *Twice.*

During the final leg of the flight, once the success of the last RV had assured his aircraft's safety, Tuxford's mind was free to consider how on earth they'd even got into such a terrible situation. At every bracket and with each new contact, the carefully constructed refuelling plan had gone more and more awry. Worn out at the end of an epic fourteen hours, he tried to pick through the bones of the mission. He knew one thing: in reporting the night's events, he decided, he wasn't going to hold back.

After taxiing to dispersal, he and his weary crew shut down the aircraft's engines and systems, unstrapped and gathered their kit. Warm tropical air filled the cabin as soon as the crew hatch was opened. As they fell out of the jet like wet rags, they were filmed by an Ops officer with a rattling 8mm movie camera. Each man was handed a cold beer before being escorted to the Ops tent for hot-debriefing by Jerry Price and Alan Bowman. Tuxford didn't pull his punches. Every tanker crew, he felt, had pushed themselves to the limit to get the Vulcan south. The memory of the disappointment he'd felt as 607 had followed them round towards the north was still fresh in his mind. No one yet knew all the facts, but Tuxford felt let down and angry. And the focus for his unhappiness was the Vulcan detachment.

Monty was no more aware of the big picture than Tuxford. And although at midday news had reached Wideawake that the Vulcan's final RV had been a success, his friend, Martin Withers, and his crew were still out there. It was also evident that they must have had a nerve-shredding time over the South Atlantic. So when the terrier-like Scot learnt from one of the American civilian air traffic controllers that a tanker had to be scrambled to bring Tux home, he began jumping to the wrong conclusions. It was clear that BLACK BUCK had come close to disaster; and as he felt all eyes start to turn on him and the Vulcan's performance, Monty, perhaps understandably, tried to look elsewhere for answers. And Tuxford's captaincy came under his scrutiny. For the Victor pilot to have put himself and his crew into such a perilous position – to have pressed on like that – Monty thought, was unforgivably irresponsible. As he met Tuxford after the hot-debriefing with Price and Bowman, he challenged him about it.

'Look, I didn't just do it off my own back,' Tuxford shot back at him. 'It wasn't my *sole* decision as commander of the aeroplane.'

'Oh, I see, it's captaincy by committee is it?'

'Well, yes, it is. That's *exactly* right. As far as I'm concerned, my crew members had a right to a say. And I can tell you that they wholeheartedly supported the view that we should continue the mission.'

'You should be court-martialled.'

'I'm not talking to you, you arsehole,' Tuxford spat and pushed past.

Nerves were frayed. Monty didn't know it yet but in lashing out, out of concern for a friend, he was attacking the man whose courage and skill had kept his friend in the air and his mission on track. As the scale of what had been achieved became apparent, a court-martial started to look very unlikely.

*

The BBC news report followed the old 'Lillibelero' theme tune. The HF radio might have left a little to be desired when trying to communicate across thousands of miles of ocean, but it picked up the World Service well enough. The headline was the same as the earlier broadcast picked up by Bob Tuxford's Victor: a lone Vulcan has successfully attacked the runway at Port Stanley. The crew, it assured them, were safe.

'I think', said Gordon Graham laconically, 'they must be talking about us . . .'

'We haven't even bloody landed yet!' Hugh Prior said, incredulous. 'And here they are broadcasting it to the world.' It was the word 'successful' that got him. As far as he was concerned, it wasn't successful until they were safely on the ground. Martin Withers enjoyed the moment. With fuel in the tanks, they could at least laugh about it. For the first time since the message had come through from John Reeve's Vulcan telling them they were on, the tension really lifted. There'd been undisguised relief at completing the final fuel transfer, but now there were smiles. The BBC was reporting the success of the raid. They must have done it.

Prior slotted a cassette belonging to Pete Taylor into the AEO's tape recorder and pressed play. Through six sets of headphones, the persistent synthesized rhythm and stirring melody of Vangelis' *Chariots of Fire* theme tune began to play. Since the Oscar-winning movie's release the previous year, the music had become something of an unofficial anthem for the Withers crew. And now, as they cruised back to Ascension after their marathon operation, it provided an appropriately rousing soundtrack.

The press arrived at Waddington before 607 had landed at Ascension. The same cameras that had been blind to her departure for Ascension two days earlier returned. The attention, flattering as it might be, was unwelcome. Enormous pressure was applied to requests for interviews and information, but John Laycock resisted it. Too much was still unclear, but it was becoming apparent that the mission would turn out to be BLACK BUCK *ONE*. Others would follow and their security and that of the crews that would fly them needed to be protected. But the radio and television reports – and the subsequent newspaper coverage – had an interesting effect on Simon Baldwin. Over the previous month he'd concentrated on nothing but trying to ensure that his CORPORATE flight could do what it was being asked to do. He'd never had the opportunity or inclination to stand back and look at it with any sense of perspective. But in capturing the attention of the media – even though he reckoned barely 30 per cent of what was being reported was accurate – the size of their achievement finally sank in. He found a piece of string and placed it over a globe, stretched between Waddington and the Falklands. *Even I'm impressed*, he thought.

His frustration with the planning and the unfortunate run-in with Monty hadn't dented Bob Tuxford's appreciation of what the Vulcan had pulled off. He knew that his crew and the men on board 607 had been through something unique and he wanted to be the first to congratulate them. He wanted to look Withers in the eyes. While three of his worn-out crew headed straight for bed, Tuxford and his AEO, Mick Beer, nicked a couple of bikes from outside the Ops tent. The two of them cycled off to the American commissary in search of something they could hand out to the returning bomber crew.

As they pedalled back down the cinder road towards the airhead carrying tins of cold beer, they realized they were going to be part of a large crowd waiting to welcome the Vulcan home.

From 41,000 feet, Bob Wright picked up Ascension on his radar and placed his markers over the airfield. Withers checked his heading indicator and gently corrected his heading. Gordon Graham called Top of Descent and Withers pulled back on the throttles to put the jet into a long shallow descent to the island. It was a clear day and Withers and Russell saw Ascension from miles out. As Withers settled on to his glide path, he noticed the ring of cloud that hung around Green Mountain. *Lovely*, he thought. At five miles out he lowered the undercarriage. Dick Russell called out the speeds.

On the concrete dispersal at Wideawake, the crowd squinted into the blue sky, watching to the west as 607's distinctive shape dropped towards them, smearing oily smoke behind her. Near her wingtips, white landing lights twinkled brightly. Below her, the main gear extended down out of the dark silhouette, reaching for the ground like the talons of an eagle.

*Two One, finals. Three greens. To land,* announced Withers over the RT as 607 covered the last few hundred yards of her long journey.

Ahead of him, above low cliffs lapped by a gentle swell, he saw the long runway stretch away towards a vanishing point. To his left, the white buildings of Georgetown stood out from the red earth that surrounded them. Beyond the capital, the golden sand of Long Beach lined the coast. The edge of the island flashed underneath them and a moment later they crossed the runway threshold at around 130 knots. Withers cut the power and checked the jet's descent with a touch of backward pressure on the stick. Fifteen hours and forty-five minutes after she'd roared into the night, 607 touched down again. With a squawk and puff of burnt rubber, the main wheels kissed the Tarmac before the full weight of the bomber settled heavily on to the hydraulic oleos of the undercarriage legs. Withers held the nose up, showing the face of the delta to slow the jet down. Gordon Graham called out the speeds. *120 . . . 110 . . . 100 . . .*

At 80 knots, Withers brought the nose down on to the track and pushed the toe-pedals to apply the brakes. Speed bled off fast. They rolled to the end of the runway, backtracked and taxied to the pan, where their Crew Chief plugged back into the intercom. Pete Taylor reached across from the jump seat and pulled the handle to open the crew hatch. The familiar call and response of the shut-down checks echoed around the cabin, while at his feet the ground crew attached the ladder.

*Transformers off . . . TRUs off . . . HP cocks . . . Fuel pumps off.*

Outside, the whistling bellow of the Olympus engines wound down abruptly as if the plug had been pulled on a giant vacuum cleaner.

*External lighting off, master off.* The six men gathered their thoughts.

*Canopy and ejection seats are safe.* Time to meet their audience.

Through the open hatch, Taylor looked down on a sea of people urging him to join them. But he didn't want to be the one to lead the crew out of the cockpit. As they waved and jostled for position, Taylor shouted down from the jumpseat.

'Wait!' he told them. 'Martin's coming down first.'

Withers clambered out of his ejection seat and down the yellow ladder to the ground, his thin hair matted to his scalp after sixteen hours under the cloth flying cap. Straightaway, surrounded by excited, friendly faces, he was handed a drink – champagne – eleven hours later than he'd expected one as he launched from Ascension the night before. Then Monty caught his eye and the look told him he'd done good. Amid cheers and clapping, the rest of the crew followed him out: Gordon Graham, Hugh Prior, Pete Taylor, Bob Wright and Dick Russell. All of them with wide grins across their faces. Wright glanced up at the bomb bay, opened during the shut-down sequence. He knew what to expect, but he was still struck by the sight of it. *Nothing.* All that was left was a bag of safety pins and nowhere to put them. Someone, he thought, would know what to do with the paperwork.

Eventually Tux managed to fight his way through the scrum to offer Withers a beer. He tried to steal a moment with him.

'Well done,' Tux told him, 'you did the job.'

But the bomber pilot seemed overwhelmed; didn't recognize him. While Withers acknowledged the gesture, there was no sign that he realized Tux was anyone but another well-wisher. And if he had recognized him, his reaction might have been cool. Withers still felt let down by the long-slot tanker. All he knew at this point was that its captain had left him very short of fuel, a very long way from home.

Tuxford and Beer hung around for a little while longer before leaving the happy circus to go and get their heads down at last.

They had needed one Nimrod, two Vulcans, thirteen Victors, nineteen separate in-flight refuellings, forty take-offs and landings, forty-two 1,000lb bombs, ninety aircrew and over 1.5 million pounds of aviation fuel, but BLACK BUCK, the most ambitious and complex offensive operation the RAF had mounted since the end of the Second World War, was over.

At Waddington, long after 607 had come to her final stop, John Laycock finally received his copy of the Operation Order. *Typical*, he thought, affording himself a contented smile, *must have arrived by pony . . .*

And on the outside of the Vulcan detachment's crew clothing and equipment tent, they now had a legend to match the 'Victor Battle Fleet' board that stood propped up outside the Victor's tent. 'VULCANS', it soon read in big letters chalked up on the green canvas, 'DO IT FOR REAL'.

# Chapter 44

At the raid's successful conclusion, George Chesworth spoke to Air Commander Sir John Curtiss on the line from Northwood.

'Right, Chief of Staff,' Curtiss began, 'I want the same again for tonight!'

Satisfied with the outcome, and unaware of how fine the margins had been, it seemed a reasonable enough demand to Curtiss. But Chesworth, who'd been witness to just how close run a thing it had been, who'd endured the valve-bouncing tension of the Ops tent, knew it simply couldn't be done. The crews were spent, the aircraft needed servicing and, most important of all, they needed to establish exactly how and why such a carefully worked out refuelling plan had gone so wrong.

'No way, sir,' he told his boss.

'What do you mean "no way"? I want the same again for tonight!' insisted the gruff New Zealander.

'We can't do it because we haven't got the aeroplanes, we haven't got the crews and, more importantly, you don't realize just how close it was. We don't know why what happened did happen.'

Curtiss wasn't at all happy, but the conversation did allow him to pass on a reaction from the Prime Minister to the success of the first raid. Chesworth conveyed it to the Vulcan crew as they endured their hot-debriefing.

'She is *very* pleased,' he was able to tell them.

*

Margaret Thatcher had heard news of the raid's success while eating breakfast. Well versed in its difficulty following her briefings by Sir Michael Beetham, she believed that the effort had been 'stupendous'. As Home Secretary and a member of the War Cabinet, Willie Whitelaw happily acknowledged to Beetham over lunch the following day at Chequers that the RAF had done *exactly* what it said it would do. The Chief of the Air Staff recorded his satisfaction in his diary.

'A GREAT DAY FOR THE AIR FORCE!' he wrote.

In purely physical terms, the damage to the runway was substantial – this was the stated aim. At the runway's mid-point, the southern third of its 130-foot width had been obliterated. The full extent of the damage was later measured by JARIC at 115 feet across and 84 feet deep, and although it was hastily filled, the repair was botched and the patched-up surface never stopped subsiding. The crater put an end to any remaining hopes Argentine forces had of using the runway for their fast jets. And while Hercules transports continued to use the strip until the end of the war, the damage complicated their task to the extent that, on one occasion, one of the big transports nearly crashed on take-off. To the raid's critics this seemed a miserly reward for the effort involved, but their reaction entirely ignores the strategic impact of the raid. And it was considerable. BLACK BUCK was directly responsible for creating circumstances in which the British could win the war. On the Falkland Islands themselves, the bombs shook the occupying Argentinians to the core. A predominantly conscript invasion force around Stanley had viewed the taking of the islands in much the same way as they would the Argentine football team being 2–0 up at half-time. For them, the game was in the bag. They'd been told over and over again that the British would not retake them by force. At just before a quarter to five in the morning on 1 May, their morale took a hammer blow.

What Beetham had hoped for when it was first broadcast that the V-force was being prepared to fight was delivered in spades. He wanted to create doubt in the minds of the junta about British intent and capability. *Were the mainland bases under threat? Was Buenos Aires at risk?* That doubt saw the immediate redeployment of Argentina's entire Mirage fighter force to the north of the country, out of range of the Falklands, to defend targets that played no part in British plans. From this moment on, the tiny force of Royal Navy Sea Harrier air defence fighters aboard the two carriers, on which British hopes were pinned, had the odds dramatically cut in their favour. They were free to concentrate on tackling the threat of Argentine strike aircraft. The statistics speak for themselves: during the six weeks of the war, twenty-eight Fleet Air Arm Sea Harriers shot down twenty enemy aircraft plus three probables. Not a single Sea Harrier was lost in air-to-air combat.

But there was a third, unexpected, consequence of the raid, and one that's never really been properly appreciated. The 1 May attack on Stanley airfield was, believed Admiral Lombardo, the Argentine Commander of Combined Operations, to be the prelude to a full-scale amphibious landing by the British. As a consequence, Admiral Allara, Commander of the Argentine Navy, was ordered to launch an immediate offensive against the British task force. It was a disastrous decision.

Two Argentine battle groups launched a pincer movement on British ships sailing 150 miles to the north-east of the islands. To the north, the Argentine carrier *Veinticinco de Mayo* was preparing her squadron of Skyhawk fighter-bombers to strike at the British task force. To the south, the cruiser *General Belgrano* and two destroyer escorts were to act as a decoy, drawing ships away from the main British fleet before picking them off with sea-skimming Exocet missiles fired from the two Type 42 destroyers.

On the afternoon of 2 May, the crew of HMS *Conqueror* enjoyed a lunch of roast lamb while they hovered unseen beneath the keel of the *Belgrano*. She'd been stalking the Argentine ship for a day and a half. At 18.57 Zulu, Commander Chris Wreford-Brown, the boat's Captain, gave the order to fire three Mk 8 torpedoes at the old ex-US Navy cruiser – a survivor of the Japanese attack on Pearl Harbor. Two of the torpedoes struck and, within an hour, she had sunk. Of *Belgrano*'s complement of 1,042, 368 lost their lives in the freezing South Atlantic.

Aboard Roger Lane-Nott's boat, HMS *Splendid*, the signal telling them of *Conqueror*'s attack was greeted with quiet satisfaction. The job of a hunter-killer submarine was a brutal one, but *Splendid*'s company recognized the effectiveness with which their sister-ship had carried out her work. For all his admiration for the skill with which Wreford-Brown had carried out his attack, though, Lane-Nott couldn't help a feeling of intense professional envy. His own efforts had been frustrated. It should have been *Splendid*, he thought.

The morality and legality of the decision to attack the *Belgrano* have been hotly debated ever since, but in military terms it was decisive: the entire Argentine Navy, which simply had no answer to the threat posed by the British hunter-killer submarines, retreated to Argentine territorial waters and played no further part in the war.

As a direct consequence of decisions provoked by the raid on Stanley airfield, the Argentinians lost the use of both their air defence fighters and their Navy. And in a war fought 8,000 miles from home, the odds against a British victory were shortened.

Four further BLACK BUCK missions were flown. John Reeve and his crew got their chance on 3 May. Two raids were flown against Argentine radar installations by Neil McDougall and his crew, who, while Withers, Reeve and Monty were deployed to Ascension, had stayed at Waddington as American AGM-45 Shrike anti-radar missiles were hurriedly married to the Vulcan airframe by men with American accents who purported to be South African. On McDougall's second mission his crew taunted and teased the Argentine defences to try to pull them on to the punch. They'd dropped into the Oerlikon kill zone around Stanley and dodged flak that zipped around the night sky like lethal fireflies. Then, having successfully fired back, they tested Monty's suggestion that classified documents be thrown out of the crew hatch into the sea inside the ration tin when a broken probe forced them to divert to Rio's Galeão International Airport. Saving the aircraft on that occasion demanded a brilliant piece of flying from McDougall that won him the Distinguished Flying Cross. Martin Withers flew one more mission, but Monty was destined always to be the bridesmaid. He launched in the reserve Vulcan four times, but, to his lasting regret, turned back for Ascension while the Primary continued south on each occasion.

All of the subsequent missions benefited from a completely revised refuelling plan, designed by Jerry Price and the Victor planning team to get as much as 30,000lb more fuel into the formation flying south. It was soon realized that on BLACK BUCK the Vulcan, flying at close to, and sometimes above, its maximum weight for much of the flight south and making continual small throttle adjustments to stay in formation, was burning nearly one and a half times the amount of fuel that Vulcan crews, over twenty years of training, had grown used to. There had, of necessity, been a degree of estimation in the fuel planning: there had simply been no figures available to refer to. On top of this, in order to stay in formation, neither the Victors nor the Vulcans were flying at their most fuel-efficient cruise height. Trying to force together the flight profiles of two such distinct types was an unhappy compromise. When strong headwinds led to the cancellation of a raid on 16 May, it only served to underline how little room for error even the revised plan carried.

In an ideal world, 'One Bomb' Beetham – as some who didn't properly grasp the ambition or success of the raid had unfairly tagged him – would have liked to have put *ten* Vulcans over Stanley, but it couldn't be done; the resources just weren't there. His Air Force had done everything it said it would do and more – without BLACK BUCK, the war would have been harder to win. In the event, one bomber was enough.

And that bomber, the magnificent delta-winged Avro

Vulcan, just months before it was destined for the scrapheap, entered the *Guinness Book of Records* for having flown, at nearly 8,000 miles, 'the longest-range attack in air history'. Despite the eventual Argentine surrender on 14 June, the Vulcans soldiered on as bombers with 44 Squadron under Simon Baldwin until December 1982 – given a stay of execution as a contingency against further Argentine aggression. Had they retired in July as planned, nothing else in the RAF could have done the job. On 8 November 1982, in conditions of great secrecy, one of Strike Command's recently acquired Panavia Tornado GR1s, accompanied by a Buccaneer S2, took part in exercise STORM TRAIL. The aim was to demonstrate the offensive reach of the new strike jet by staging a mock attack on RAF Akrotiri in Cyprus from the UK. The Tornado took off from RAF Marham. Strict conditions on the air-to-air refuelling were put in place – not above 28,000 feet and not in cloud – because the Tornado's anti-icing systems weren't yet fully operational. Both limits had to be busted in order for the mission to succeed. At times, the Tornado, always asthmatic at altitude, had to rely on the Victor tankers supporting the mission to shepherd it along. It made it there and back, though. Just. But the Tornado's warload on STORM TRAIL was a tiny fraction of that carried by Vulcans on the BLACK BUCK missions; the distance from the UK to Cyprus, barely 2,000 miles.

For his flight into the unknown, Martin Withers was awarded the Distinguished Flying Cross while his crew were Mentioned in Dispatches. Withers' citation recorded that he had displayed qualities of 'leadership, determination and presence of mind which were an inspiration to his crew'. He took them with him to London when he was presented with his medal.

For his part, Bob Tuxford was awarded the Air Force Cross – his crew all received the Queen's Commendation for Valuable Service in the Air. Tux also received a personal letter from Sir Michael Beetham congratulating him on his 'epic flight'.

Shortly after the end of hostilities, Tuxford's wife Eileen was at home alone watching a documentary about the Falklands War on television when the telephone rang. She picked up and a voice she didn't recognize introduced himself as Martin Withers' father. He'd been watching the same programme and had felt moved to say something.

'If it hadn't been for your husband's AFC,' he told her, 'my son wouldn't have got his DFC.'

On Ascension Island the day after the raid, when its fragile tapestry had become apparent to all involved, Bob Tuxford was enjoying a drink with Beer, Keable, Rees and Wallis in the American commissary. The group looked up to see Martin Withers' Vulcan crew crossing the noisy bar to join them. Withers was carrying a tray of beers which he set down on the table and pushed towards Tuxford.

'Well done, guys,' Withers said, 'and thank you.' It didn't need much more than that.

# Epilogue

## The Old Lags

*The raid had three advantages, really. The first advantage was to give the people at that time a little fillip. The news had been all bad until then. The second advantage was to cause the Japanese to worry and feel that they were vulnerable, and the third and most useful part of the raid was that it caused a diversion of aircraft and equipment to the defense of the home islands which the Japanese badly needed in the theaters where the war was actually being fought.*

Brigadier General James Doolittle, USAAF, leader of the April 1942 'Doolittle Raid' on Tokyo, reflects, years later, on its impact

At just after nine o'clock in the evening on 1 May 1982, television audiences around Britain tuned in to BBC1 to watch the big hair and shoulderpads of a new American drama called *Dynasty*. As they settled into their sofas, in London over 700 veterans of the Second World War gathered under the heavy chandeliers of the Grosvenor House ballroom for the annual Bomber Command Association dinner. Every year since 1977, they'd met at the Park Lane hotel to keep alive the memory of their wartime contribution. Some had attended a memorial service earlier in the day at the Royal Air Force church of St Clement Danes at the eastern end of the Strand, but most had come to the capital especially for the evening's reunion. They'd been well fed and watered when Air Chief Marshal Sir Michael Beetham rose from his chair to reply to the toast on behalf of the Royal Air Force. As a Bomber Command veteran himself he was one of them and that, at any other time, would have been enough to guarantee a warm reception. Today, though, just a few hours earlier, Flight Lieutenant Martin Withers had shut down the engines of his Vulcan bomber on a remote airfield in the mid-Atlantic after completing an epic mission ordered by Beetham himself. The RAF strategic bomber force had been in action again and that event held a significance in this company that it could hold nowhere else. Some of the audience had gone on, after the war, to fly the Vulcans and

Victors of the V-force. One or two of the names of the men who'd taken part in BLACK BUCK might even have been familiar to them. Beetham felt at home and spoke with pride on the day of another extraordinary RAF achievement.

And yet the veterans' most enthusiastic reaction was reserved for someone else. The room fell silent as the Guest of Honour, wearing thick, black-rimmed spectacles, rose to speak. Although ninety years old and reliant on a pair of hearing aids, Marshal of the Royal Air Force Sir Arthur 'Bomber' Harris remained a pungent, witty after-dinner speaker. And 'Old Butch', as he was known to his crews, was adored by them. They shared with him the hurt that came from knowing their role in Hitler's defeat had not been properly recognized by their country. Indeed, it seemed sometimes that she was almost ashamed of what they had done. Harris spoke for twenty minutes without notes, captivating an audience that hung on his every word and afterwards sat late into the night, finding time for all who asked for it. Stung into silence by the controversy surrounding his wartime bombing campaign he had only recently begun to talk of it again, mainly because of the encouragement of the veterans. He was profoundly moved by the affection shown to him by his 'old lags'. Sir Michael Beetham felt privileged to have become friendly with Harris in his years as Chief of the Air Staff. The two men sat next to each other at dinner. But Harris was not the only legendary wartime leader in attendance. Another honoured guest was the 86-year-old Lieutenant General James H. Doolittle, Commander of the US 8th Air Force and Harris's American counterpart towards the end of the war. 'Bert' Harris counted Doolittle as one of the closest of his friends. And his presence today had a particular resonance.

In April 1942, Doolittle had led an ultra-long-range raid on Tokyo that marked the beginning of America's response to the bombing of Pearl Harbor. For a while, America had been powerless to respond to the unexpected attack on her Hawaiian naval base. But the audacity and ingenuity of the Doolittle's B-25 strike on Tokyo had shaken the Japanese.

Ironically, one of those who appreciated the impact of the 'Doolittle Raid' was the then Argentine commercial attaché to Japan.

'It caught the Japs by surprise,' he reported, 'their unbounded confidence began to crack.'

Forty years on, the RAF's similarly unexpected raid had just had a comparable effect on his own countrymen – a fact not lost on Doolittle and his companions at the Grosvenor House dinner. As they discussed the Vulcan raid, Sir Michael Beetham was gratified by Harris's approval. The old man was delighted with news of the bomber's success.

'We can't be kicked around without retaliating,' Harris said, reflecting on the decision to take out the runway. 'I would have done exactly that.' He went on, warming to his theme: the aircrews involved in BLACK BUCK, he was in no doubt, were of 'the same breed' as those he used to command.

Harris's only note of criticism was appropriate given the name by which he was now best known. Ideally, he said, he might have liked to use heavier bombs; make bigger craters. But, as he had the grace to acknowledge, 'it is an awfully long way to carry them'.

# Glossary

**18228** part number for the Vulcan's Radar Warning Receiver

**90 Way** The unit controlling the dropping of the Vulcan's bomb-load. So called because, supposedly, it offered ninety different options

**A-4 Skyhawk** US-made single-engine, single-seat naval attack aircraft

**AARI** Air-to-Air Refuelling Instructor

**AEO** Air Electronics Officer

**AFC** Air Force Cross

**AIM-9 Sidewinder** American-made heat-seeking air-to-air missile

**Alpha Jet** Franco-German advanced jet-training aircraft

**Amtrac** Armoured Personnel Carrier

**anti-metric depth** An imperial depth that's not directly equivalent to an obvious metric depth such as 50, 100, 150 or 200 metres

**AOC** Air Officer Commanding

**APC** Armoured Personnel Carrier

**AS12** air-to-surface missile carried by British Wasp helicopters

**AS-37 Martel** Anglo-French air-to-surface missile

**ASI** Ascension Island

**astro-navigation** Establishing one's position using a sextant and starcharts

**B-52 Stratofortress** American eight-engined heavy bomber

**Balbo** Slang for a large formation of aircraft. After Italo Balbo, an Italian who, in 1933, flew a squadron of twenty-two flying boats from Italy to the United States

**BAM Malvinas** Base Aérea Militar Malvinas

**Bear** The NATO reporting name for the TU-95, a swept-wing Soviet patrol bomber powered by four turboprop engines

**Belfast** British turboprop transport aircraft

**Bingo Fuel** A preplanned fuel level at which an aircraft has to turn for home

**Bison** The NATO reporting name for the M-4, a Soviet four-jet patrol bomber

**Bone Dome** protective flying helmet

**Buccaneer** British low-level strike aircraft

**Burn-Out Zone** The zone where a weapon is inaccurate but still potentially lethal

**C-130 Hercules** US-made turboprop transport aircraft

**C-141** US-made four-jet transport aircraft

**Carousel** an inertial navigation system

**Dagger** Israeli version of the Mirage jet

**Dash 10** A wing-mounted podded radar jammer used by the Vulcan during the BLACK BUCK raids

**DFC** Distinguished Flying Cross

**dihedral** angled upwards from horizontal

**drogue** Also known as the basket, this is at the end of the hose trailed from the Victor's HDU. Shaped like a shuttlecock, it couples with the receiver's probe to allow fuel to flow between the two aircraft

**DV** Direct Vision

**ECM** Electronic Counter-Measures

**EPIRB** Emergency Position-Indicating Radio Beacon

**Exocet** French air-, surface- or submarine-launched anti-ship missile

**F4 Phantom** American-built two-seat fighter-bomber

**F95** aerial camera used by the RAF

**FAA** Fuerza Aérea Argentina: the Argentine Air Force

**Fansong** Soviet fire-control radar used with the SA-2 surface-to-air missile

**FIBS** Falkland Islands Broadcasting Service

**FIDF** Falkland Islands Defence Force

**FIGAS** Falkland Islands Government Air Service

**fire-control radar** Radar that directs the fire of anti-aircaft guns or surface-to-air missiles

**flameout** extinction of the flame in a jet engine's combustion chamber

**GADA 601** Grupo de Artillería de Defensa Aérea: an Argentine Army anti-aircraft unit

**gash** RAF slang for rubbish

**Gnat** British advanced jet-training aircraft

**GPI6** Ground Position Indicator Mk 6

**GPMG** General Purpose Machine-Gun

**green porridge** RAF slang for the H2S radar display used by Vulcan and Victor Navigator Radars

**Gun Dish** Soviet fire-control radar used with the ZSU-23-4

**H2S** radar carried by Vulcans, Victors and Valiants

**HDU** Hose Drum Unit: the mechanism that winds and unwinds the Victor's refuelling hose

**HF** high-frequency

**HP cock** high-pressure cock

**Humphrey** nickname for HMS Antrim's Wessex helicopter

**IFF** Identification Friend or Foe: a radio transponder broadcasting on prearranged frequencies to confirm identity

**INS** Inertial Navigation System

**JARIC** Joint Air Reconnaissance Intelligence Centre at RAF Brampton in Cambridgeshire

**Jet Provost** British basic jet-training aircraft

**JPT** jet pipe temperature

**KC-135** US-made aerial tanker

**KH11** American spy satellite

**Kill Zone** The zone in which a weapon is accurate and lethal

**LADE** Líneas Aéreas de Estado: airline operated by the Argentine Air Force

**Lightning** single-seat British jet fighter

**LP cock** low-pressure cock

**Mae West** RAF nickname for aircrew's life jackets

**MEZ** Maritime Exclusion Zone

**Mirage** French-made single-engine, single-seat fighter-bomber

**MRR** Maritime Radar Reconnaissance

**NATO** North Atlantic Treaty Organization

**NBS** Navigation and Bombing System

**NVGs** night-vision goggles

**OCU** Operational Conversion Unit

**ODM** Operating Data Manual

**Oerlikon** Swiss-made radar-guided 35mm anti-aircraft cannon

**Omega** very-low-frequency radio navigation system

**Operation ALPHA** Argentine plan to establish sovereignty on South Georgia

**Operation BLACK BUCK** The codename given to RAF Vulcan raids during the Falklands War

**Operation BLUE** Argentine plan to seize the Falkland Islands

**Operation CORPORATE** The codename given to the British operation to retake the Falkland Islands

**Operation PARAQUAT** The codename for the British operation to retake South Georgia

**PEC** Personal Equipment Connector

**pop up** To ascend briefly from low level in order to deliver weapons

**PRF** Pulse Recurrence Frequency: picked up by an RWR and used by the AEO to distinguish one radar from another

**probe** The device through which a receiver takes on fuel during air-to-air refuelling

**QFI** Qualified Flying Instructor

**QRA** Quick Reaction Alert

**Radar Altimeter** Measures altitude by transmitting radar pulses directly downwards which reflect back to the radar aerial. In contrast to a barometric altimeter, it measures actual distance from the ground rather than indicating height above sea level

**RAT** Ram Air Turbine: source of emergency electrical power used in the event of engine failure

**RED FLAG** The realistic air warfare exercises held in Nevada, USA

**Red Rag** The codename for the BLACK BUCK Operations team on Ascension

**Red Shrimp** radar jammer fitted to the Vulcan

**retarded bomb** A bomb fitted with a drag parachute in order to prevent an aircraft flying at low level being damaged by the blast from its own weapons

**Rheinmetall** German-made 20mm anti-aircraft cannon

**Roland** Franco-German radar-guided surface-to-air missile

**rotate** The point at which an aircraft takes off

**RT** radio telephony

**RV** rendezvous

**RWR** Radar Warning Receiver

**SA-2** Soviet surface-to-air missile: NATO reporting name Guideline

**Saints** nickname for St Helenians

**SAM** surface-to-air missile

**SCSYS** Satellite Communication System; pronounced 'Sixsis'

**Sea Harrier** British V/STOL single-seat naval fighter-bomber

**Sea King** British naval helicopter

**SHAR** Royal Navy nickname for the Sea Harrier FRS1

**Skybolt** An air-launched ballistic missile, cancelled in the 1960s

**Skyguard** Swiss-made fire-control radar

**SLR** Self-Loading Rifle

**Spadeadam** electronic-warfare range in Cumbria

**stick spacing** distance between each bomb in a stick of bombs

**Super Étendard** French-made single-engine, single-seat naval attack aircraft

**Superfledermaus** Swiss-made fire-control radar

**TACAN** Tactical Air Navigation: a UHF transponder that provides information on range and bearing

**TEZ** Total Exclusion Zone

**TFR** Terrain-Following Radar

**Tiger Cat** British-made optically guided surface-to-air missile

**Tornado GR1** British/German/Italian-built two-seat, swing-wing strike aircraft

**TPS-43** American-made long-distance search radar

**TPS-44** American-made search radar

**TRU** Transformer Rectifier Unit

**U-2** American high-altitude reconnaissance aircraft

**UHF** ultra-high frequency
**VC10** A four-jet British airliner used by the RAF as a transport aircraft
**Verey flare** coloured flare fired from a pistol
**VHF** very-high frequency
**V/STOL** Vertical/Short Take-Off and Landing
**Wasp** British ship-borne helicopter
**Wessex** British helicopter
**WRAF** Women's Royal Air Force
**ZSU-23-4** Soviet radar-laid anti-aircraft cannon
**Zulu** Greenwich Mean Time

# Bibliography

## BOOKS

Barker, Nick, *Beyond Endurance: An Epic of Whitehall and the South Atlantic Conflict*, Leo Cooper, 1997.

Beckett, Andy, *Pinochet in Piccadilly: Britain and Chile's Hidden History*, Faber and Faber, 2002.

Briasco, Jesus Romero, and Salvador Mafe Huertas, *Falklands: Witness of Battles*, Federico Domenech, 1985.

Brickhill, Paul, *The Dambusters*, Pan, 1954.

Brookes, Andrew, *V Force: The History of Britain's Airborne Deterrent*, Jane's, 1982.

Brookes, Andrew, *Handley Page Victor*, Ian Allan, 1998.

Brown, Dale, *Flight of the Old Dog*, HarperCollins, 1988.

Brown, David, *The Royal Navy and the Falklands War*, Leo Cooper, 1987.

Bulman, Craig, *The Vulcan B.Mk2 from a Different Angle*, Pentland Press, 2001.

Burden, Rodney, Michael Draper, Douglas Rough, Colin Smith, and David Wilton, *Falklands: The Air War*, Arms and Armour Press, 1986.

Burns, Jimmy, *The Land That Lost Its Heroes: How Argentina Lost the Falklands War*, Bloomsbury, 1987.

Carballo, Captain Pablo Marcos, *Dios y los Halcones*, Editorial Abril SA, 1983.

Chartres, John, *BAe Nimrod*, Ian Allan, 1986.

Cobham, Alan J., *My Flight to the Cape and Back*, A&C Black, 1926.

Cruddas, Colin, *In Cobham's Company: Sixty Years of Flight Refuelling Limited*, Cobham, 1994.

Cruddas, Colin, *Cobham: The Flying Years*, Chalford, 1997.

Deighton, Len, *Bomber: Events Relating to the Last Flight of an RAF Bomber over Germany on the Night of June 31st, 1943*, HarperCollins, 1978.

Delve, Ken, *RAF Marham: The Operational History of Britain's Front-line Base from 1916 to the Present Day*, Patrick Stephens, 1995.

Downey, Bob, *V-Bombers*, Arms and Armour Press, 1985.

Ethell, Jeffrey, and Alfred Price, *Air War South Atlantic*, Sidgwick and Jackson, 1983.

Flintham, Victor, *Air Wars and Aircraft: A Detailed Record of Air Combat, 1945 to the Present*, Arms and Armour Press, 1989.

Ghione, Sergio, *Turtle Island: A Journey to Britain's Oddest Colony*, Allen Lane, 2002.

Goodwin, Barry, *The 'FOB'S KID' Syndrome: Vulcan Bombers in Action*, Airlife, 2001.

Gray, Anthony, *The Penetrators*, Mayflower, 1967.

Gunston, Bill, and Peter Gilchrist, *Jet Bombers: From the Messerschmitt Me262 to the Stealth B2*, Osprey, 1993.

Hastings, Max, and Simon Jenkins, *The Battle for the Falklands*, Michael Joseph, 1983.

Hill, Richard, *Lewin of Greenwich: The Authorised Biography of Admiral of the Fleet Lord Lewin*, Weidenfeld & Nicholson, 2000.

Hobson, Chris, with Andrew Noble, *Falklands Air War*, Midland, 2002.

Inskip, Ian, *Ordeal by Exocet: HMS Glamorgan and the Falklands War 1982*, Chatham, 2002.

Jackson, Bill, and Dwin Bramall, *The Chiefs: The Story of the United Kingdom Chiefs of Staff*, Brassey's, 1992.

Jackson, Robert, *World Military Aircraft since 1945*, Ian Allan, 1979.

Jackson, Robert, *Avro Vulcan*, Patrick Stephens, 1984.

Jones, Barry, *V-Bombers: Valiant, Vulcan and Victor*, Crowood Press, 2000.

Junger, Sebastian, *The Perfect Storm: A True Story of Men against the Sea*, Fourth Estate, 1997.

Kon, Daniel, *Los Chicos De La Guerra*, New English Library, 1983.

Laming, Tim, *The Vulcan Story: 1952–2002*, Cassell, 2002.

Leach, Henry, *Endure No Makeshifts: Some Naval Recollections*, Leo Cooper, 1993.

Middlebrook, Martin, *Task Force: The Falklands War, 1982*, Penguin, 1987.

Middlebrook, Martin, *The Berlin Raids: RAF Bomber Command Winter 1943–44*, Penguin, 1990.

Middlebrook, Martin, *The Fight for the 'Malvinas'*, Penguin, 1990.

Middleton, Donald, *Tests of Character: Epic Flights by Legendary Test Pilots*, Airlife, 1995.

Mondey, David, *The Hamlyn Concise Guide to British Aircraft of World War II*, Hamlyn, 1982.

Nelson, Craig, *The First Heroes: The Extraordinary Story of the Doolittle Raid – America's First World War II Victory*, Corgi, 2003.

Nott, John, *Here Today, Gone Tomorrow: Recollections of an Errant Politician*, Politicos, 2002.

Perkins, Roger, *Operation Paraquat: The Battle for South Georgia*, Picton Publishing, 1986.

Prest, Robert, *F4 Phantom: A Pilot's Story*, Corgi, 1981.

Probert, Henry, *Bomber Harris: His Life and Times*, Greenhill, 2003.

Rice, Desmond, and Arthur Gavshon, *The Sinking of the Belgrano*, Secker and Warburg, 1984.

Ring, Jim, *We Come Unseen: The Untold Story of Britain's Cold War Submarines*, John Murray, 2001.

Ross, A. E., *Through Eyes of Blue: Personal Memories of the RAF from 1918*, Airlife, 1982.

Skinner, Michael, *Red Flag: Air Combat for the '80s*, Presidio Press, 1984.

Smith, John, *74 Days: An Islander's Diary of the Falklands Occupation*, Quetzal, 2002.

Thatcher, Margaret, *The Downing Street Years*, HarperCollins, 1993.

Thomas, Gordon, and Max Morgan-Witts, *Ruin from the Air: The Atomic Mission to Hiroshima*, Hamish-Hamilton, 1977.

Thompson, Julian, *No Picnic*, Cassell, 2001.

Trubshaw, Brian, with Sally Edmondson, *Test Pilot*, Sutton, 1998.

Wagstaff, William, *Falkland Islands*, Bradt, 2001.

Ward, Commander 'Sharkey', *Sea Harrier over the Falklands*, Orion, 1993.

Weinberger, Caspar, *Fighting for Peace: Seven Critical Years in the Pentagon*, Michael Joseph, 1990.

West, Nigel, *The Secret War for the Falklands: The SAS, MI6, and the War Whitehall Nearly Lost*, Little, Brown, 1997.

Woodward, Admiral Sandy, with Patrick Robinson, *One Hundred Days*, HarperCollins, 1992.

Wynn, Humphrey, *RAF Nuclear Deterrent Forces*, HMSO, 1994.

# WEBSITES

www.aopa.org Tips for Maintaining and Regaining Situational Awareness by Michael P. Collins

www.avrovulcan.org.uk Vulcans in Camera

www.britains-smallwars.com Britain's Small Wars 1945–2003

www.designation-systems.net Directory of US Military Rockets and Missiles

www.fleetairarmarchive.net Fleet Air Arm Archive 1939–1945

www.geocities.com/layedwyer Ascension Island: A Partial Military History

www.gladwell.com The Art of Failure by Malcolm Gladwell (originally published in the *New Yorker*)

www.heritage.org.ac Ascension Island Historical Society

www.lynnesdiaries.freeserve.co.uk Brigands to V-Bombers

www.northwood.mod.co.uk PJHQ Northwood

www.rafmarham.co.uk RAF Marham

www.raf.mod.uk The Vulcan Engineering Detachment on Ascension by Squadron Leader Mel James www.raf-waddington.com RAF Waddington

www.samueljohnson.com Thoughts on the Late Transactions Respecting Falkland's Islands

www.scientificamerican.com What Happens When Lightning Strikes an Airplane? Edward J. Rupke

www.thunder-and-lightnings.co.uk Thunder and Lightnings

www.tvoc.co.uk Vulcan to the Sky

www.xl426.com The Vulcan Restoration Trust

www.xm655.com The 655 Maintenance and Preservation Society

## MAGAZINES, JOURNALS AND PERIODICALS

*Air Forces Monthly*, November 1992

Bond, Steve, 'RAF in the 1950s', *Flypast*, April 1990

Brocklebank, Roy, 'The Final Countdown', *Aeroplane*, March 2005

Brookes, Wing-Cdr, 'Vulcans vs Buffs', *Allied Airpower – Enduring Co-operation*

Burney, Allan, 'Ascension Island: Staging Post to the Falklands – Part 1', *Aircraft Illustrated*, November 1982

Calvert, Denis J., 'To Intercept a Bear', *Aircraft Illustrated*, December 1984

*Cape Argus*, July 1959

Carlson, Ted, 'Red Flag – Showdown in Nevada', *Top Gun Combat – Take My Breath Away*

'Classics Compared: Avro Vulcan and Rockwell B-1B', *Air International*, June 2004

'Five Black Bucks, The', *Air International*, December 1982

Foster, Peter R., 'Victor Force: Part One', *Aircraft Illustrated*, September 1986

—, 'Victor Flight', *Aircraft Illustrated*, October 1986

Gething, Michael J., 'The Black Buck Raids', *Vulcan News*, November 2000

Gunston, Bill, 'Spadeadam: Space Springboard or White Elephant?', *Flight*, 16 September 1960

—, 'The V-bombers – Avro Vulcan – Part 1', *Aeroplane Monthly*, October 1980

—, 'The V-bombers – Avro Vulcan – Part 2', *Aeroplane Monthly*, November 1980

—, 'The V-bombers – Avro Vulcan – Part 3', *Aeroplane Monthly*, December 1980

—, 'The V-bombers – Handley Page Victor – Part 1', *Aeroplane Monthly*, January 1981

—, 'The V-bombers – Handley Page Victor – Part 2', *Aeroplane Monthly*, February 1981

—, 'The V-bombers – Handley Page Victor – Part 3', *Aeroplane Monthly*, March 1981

Jackson, Paul, 'Avro Vulcan', *Wings of Fame*, Volume 3

Jenkins, Simon, 'An Unnecessary War', *The Times*, 2 April 2002

*Jets*, Summer 2000

*Jets*, Vulcan Special, Winter 1999

Lambert, C. M., 'Bomex by Vulcan', *Flight*, 18 July 1958

Leach, Sqn Ldr Ray, 'Life with the Last Vulcan', *Flypast*, May 1988

'Louisiana Bomb Run', *Air International*, March 1980

*Marham News*, South Atlantic Special 1982

Mellow, Craig, 'God Save the Vulcan!' *Air and Space Smithsonian*, December 2003/January 2004

Panavia Tornado advertisement, *Air International*, July 1981

'Petrol Pumps in the Sky', *Air International*, December 1976

Pinney, Wing Cdr Phil, 'Red Flag 77–9', *Royal Air Force Yearbook 1978*

Price, Dr Alfred, 'Black Buck to the Falklands', *Royal Air Force Air Power Review*, vol. 5, no. 2, Summer 2002

Prins, François, 'Old Vic Soldiers On', *Aircraft Illustrated*, September 1988

Rawlings, J. D. R., 'Dambusting Navigator', *Air Pictorial*, September 1975

'Readiness is Red Flag', *Air International*, May 1981

Rodwell, Robert R., 'Lo-Hi Victor', *Flight International*, 6 May 1965

*Royal Air Force Historical Society Journal*, 30

Stuttaford, Dr Thomas, 'How to Survive the Cruel Sea', *The Times*, 12 August 2004

Talliss, Jack, 'Black Buck Raid', *Air Forces Monthly*, May 1992

Thomas, Sqn Ldr David and Tim Laming, 'Flying the Vulcan', *Aircraft Illustrated*, December 1992

'V-bomber Salute', *Flypast*, July 2002

'Victor K2 Sortie', *Aircraft Illustrated*, August 1982

*Vulcan, The*, Falklands Special, May 2002

'Vulcan at 50', *Flypast*, August 2002

# VIDEOS

*Britain's Cold War Super Weapons*, Blakeway Productions, 2005

*Early Vulcan and Victor Development*, Aviation Video International

*Flight Sortie*, Wolf Video Productions, 1995

*Handley Page Victor K Mark 2, The*, Wolf Video Productions, 1995

*HeavyLift Cargo Airlines: Shorts Belfast*, Just Planes Videos

*Marham Victors*, Aviation Video International

*Thunderball* (dir. Terence Young), MGM, 1965

*V-Force*, Aviation Video International

*V-Force: Britain's Nuclear Bombers*, DD Video, 1998

*Vickers Valiant – First V-bomber is 50*, Ken Wixey, *Flypast*, May 2001

*Victor: Last of the V-Force*, DD Video, 1995

*Vulcan: A Farewell to Arms*, DD Video

*Vulcan Bomber Mark 2*, Wolf Video Productions, 1995

*Vulcan Squadron*, Bygone Films 1995

*Vulcan Story, The*, Leisure View Video, 1998

*Waddington Vulcans*, Aviation Video International

*Where the Big Birds Fly*, Yorkshire Television

## UNPUBLISHED ACCOUNTS

Knight, Air Vice Marshal Sir Michael, 'A Background to
   Operation "Black Buck 1"'
Laycock, Group Captain John
Montgomery, Group Captain Alastair
Russell, Flight Lieutenant Dick, AFC
Weightman, Flt Lt G. R., 'First Contacts!'
Withers, Flight Lieutenant Martin, DFC

## INTERVIEWS

Detailed in the acknowledgements

---

### VULCAN TO THE SKY

If you've enjoyed *Vulcan 607*, why not find out more about the campaign to return XH558, the last airworthy Vulcan bomber, to the sky. Supported by a Lottery Heritage Fund grant of £2,734,000 and 'donor' support of £1.5m, together with partnership with BAE Systems plc and Marshalls Aerospace, the Vulcan Operating Company – the engineering subsidiary of the Vulcan to the Sky Trust which owns the aircraft for the nation – expects to begin test-flying XH558 in summer 2006. Of the aircrew who took part in the BLACK BUCK Raids, both Martin Withers and Barry Masefield have signed up to fly her.

Funds are still needed, and there are a number of different ways in which you can support the project, from donations to buying merchandise to sponsoring individual XH558 components. Read more about Vulcan to the Sky online at: www.vulcantothesky.com

or contact them at:    Vulcan to the Sky
PO BOX 3240
Wimborne
Dorset
BH21 4YP
England

Freephone: 0800 083 2022
Tel / Fax: 0044 (0) 1258 841 274
Email: vulcantothesky@aol.com

# Appendix 1

## Vulcan Cutaway

# Avro Vulcan B Mk 2

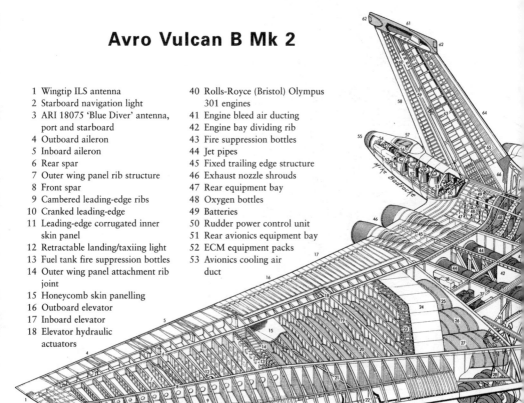

1 Wingtip ILS antenna
2 Starboard navigation light
3 ARI 18075 'Blue Diver' antenna, port and starboard
4 Outboard aileron
5 Inboard aileron
6 Rear spar
7 Outer wing panel rib structure
8 Front spar
9 Cambered leading-edge ribs
10 Cranked leading-edge
11 Leading-edge corrugated inner skin panel
12 Retractable landing/taxiing light
13 Fuel tank fire suppression bottles
14 Outer wing panel attachment rib joint
15 Honeycomb skin panelling
16 Outboard elevator
17 Inboard elevator
18 Elevator hydraulic actuators

40 Rolls-Royce (Bristol) Olympus 301 engines
41 Engine bleed air ducting
42 Engine bay dividing rib
43 Fire suppression bottles
44 Jet pipes
45 Fixed trailing edge structure
46 Exhaust nozzle shrouds
47 Rear equipment bay
48 Oxygen bottles
49 Batteries
50 Rudder power control unit
51 Rear avionics equipment bay
52 ECM equipment packs
53 Avionics cooling air duct

19 No. 7 starboard fuel tank, total internal capacity 9,260 Imp gal (42,096 litres)
20 No. 5 starboard tank
21 Diagonal rib
22 Leading-edge de-icing air duct
23 Wing stringers
24 Parallel chord wing skin panels
25 No. 6 starboard fuel tank
26 No. 4 starboard tank
27 No. 3 starboard tank
28 Main undercarriage leg strut and shock absorber
29 Eight-wheel main undercarriage bogie
30 Mainwheel bay door
31 Fire suppression bottles
32 Inboard leading-edge ribs
33 De-icing air supply
34 Fuel collectors and pumps
35 Main undercarriage wheel bay
36 Drag link and retraction actuator
37 Airborne Auxiliary Power Plant (AAPP)
38 Electrical equipment bay
39 Starboard engine bays

54 'Red Steer' tail warning radar equipment
55 Aft radome
56 Twin brake parachute housing
57 Parachute door
58 Rudder rib structure
59 Rudder mass balances and seals
60 Fin de-icing air vent
61 Fin tip antenna fairing
62 Passive ECM antennae, fore and aft
63 Two-spar fin torsion box structure
64 Fin leading-edge rib structure
65 Corrugated inner skin/de-icing ducting
66 HF antenna
67 Fin de-icing air supply
68 Bomb bay rear bulkhead
69 Bomb bay roof arch frames
70 De-icing bleed air pre-cooler air intake
71 VHF antenna
72 Port Olympus 301 engines
73 Engine bay shroud ribs
74 Port jet pipe fairing
75 Electrical equipment bay

76 Chaff/flare launchers
77 'Green Satin' doppler navigational equipment bay
78 Elevator mass balances and seals
79 Elevator hydraulic actuators
80 Port inboard elevator
81 Port outboard elevator
82 Port inboard aileron
83 Aileron mass balance and seal
84 Control rods
85 Aileron power control units
86 Ventral actuator fairings
87 Port outboard aileron
88 Wingtip localizer antenna
89 Port navigation light
90 Cranked and cambered leading-edge panel
91 Fuel tank fire suppression bottles
92 Outer wing panel joint rib
93 No. 7 port fuel tank
94 No. 5 port tank
95 Leading-edge de-icing air duct
96 No. 6 port fuel tank
97 No. 4 port tank
98 No. 3 port tank
99 Port main undercarriage bay

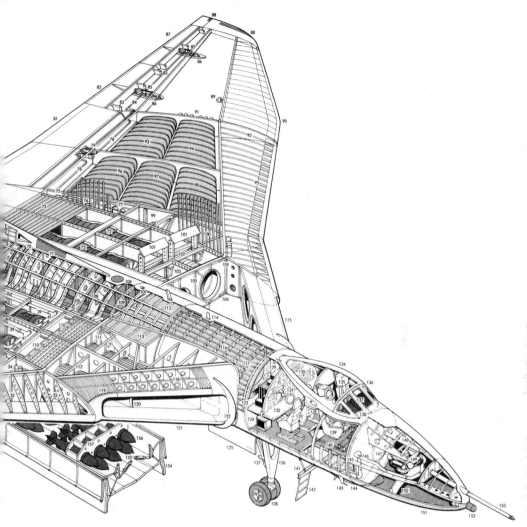

100 Skin support stringers
101 Port airbrake panels
102 Airbrake drive mechanism
103 Intake ducts
104 Wing spar attachment joints
105 Centre-section front spar transverse main frame
106 DF loop antenna
107 Anti-collision light
108 Bomb bay longerons
109 Bomb bay front bulkhead
110 Starboard airbrake housings
111 Boundary layer bleed-air duct
112 Starboard intake duct structure
113 No. 2 fuselage fuel tanks, divided port and starboard
114 UHF antenna
115 Port engine intake
116 No. 1 fuselage fuel tanks, divided port and starboard
117 Fuselage frame and stringer structure
118 Intake lip structure
119 De-icing air duct corrugated inner skin

120 Intake divider
121 Starboard air intake
122 Boundary layer splitter plate
123 Forward fuselage section joint frame
124 Rear pressure bulkhead
125 Nosewheel doors
126 Nose undercarriage shock absorber leg strut
127 Hydraulic steering jack
128 Twin nosewheels
129 Avionics equipment bay
130 Rearward-facing crew members' stations, Tactical Navigator, Radar Navigator and Air Electronics Officer
131 Cabin side windows
132 Chart table
133 Assisted exit swivelling crew seats
134 Jettisonable cockpit canopy, dinghy stowage beneath
135 First Pilot's Martin-Baker Mk 4 ejection seat
136 Windscreen panels

137 Instrument panel shroud
138 Windscreen wipers
139 Co-pilot's ejection seat
140 Flight deck floor level
141 Entry hatch
142 Extending boarding ladder
143 Pitot head
144 Ventral bomb aiming fairing, unused on B Mk 2 aircraft
145 Aircraft destructor
146 Air refuelling supply pipe
147 Forward pressure dome
148 Radar mounting structure
149 H2S radar equipment pack
150 Rotating radar scanner
151 Radome
152 Terrain Following Radar antenna
153 Flight refuelling probe
154 Bomb bay doors
155 Bomb door hydraulic actuators and hinge links
156 1,000lb (454kg) HE bombs
157 Seven-round bomb carrier, maximum load, three (21,000lb)

# Appendix 2

## Victor Cutaway

# Handley Page Victor K2

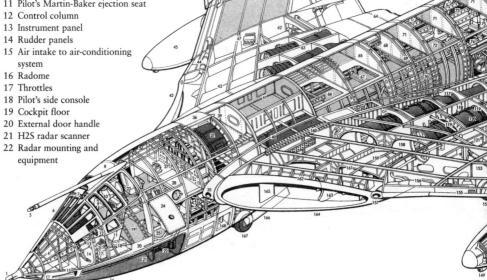

1 Nose probe
2 Control feel system pressure intake
3 Nose compartment windows
4 Nose construction
5 In-flight refuelling probe
6 Windscreen
7 Refuelling searchlights
8 Jettisonable roof hatch
9 Co-pilot's Martin-Baker ejection seat
10 Pilot's roof hatch windows
11 Pilot's Martin-Baker ejection seat
12 Control column
13 Instrument panel
14 Rudder panels
15 Air intake to air-conditioning system
16 Radome
17 Throttles
18 Pilot's side console
19 Cockpit floor
20 External door handle
21 H2S radar scanner
22 Radar mounting and equipment

23 Rearward-facing crew members' seats – AEO port, Nav Plotter centre, Nav Radar starboard
24 Cockpit door
25 Entry steps
26 Front fuselage construction
27 Rear-view periscope
28 Rearward-facing crew members' work table
29 Cabin side window
30 Air-conditioning system
31 Nose freight compartment
32 Instrument panels
33 Radio and electronics racks
34 Pressure bulkhead
35 Air-conditioning intake
36 Starboard emergency life raft hatch
37 Port life raft pack
38 Forward fuselage connecting construction

39 Wing spar bulkhead
40 Wing centre-section fuel tank
41 Overwing fuel tank
42 Starboard engine intake
43 Intake ducts
44 De-icing air system
45 Underwing fuel tank
46 Starboard wing fuel tanks
47 Fuel flow proportioner
48 De-icing connector to outer wing
49 Vortex generators
50 Starboard Flight Refuelling FR20B refuelling pod
51 Power turbine propeller
52 Pylon mounting
53 Pitot head
54 Starboard wingtip
55 Starboard aileron
56 Trim tab
57 Refuelling hose
58 Trailing-edge fairing
59 Starboard flap

60 Flap track fairing
61 Flap mechanism
62 Starboard main undercarriage bay
63 Starboard engine bays
64 Exhaust pipe fairing
65 Bomb bay roof forward fuel tank
66 Forward refuelling bomb bay tank
67 Tank mountings
68 Fuel flow proportioner
69 Fuselage double frames
70 Fuselage stringer construction
71 Bomb bay roof aft fuel tanks
72 Air refuelling bomb bay tank
73 Bomb bay roof structure
74 Flight Refuelling FR17B hose reel unit
75 Hose reel jack
76 Reel drive motor
77 Air system piping
78 Bomb bay aft bulkhead

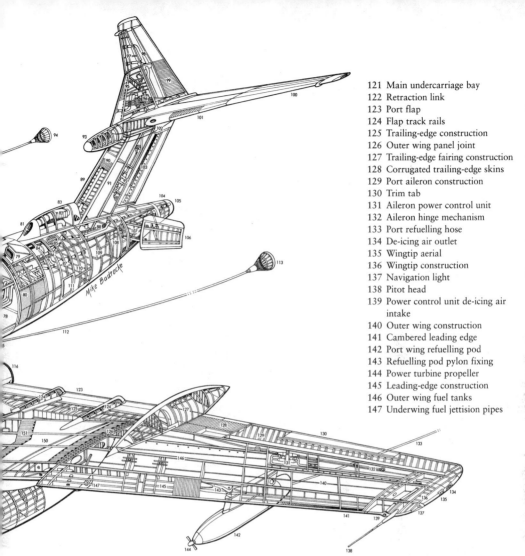

121 Main undercarriage bay
122 Retraction link
123 Port flap
124 Flap track rails
125 Trailing-edge construction
126 Outer wing panel joint
127 Trailing-edge fairing construction
128 Corrugated trailing-edge skins
129 Port aileron construction
130 Trim tab
131 Aileron power control unit
132 Aileron hinge mechanism
133 Port refuelling hose
134 De-icing air outlet
135 Wingtip aerial
136 Wingtip construction
137 Navigation light
138 Pitot head
139 Power control unit de-icing air
   intake
140 Outer wing construction
141 Cambered leading edge
142 Port wing refuelling pod
143 Refuelling pod pylon fixing
144 Power turbine propeller
145 Leading-edge construction
146 Outer wing fuel tanks
147 Underwing fuel jettision pipes

79 Retractable Ram Air Turbine
   intakes
80 Rear fuselage fuel tank
81 Air system intake
82 Heat exchanger
83 Fin root fairing
84 Ram Air Turbine
85 Air exhaust louvres
86 Turbine intake jack
87 Tailplane de-icing air system
88 Fin root fixing
89 Fin leading edge
90 Corrugated inner skin
91 Fin construction
92 Rudder control unit
93 Tailplane fairing
94 Starboard refuelling drogue
95 Starboard tailplane construction
96 Elevator power control unit
97 Elevator construction
98 Tailplane de-icing air system
99 Corrugated tailplane inner skin

100 Port elevator
101 Port tailplane
102 Tailplane fixings
103 Rudder construction
104 Tailplane fairing
105 Fuel jettison pipe
106 Port airbrake, open
107 Airbrake hinges
108 Airbrake jack
109 Tailplane support construction
110 Rear fuselage freight compartment
111 Freight compartment door
112 Centre refuelling hose
113 Centre drogue
114 Retractable drogue fairing
115 Signal lights to receiver
116 Port engine exhausts
117 Port inner engine bay
118 Port outer engine bay
119 Engine mounting beams
120 Rolls-Royce Conway 201
   (RCo17) engine

148 Underwing fuel tank
   construction
149 Pressurizing air intake
150 Inner wing fuel tanks
151 Corrugated skin sandwich
   panels
152 Main undercarriage leg
153 Undercarriage strut
154 Eight wheel bogie
155 Leading-edge de-icing air duct
156 De-icing air system
157 De-icing air intake
158 Rear spar spectacle frame
159 Intake duct construction
160 Wing attachment joint
161 Front spar spectacle frame
162 Intake lip construction
163 Intake duct divider
164 Port engine air intake
165 Intake guide vane
166 Nosewheel bay door
167 Twin nosewheels
168 Battery bay

# Picture Acknowledgements

Although every effort has been made to trace copyright holders and clear permission for the photographs in the book, the provenance of a number of them is uncertain. The author and publisher would welcome the opportunity to correct any mistakes.

*First section*

Cover of *The Aeroplane*: © Aeroplane Monthly; Victor prototype: © T R H Pictures; upside down Victor: © The Handley Page Association; Vulcan prototype: © The Flight Collection

Withers and crew: © BAE Systems; Nellis AFP: © Crown; Vulcan at Nellis: © Alastair Montgomery; Port Stanley: © Imperial War Museum FKD 2070; Argentine Air Force C-130 Hercules: © Imperial War Museum FKD 2181; armoured troop carriers: © Imperial War Museum FKD 2173

Air Chief Marshal Sir Michael Beetham: © Crown; RAF Waddington: © Alastair Montgomery; Wing Commander Simon Baldwin: © Simon Baldwin; work on the Victors: © Crown; RAF Marham: © Crown

Bombing Garvie Island sequence: © Crown; over Spadeadam: © John Duggan; in-flight refuelling: © Crown; no room for error: © Crown

Victor arrives at Ascension: © Barry Neal; Ascension from the air: © Crown; flight-crew tents: © Bob Tuxford

*Second section*

Fuel flows: © John Reeve; Victor with drag chute: © Crown; damaged fuselage: © Bob Tuxford

HMS *Endurance*: © Imperial War Museum FKD 1178; crashed Wessex: © Imperial War Museum FKD 53; Wessex over South Georgia: © Imperial War Museum FKD 4896; Argentine air defences x 2: © Imperial War Museum FKD 2916, FKD 2917

29 April 1982; arrival at Wideawake: © Mel James; backtracking down runway: © Mel James; BLACK BUCK planning: © Bob Tuxford; Reeve crew on Ascension: © John Reeve

Dash-10 pod: © Mel James; Vulcan's bomb bay: © Mel James; dusk at Wideawake; flight planning: © John Reeve; map of alternative attack plans: © Alastair Montgomery; BLACK BUCK briefing: © John Reeve

Vulcan, pre-flighted at Wideawake: © John Reeve; minutes to go: © John Reeve

*Third section*

*40 Degrees South*: © Ronald Wong; Vulcan cockpit

Rheinmetall shells: © Spiegel TV; Oerlikon; Roland surface-to-air missile; radar-guided Roland; Splash One: © Royal Australian Air Force

Radar screen: © John Reeve; reconnaissance picture of Port Stanley: © Ministry of Agriculture; bomb release: © Crown; Battle Damage Assessment: © Crown; cratered runway: © Imperial War Museum FKD 872; close-up view of crater: © Imperial War Museum FKD 297

Victor tanker: © John Reeve; rare refuelling shot: © Crown; final approach to Wideawake: © John Reeve; Tuxford crew: © Bob Tuxford; seconds from touchdown: © Alastair Montgomery; Vulcan 607 touches down: © Mel James; Martin Withers: © Mel James

'Vulcan Victory': © Sunday Mirror; the Avro Vulcan B2: © Dick Clements

# Index